# Practical AI on the
# Google Cloud Platform
*Utilizing Google's State-of-the-Art*
*AI Cloud Services*

*Micheal Lanham*

Beijing · Boston · Farnham · Sebastopol · Tokyo

**Practical AI on the Google Cloud Platform**

by Micheal Lanham

Published by O'Reilly Media, Inc., 1005 Gravenstein Highway North, Sebastopol, CA 95472.

O'Reilly books may be purchased for educational, business, or sales promotional use. Online editions are also available for most titles (*http://oreilly.com*). For more information, contact our corporate/institutional sales department: 800-998-9938 or *corporate@oreilly.com*.

**Acquisitions Editor:** Jonathan Hassell
**Development Editor:** Melissa Potter
**Production Editor:** Kate Galloway
**Copyeditor:** Piper Editorial, LLC
**Proofreader:** Arthur Johnson

**Indexer:** Judith McConville
**Interior Designer:** David Futato
**Cover Designer:** Karen Montgomery
**Illustrator:** Kate Dullea

November 2020:     First Edition

**Revision History for the First Edition**

2020-10-20:   First Release

See *http://oreilly.com/catalog/errata.csp?isbn=9781492075813* for release details.

978-1-492-07581-3

[LSI]

# Table of Contents

# Preface

This book was developed for an audience that I regularly see at my local Deep Learning Meetup group, a group of young, very eager, and very intelligent people wanting to understand and use the latest AI. Except, their dreams are often crushed or soured when they realize that the mathematics or programming they took in school is not the math they need to use for AI. For those who learn the correct math and programming, they then face the roadblock of building real, working AI—often with limited resources. While many companies see the value in investing in AI, the amount they are currently willing to invest is very small. In fact, developing cutting-edge AI can be quite expensive computationally, and that equals money.

Google likely encountered the same audience I had seen at my Meetup groups—very young and keen newbies eager to learn but missing certain resources—when it decided to build its first AI cloud platform. However, what likely solidified that decision was seeing the same mentality expressed in corporations and businesses worldwide. Companies were essentially in the same boat as those trying to learn this new AI tech. Providing an entire AI platform with state-of-the-art models and other training tools in the cloud was a no-brainer. And so it was born, Google AI on the Google Cloud Platform (GCP).

Of course, what the next wave of AI/machine learning will look like remains to be seen. Will it be a set of automation tools that make our lives easier, or will it be something else? While I agree that automation tools like robot cleaners, self-driving cars, and so on will be a part of it, they won't be the only part. What I see is the potential for a whole new wave of AI assistant or AI automation assistant apps. These could be smart assistants that provide the following services:

*Self help*
> From assisting with maintaining physical training to just managing your weight, this will likely be a major part of what we use AI for in the future.

*Personal automation*

Google has already shown how personal assistants will be able to book your next hair appointment, but this could be taken a step further—perhaps automating a series of tasks to create a vacation, or an adventure vacation.

*Financial management*

Imagine having Warren Buffett as your personal financial advisor, except instead of him, you get an AI assistant that can and will manage all your money for you. That includes setting up and making investments and so on. An AI that would work 24/7 managing your money and making extra money for you won't be a hard app to sell.

*Care assistants*

As the world ages, the number of personal-care assistants needed to help with aging will also increase. For the most part this will be physical care, but it will likely include more mundane tasks like remembering medication or making appointments. However, this could progress to having real medical diagnosticians that would be better able to track your whole medical history throughout your life.

*Teachers*

Perhaps an AI teacher would allow you to better manage and track your learning goals. This AI agent could progress with you and manage your education and even accreditations throughout your lifetime. Imagine hiring an AI bot that not only trained you, but also accredited your training to others.

*Entertainment*

People in the AI community have been writing or trying to write self-aware chatbots for decades. Examples of this have been the focus of several movies, including the Oscar winner *Her*. *Her* features a Siri-like AI that is (or becomes) self-aware and falls in love with a human. The AI in *Her* was developed more as a general assistant and was not intended as a love bot—at least it is not portrayed that way in the movie. But perhaps the intention could be to build love or companion AI in a variety of forms. You could have imaginary AI friends for the lonely child, or replicas of old or deceased celebrities for those aging, and so on. The possibilities in this area are endless.

*Protection*

Imagine if you had an AI that could protect you in multiple ways, from guarding your finances to just looking behind your back when you walk home late at night. These could be separate AI or perhaps combined.

*Everything else*

The list of these types of AI agents could go on and on, and it remains to be seen what will become practical in this brand-new space.

While the goal of this book is to teach you how to use the Google AI platform for a variety of reasons, it is my hope that you will think about how these services could be used to power these types of AI assistants.

Of course, you may not be ready to pull all of the resources together to build an AI assistant. Therefore, I have also made this book accessible for you by showing the base case for using the service or system, and how best to use it. That way you will be able to use the system immediately and then perhaps later move on to building a full, working AI assistant. For those of you looking to just build business AI, I have also shown plenty of examples with that in mind.

## Who Should Read This Book

You will enjoy this book if you're eager to learn and enjoy working with or seeing plenty of coding examples. I have tried to make this book accessible by minimizing the discussion of mathematics. However, you may find yourself needing some math refreshers or tutorials to grasp certain core concepts. Training models can and will take time, so patience is a must. As well, you need to understand that you will most certainly fail at what seem to be the most rudimentary of tasks. The important thing to remember is that AI is just hard; it takes dedication and commitment to understand it.

## Why I Wrote This Book

I wanted to write this book because Google had developed all of this cool AI that no one seemed to be using. Then I realized I wanted to write this book to help those looking for their place in AI. That sounds really cheesy until you understand my involvement in AI. I first learned of AI as a young man in the 1980s. It wasn't until the later 1990s that I took a serious look back at advanced neural networks, only to be disappointed again by their lack of progress. Instead, I relied on some traditional data science and later ventured into various genetic learning strategies. Over many years I returned to deep learning and AI only to be disappointed time and again, until recently.

It was through a recent project only a few short years ago that I took a look back at deep learning and realized how far it had come. However, unlike many, I had a broad base of understanding of the concepts and mathematics. Being exposed to deep learning over many, many years previously and keeping up with research gave me a significant advantage that allowed me to pick up the technology quicker than most. Then, when I sought the help of others, it occurred to me that most people were eager to learn but were unable to do so because of their frustrations with what was being taught. From those frustrations I spun out a group of introductory workshops aimed at providing a tutorial on deep learning. Through hosting those sessions and the very positive response I received, I decided I wanted a bigger voice, and therefore writing a book made sense. So a big reason for writing this book is to help others bypass the same frustrations I have succumbed to over the years. I hope that alleviating those frustrations will give newcomers more energy to tackle tougher problems more successfully in the future.

## Navigating This Book

This book is best read from start to finish, but of course you are likely a technical professional who needs to find their way and get answers as quickly as possible. With that in mind, use the following summary to help you decide the best place to start or perhaps just to refresh your knowledge if you return to the book later as a reference:

*Chapter 1, Data Science and Deep Learning*
    This chapter is the best place to start if you are newish to data science, machine learning, or deep learning. If you have only a basic understanding of any of those topics, you will not want to miss this chapter. You should bypass this chapter only if you consider yourself a master of deep learning.

*Chapter 2, AI on the Google Cloud Platform*
    This is a gentle introduction to the available AI services on Google and how those services are structured. From there we will look at how to use the Google Colab service to build our first working deep learning network.

*Chapter 3, Image Analysis and Recognition on the Cloud*
    In this chapter we take a look at how deep learning networks perform image recognition, and the tools they use to do this. We will look at building a similar image classification network, and then we will move on to using the Google Vision AI service.

*Chapter 4, Understanding Language on the Cloud*
    Natural language processing, or NLP, is one area where deep learning systems are making unbelievable progress. In this chapter we first learn how a deep learning system can process language, and then we build a simple language processor.

*Chapter 5, Chatbots and Conversational AI*
    Google provides a natural language chatbot service called Dialogflow that does a variety of language processing tasks. In this chapter we'll use Dialogflow as a chat agent for a variety of tasks.

*Chapter 6, Video Analysis on the Cloud*
    Video analysis is really an extension of image analysis, and in this chapter we see that Google has developed a service for doing just that. Later, we will review a variety of examples that use this service.

*Chapter 7, Generators in the Cloud*

AI can be used for a number of tasks, but one showing extreme promise is generation of content. AI content generation is where deep learning models generate unique and new content on their own. We take a look at how they do it in this chapter.

*Chapter 8, Building AI Assistants in the Cloud*

As AI advances, we need to look at new and more powerful means to develop agents for various applications and uses. In this chapter we look at more advanced forms of AI that can be used to power AI assistants.

*Chapter 9, Putting AI Assistants to Work*

In this chapter we put the culmination of this book's instruction to use in a single project. We build an agent assistant that can help us determine if the foods we eat are good or bad for us.

*Chapter 10, Commercializing AI*

Understanding how to take your idea from proof of concept to commercial app is challenging. In this chapter we look at the steps to commercialize a full AI agent app.

# A Note on the Google AI Platform

AI is currently progressing at a ferocious rate, and many aspects of AI are breaking and/or quickly becoming dated. It is quite likely that parts of this book could become outversioned, but not to fear. Many of the examples in this book are based on very common tasks, and in many cases Google may have similar and more up-to-date examples. Therefore, if at any time throughout this book you encounter an issue, do a quick Google search and you may see the answer to your problem in a number of places.

You will likely find that many of the code examples early on this book use very common blocks of code, and this is very much intentional. However, make sure you understand all the details of that code, including any minor changes. Many times what appears to be just a minor difference turns out to be the reason the code was failing. Be sure you pay attention to details and understand how the code works, including the inputs and outputs.

Another thing to note about the Google AI platform is that it is mostly free, but is also a paid service. I will often recommend areas that warrant caution to avoid costly mistakes. However, it is still up to the reader to be wary of their own cloud usage, as well as the security of that usage. Please be aware that costly mistakes can and often do happen because of a lack of awareness. Just be careful when using cloud services.

# Things You Need for This Book

Working through the examples in the book will require you to have the following knowledge or resources:

*Python*
> You should have a good grasp of the Python language, and know how to run scripts on your own.

*Desktop computer*
> All of the examples are provided online and in cloud services, but it is still recommended you do this on a wider-screen desktop computer for better results. Of course, for those diehards out there, using a phone will always be an option.

*Mathematics*
> For best results, you want to have an interest in math. You don't have to be a genius in mathematics, but an understanding at the high school or postsecondary level is recommended.

*Fortitude*
> You need the ability to persevere through extremes, and developing AI will certainly challenge that. You will have many ups and downs learning and doing AI. Be prepared to be humble and get tough—you will need it.

*Google*
> Googling is a skill that apparently not all people have. Make sure to keep yours current, and use Google to enhance your knowledge.

# Conventions Used in This Book

The following typographical conventions are used in this book:

*Italic*
> Indicates new terms, URLs, email addresses, filenames, and file extensions.

`Constant width`
> Used for program listings, as well as within paragraphs to refer to program elements such as variable or function names, databases, data types, environment variables, statements, and keywords.

**`Constant width bold`**
> Shows commands or other text that should be typed literally by the user.

*`Constant width italic`*
> Shows text that should be replaced with user-supplied values or by values determined by context.

This element signifies a tip or suggestion.

 This element signifies a general note.

 This element indicates a warning or caution.

# Using Code Examples

Supplemental material (code examples, exercises, etc.) is available for download at *https://github.com/cxbxmxcx/Practical_AI_on_GCP*.

If you have a technical question or a problem using the code examples, please send an email to *bookquestions@oreilly.com*.

This book is here to help you get your job done. In general, if example code is offered with this book, you may use it in your programs and documentation. You do not need to contact us for permission unless you're reproducing a significant portion of the code. For example, writing a program that uses several chunks of code from this book does not require permission. Selling or distributing examples from O'Reilly books does require permission. Answering a question by citing this book and quoting example code does not require permission. Incorporating a significant amount of example code from this book into your product's documentation does require permission.

We appreciate, but generally do not require, attribution. An attribution usually includes the title, author, publisher, and ISBN. For example: "*Practical AI on the Google Cloud Platform* by Micheal Lanham (O'Reilly). Copyright 2021 Micheal Lanham, 978-1-492-07581-3."

If you feel your use of code examples falls outside fair use or the permission given above, feel free to contact us at *permissions@oreilly.com*.

# O'Reilly Online Learning

 For more than 40 years, *O'Reilly Media* has provided technology and business training, knowledge, and insight to help companies succeed.

Our unique network of experts and innovators share their knowledge and expertise through books, articles, and our online learning platform. O'Reilly's online learning platform gives you on-demand access to live training courses, in-depth learning paths, interactive coding environments, and a vast collection of text and video from O'Reilly and 200+ other publishers. For more information, visit *http://oreilly.com*.

# How to Contact Us

Please address comments and questions concerning this book to the publisher:

O'Reilly Media, Inc.
1005 Gravenstein Highway North
Sebastopol, CA 95472
800-998-9938 (in the United States or Canada)
707-829-0515 (international or local)
707-829-0104 (fax)

We have a web page for this book, where we list errata, examples, and any additional information. You can access this page at *https://oreil.ly/practical-ai-google-cloud*.

Email *bookquestions@oreilly.com* to comment or ask technical questions about this book.

For news and information about our books and courses, visit *http://oreilly.com*.

Find us on Facebook: *http://facebook.com/oreilly*

Follow us on Twitter: *http://twitter.com/oreillymedia*

Watch us on YouTube: *http://www.youtube.com/oreillymedia*

# Acknowledgments

I would really like to thank the team at O'Reilly for all their help and support in my journey writing this book. It has been a pleasure to write this book, and the team at O'Reilly is certainly a big part of that. In particular, many thanks to my acquisitions editor, Jonathan Hassell, who was a great help in narrowing the scope of this project and making it more accessible. My content development editors, Angela Rufino and

Melissa Potter, have also been a tremendous asset in keeping my content on track and focused.

As always, I would like to thank my family for all their help and support. None of this extracurricular writing would be possible without their assistance and support. From grudgingly posing for photos to stressfully making graphics, they have always helped out where I needed it, and I can't thank them enough for that. A special thanks goes to my partner, Rhonda, my angel who has taken care of me and is someone I think of while writing almost every word. To my children, all nine of them, I cherish the time I have spent with all of them, and each of them has likewise inspired me to write in some way.

A big part of this work is the result of me giving talks for my Deep Learning Meetup in Calgary. It is from that group and through many of those sessions that the contents of this book were born. The Perceptron Game was developed for, and as a result of, my teaching free sessions on introductory deep learning for this group. It is from those teachings that I have been able to extract value and insight to help me write this book, and I would like to thank all those who attend the Calgary Deep Learning Meetup.

Lastly, I want to thank the elephant in the room, Google. On so many levels, Google makes our growth in technology, and AI in particular, possible. I don't think enough credit can and will be given to Google and to a greater extent the vast army of people who work there. There are many that you might call AI rock stars working at Google, but this acknowledgment is more for those "regular" people pushing their limits to make the world a better place. Of course, there is currently uncertainty around whether AI will make the world a better place. My hope is that, with Google leading the charge, we are on the right track.

# CHAPTER 1

# Data Science and Deep Learning

Only 20 years have passed since the beginning of the new millennium, and we have thrust the bulk of our technological knowledge into the machine age—an age that, it has been suggested, will bring more change than our earlier discovery of electricity. Change so massive that some believe that all life on our planet will be affected in some way, good or bad. Technologists refer to this change or revolution as *machine learning* or, more recently, as the dawn of artificial intelligence. While it remains to be seen how intelligent we can make machines, one thing is for sure: this new wave of technology is now everywhere. Developers all over the globe are struggling to make sense of this field and keep up with the changes, as well as trying to benefit from new tools and techniques. Fortunately, companies like Google have realized the difficulties and expense of crafting this powerful new AI and are now commercializing powerful AI services on the cloud. It is the goal of this book to guide the reader through the use of these new and growing AI-powered cloud services from Google.

There is a growing list of other cloud AI providers providing competition for Google, including Microsoft, Amazon, IBM, and many others.

In this chapter we introduce a number of base concepts about machine learning and data science as well as introduce the field of deep learning. The following is a list of topics we will cover in this chapter:

- What Is Data Science?
- Classification and Regression
- Data Discovery and Preparation

- The Basics of Deep Learning
- Understanding How Networks Learn
- Building a Deep Learner

# What Is Data Science?

Data science is the practice of applying statistical methods to data in order to ascertain some further characteristics about said data. This could be for the purpose of predicting some future event or classifying some observation of an event. Anyone who has ever checked the weather for the next day has used data science in the form of predicting the weather. In fact, humans have been intuitively practicing data science for thousands of years, and it all started when we learned to predict the weather for tomorrow given the weather from the past.

While we may have been practicing data science in many forms for thousands of years, from weather prediction to engineering, it wasn't until quite recently that the actual field of data science became well known and coveted. This was due primarily to the big data revolution, which began about 10 years ago. This spawned a broader outlook on computer-aided learning about data, which collectively became known as machine learning.

Since machine learning originates from the application of data science, it only makes sense that the two would share a common vocabulary and methodology. As such, we often recommend that anyone seriously interested in developing advanced AI tech like deep learning learn some data science. This will help you not only better grasp the terminology, but also understand the origin or purpose of many techniques. We will address the primary topics in this book, but I suggest that you learn more about data science on your own.

There are plenty of free courses available online. Just use your favorite search engine and search for "free data science course."

Now that we understand what data science is and how it relates to machine learning and deep learning, we will move on to looking at how we make sense of data.

# Classification and Regression

Data science has developed many ways of exploring and making sense of data, and we often refer to this whole practice as *learning*. The greater area of machine learning encompasses all forms of learning, including deep learning; reinforcement learning;

and unsupervised, semisupervised, and supervised learning, to name just a few. Figure 1-1 shows an overview of the various forms of learning and how they relate to one another.

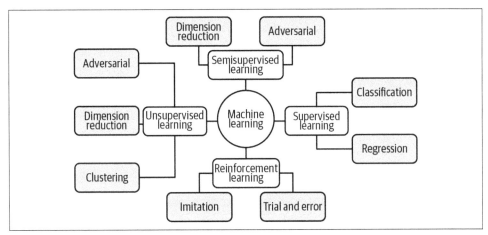

*Figure 1-1. Forms of learning that machine learning encompasses*

As you can see from Figure 1-1, there is a diverse set of learning methodologies (the unshaded boxes) that encompass machine learning as a whole. Within each learning branch we have also identified the key problems or tasks this learning attempts to tackle, shown with rectangles. Each of these subproblems or tasks spawns numerous additional applications. We use the term *adversarial* for both semisupervised and unsupervised learning to denote the class of algorithms that self-learn by training against themselves or other similarly matched algorithms. The most famous form of adversarial learner is the GAN, or generative adversarial network. We won't have much time to go into detail about the methods of unsupervised, semisupervised, or reinforcement learning in this book. However, after gaining the knowledge in this book, and this chapter in particular, you may want to explore those forms on your own later.

At the middle right of Figure 1-1 is the area of supervised learning and its various branches. This is what we will focus on in this text, particularly the areas of regression and classification. Supervised learning is so named because it requires that the data first be labeled before being fed into the learning algorithm. An example is a dataset showing the amount of accumulated rainfall in millimeters (30 millimeters = 1 inch) over the course of 12 months, shown in Table 1-1.

*Table 1-1. Mythical rainfall over months*

| Month | Min rainfall | Max rainfall | Total rainfall |
|---|---|---|---|
| 1 | 22 | 30 | 24 |
| 2 | 22 | 25 | 48 |
| 3 | 25 | 27 | 75 |
| 4 | 49 | 54 | 128 |
| 5 | 8 | 8 | 136 |
| 6 | 29 | 47 | 168 |
| 7 | 40 | 41 | 209 |
| 8 | 35 | 63 | 263 |
| 9 | 14 | 25 | 277 |
| 10 | 45 | 57 | 333 |
| 11 | 20 | 39 | 364 |
| 12 | 39 | 51 | 404 |

The data shows monthly precipitation values from fictional ground stations in a mythical country or location. To keep things simple, we are going to contrive our data for the first few examples. Over the course of the book, though, we will look at plenty of real datasets. As we can see, the data is labeled with a number of attributes: month, minimum rainfall, maximum rainfall, and total accumulated rainfall. This will work as an excellent example of labeled data, which we can use to perform supervised learning of regression and classification later in this chapter. Before that, let us take a close look at regression in the next section.

## Regression

*Regression* is the process of finding the relationship between dependent variables and independent variables. The most common form of regression is linear regression, so named because it assumes a linear relationship between variables. Figure 1-2 is an example of drawing a line of regression through that set of weather data previously shown in Table 1-1. Plotted was the independent variable month against the dependent last column, total rainfall. For this simple example, we use only two variables. The plot was generated with Google Sheets, which provides linear regression as a data analysis tool out of the box, using the Trendline option under Customize Series.

Independent variables in an equation are separate and outside the influence of other variables. The variable $x$ in the equation $y = mx + b$ is the independent variable. The dependent variable is $y$ because it is derived from $x$.

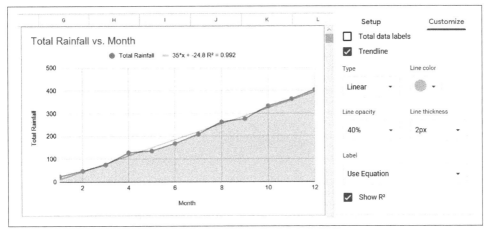

*Figure 1-2. Linear regression of total rainfall versus month*

Placing a trendline is the same as performing regression against our plotted data. In this case we plotted the month number against the accumulated total rainfall for the year. Using the total accumulation of rain rather than an actual amount per month likewise simplifies our placement of a trendline. The regression we are using in the example is linear, and Google Sheets also allows us to derive and show the equation of the line. Check the charts legend and note the equation is in the form $y = mx + b$, or in other words, linear. You will also notice in the legend another value called $R^2$, or what we call *R squared*. R squared is used as a measure of goodness of fit (i.e., how well the predicted values from regression match the actual data), and because the value ranges to a maximum of 1.0, it often provides a good baseline measure. However, R squared is not our preferred method for determining goodness of fit, and we will talk about better methods in the next section.

## Goodness of Fit

The primary problem with R squared is that it actually does not measure goodness of fit. What we find is that the more varied the data is, the larger the standard deviation is, and the lower the values of R squared are. Thus, R squared generally indicates lower values over more diverse and larger datasets, and this makes it useless in deep learning. Instead we apply an error function against our predicted and actual values, taking the difference squaring and then averaging it. The result of this is known as the average or *mean squared error* (MSE). Figure 1-3 shows how we would calculate the MSE from our last example. Inside the diagram is the equation that essentially means we take the expected, predicted value with regression and subtract that from the actual. We square that number to make it positive and then sum all of those values. After that, we divide by our total samples to get an average amount of error.

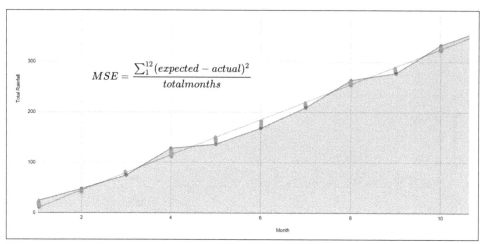

$$MSE = \frac{\sum_1^{12} (expected - actual)^2}{total months}$$

*Figure 1-3. Calculating MSE for regression*

MSE is a relative measure of error and is often specific to your dataset. While MSE does not give us a general quality of fit like R squared, it does give us a relative indication of goodness of fit. This means that lower values of MSE indicate a better goodness of fit. There are other similar measures we can use to determine how well a regression model fits to the data. These include root mean squared error (RMSE), which is just the root of MSE, and mean absolute error (MAE), which measures the independent difference between variables. Determining goodness of fit will ultimately determine the quality of our models and is something we will revisit often throughout the rest of the book.

In the next section we look at a different form of regression: logistic regression, or what we commonly refer to as *classification*.

## Classification with Logistic Regression

Aside from regression, the next common problem we will look to solve is classifying data into discrete classes. This process is known as classification, but in data science we refer to it as logistic regression. Logistic means *logit* or *binary*, which makes this a binary form of regression. In fact, we often refer to this form of regression as regression with classes or binary regression, so named because the regression model does not predict specific values, but rather a class boundary. You can think of this as the equation of regression being the line that separates the classes. An example of how this looks/works is shown in Figure 1-4.

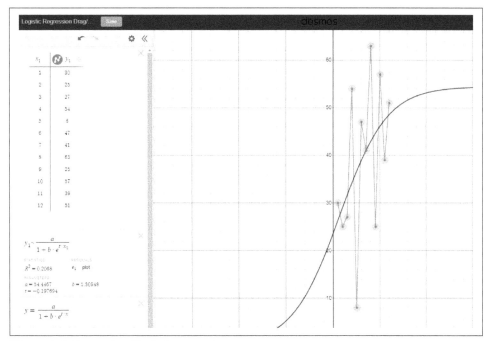

*Figure 1-4. Example of logistic regression*

In Figure 1-4, we see our example rainfall data again, but this time plotted on month and maximum rainfall for a different year. Now the purpose of the plot is to classify the months as rainy (wet) or dry. The equation of regression in the diagram denotes the class break between the two classes of months, wet or dry. With classification problems, our measure of goodness of fit now becomes how well the model predicts an item is in the specific class. Goodness of fit for classification problems uses a measure of accuracy, or what we denote as ACC, with a value from 0 to 1.0, or 0% to 100%, to denote the certainty/accuracy of data being within the class.

The source for Figure 1-4 is a free data science learning site called Desmos. Desmos is a great site where you can visualize many different machine learning algorithms. It is also highly recommended for anyone wanting to learn the fundamentals of data science and machine learning.

Referring back to Figure 1-4, it is worth mentioning that the logistic regression used here is a self-supervised method. That means we didn't have to label the data to derive the equation, but we can use supervised learning or labeled data to train classes as well. Table 1-2 shows a sample rainfall dataset with classes defined. A class of 1 indicates a wet month, while a class of 0 denotes a dry month.

*Table 1-2. Months classified as wet or dry*

| Month | Dry/Wet (0 or 1) |
| --- | --- |
| 1 | 1 |
| 2 | 0 |
| 3 | 0 |
| 4 | 1 |
| 5 | 0 |
| 6 | 1 |
| 7 | 0 |
| 8 | 1 |
| 9 | 0 |
| 10 | 1 |
| 11 | 0 |
| 12 | 1 |

It is easy to see from Table 1-2 which months break into which classes, wet or dry. However, it is important to note how we define classes. Using a 0 or 1 to denote whether a data item is within a class or not will become a common technique we use later in many classification problems. Since we use accuracy to measure fit with classification, it also makes this type of model more intuitive to train. If your background is programming, though, you may realize that you could also classify our sample data far more easily with a simple `if` statement. While that is true for these simple examples of single dependent variable regression or classification, it is far from the case when we tackle problems with multiple dependent variables. We will cover multivariable learning in the next section.

## Multivariant Regression and Classification

The example problem we just looked at was intended to be kept simple in order to convey the key concepts. In the real world, however, data science and machine learning are far from simple and often need to tackle far more complex data. In many cases, data scientists look at numerous independent variables, or what are referred to as *features*. A single feature denotes a single independent variable we would use to describe our data. With the previous example, we looked at only one independent variable, the month number for both problems of regression and classification. This allowed us to derive a relationship between that month number (a feature) and a dependent variable. For regression, we used total monthly rainfall to determine the linear relationship. Then for classification we used maximum monthly rainfall to determine the month's class, wet or dry. However, in the real world we often need to consider multiple features that need to be reduced to a single value using regression or classification.

The data science algorithms we look at here for performing regression and classification were selected because they lead into the deep learning analogs we will look at later. There are numerous other data science methods that perform the same tasks using statistical methods that we will not spend time on in this book. Interested readers may wish to explore a course, book, or video on data science later.

In the real world, data scientists will often deal with datasets that have dozens, hundreds, or thousands of features. Dealing with this massive amount of data requires more complex algorithms, but the concepts for regression and classification are still the same. Therefore, we won't have a need to explore finer details of using these more complex classic statistical methods. As it turns out, deep learning is especially well suited to learning data with multiple features. However, it is still important for us to understand various tips and tricks for exploring and preparing data for learning, as discussed in the next section.

# Data Discovery and Preparation

Machine learning, data science, and deep learning models are often very much dependent on the data we have available to train or solve problems. Data itself can represent everything from tabular data to pictures, images, videos, document text, spoken text, and computer interfaces. With so much diversity of data, it can be difficult to establish well-defined cross-cutting rules that we can use for all datasets, but in this section we look at a few important considerations you should remember when handling data for machine learning.

One of the major hurdles data scientists and machine learners face is finding good-quality data. Of course, there are plenty of nice, free sample datasets to play with for learning, but when it comes to the real world, we often need to prepare our own data. It is therefore critical to understand what makes data good or bad.

## Bad Data

One characteristic of bad data is that it is duplicated, incomplete, or sparse, meaning it may have multiple duplicated values or it may be missing values for some or many features. Table 1-3 shows an example of our previous mythical rainfall data with incomplete or bad data.

*Table 1-3. Mythical rainfall over months (missing data)*

| Month | Min rainfall | Max rainfall | Total rainfall |
|---|---|---|---|
| 1 | 22 | 30 | 24 |
| 2 | 22 | 25 | 48 |
| 3 | 25 | | |
| 4 | 49 | 54 | 128 |
| 5 | 8 | 8 | 136 |
| 6 | | 47 | 168 |
| 7 | 40 | 41 | 209 |
| 8 | 35 | | |
| 9 | 14 | | 277 |
| 10 | 45 | 57 | 333 |
| 11 | | | |
| 12 | 39 | 51 | 404 |

Now, if we wanted to perform linear regression on the same dataset, we would come across some issues, the primary one being the missing values on the labeled dependent variable total rainfall. We could try and replace the missing values with 0, but that would just skew our data. Instead, we can just omit the data items with bad data. This reduces the previous dataset to the new values shown in Table 1-4.

*Table 1-4. Mythical rainfall over months (cleaned data)*

| Month | Min rainfall | Max rainfall | Total rainfall |
|---|---|---|---|
| 1 | 22 | 30 | 24 |
| 2 | 22 | 25 | 48 |
| 4 | 49 | 54 | 128 |
| 5 | 8 | 8 | 136 |
| ... | ... | ... | ... |
| 7 | 40 | 41 | 209 |
| ... | ... | ... | ... |
| 10 | 45 | 57 | 333 |
| 12 | 39 | 51 | 404 |

Plotting this data in Google Sheets and applying a trendline produces Figure 1-5. As you can see in the figure, the missing values are not much of an issue. You can clearly see now how removing the null values also shows us how well regression performs. Pay special attention to where the missing months should be, and look at how well the trendline or regression equation is predicting these values. In fact, data scientists will often remove not only bad data with missing null values, but also good data. The reason they remove good data is to validate their answer. For instance, we can go back to our full sample data as shown in Table 1-1 and use some of those values to validate our regression. Take month 3, where the accumulated value is 75. If we consider the predicted value for month 3 from Figure 1-5, we can see the value is predicting around 75. This practice of removing a small set of data for testing and validating your answers is fundamental to data science, and is something we will cover in the next section.

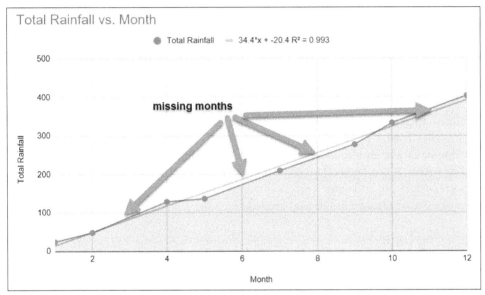

*Figure 1-5. Example of regression with reduced data*

## Training, Test, and Validation Data

A fundamental concept in data science is breaking source data into three categories: training, test, and validation. We set aside the bulk of the data, often about 80%, for training. Then we break the remaining data down into 15% test and 5% validation. You may initially think this could compromise your experiment, but as we saw, removing small amounts of data increased the confidence in our model. Since model confidence is a key criterion for any successful machine learning model, removing a small percentage of data for testing and validation is seen as trivial. As we will see, setting aside data for testing and validation will be critical for evaluating our performance and baselining our models.

Another critical purpose for breaking out data into test and validation is to confirm that the model is not over- or underfitting. We will cover the concepts of over- and underfitting when we get to deep learning later in this chapter.

## Good Data

Aside from the obvious missing, duplicate, or null features, characterizing data as good is subjective to the machine learning technique. When using all classical data science methods, we almost always want to verify the dependency between variables. We do this to make sure the two dependent variables are not strongly dependent on one another. For instance, in our previous rainfall example, the total accumulated rainfall per month would be heavily dependent on the maximum monthly rainfall. Therefore, most classic data science methods would discourage using both variables since they heavily depend on each other. Instead, those methods strongly encourage variable independence, but again, this is often not the ideal when it comes to the real world. This is also where we see the true benefit of deep learning methods. Deep learning has the ability to work with independent, dependent, and sparse or missing data as well as if not better than any other statistical method we have at our disposal. However, there are still some common rules we can use to prepare data for all types of learning, as discussed in the next section.

## Preparing Data

The type of preparation you need to perform on your data is quite dependent on the machine learning algorithm being employed and the type of data itself. Classical statistics–based methods, like the ones we used for regression and classification earlier, often require more data preparation. As we saw, you need to be careful if the data has null, duplicate, or missing values, and in most cases you either eliminate those records or annotate them in some manner. For example, in our previous rainfall example, we could have used a number of methods to fill in those missing data values. However, when it comes to deep learning, as we will see shortly, we often throw everything at the learning network. In fact, deep learning often uses data sparsity to its advantage, and this strongly goes against most classic data science. If anything, deep learning suffers more from too-similar data, and duplicated data can be especially problematic. Therefore, when preparing data for deep learning we want to consider some basic rules that are outside the norm for data science:

*Remove duplicated data*
> Duplicated data is often an issue for deep learning, and for data science in general. Duplicates provide extra emphasis to the duplicated rows. The one exception to this will be time-based data, or where duplicate values have meaning.

*Maintain data sparsity*

Avoid the temptation to fill in data gaps or remove data records due to missing values. Deep learning networks generalize data better when fed sparse data or when the network itself is made sparse. Making a network layer sparse is called *dropout*, which is a concept we will cover in later chapters.

*Keep dependent variables*

Data scientists will often reduce the number of features in large datasets by removing highly dependent features. We saw this in our rainfall example where the total rainfall in a month was highly dependent on the maximum rainfall in that month. A data scientist would want to remove the dependent feature, whereas a deep learner would likely keep it in. The reason for this is that, while the feature is observed to be highly dependent, it may still have some independent effect.

*Increase data variability*

In most data science problems, we often want to constrain data variability in some manner. Reducing data variation allows a model to train quicker and results in a better answer. However, the opposite is often the case with deep learning, where we often want to expose the model to the biggest variation to encourage better generalization and avoid false positives. We will explore why this can be an issue in later chapters.

*Normalize the data*

Normalizing the data is something we will cover in more detail as we go through the various examples. We do this in order to make features unitless and typically range in value from –1 to +1. In some cases you may normalize data to 0 to 1. In any case, we will cover normalization later when it pertains to the relevant sample.

Aside from applying these general rules to your data, you will also want to understand what it is you want from your data and what your expectations are. We will cover this in more detail in the next section.

## Questioning Your Data

One key observation we need to make with any dataset before applying a data science or machine learning algorithm is determining how likely the expected answer is. For example, if you are training an algorithm to guess the next roll on a six-sided die, you know that an algorithm should guess correctly one out of six times, or 1/6th, at a minimum. If your trained algorithm guessed the correct answer 1 out of 10 times on a 6-sided die then this would indicate very poor performance since even a random guess is likely correct 1 out of 6 times. Aside from understanding the baseline expectation, here are some other helpful questions/rules, again skewed more toward deep learning:

*Evaluate baseline expectation*

Determine how likely a random guess is to get the correct answer.

*Evaluate maximum expectation*

How likely is your model to get the best answer? Are you constraining your search to a very small space, so small that even finding it could be problematic? For example, assume we want to train a network to recognize cats. We feed it 1 picture of a cat and 10,000 pictures of dogs, which we train the network to recognize. In that case, our algorithm would have to correctly identify 1 cat out of 10,001 pictures. However, with deep learning, since our network was trained on only one cat picture, it will only recognize one exact, more or less, cat. The takeaway here is to make sure the data covers as much variety as possible—the more, the better.

*Evaluate least expectation*

Conversely, how likely is your algorithm to get the wrong answer? In other words, is the random guess or base expectation very high to start? If the base expectation is above 50%, then you should reconsider your problem in most cases.

*Annotate the data*

Are you able to annotate or add to the data in some manner? For instance, if your dataset consists of dog pictures, what if you horizontally flipped all pictures and added those? This would in essence duplicate your data and increase your variability. Flipping images and other methods will be explored later in relevant exercises.

Make sure to always review the first three rules from this list. It is important to understand that the questions have answers in your data, and that the answers are obtainable. However, the opposite is also very true, and you need to make sure that the answer is not so obvious. Conversely, unsupervised and semisupervised learning methods are designed to find answers from the data on their own. In any case, when performing regression or classification with supervised learning, you will always want to evaluate the expectations from your data.

A common practice now is to construct unsupervised and semisupervised deep learning networks to extract the relevant features from the data, and then train on those new features. These networks are able to learn, on their own, what features have relevancy. This practice is known as *autoencoding*, and is one of the first types of networks we will learn later in this chapter.

# The Basics of Deep Learning

Deep learning and the concept of connected learning systems that function similarly to a biological brain have been around since the 1950s. While deep learning is inspired by biology, it in no way attempts to model a real biological neuron. In fact, we still understand very little of how we learn and strengthen the connections in any brain; however, we will need to understand in great detail how the connections strengthen or weaken—how they learn—in the deep learning neural networks we build.

 *The Deep Learning Revolution* by Terrence J. Sejnowski (MIT Press) is a fantastic book on the history and revolution of deep learning. Sejnowski is considered a founding father of deep learning, which make his tales about its history more entertaining.

In early 2020, state-of-the-art deep learning systems can encompass millions of connections. Understanding how to train such megalithic systems is outside the scope of this book, but using such systems is not. Google and others now provide access to such powerful deep learning systems through a cloud interface. These cloud interfaces/services are simple to use, as we will see in later chapters. However, understanding the internal workings of a deep learning system will make it easier to identify when things go wrong and how to fix them. As well, understanding the simplicity of these systems will likely take away any apprehension or intimidation you feel about deep learning. Therefore, we will start with the heart of the deep learning network, the perceptron.

The perceptron is central to a deep learning system. You can think of the perceptron as being analogous to the engine in a car, except in a car there is a single engine, while in a deep learning system there may be thousands of perceptrons all connected in layers. Figure 1-6 shows a single perceptron with a number of input connections and a single output controlled by an activation function.

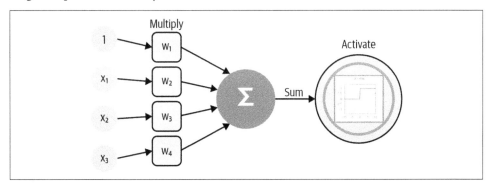

*Figure 1-6. A simple model of the perceptron*

We can picture all activity flowing through Figure 1-6 from the left to the right. Starting at the far left, the inputs are labeled $X_1$ to $X_3$ to show three inputs. In a real network the number of inputs could be in the thousands or millions. Moving from the inputs, we then multiply by a weight for each input denoted $W_1$ to $W_4$. The weights represent how strong the connection is; thus a higher-value weight will have a stronger connection. Notice that we multiply the first weight by one; this is for the bias. After all the weights are multiplied by the inputs, they are summed at the next step, denoted by the Greek symbol $\Sigma$ for summation. Finally, the total sum is pushed through an activation function and the result is output, which is dependent on the activation function. It may help to think that the activation function controls how the perceptron fires and passes its output along. This whole process is called a forward pass through the network; it is also called inference, or how the network answers.

Generally, we will try to minimize the use of math to explain concepts in this book. However, math is a core element of this technology, and it is sometimes easier and more relevant to express concepts in terms of math equations. Therefore, we will start by showing how a perceptron fires mathematically, as shown in Equation 1-1.

*Equation 1-1.*

$$y = W_1 + \sum_{i=1}^{n} x_i \times W_{i+1}$$

Where:

$y$ = output sent to activation function
$W$ = a weight
$x$ = an input

Equation 1-1 shows the summation part of the forward pass through a single perceptron. This is just where the weights are multiplied by the inputs and everything is added up. It can also be helpful to view how this looks in code. Example 1-1 shows a function written in Python that performs the summation step in a perceptron.

*Example 1-1.*

```
def summation(inputs, weights):
        sum = weights[0]
        for i in range(len(inputs)-1):
                sum += weights[i + 1] * inputs[i]
        return sum
```

After summation the result is passed into an activation function. Activation functions are critical to deep learning, and these functions control the perceptron's output. In the single perceptron example, an activation function is less critical, and in this simple example we will just use a linear function, shown in Example 1-2. This is the simplest function, as it just returns a straight mapping of the result to the output.

*Example 1-2.*

```
def act_linear(sum):
        return sum
```

Example 1-3 shows a step activation function, so named because the output steps to a value when the threshold is reached. In the listing, the threshold is >= 0.0 and the stepped output is 1.0. Thus, when a summed output is greater than or equal to zero, the perceptron outputs 1.0.

*Example 1-3.*

```
def act_step(sum):
        return 1.0 if sum >= 0.0 else 0.0
```

 The code examples here are meant for demonstration only. While the code is syntactically correct and will run, don't expect much from the output. This is because the network weights still need to learn. We will cover this later in this chapter.

Finally, we can put all of this code together in Example 1-4, where we have written a forward_pass function that combines summation and the earlier linear activation function.

*Example 1-4.*

```
def forward_pass(inputs, weights):
  return act_linear(summation(inputs, weights))

print(forward_pass([2,3,4],[2,3,4,5]))
```

Can you predict the output of Example 1-4 and previous related listings? Try to predict the outcome without typing the code into a Python interpreter and running it. We will leave it as an exercise for the reader to find the answer on their own. While the code in the previous example may seem simple, there are a number of subtle nuances that often trip up newcomers. Therefore, we will reinforce the concept of the perceptron further in the next section by playing a game.

## The Perceptron Game

Games and puzzles can be a fun, engaging, and powerful way to teach abstract concepts. The Perceptron Game was born out of frustration from teaching students the previous coding example and realizing that 90% of the class often still missed major and important concepts. Of course, many other deep learners, including the godfather himself, Dr. Geoff Hinton, have been said to use variations of a similar game.

This version can be played as a solitaire puzzle or as a group collaboration. It really depends on how many friends you want to play with. One thing to keep in mind before inviting the family over is that this game is still heavily math-focused and may not be for everyone.

You can find all of the printable materials for the game in the book's source code download for Chapter 1 (*https://github.com/ cxbxmxcx/Practical_AI_on_GCP*).

The play area for the Perceptron Game is a perceptron, or in this case a printed mat like that shown in Figure 1-7. This is the same figure we saw previously, but this time it is annotated with some extra pieces. Aside from printing out the play area, the perceptron mat, you will need to find about eight six-sided dice. You can use fewer dice, but the more, the better. We will use the dice as numeric placeholders. For the most part, the number on each die face represents its respective value, except for 6, which takes 0.

Thus, the value for each die face is:

$1 = 1$
$2 = 2$
$3 = 3$
$4 = 4$
$5 = 5$
$6 = 0$

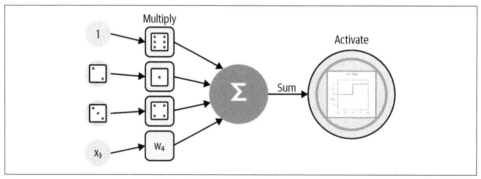

*Figure 1-7. The Perceptron Game play area with dice*

Given the die positions on the mat shown in Figure 1-7, we can see there are two inputs represented by 2 and 3. Inside the perceptron we have weights set to 0, 1, and 4 (remember that $6 = 0$). Based on these inputs and weights, we can calculate the total summation by:

1. bias = $1 \times 0 = 0$
2. input 2 = $2 \times 1 = 2$
3. input 3 = $3 \times 4 = 12$

Total sum = $0 + 2 + 12 = 14$

The total sum now needs to be output through an activation function. For simplicity, we will say that our current perceptron does not use an activation function. This means that all of the outputs will be linear or raw values. So 14 becomes the output value for the perceptron, except assume that the real answer we want, the labeled answer, is 10. That means the perceptron has to learn the weights through mirco-adjustments to provide the right output. Fortunately, there is a relatively simple equation, Equation 1-2, that can do that.

*Equation 1-2.*

$$W_i = W_i + \alpha(L - O)$$

Where:

$L$ = the labeled value
$O$ = the output from the perceptron
$W$ = the weight to be adjusted
$\alpha$ = training constant

Equation 1-2 adjusts each weight by a factor controlled by alpha ($\alpha$), and which is a result of the difference in actual value and one predicted (forward pass) in the perceptron. Going back to our last example, we can correct one of the sample weights shown by substituting values into Equation 1-2 and assuming a value of 0.1 for $\alpha$ and the weight to be 4 (above example), we get Equation 1-3.

*Equation 1-3.*

$$3.6 = 4 + 0.1(10 - 14)$$

Thus, from Equation 1-3 we can see the new value for the weight would be 3.6. Now, if we put those values back into the equation, the new output for the perceptron would be 12.8. However, the right answer is still 10. This is okay because we don't want to adjust a single weight too quickly. Remember that this is only one input, and we may need to adjust for thousands or millions of inputs, which is why we only set $\alpha$ to a small value. By using only a small value, we can then incrementally go through the inputs over and over again until the perceptron weights learn. Going back to the previous example with actual answer 10 and output 14, we can perform weight updates iteratively, as shown in Table 1-5.

*Table 1-5. Perceptron learning*

| X1 | X2 | W1 | W2 | Label | Ouput | Error |
|----|----|-----|-------|-------|--------|-------|
| 2 | 3 | 1 | 4 | 10 | 14 | 4 |
| 2 | 3 | 0.6 | 3.6 | 10 | 12 | 2 |
| 2 | 3 | 0.4 | 3.4 | 10 | 11 | 1 |
| 2 | 3 | 0.3 | 3.3 | 10 | 10.5 | 0.5 |
| 2 | 3 | 0.25 | 3.25 | 10 | 10.25 | 0.25 |
| 2 | 3 | 0.225 | 3.225 | 10 | 10.125 | 0.125 … |

By iteratively adjusting weights, we can see how the perceptron converges to an answer for a single set of inputs. We of course want to look at far more complex problems, hence the reason for the game.

 Before you throw this book down and yell, "Eureka! I know how neural networks learn," wait and take a step back. Real networks use a far more complex method called *backpropagation*, which is coming up in this chapter.

The goal of the Perceptron Game is to find the weights that will solve for the correct outputs. In Table 1-6, there is a list of single inputs and the expected outputs. What you need to do is find the weights (weight 1 for the bias and weight 2 for the input) that will let the perceptron predict the correct output.

*Table 1-6. Game 1*

| X1 | Expected output |
|----|------------------|
| 4 | 14 |
| 3 | 11 |
| 2 | 8 |
| 1 | 5 … |

Now you have a number of options to use to learn or set the weights. You can:

- Guess: As a human you may be able to intuitively figure the answer out in your head. Try to guess what the weights are first.
- Use the random method: Use the dice and roll random values. Then try those random values and see if those work. As a hint, the bias (weight 1) and input 1 (weight 2) weights are not the same value and are not zero (6 on a die).

- Use Equation 1-2: Use the equation we looked at earlier to solve for the weights. If you get stuck, this may be a good method to fall back on.
- Use programming: We will frown upon programming as a solution in this chapter, but only in this chapter. Leave it for later.

 Even if you guess the answer quickly, try using the random method as well. Understanding how different methods solve for the weights is the point of this exercise.

The answer to this problem (and the others) is provided at the end of the chapter. We didn't want readers to spot the answers while doing the problem. When you are done, check your answer at the back of the chapter and then move on to the next perceptron puzzles in Tables 1-7 and 1-8.

*Table 1-7. Game 2*

| X1 | X2 | Expected output |
|----|----|-----------------|
| 4 | 2 | 8 |
| 3 | 1 | 5 |
| 2 | 0 | 2 |
| 1 | 3 | 7 |
| 0 | 4 | 8 |
| 5 | 5 | 15 |

*Table 1-8. Game 3*

| X1 | X2 | X3 | Expected output |
|----|----|----|-----------------|
| 4 | 2 | 1 | 8 |
| 3 | 1 | 0 | 5 |
| 2 | 0 | 2 | 2 |
| 1 | 3 | 3 | 7 |
| 0 | 4 | 4 | 8 |
| 5 | 5 | 5 | 15 |

There can be multiple answers to these games depending on how you solve them. We arrived at the answers at the end of the chapter by guessing, and yours may differ if you used Equation 1-2, for instance. Either way, if your perceptron is able to regress the right output and you understand how this is done, you are well on your way.

With regression under our belt, it is time to move on to classification. Now we are interested in classifying something as either in a class or not; that is, a day is wet or dry, cold or hot, cloudy or sunny. However, to do this correctly, we have to step our output through an activation function. Using an activation function, particularly the step function, will allow us to better classify our output. Refer back to Example 1-3 to review the step function, but essentially, if the output is less than zero, nothing is output; 1.0 is output otherwise. Now, if we consider the game in Table 1-9, the output is shown as a class 0 or 1.

*Table 1-9. Game 4*

| X1 | Expected output |
|----|-----------------|
| 4  | 0               |
| 3  | 0               |
| 2  | 1               |
| 1  | 1...            |

Programmatically, you could likely solve Game 4 in seconds, but what weights would you need to solve the perceptron that could properly classify those outputs? Well, the problem is that it can't be done using our toolset thus far. Go ahead and try Equation 1-2, but you'll find that it doesn't work—not for a single perceptron anyway. However, we can solve this by adding a couple more perceptrons, as shown in Figure 1-8. In this figure, we can see three perceptrons connected, two input and one output. We call each set of perceptrons a *layer*. Therefore, the figure has an input layer with two perceptrons and one output layer with a single perceptron. Inside these perceptrons there are four input weights (bias + input × 3) in the input layer and two weights in the output layer. Are you able to balance these weights now to provide the correct output? Give it a try.

> In classroom settings, we typically have students form groups and pretend each is a perceptron. They are then told to organize themselves in layers and solve the various weights in the problem.

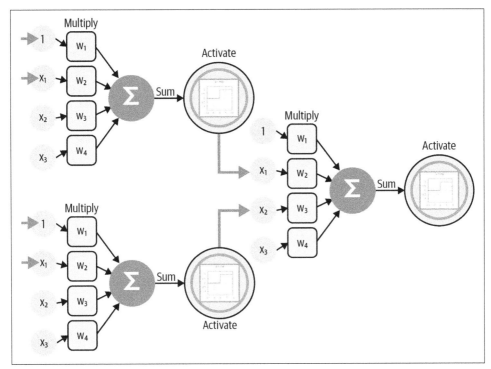

*Figure 1-8. Multilayer Perceptron Game 4*

For the last game (Table 1-10), we want to increase the number of outputs from one class output node to two. This means we also need to put two perceptrons in the output layer.

*Table 1-10. Game 5*

| X1 | X2 | X3 | Y1 | Y2 |
|----|----|----|----|----|
| 4 | 0 | 2 | 0 | 1 |
| 5 | 1 | 3 | 0 | 1 |
| 3 | 2 | 4 | 0 | 1 |
| 2 | 3 | 5 | 1 | 0 |
| 1 | 4 | 0 | 1 | 0 |
| 0 | 5 | 1 | 1 | 0 |

Likewise, we are adding another input, and therefore it makes sense to also add another input perceptron. We then end up with the multilayer perceptron network shown in Figure 1-9. The figure shows a network with 3 input perceptrons each taking 3 inputs for a total of 12 weights ([3 input + bias] × 4). Then in the second (output) layer of 2 perceptrons, we have 8 weights ([3 input + bias] × 2) for a total of 20 weights. The game is far more simple than it first appears, and the trick is to follow the zeros.

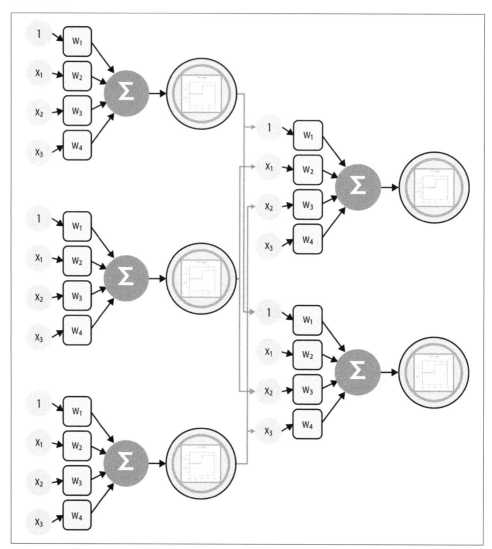

*Figure 1-9. Multilayer Perceptron Game 5*

After you solve each problem, consult the end of the chapter for the answer. You may be able to solve the games completely in your head, but it can also help to physically use a mat and dice to try to solve the games randomly. However, you should also consider at this point how you might apply Equation 1-2, the perceptron learning equation, to a multilayer perceptron. The short answer is that you can't, and we will look at why this is the case in the next section.

# Understanding How Networks Learn

As we've seen by playing the Perceptron Game, when we start to combine multiple perceptrons into layers, things get complicated quickly. We call those multilayer perceptron models neural networks or advanced neural networks, or more recently, deep learning systems. Whatever we call them, when we scale from a single perceptron to even just a few, solving for the amount to update a single weight in the entire system becomes very complicated. You likely already realized that when playing the game, but hopefully you also figured out that solving the weights becomes systematic. That is, once you have one weight figured out, you can move backward and solve the rest. This system of solving the weights by moving backward is how we solve the weights in networks today. That system is called backpropagation, and we will delve into greater detail on it next.

 As you've already seen, there are numerous ways to solve the weights in a network. Randomizing was often a good solution before networks became far too complex. However, the preferred method is now backpropagation, though that may change in the future.

## Backpropagation

While Equation 1-2 will work for updating or learning the weights in a single perceptron, it is not able to find the updates across an entire network. In order to do this, we fall back to calculus, which is able to determine how much change or effect each weight has on the network output. By determining this, we can work backward and determine how much each weight in the network needs to be updated or corrected. This system is called backpropagation. The complicated parts come from calculus, but fortunately the whole system can be automated with a technique called *automatic differentiation*. However, it still is important to intuitively understand how this system works in the event something goes wrong. Problems will and do often happen, and they are the result of something called vanishing or exploding gradients. Therefore, to help you understand if you have a vanishing or exploding gradient, we will explore backpropagation in some detail.

In order to determine the amount of change of each weight, we need to know how to calculate the amount of change for the entire system. We can do this by taking the equation that gives us the forward answer, or prediction, and differentiating it with calculus. Recall that calculus gives us the rate of change of an equation or system. For basic calculus with one variable, this is elementary, and Figure 1-10 shows how a function can be differentiated at a single point to find the gradient or change at that point.

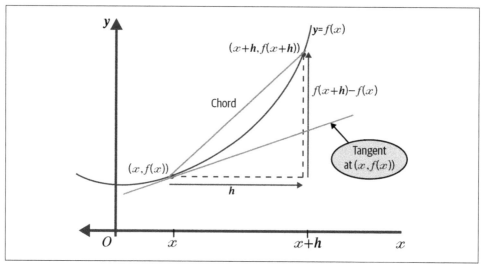

*Figure 1-10. Finding the gradient of a point on a function*

 If you have a foundational knowledge of calculus, you should be able to understand the upcoming material even if it has been some time since you practiced calculus. However, those readers with no knowledge of calculus should explore that material further on their own. There are plenty of free videos or courses online that can provide this knowledge.

Now that we understand why calculus is essential, we can move on to solving our equations. However, with a multilayer perceptron, each perceptron has its own weights, summation, and activation functions, so differentiating all of this sounds quite complex. The short answer is yes, it very much used to be, but we have found tricks to dramatically simplify the problem. If we consider that each layer of perceptrons uses the same activation function, then we can treat the entire layer as a linear system of equations, thus reducing a single layer down to a single function such as *f()*. Incidentally, reducing a layer down to a linear system of equations, or in other words a matrix, reduces the computational complexity immensely as well. This is how all deep learning systems work internally today, and this is what makes processing a layer through a network so fast. It is also the reason that deep learning systems now surpass humans in many tasks that we previously thought we would never be surpassed on.

Included in your required math background is linear algebra. Linear algebra helps us solve linear systems of equations and create some cool 3D visuals, like games. It is another mathematical tool that can help you understand deep learning and other systems, likely more so than calculus.

By reducing an entire layer down to a system of equations, we can then assume a single function $f()$. Each successive function then would apply itself to f, such as $g(f())$, where the $g$ function is a second or successive layer in a network. Remember that the output from the first layer feeds into the second layer, or function, and so on. We can solve this function by using the chain rule, as demonstrated in Equation 1-4.

*Equation 1-4.*

$$h(x) = g(f(x))$$

$$\frac{dh}{dx} = \frac{dg}{df}\frac{df}{dx}$$

In Equation 1-4, we can use the chain rule from calculus, which tells us that any equation in the first form can then be differentiated in the second form. This gives us a method to differentiate each of the layers, and then by using some more math magic, we can derive the set of specific weight update equations shown in Figure 1-11.

$$x_{i,j}^l = \sum_m \sum_n w_{m,n}^l o_{i+m,j+n}^{l-1} + b_{i,j}^l$$

$$o_{i,j}^l = f(x_{i,j}^l)$$

$$\delta_{i,j}^l = \frac{\partial E}{\partial x_{i,j}^l}$$

$$\frac{\partial E}{\partial x_{i',j'}^l} = \sum_{m=0}^{k_1-1} \sum_{n=0}^{k_2-1} \delta_{i'-m,j'-n}^{l+1} w_{m,n}^{l+1} f'(x_{i',j'}^l)$$

$$\frac{\partial E}{\partial w_{m',n'}^l} = \sum_{i=0}^{H-k_1} \sum_{j=0}^{W-k_2} \delta_{i,j}^l o_{i+m',j+n'}^{l-1}$$

*Figure 1-11. Finding the gradient weight*

Figure 1-11 shows the high-level steps of reducing the perceptron forward function at the top of the figure into a gradient weight function we can use to update weights in training at the bottom. The mathematics show how the forward function is first derived with respect to $x$, the inputs, into the second-to-last equation, where the last equation differentiates the function with respect to the weights ($w$). By differentiating with respect to $w$, we can determine the gradient or amount of change each weight contributes to the final answer.

This equation shows the calculus for deriving the gradient of change for each weight. Gradients represent an amount and direction of change. Thus, by finding the gradient, we can understand the amount the individual weight or parameter contributed to the output error. We can then reverse the gradient and adjust the weight in the opposite direction. Keep in mind that each time we change a weight, we want to change the smallest amount possible. This way a change in the weight won't cause another weight to get unbalanced. This can be quite tricky when we train thousands or millions of weights, so we introduce a learning rate called *alpha*. Remember that we used alpha in our single perceptron example to set the amount of change or improvement in each iteration, and the same applies here. Except in this case, we need to make alpha a much smaller value, and in most cases the value is 0.001 or less.

Alpha, the learning rate of a network, is a common parameter we will see over and over again, and it is used to tune how fast a network trains. Set the value too low, and the network learns very slowly, but it may avoid certain training pitfalls. Set alpha too high, and the network learns quickly but then will likely become unstable. Instead of converging to an answer, it will likely give a wrong answer. These issues occur because the network may get stuck in some local minimum, as shown in Figure 1-12, where the goal of any network is to find the global minimum or maximum value.

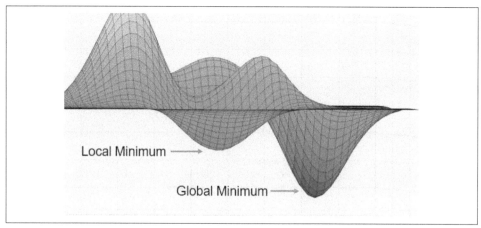

*Figure 1-12. Local minimum versus global minimum*

# Optimization and Gradient Descent

The whole process of backpropagation is further described as using gradient descent, so named because backpropagation finds the gradient that describes the impact of an individual weight. It then reverses the direction of the gradient and uses that to find the global minimum of the solution. We refer to this entire process of optimizing a solution to a global minimum as *optimization*, because we reduce the total errors of a solution to a global minimum. Optimization itself is fundamental to data science and is used to describe the method that minimizes the errors of a method. Minimizing error is relative to the function being performed—either regression or classification, for instance—and uses the specific function error metric to determine performance. For example, with regression we may minimize on MSE.

Optimizers come in several variations, but many of the ones we use for deep learning are based on gradient descent, the backpropagation method. Here is a list of optimizers we will cover in this book:

*Gradient descent*
> This is the base algorithm, and it works as described in the section on backpropagation.

*Stochastic gradient descent (SGD)*
> This is an improved version of gradient descent that uses random batch sampling to improve on generalization. This is the actual standard, and we will devote a whole section to this method later.

*Nesterov*
> This method introduces the concept of momentum. Momentum is like an additional speed control for SGD and allows it to converge quicker. Nesterov provides an additional speed boost to momentum as well.

*AdaGrad*
> This is a form of gradient descent that adjusts to how frequent the data is. This, in turn, gives it an advantage when handling sparse data. Data associated with infrequent features with higher value will benefit more when using AdaGrad. However, this method does suffer from diminishing learning rates. This method also introduces the concept of adaptive learning rates.

*AdaDelta*
> This method is based on AdaGrad but improves on it by not requiring an initial learning rate (alpha) as the algorithm will adjust on its own. It also manages the diminishing learning rates better.

*RMSprop*
> This is a version of AdaDelta that was independently developed by Geoff Hinton.

*Adaptive Moment Estimation (Adam)*

This is an extension to AdaDelta and RMSprop that allows finer control over the momentum parameters. Adam is also one of the more popular optimizers you may encounter in recent papers.

*AdaMax*

This is an improvement to Adam that updates the momentum parameters.

*Nadam*

This is a combination of Nesterov and RMSprop, which is like supercharging the momentum on RMSprop.

*AMSGrad*

This is a new gradient descent algorithm with momentum that intends to improve on methods like Adam where it is shown that using SGD with momentum works just as well or better. This method is becoming the go-to when Adam does not perform as well as may be expected.

This list has doubled since 2012, and it likely could double again in a few short years.

 You may find yourself generally sticking to a few standard optimizers for various classes of problems. A lot of this depends on the problem you are trying to solve and the data you are using. We will of course explore further details about optimizers in later chapters as we solve particular problems.

# Vanishing or Exploding Gradients

Generally, the whole system of backpropagation (gradient descent) and finding the partial derivative with respect to each weight works automagically (*https://oreil.ly/_e5qM*). That is, most deep learning libraries like Keras, TensorFlow, and PyTorch provide automatic differentiation of the partial derivative of a network out of the box. While this is incredibly powerful, and a blessing for those of us who used to do it by hand, it still has some problems. While we generally won't encounter these issues until we look at larger and more complex networks, it is worth mentioning here.

Occasionally, and for a variety of reasons, the gradient descent optimization algorithm may start to calculate exploding or vanishing gradients. This may happen for the various optimizers we covered earlier. Remember, a gradient denotes the amount and direction a weight contributes to the network. An optimizer may start to calculate an incredibly large value for a gradient, called an *exploding gradient*, or conversely, very small or *vanishing gradients*. In the case of exploding gradients, the network will start to generally overpredict, while in the case of vanishing gradients, the network will just stop learning and freeze. To help diagnose these issues early, use the following guide:

- The network does not improve after $x$ number of iterations.
- The network is unstable, and you see large changes in error moving from positive to negative.
- The network appears to go backward in learning.

The best way to diagnose these issues is by watching and monitoring how your network trains. In most cases, you will want to closely observe your network training for the first several thousand iterations. In the next section, we'll discuss further optimization when training networks.

## SGD and Batching Samples

One problem we may come across when training thousands of data through a network is that the process can take a long time and isn't general enough. That is, if we update our network for each individual weight, we may find elements that cancel each other out. This can be further compounded if the data is pulled from the same order. To alleviate these problems, we introduce a random batching approach to updating our network. Batching the data into groups and then applying changes averaged across those groups better generalizes the network, which is usually a good thing. Furthermore, we randomize this batching process so that no two batches are alike and data is further processed randomly. This whole technique is called stochastic gradient descent when used with backpropagation to train a deep learning network.

We use the term *stochastic* to mean random since we are now pulling random groups of samples. The gradient descent part is the heart of backpropagation optimization, as we already learned. SGD is the standard optimizer, as we saw earlier. There are plenty of variations to SGD that are more powerful, and we will explore those as well. The important thing to remember about SGD and other optimizers is that they use batches of data and not individual samples. As it turns out, since we are using linear systems of equations, this also becomes more computationally efficient.

`batch_size` is used to determine updates to the network. Typical batch sizes are 32–256 for large dataset sizes. The batch size is a deceptive parameter that may or may not have an incredible impact on network training. It generally will be one of the first parameters you tune to enhance a network. Smaller values of batch size reflect large changes in training, while larger batches reduce changes.

Another improvement to batching is minibatching, which is when we break up the batches into smaller batches. These smaller and also random batches have been shown to increase data variance further, which is a good thing. This in turns leads to better generalization and, of course, better training.

There is also a third option—or should we say, the original option. Originally, data was just batched, and the method was called batch gradient descent. The major problem with this was that the batches were always the same. This reduced the data variance, which, as we now know, led to decreased training performance and learning. Batch gradient descent is an option, but not one you will choose very often.

## Batch Normalization and Regularization

Batch normalizing is an additional process we may perform as the inputs flow through the network. Normalizing the data in a batch or after it processes through a layer allows for more stable networks by avoiding vanishing and exploding gradients. Regularization is the same process, but it typically involves balancing internal network weights using the L1 or L2 norm. We use the term *norm* to refer to a normalization of the vector space, or as performed in linear algebra, normalizing a vector. The L1 or L2 refers to the distance used to calculate the vector's magnitude. In calculating the L1 norm, we use what is referred to as the taxi cab or block distance, while the L2 norm is the more typical euclidean distance. An example of calculating the L1 and L2 norm is shown in Equation 1-5. Notice the subtle but important difference between the two calculations.

*Equation 1-5.*

$$||X||_1 = |3| + |4| = 7$$

$$||X||_1 = |3|^2 + |4|^2 = \sqrt{9 + 16)} = \sqrt{25)} = 5$$

Normalization and regularization can be important ways to optimize deep learning, as we will see when we start building networks.

## Activation Functions

We already covered the absence of an activation function or just straight linear output of a network. We also looked at the step activation function, which essentially steps the output and is very useful in classification problems. We will use a variety of activation functions that are specific to regression or classification. However, in many cases we may use broader functions to work between hidden layers of networks that will work on either problem. Much like optimizers, there are a variety of activation functions that are more useful for certain problems and data types. There is often no hard-and-fast rule for which to use, and a lot of your experience working with these functions will come through hard work. Another option is to digest several papers and take recommendations from those. While that can work, and is quite useful anyway, you often have to be careful that their problems and network design align well

---

with your own problem. The following are the more common activation functions you may come across and will likely use in this book:

*Linear*
> Essentially the absence of an activation function. The output from summation is sent directly to output. This, as we've seen, is a perfect function for regression problems.

*Step*
> We've seen a basic implementation of a step function in Example 1-3. Use this one for classification problems.

*Sigmoid or logistic activation*
> This is also called the *squishification* function because it squishes the output to a value between 0.0 and 1.0. It was the first common activation function because it was so easy to differentiate when calculating backpropagation by hand. Figure 1-13 shows the sigmoid function and how it resembles logistic regression. This method is used for classification.

*Tanh or hyperbolic tangent function*
> This squishes the output to between −1 and +1 and is most effective for classification problems.

*ReLU (rectified linear unit)*
> This is a combination of the step and linear functions. This function is used for regression and is quite often in between hidden layers.

*Leaky ReLU*
> Exactly like ReLU, but with a leaky step function. This function is quite effective in controlling vanishing or exploding gradients. Leaky ReLU works best between layers.

*Parametric ReLU (PReLU)*
> This is a leaky ReLU function that provides further control with parameters. Again, it is best used between layers, but it also works for regression.

*ELU (exponential linear unit)*
> This provides an exponential rather than a linear response. This method works for regression problems and between layers.

*Softmax*
> This is for classification problems where the output is represented by a probability vector that denotes how well an output ranging from 0.0 to 1.0 fits within a set of classes. The total sum of the output of all classes equals 1.0, or 100%. If we go back to the Perceptron Game and review the classification problems, we needed two output neurons to denote our separate classes. Softmax would allow us to

reduce our output to one neuron that can output a vector of the classes and probabilities of being within each class.

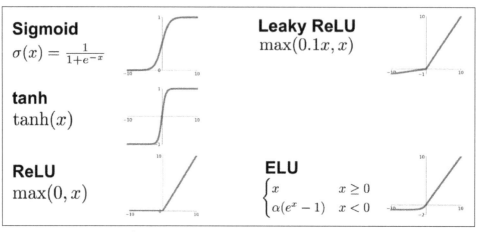

*Figure 1-13. Activation functions*

The sample set of activation functions in Figure 1-13 has also almost doubled in just under a decade. If you are training deep learning networks, you need to keep current with the best activation and optimization functions and so on. Fortunately, when using AI (deep learning) services provided by Google, the cloud services manage most of that or, as we will see, provide help along the way.

## Loss Functions

As we saw when we talked about goodness of fit earlier in this chapter, our methods (or what we call *models*) need a way to determine the amount of error. We may also use the terms *loss* or *cost* to denote the total amount of error. Recall that our goal is to minimize this error, loss, or cost by using some variation of gradient descent optimization. As we've seen with MSE, loss or error functions also are differentiated by the goal of the network, be it regression or classification. Below is a quick preview of loss functions you will likely encounter in this book, or as you explore deep learning solutions on your own:

*MSE (mean squared error)*
> We covered this method earlier when we looked at regression. MSE represents the mean error distance squared.

*RMSE (root mean squared error)*
> This is the square root of MSE. This variation is useful when trying to better understand the variance of your model.

*MSLE (mean squared logarithmic error)*
This denotes the MSE on a logarithmic scale. This method is useful for large ranges of numbers—that is, when values range from zero to billions or more.

*MAE (mean absolute error)*
This measures the error distance between two variables or features. Thus, in a 2D (x, y) regression plot, error would be measured on the x- and y-axes, both vertically and horizontally. In MSE, the measure of error is only the vertical difference on the y-axis.

*Binary classification functions*
There is a whole list of base error functions that measure classification on outputs. They determine the amount of error an input is within a class (1) or not within a class (0), which works well for binary problems.

*Binary cross-entropy loss*
With classification problems, it works better mathematically to classify in terms of probability within a class rather than to just use binary classification as above. That means this becomes the preferred method, and one we will discuss at length when we get to those later chapters.

*Hinge loss*
This is a binary classification loss function similar to cross-entropy. It differs in that it allows classification to range in values from [−1,1]. Standard cross-entropy uses values in the range [0,1].

*Squared hinge loss*
This is an extension of hinge loss.

*Multiclass classifier*
This is useful for when you want to class an input into multiple classes. For example, a picture of a dog fed into a network could be identified as a dog, and perhaps a specific dog breed and color.

*Multiclass cross-entropy loss*
This is the same approach we use in binary cross-entropy, except it's used for multiple class problems. It is the preferred and standard approach.

*Spare multiclass cross-entropy loss*
This deals with the problem of identifying data over a large number of classes. Datasets as large as 11,000 classes have been released in just the last year. Even with 18 million images fed into a classifier, with that many classes, that still only leaves about 1,600 images per class.

*Kullback–Leibler divergence loss (KL divergence)*
This is an advanced function that determines the amount of error between distributions of data. It is not well-suited to multiclass classification problems but does well for adversarial training.

Use this list of loss functions as a reference. We will explore the more important loss functions more closely in later examples. In the next section, we look at building a simple multilayer perceptron network.

 Adversarial training is a form of network training that we find in autoencoders and generative adversarial networks, or GANs. They are so named because they pit networks against each other.

# Building a Deep Learner

We already understand how to build a network, but when doing the backpropagation with automatic differentiation and all the other parts, it really makes more sense to use a library like Keras, TensorFlow, PyTorch, and so on. All of these libraries are available on a local machine, which is sometimes required for data privacy concerns. For this book, we will use the cloud to build all of our networks. However, it can be useful to look at code examples of how deep learning networks are built with other libraries in Python. Example 1-5 shows an example of a simple classifier network, one that could be used to solve our Perceptron Game 5 problem.

*Example 1-5.*

```
model = Sequential()
model.add(Dense(3, input_dim=2, activation='relu'))
model.add(Dense(2, activation='sigmoid'))

# compile the keras model
model.compile(loss='binary_crossentropy', optimizer='adam', metrics=['accuracy'])

# fit the keras model on the dataset
model.fit(X, y, epochs=1000, batch_size=10)
```

The example Keras code shown in Example 1-5 builds a deep learning network with three input nodes and a second output layer with two output nodes. We refer to perceptrons as *nodes* here to makes things more generic. Not all nodes in a future network may follow a perceptron. The code starts by denoting a variable called a model of type Sequential. The model denotes the entire deep learning network, which in this case is denoted as Sequential. Sequential here just means continually connected. After that, each layer is added with an add statement, the first layer being three nodes with an input dimension of 3 and a ReLU activation function. Don't worry too much about the new activation functions just now—we will cover them later. Next, the output layer is added with a sigmoid function. Then the entire model is compiled, which means it is set up for backpropagation. Finally, the model calls `fit`, which means it will iterate through the data for 1,000 epochs or iterations, batching the learning process in groups of 10.

Example 1-5 shows how accessible and powerful this technology has become. What can be done in six lines of Python code using the Keras library likely took hundreds of lines of code just a few years ago. However, as accessible as this technology is, it still requires an immense amount of data and processing power to be effective. While data can be accessed for free or may be available from your organization, computational processing is often another matter entirely, and this is why we focus on using cloud resources for all of the networks in this book.

> Keras is a great library that can quickly get you programming deep learning models. Be sure to check out the Keras website (*https://keras.io*) for more information and tutorials to help you get started.

Fortunately, there is a free tool available from Google that will allow us to set up a multilayer network quickly and train it in minutes—yes, minutes. Open the TensorFlow Playground site (*https://playground.tensorflow.org*), as shown in Figure 1-14.

As soon as you open that site, you will see there are two inputs denoted $X_1$ and $X_2$ shown as two shaded boxes. These boxes represent distributions of data. You can think of a distribution as an endless box of data. Each time you reach into the box and pull a sample at random, the value of the sample is determined by the distribution. This is an important concept and is further explained in Figure 1-15. In the figure, we can see two distributions. If we guess a value of 0.5 (x) and apply it to each distribution, we get a value of 0.5 for uniform and perhaps 1.7 for normal. This is because the data is skewed by the shape of the distribution. This is an important concept to grasp, and it is one we will revisit later.

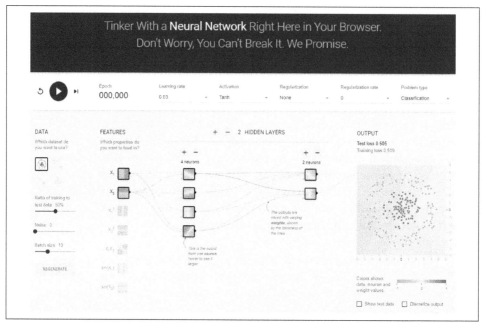

*Figure 1-14. TensorFlow Playground*

 Being able to understand distributions and probability is fundamentally important to data science, and in turn, deep learning. If you find you lack some knowledge in statistics or probability theory, you should brush up. Again, there are plenty of free materials online.

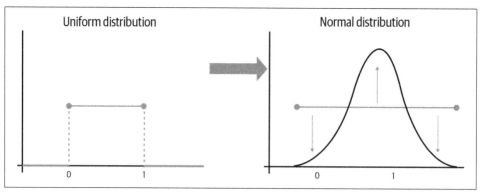

*Figure 1-15. Comparison of normal and uniform distributions*

Getting back to Figure 1-14 and TensorFlow Playground, we can see that inside the network there are two hidden layers with an input layer of four neurons and an output layer of two neurons. Pressing the Play button on the left will start the network training, and you will see how the network classifies the output as the epochs progress. In the end, the loss is minimized, and the fit looks quite nice. However, at this point and always, we want to understand whether we can optimize the network in some manner.

## Optimizing a Deep Learning Network

After we have our inputs flowing through the network and can see that the outputs are training effectively, our next step is always to optimize a network. We want do this step before any data validation as well. Recall that we always want to break our input data into three sets of data for training, testing, and validation. Before doing that, though, there are few simple tricks we can apply to this model or to any network:

*Learning rate = alpha (α)*
Determine what effect adjusting the learning rate up or down has on the network. Adjust the learning rate to 0.01 and replay the sample. Then adjust the rate to 0.1. Which learned faster?

*Activation function = tanh*
Try various activation functions. Tanh and sigmoid work well with classification, while ReLU and linear are applicable to regression.

*Regularization and regularization rate*
Regularizing data is a form of normalizing data between layers. We do this to avoid those exploding or vanishing gradients that can happen if a weight gets too large or small.

*Hidden layers*
Increase the number of hidden layers, and thus neurons, in the network. Determine the effect this has on the network.

*Neurons*
Increase or decrease the number of neurons on each layer of the network. Monitor the training performance of the network and watch for over- or underfitting.

Figure 1-16 shows a network being trained with a modified learning rate. Play with the network and try to optimize it to the fewest neurons while still being able to learn to classify the outputs effectively. Make sure that you do not overfit or underfit to the data.

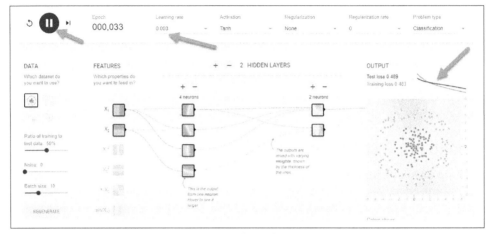

*Figure 1-16. Training a network in TensorFlow Playground*

You are unable to control the loss function aside from setting the problem type as regression or classification. Be sure to switch between the two problem types and see what effect that has on the output as well. In the next section, we look at what can happen if your network design has too few or too many layers or neurons.

## Overfitting and Underfitting

One of our primary goals in optimizing a network is to build the smallest and most concise network for the task at hand. It can be very easy to throw endless layers, neurons, and weights at a problem. The problem with this approach is that deep learning networks can actually memorize data—that is, they can learn data so well that they just remember the answer to a specific question rather than generalize an answer. This is the reason we withhold a percentage of data for both test and validation. Typically after optimizing a network to a set of training data, you then evaluate the trained network on the test dataset. If the network predicts comparative results, we say it has generalized to the training data. In some cases, running the test set may generate very bad predictions, and this often indicates the network has been overtrained or overfitted to the data.

Breaking data into training, test, and validation sets provides two phases of confirmation of your model. You can use the test dataset as a first-pass test against your trained model, and the validation set can be used as a second-pass test against the model. In more critical applications, you may have more phases of test/validation data.

Over- and underfitting is a critical element to building successful networks, so it is a topic we will revisit over and over again throughout this book. It is easy to see how we can over- and underfit using TensorFlow playground. Figure 1-17 shows the results of over- and underfitting the neural network. Add or remove layers and neurons to see if you can create the same over- and underfit patterns. You may also have to alter the learning rate, the activation function, or the number of epochs you run. On the bottom-left side of the interface, there are also options to set the ratio of training to test data, as well as noise and batch size.

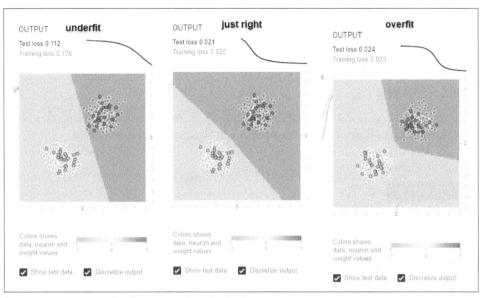

*Figure 1-17. Example of over- and underfitting*

## Network Capacity

The capacity of a network, or the number of neurons and weights in a network, describes its capacity to learn the required data. If your network is small, with only a few layers and neurons, you would not expect such a network to learn a large dataset. Likewise, a network that is too large, with lots of layers and neurons, could become able to memorize the data. Again, this is the reason we break out test and validation datasets to confirm how well a network performs after training.

Hopefully you can now appreciate how simultaneously easy and difficult building deep learning networks can be. On the surface, stacking layers and designing networks is like combining Lego blocks that wrap around complex systems of equations. Building deep learning models takes attention to detail and patience—lots of patience. Fortunately, using the Google Cloud Platform will wrap many of the complex details and provide a performant platform that should reduce training times, thus allowing you to conduct more experiments in the same amount of time.

# Conclusion

Deep learning has become the cornerstone of the new wave of AI tech that is sweeping the globe. The thing we need to remind ourselves, though, is that the foundation of this AI is still based on old tech like data science. This means we still need to understand the tenets of data science in order to be successful AI practitioners. That in turn means that understanding the data is also a requirement for anyone looking to be successful. Sadly, this fact is often lost on eager newcomers looking to build cool AI, only to find nothing they try works. Almost always this speaks to a lack of understanding of the fundamentals and the data. Hopefully you can appreciate the importance of data science and keep that in mind as we move into deeper AI. In the next chapter, we will begin exploring AI on the Google Cloud Platform.

## Game Answers

Here are the answers for the Perceptron Games 2 and 3. Some of the games may allow for multiple solutions, and this may mean your solution is not listed.

*Table 1-11. Game 2*

| W1 | W2 | W0 or bias |
|----|----|-----------|
| 1  | 2  | 0         |

*Table 1-12. Game 3*

| W1 | W2 | W3 | W0 or bias |
|----|----|----|-----------|
| 1  | 2  | 0  | 0         |

### Game 5

There are multiple solutions for Game 5, and we leave it up to the reader to find them on their own. The solution to Game 5 is not important, however; what is important is that you understand how a fully connected network functions.

# CHAPTER 2

# AI on the Google Cloud Platform

Since the implementation of the first self-driving cars, Google has had a predominant hand in shaping the AI landscape. The company has embraced all aspects of AI development, from text and speech recognition and translation to deep reinforcement learning, and it has acquired or recruited some of the best and brightest minds in the AI space. From this, Google is now providing its expertise in AI as a complete suite of services. While others are competing to do the same, Google is certainly the first place you should look when building any AI application in the future.

In this chapter, we provide an overview of the many powerful AI services Google currently provides on its cloud platform. From there we will look at how you can sign up and start working with these services. Then we will dive in and work hands-on with Google Colab and build a couple of deep learning examples with Keras. After that, we will expand on those examples by using the AutoML Tables service to upload and work with our own sample datasets. Finally, we will review the Google Cloud Shell and look at other utilities we will need over the course of the book.

In this chapter, we start coding and working with cloud services. As such, you may find it helpful to have a computing device with a larger screen and keyboard to work with the coding examples.

Here is a brief summary of the main content we will cover in this chapter:

- AI Services on GCP
- Google Colab Notebooks
- AutoML Tables
- The Cloud Shell
- Managing Cloud Data

# AI Services on GCP

GCP was launched in the spring of 2008 with the App Engine platform. Since then, the platform has grown to encompass several services, including computing, storage, networking, security, big data, IoT, and of course, AI. While Google is often considered just behind Amazon with respect to general cloud services, the same can certainly not be said for its AI services. Google has devoted considerable infrastructure and development efforts to developing the next wave of AI, and it has been doing so since its investment in self-driving cars in 2006. The AI teams at Google, consisting of Google Brain, DeepMind, and others, are considered the best of the best, hands down. It therefore makes sense that Google has and will set the standards for AI services. However, even with these high standards, there are still many other challengers producing comparable products. In the end, you may find yourself looking to other services, but in this book, we will stick with Google for now.

Figure 2-1 outlines the structure of how the AI services within the GCP are organized. At the outside is the AI Hub, which is essentially the container for everything AI and GCP. Inside the hub are the main components: the building blocks and the platform. The AI building blocks consist of the various predeveloped, trained, and tuned AI models for everything from Vision to language, speech, recommendations, and more. These blocks are consumed by the platform services in the AI Platform, which is denoted in Figure 2-1 by the arrow. Throughout this book, we will look at how to integrate those AI building blocks into the AI Platform. We will start with the main hub next.

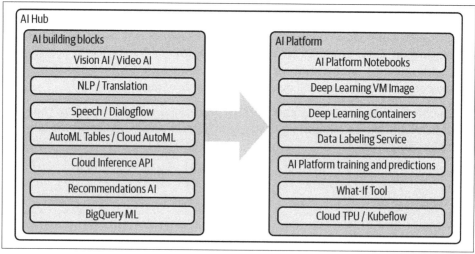

*Figure 2-1. Google AI Hub, building blocks, and Platform*

# The AI Hub

Your first gateway to accessing the AI services on GCP is through the AI Hub (*https:// aihub.cloud.google.com*). When you go to the page, you will be required to log in with a Google account. If you do not have one, you will need to create one. After you sign in to your Google account, you will be directed to the AI Hub page, as shown in Figure 2-2. This dashboard page will be your main entry point into the many services we use throughout this book. Before jumping into those services, we will look at the main navigation items that will be of interest.

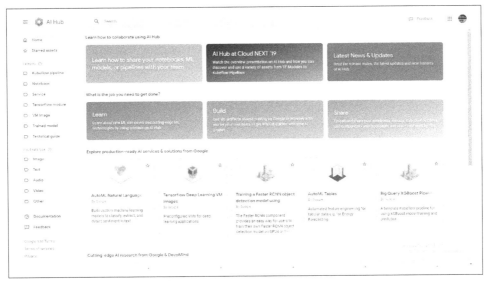

*Figure 2-2. The Google AI Hub*

On the navigation bar on the left in Figure 2-2, we see two main headings: "Category" and "Input data type." The Category heading represents the platform category that you want to run an AI service or building block on. The Input data type area represents a point of entry into importing various forms of data (image, text, audio, video, and other) on the cloud platform. You can then use this data in the various platform AI services or building blocks you use or develop on your own.

> Using many of the AI building blocks and platform services requires authorizing a payment account because these services may be billed for use. However, Google does provide a rather generous amount of credits in order to test development.

# AI Platform

The AI Platform represents the backend services, models, or containers that host your AI building blocks or process data. As such, when starting to build any AI service, your first task is to decide which platform will host your service. Of course, services and platforms are interchangeable, and you may transfer an AI service developed on one platform to another. However, you do still need to select a development or test platform first. We will primarily be working with the Notebook platform for most coding exercises, but it will be useful to offer a broad overview of all platforms here:

*Kubeflow Pipelines*
> Kubeflow itself is an open source project from Google. The pipeline part is about deploying apps within the Kubernetes container engine. Container engines like this simplify deployment immensely.

*Notebook*
> This represents the Google Colab notebook platform, which is a derivative of Jupyter Notebooks. The Google Colab notebook will be our primary coding surface for most development projects.

*Service*
> Services come in many different forms, from AI building blocks like Vision to the human data labeling service, including the ability to enroll in potential Workshop experiments. Service in this case is perhaps misnamed in that it does not represent hosting AI services.

*TensorFlow module*
> In this case, TensorFlow represents the container for the model for processing data. This platform module represents state-of-the-art TensorFlow models for image classification and natural language processing.

*VM Image*
> This allows you to run your code, service, or module on your own VM server. This is useful when you need finer access control on performance and data management. However, a running VM Image will consume services, and therefore money. This will likely be your most expensive option for deploying AI services.

*Trained Model*
> This platform allows you to run a trained model, usually TensorFlow (Keras) or PyTorch in a container. This limits the model to being used only as needed, and is often the most economical for full-time production services.

While the word *platform* is a bit of a misnomer for all the functions within the AI Platform, it is still helpful to understand all the potential uses for AI on the GCP. In the next section, we look at the higher-level building blocks we will focus on throughout this book.

## AI Building Blocks

Our primary focus for the rest of this book will be to look in detail at the robust commercial set of AI services Google is currently providing as blocks. We will spend considerable time looking at each block in detail, as well as looking at how to integrate multiple blocks together. The following is a summary of the various blocks, what they can be used for, and in what particular section or chapter we will focus on that block:

*Vision AI*
> In Chapter 3, we will look at how to use the Vision block for various forms of image recognition and search tasks.

*Video AI*
> In Chapter 4, we look at using the Video block to index and detect various tasks or items within video.

*NLP/Translation*
> In Chapters 5, and 6, we will spend plenty of time looking at all service blocks with respect to language and speech.

*AutoML Tables*
> Later in this chapter, we begin to explore the power of AutoML and how well it can build and train models for simpler problems.

*BigQuery ML*
> We will address data queries that use this block in various sections throughout the book. Starting with this chapter, we will look at how to move data with BigQuery.

These building blocks will be essential elements to the many applications and models we build throughout this book. They also provide us with the greatest path to success in building real-world AI applications you can put in place to power your business or commercial applications. With that basic understanding of the platform and building blocks, we can move on to working with the first platform component.

## Google Colab Notebooks

The Notebook platform is a derivation of a popular open source project we often use for data science and deep learning called Jupyter Notebooks. You typically run Jupyter as a service on a development machine and then open the interface in a web browser. The version Google ported to the GCP is called Colab. Colab is essentially Jupyter Notebooks on GCP running in your browser, but since it is GCP-focused, it provides so much more. It allows you to seamlessly integrate GCP data services with cloud AI services. It will be an essential driver in many of the projects we work on in this book. Therefore, we will walk through a few exercises that show you how to build deep learning models with Keras on Colab.

## Building a Regression Model with Colab

The best way to learn is by doing, and this is certainly the case with deep learning and AI in general. Therefore, in this section, we walk through building a regression model using Keras. Keras is a high-level deep learning Python library that will allow us to build our own models quickly. While we won't build many deep learning models at this level of detail, it is important to understand this foundational process. That way, when something goes wrong, you will be able to diagnose the issue on your own, thus avoiding technical frustrations and errors in potentially critical applications.

In Example 2-1, we look at developing a Keras deep learning model for performing regression analysis on Google Colab. Notebooks are meant to be developed in stages, and this will be perfect for this and many other exercises. Likewise, we will break the entire regression exercise into subexercises that you can reuse on your own later.

*Example 2-1. Setting up the environment*

- Open the Colab site (*https://colab.research.google.com*) in your web browser. If you have not signed up for GCP and the AI services, you will need to do so now.
- Figure 2-3 shows the dialog you will face when going directly to Colab. Click the New Python 3 Notebook button to create a new notebook.
- Inside this empty notebook will be one code cell. Each cell can contain code or text. Enter the following code in the cell:
  ```
  In [1]: !pip install seaborn
  ```
- The ! before a command routes that command to the shell. Thus, this command does a pip install of the Seaborn library for plotting.
- After the code is entered, click the black arrow beside the cell to execute the code. You should see the command execute, and the Seaborn library will be installed on the shell.

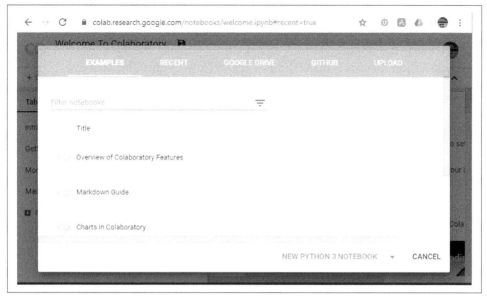

*Figure 2-3. Starting Google Colab*

- Next, click the + Code button in the header to add a new code cell, and enter the following setup code:

```
from __future__ import absolute_import, division, print_function,
                        unicode_literals

import pathlib

import matplotlib.pyplot as plt
import pandas as pd
import seaborn as sns

try:
 # %tensorflow_version only exists in Colab.
 %tensorflow_version 2.x
except Exception:
 pass
import tensorflow as tf

from tensorflow import keras
from tensorflow.keras import layers

print(tf.__version__)
```

- This code just does a number of imports and then sets up the TensorFlow back-end. TensorFlow is the deep learning engine that powers Keras. You can build models directly in TensorFlow, but that requires a greater understanding of the basic math than we previously covered. As such, we will stick with Keras.

- Make sure the cell is error free, and run it by pressing the black arrow. The only output from this cell is the version of TensorFlow you just installed.

You may find yourself using the first subexercise over and over again as you work your way through building and training models. Now, with the environment set up, we want to move on to Example 2-2.

*Example 2-2. Importing data*

- Continuing from the last notebook, Example 2-1, create a new cell and enter the following code:

```
dataset_path = keras.utils.get_file("housing.data",
  "http://archive.ics.uci.edu/ml/machine-learning-databases/housing/
  housing.data")
dataset_path
```

- The above code sets a variable with the `dataset_path`. The path is where a Keras utility will get the file from a sample data archive and download it for our regression experiment.

- Run the code by pressing the black arrow. You will see the utility download the file and then print the path where the file is stored local to the notebook.

- We next need to load our data into a data container called a *data frame*. The Pandas library we imported in setup will allow us to load and parse the data we just downloaded into a data frame. In the next section of code, we label the columns and parse the data into a data frame:

```
column_names = ['CRIM','ZN','INDUS','CHAS','NOX','RM', 'DIS', 'RAD', 'TAX',
                'PTRATIO', 'B', 'MEDV']
raw_dataset = pd.read_csv(dataset_path, names=column_names,
                          na_values = "?", comment='\t',
                          sep=" ", skipinitialspace=True)

dataset = raw_dataset.copy()
dataset.tail()
```

- The first line of code sets up the column names. These names were obtained from a sister file in the same housing folder on the archive site.

- Next, Pandas pd uses `read_csv` to parse the downloaded dataset given the rules in the function call.

- Finally, the code completes by doing a copy and then outputs the tail of the data frame.

- Execute the code by pressing the black arrow. The code will run, and you should see the output shown in Figure 2-4.

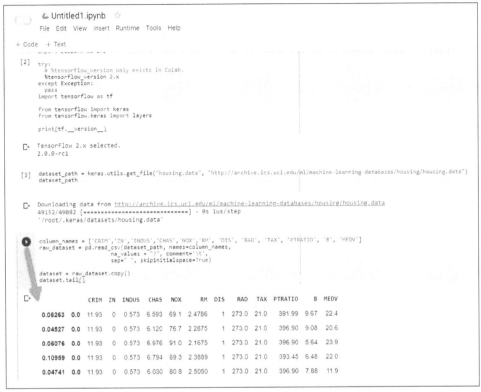

*Figure 2-4. Executing code in Colab*

The archive we pulled the data from has plenty of sample datasets you can revisit on your own or as part of other learning. Code for this import method is just one way of getting data into Colab—we will review a few other methods throughout this chapter.

After importing the data, our next step as a data scientist would be to analyze and clean the data. Even as AI practitioners of deep learning, we are still bound by rules of expectation and probability to understand our data. While deep learning purists prefer to consume any and all data, our current method will be to analyze and understand the data. We also do this because the dataset is relatively small, as we will see. In the next exercise, Example 2-3, we look at techniques for cleaning, splitting, and inspecting the data.

*Example 2-3. Cleaning, splitting, and inspecting data*

- Since our dataset is quite small, we will want to clean any null or not-a-number (NaN) values from it. We can do this by creating a new cell and entering the following code:

```
dataset.isna().sum()
```

- This will identify the number of null or NaN values in the dataset. Assuming there are some, we can remove them by running the following code:

```
dataset = dataset.dropna()
```

- After cleaning the data, we need to move on to splitting the data into a training set and test set. Recall from the first chapter that we split our data up like this to reaffirm that our results are not over- or underfitting.

- Create a new cell and enter the following code:

```
train_dataset = dataset.sample(frac=0.8,random_state=0)
test_dataset = dataset.drop(train_dataset.index)
```

- This code splits up the dataset randomly into a training section, consisting of .8, or 80% of the data, with the remainder of the data going to the test_dataset. Run this cell to break up the data into test and training sets.

- We can now inspect the data for any obvious characteristics we should be aware of. Run the following code in a new code cell:

```
sns.pairplot(train_dataset[["CRIM", "INDUS", "TAX", "MEDV"]],
             diag_kind="kde")
```

- Running the last cell will generate the correlation cross plot in Figure 2-5. A correlation cross plot shows the relationship between various features in a dataset. In data science, we often remove features that show little or no relationship with the target feature or sibling features.

- Next, we want to review the basic statistics of each feature using the following code:

```
train_stats = train_dataset.describe()
train_stats.pop("MEDV")
train_stats = train_stats.transpose()
train_stats
```

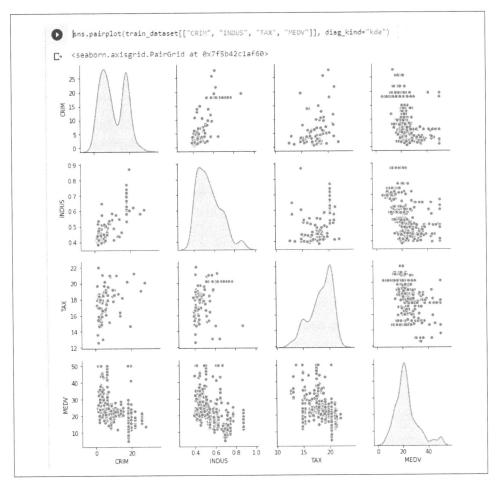

```
sns.pairplot(train_dataset[["CRIM", "INDUS", "TAX", "MEDV"]], diag_kind="kde")
```

<seaborn.axisgrid.PairGrid at 0x7f5b42c1af60>

*Figure 2-5. Correlation cross plot*

- Run the last cell, and the basic descriptive statistics describing each feature will be output. This is something all data scientists will perform as a basic analysis step. Deep learners may perform this step in order to understand the variability of the data. However, a deep learning purist may still ignore these values.

Deep learning purists will prefer to consume all data, even with the realization that not all data may be relevant. Why? Well, they believe that we need to eliminate all human bias in any AI experiment. The purists still clean the data, but they use other deep learning embedding and encoding techniques. These techniques learn the relevance from the data itself and are thus becoming more powerful all the time. Readers interested in this subject should search for "autoencoding with deep learning." Keep in mind that even a purist would consider this method only when given a sufficient amount of variable data.

With the data cleaned, split, and inspected, we can move on to preparing the data. We want to identify the parts of the data that represent our target value. In our regression problem, we are selecting one column or feature as our target. We then need to split this value off into labels. Let's see how that is done in Example 2-4.

If at any time you find that cells are not running correctly, it may be because your code is out of order, meaning you may have run cells before you should have. It is often better to rerun previous cells before running new cells. In fact, if the notebook seems to start failing, just go back to the beginning and start again.

*Example 2-4. Preparing data*

- Since we are using supervised learning, this requires us to label the data. We label and split the target columns from the original test and training datasets with the following code:
```
train_labels = train_dataset.pop('MEDV')
test_labels = test_dataset.pop('MEDV')
```

- The target feature in this regression problem will be MEDV, and we essentially pop it off the data frame and into a single column data frame with the preceding code.

- Run the code and the new variables will set.

- Next, we want to normalize the data. We normalize a feature by subtracting from the mean and then dividing by the standard deviation. The end result produces data within one standard deviation of the mean. We do this so that not a single feature overrides other features. There are many other forms of normalization we will use on other examples.

- We will normalize the data by creating a new function and then executing that in the same cell, with the following code:
```
def norm(x):
  return (x - train_stats['mean']) / train_stats['std']
```

```
normed_train_data = norm(train_dataset)
normed_test_data = norm(test_dataset)
```

- You can confirm this step was taken by outputting the tail from either test or train data frames using the following code:
```
normed_train_data.tail()
normed_test_data.tail()
```

- Running this code will output the tail values from the respective data frame.

With the data now prepared, we can move on to building the model or deep learning network in Keras that we will train to solve our problem. In Example 2-5, we build a neural network model that we feel is suited to solving our problem.

*Example 2-5. Building the model*

- In order to explain the construction of the next function well, we are going to break this cell up into code sections, starting first with the function definition:
```
def build_model():
```

- Simple enough—then the first line will build the entire model with this code:
```
model = keras.Sequential([
  layers.Dense(64, activation='relu',
              input_shape=[len(train_dataset.keys())]),
  layers.Dense(64, activation='relu'),
  layers.Dense(1)
])
```

- Make sure this line is indented as it needs to be part of the function. This line creates an entire Sequential fully connected network that has 64 input neurons of input_shape, which is the length of our input parameters. That is followed by a second layer of 64 neurons, a hidden middle layer. The third and final layer reduces to one output neuron that will output our learned result.

- Next, we set up the optimizer. In this case, we use the RMSprop optimizer with the following code:
```
optimizer = tf.keras.optimizers.RMSprop(0.001)
```

- Again, make sure the line is indented. We could have, of course, used a variety of other optimizers on this problem.

- The last step is to compile the model with the optimizer and a set of metrics using the following code:
```
model.compile(loss='mse',
             optimizer=optimizer,
             metrics=['mae', 'mse'])
```

- Compiling is where a model is set up for the backpropagation process. This is where the automatic differentiation calculates the required functions for learning.

- Finally, after compiling, we return the model with the following:
```
return model
```

- Finish entering the code, and then execute the cell. With the function built, we can now create a model with the following code:
```
model = build_model()
```

- Run and execute that last line of code to build and set the model.

- After the model is set, you can output a summary of the model by running the following code in a new cell:
```
model.summary()
```

- The summary output of this model is shown in Figure 2-6. In the figure, you can see each layer in order of processing as well as the size and type. The `Param #` represents the number of weights in each layer. Notice that for this problem we are using almost 5,000 weights.

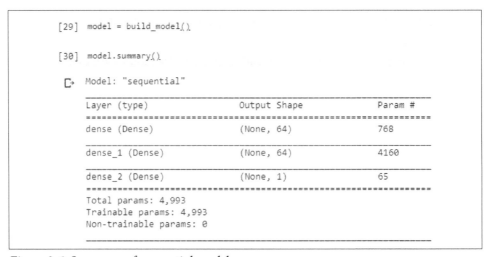

Figure 2-6. Summary of sequential model

With the network model built, we can move on to training it. Remember that we train a network by showing it batches of labeled samples. The goal of the network will be to minimize the error on the loss function, which in this case is MSE, or mean squared error. In Example 2-6, we train the model to learn from the data.

Example 2-6. Training a network

- Before we start training, we want to do a simple test and run a number of samples through the `predict` function of the model with the following code:

```
example_batch = normed_train_data[:10]
example_result = model.predict(example_batch)
example_result
```

- That code extracts 10 rows of data and pushes them through the `predict` function. Then the results are output. Run the cell and look at the results. The results will not make much sense yet because the model has yet to be trained.

- We will be able to train the model in one line of code, but we will also want to see the training progress. In order to do that, we want to create a new small helper class to output progress.

- Enter the following code in a new cell and execute it:
```
class PrintDot(keras.callbacks.Callback):
  def on_epoch_end(self, epoch, logs):
    if epoch % 100 == 0: print('')
    print('.', end='')
```

- Next, we define the number of epochs or training iterations we want to train the model on. Recall that one training iteration is one full pass of all data through the network. Create a new cell and execute it with the following code:
```
EPOCHS = 10000
```

- The important thing to understand here is that one epoch is one full pass of all training data. If you find that training is taking too long, you can reduce this number to 1,000.

- We can now train the model by entering the following code in a new cell and executing it:
```
history = model.fit(
  normed_train_data, train_labels,
  epochs=EPOCHS, validation_split = 0.2, verbose=0,
  callbacks=[PrintDot()])
```

- This code sets up the model for training and feeds it the data `normed_train_data` and `train_labels` labels. We can also see that the model is running with a validation split. That provides us with another step in tracking our network progress.

- As the cell runs, you will see a dot print for each 100 epochs. Refer back to the `PrintDot` class if you need to understand this.

- At the end of this training session, we want to review some of the history by running code in a new cell:
```
hist = pd.DataFrame(history.history)
hist['epoch'] = history.epoch
hist.tail()
```

- Figure 2-7 shows the tail output from the training history. The goal of any training is to see our loss function converge. However, the output in Figure 2-7 shows that the loss function is not converging. Instead it is wobbling about, which is likely being caused by a vanishing gradient of some type.

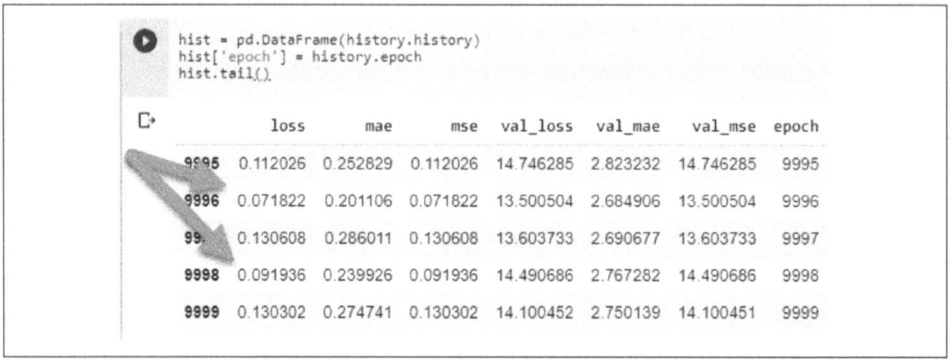

```
hist = pd.DataFrame(history.history)
hist['epoch'] = history.epoch
hist.tail()
```

|      | loss     | mae      | mse      | val_loss  | val_mae  | val_mse   | epoch |
|------|----------|----------|----------|-----------|----------|-----------|-------|
| 9995 | 0.112026 | 0.252829 | 0.112026 | 14.746285 | 2.823232 | 14.746285 | 9995  |
| 9996 | 0.071822 | 0.201106 | 0.071822 | 13.500504 | 2.684906 | 13.500504 | 9996  |
| 99.  | 0.130608 | 0.286011 | 0.130608 | 13.603733 | 2.690677 | 13.603733 | 9997  |
| 9998 | 0.091936 | 0.239926 | 0.091936 | 14.490686 | 2.767282 | 14.490686 | 9998  |
| 9999 | 0.130302 | 0.274741 | 0.130302 | 14.100452 | 2.750139 | 14.100451 | 9999  |

*Figure 2-7. Output of training history*

We trained our model, but as we've seen, there is a hint that the model wasn't converging well. What we need now is a way to explore the training history through a plot. Fortunately, we have already set up a plotting library in this example and can do just that in Example 2-7.

*Example 2-7. Training a network*

- Create a new cell and enter the following function code:

```
def plot_history(history):
  hist = pd.DataFrame(history.history)
  hist['epoch'] = history.epoch

  plt.figure()
  plt.xlabel('Epoch')
  plt.ylabel('Mean Abs Error [MEDV]')
  plt.plot(hist['epoch'], hist['mae'],
          label='Train Error')
  plt.plot(hist['epoch'], hist['val_mae'],
          label = 'Val Error')
  plt.ylim([0,5])
  plt.legend()

  plt.figure()
  plt.xlabel('Epoch')
  plt.ylabel('Mean Squared Error [$MEDV^2$]')
  plt.plot(hist['epoch'], hist['mse'],
          label='Train Error')
  plt.plot(hist['epoch'], hist['val_mse'],
          label = 'Val Error')
  plt.ylim([0,20])
```

```
plt.legend()
plt.show()
```

- This large block of code just outputs some plots that will display how well the model fits to training and an internal validation set. Recall that we also set a 0.2 or 20% rate on internal validation when building the model. That means 20% of the data will be withheld for auto-validating the model.

- Run the function code, and then create a new cell and execute it with the following code:
```
plot_history(history)
```

- Running that block will output Figure 2-8, which shows that our model does indeed have a problem, although likely not the one we expected.

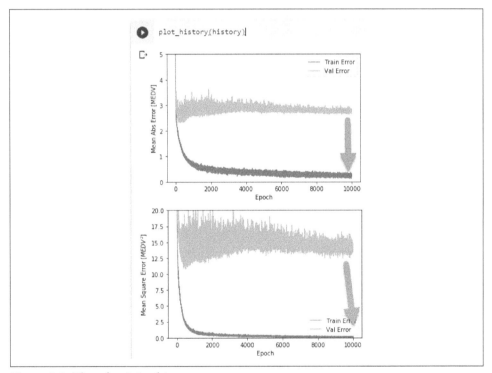

*Figure 2-8. Plot of training history errors*

We can see now that our model does indeed have issues with respect to overfitting on the data. Notice in Figure 2-8 that the errors on the training data, the bottom line, are much less than the errors on the validation line. Ideally, we want both lines to occupy the same space and have similar errors, which means the model is not over- or under-fitting. Fixing the model in this case just takes experience in understanding how networks fail. Experience can take months or years to gain, which is why we want to use those fully developed models later. Example 2-8 will show a few techniques to fix our current problem.

*Example 2-8. Tuning a network*

- From the menu, select Runtime → Run All. This will rerun all the cells and output the results again. This is also an excellent way to reset your environment if you get lost on which cell you were executing.
- Locate the cell in the notebook with the function to build the network model. Alter the function to the following code:

```
def build_model():
  model = keras.Sequential([
   layers.Dense(128, activation='relu',
                input_shape=[len(train_dataset.keys())]),
   layers.Dropout(.5),
   layers.Dense(64, activation='relu'),
   layers.Dropout(.5),
   layers.Dense(32, activation='relu'),
   layers.Dropout(.5),
   layers.Dense(1)
  ])

  optimizer = tf.keras.optimizers.RMSprop(0.001)

  model.compile(loss='mse',
                optimizer=optimizer,
                metrics=['mae', 'mse'])
  return model
```

- The code has been modified in two ways:
  - First, the layer architecture itself was modified into more of a funnel shape, as the top layer goes from 128 neurons down to the last hidden layer of 32 neurons before being output to 1.
  - Second, we added a special kind of layer called Dropout. Dropout layers drop out or randomly turn off a percentage of neurons set by the dropout rate. In this setup, we add dropout to every layer connection and set it to .5, or 50%. This means that half the neurons will fail to fire during training. The end effect is that the network generalizes better.
- After you update that code, it is best to execute the entire notebook again using the Runtime → Run All menu command.

- Running the notebook will produce Figure 2-9, and you can now see how the training and validation errors converge but then diverge again after that. Notice that the validation set is now better predicted, at least initially. This is likely an indication of too much dropout. Can you fix it?

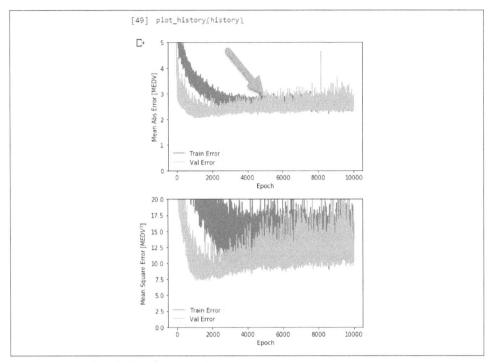

*Figure 2-9. Updated plot of training history errors*

In the last exercise, we saw how the convergence of training errors can differ based on how the model generalized. Eventually the model did reach some convergence but then deviated from overtraining. We can fix this in Example 2-9 by introducing an auto-stopping mechanism.

*Example 2-9. Auto-stopping training*

- Since most of our models will be using cloud resources, it is important to make sure we avoid overtraining. Overtraining means lost resources, and lost resources also mean lost money. This can certainly be the case when working with more complex datasets and AI tasks.
- Enter the following code in a new cell at the bottom of the notebook:

```
model = build_model()
early_stop = keras.callbacks.EarlyStopping(monitor='val_loss',
```

```
                                          patience=1000)
history = model.fit(normed_train_data, train_labels, epochs=EPOCHS,
                    validation_split = 0.2, verbose=0,
                    callbacks=[early_stop, PrintDot()])
plot_history(history)
```

- This code rebuilds the model and then, using keras.callbacks, uses a function called EarlyStopping to put a watch in place. The callback watch will monitor the training every number of iterations set by the patience or wait parameter. In this case, it is set to 1,000.

- We then fit the model again using the new callback early_stop and then plot the history, as shown in Figure 2-10.

- Run the code, and you should see the output generated in Figure 2-10.

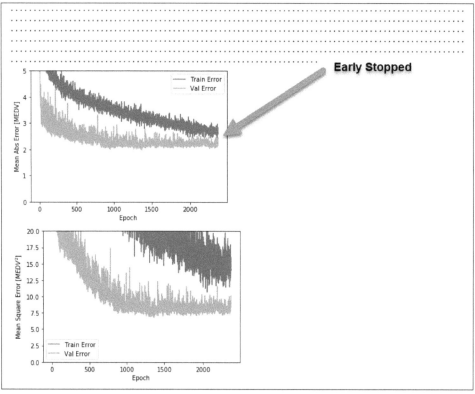

*Figure 2-10. Example of early training stopping*

With our model corrected and not overtraining, we can move on to doing predictions with our reserved test dataset. Running another test against the model this way assures us that the model is robust enough for the real world. In Example 2-10, we look at how to make predictions and do a final evaluation of the trained model.

*Example 2-10. Evaluating a trained model*

- When we are satisfied with training the model, it is time to do a proper evaluation and final assessment to make sure it is ready for the real world. We can do that by running `evaluate` on the model with the following code:

```
loss, mae, mse = model.evaluate(normed_test_data, test_labels, verbose=0)

print("Testing set Mean Abs Error: {:5.2f} MEDV".format(mae))
```

- Run that code in a new cell at the end of the notebook. Notice that we run `evaluate` against the test data and labels. The output will show the MAE of the training error in MEDV, or median household value, against the test data.

- We can go a step further and plot those predictions by running the test data through the model and then plotting the results. This can simply be done with the following code:

```
test_predictions = model.predict(normed_test_data).flatten()

plt.scatter(test_labels, test_predictions)
plt.xlabel('True Values [MEDV]')
plt.ylabel('Predictions [MEDV]')
plt.axis('equal')
plt.axis('square')
plt.xlim([0,plt.xlim()[1]])
plt.ylim([0,plt.ylim()[1]])
_ = plt.plot([-100, 100], [-100, 100])
```

- The first line in the code is where `model.predict` is called against the `normed_test_data`. Then the data is plotted with the plot code. The top plot in Figure 2-11 shows the predicted output with a regression line through it.

- Finally, we want to get a sense of the distribution of the errors. Not every model we develop will be perfect, and it is important to understand how well a model predicts. We can do that by generating a histogram of errors with the following code:

```
error = test_predictions - test_labels
plt.hist(error, bins = 25)
plt.xlabel("Prediction Error [MEDV]")
_ = plt.ylabel("Count")
```

- Enter that code in a new cell and run it. You should see the results, as shown in the bottom of Figure 2-11. The output is not as smooth as we like because of the small dataset.

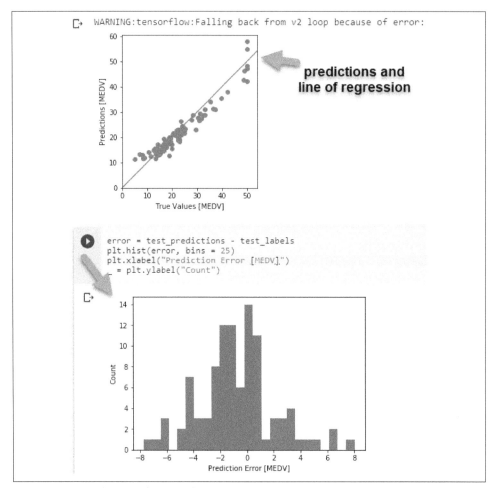

*Figure 2-11. Evaluating the model*

At this point, your decision comes down to whether the model is good enough for what you or your organization need to do. If it is, you make the journey to commercialize your new model. Since the model is already on the cloud, that should be fairly straightforward. Of course, if the model is not good enough then it is back to training and evaluation.

In this section, we learned to build and tune a model. In order to tune our model, we first altered the network architecture and then used a special layer called Dropout. Dropout layers randomly drop out neurons between activations, and this allows for better generalization across data. Tuning networks can be time-consuming and tedious, and many times it feels like a mystic art. There have even been deep learning support groups formed to discuss these problems and alleviate frustrations. Of course, this is nothing new to Google, which has worked in this space for over a decade. This is why Google has invested so heavily in AutoML, and that is the first AI building block we will cover in the next section.

# AutoML Tables

Anyone who has worked developing models knows that there are countless variations and ways to solve a problem. As we have seen, the plethora of network architecture and training options can not only intimidate developers, but also leave them unable to decide on the best network and just going back and forth between configurations for weeks or even months. To address this problem, a new form of meta or training the trainer called AutoML was introduced. AutoML is essentially machine learning on top of machine learning. This is great because it allows us to try various configurations automatically.

 AutoML Tables on GCP currently runs about $20 per hour. When training AutoML, you must train in increments of an hour, and the range is from 1 to 72 (one hour to three days). Since the AutoML service is expensive to run, it is suggested that you run the exercises in this section only as necessary.

At this time, AutoML Tables is designed to process tabular data for building models to automatically perform either regression or classification. In Example 2-11, we see how to set up and use AutoML Tables to perform regression.

*Example 2-11. Developing an AutoML model*

- Navigate to the AutoML Tables page (*https://console.cloud.google.com/automl-tables*).

- The start of an AutoML workflow requires you to pick or import a prepared dataset. We will learn how to prepare data later, but for now, just use the Quickstart dataset. This is likely the only dataset showing on the interface.

- After you click on the Quickstart dataset, a page will load showing the data schema in Figure 2-12. The Schema tab allows you to review the features in the dataset and determine what target to choose.

- Select the Balance as the target, as shown in Figure 2-12, and then press Continue.

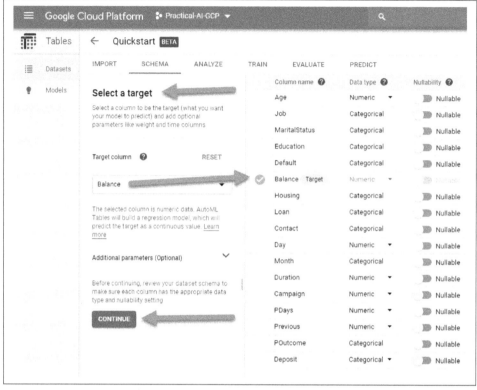

*Figure 2-12. Examining the schema*

- This will open the Analyze tab and run basic descriptive statistics on all of the column features. Notice that in this case, some of the features are categorical. Categorical features are based on classes or categories.

- Clicking on any categorical feature will display a summary of the categories it consists of. Normally, we need to break down categorical values into numeric values in some manner. This is all taken care of with AutoML Tables.

- Select the Train tab and click the Train Model button. This will prompt you to enter a few additional parameters. For this example, we will set the parameters as follows:

  — Use Regression_Balance as the name of our model. Use a unique descriptive name for this value.

  — Training budget = 1, for one hour of training time. AutoML training, at time of writing, was going for $20 per hour. Not to worry, though. Training this example will only take a few minutes, and unless you have been reckless, you should have plenty of Google credits remaining.

— Input feature selection allows you to turn off features/columns you may not want to train this model on. This is sometimes useful when comparing multiple models. Leave this as is—the features we have will all work for this model.

— Expand the Advanced Options section to view advanced parameters:

— Early stopping = ON. Be sure this option is on. It ensures that the model will stop if it has trained all that it feels it can. This option should be on by default, but check to be sure.

- When all options are set, click the Train Model button. This will start training the model. Since we set training for an hour, expect to wait an hour for the results to return. Yep, an hour.

- Figure 2-13 shows the results returned from one hour of training on the example data. Your results may vary slightly, but not by much.

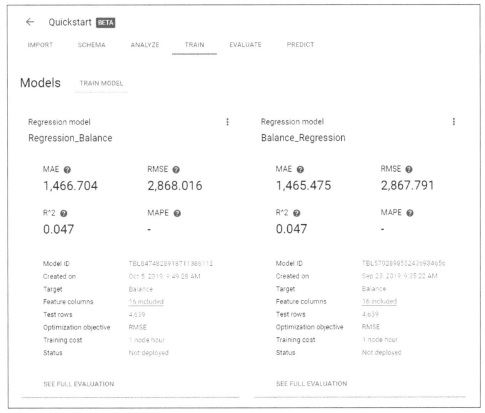

*Figure 2-13. Example generated model*

- In Figure 2-13, we can see three measures of error: MAE, RMSE, and $R^2$ or R squared. We learned earlier that R squared can be deceptive in some cases—is this such a case? The MAE seems quite low, but consider the RMSE of around 3,000, or around 900,000 MSE. Remember, RMSE is the square root of MSE.

- Click back to the Analyze tab and review the basic stats for the Balance feature again. Find the Standard deviation column and review the value. The value for Balance is around three million, which means our error of around nine hundred thousand or a million is less than one-third of a standard deviation.

There are a number of methods for breaking down categorical features into numeric values. For instance, if a feature is a category like wet or dry as we saw in Table 1-2, we could assign a value of 1 for wet and 0 for dry.

In most cases, we will aim to reduce our expected error to less than 5%. For some problems, this could be relaxed, and in other cases the expectation could require much less acceptable error. The definition of what is acceptable will be up to you and/or your organization. If the organization you are working for does not have these standards, it should consider putting them in place for when legal comes knocking.

You could certainly expect any industrial or human-intractable AI to require much higher error tolerances. However, it depends on the situation, and in many ways, on the interaction itself. A fraud detection system may have a relatively low error threshold compared to a medical application, for instance.

After the model is trained, we can then evaluate the training process itself. In Example 2-12, we will evaluate the generated model and look at predictions.

*Example 2-12. Evaluating an AutoML model*

- After training, we will generally want to evaluate the results of our model. By evaluating the model, we can get a further sense of important and not-so-important features.

- Click the Evaluate tab to open the page. The top portion reiterates the earlier error metrics, but at the bottom we can see a Feature importance plot, as shown in Figure 2-14. This plot indicates to us the importance of each feature, and how important it is with respect to other features.

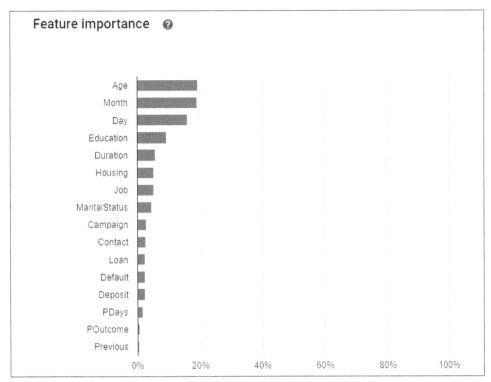

*Figure 2-14. Feature importance plot of model*

- In Figure 2-14, you can see that the Age feature is the most important and the Previous feature the least.

- At this point, we would go back and remove some less important features such as Previous, POutcome, and PDays, and then retrain the model and reevaluate. You may even repeat that process to tune the features further, perhaps even adding in other features.

- Click the View Your Evaluation Results In BigQuery link in the middle of the page. This will direct you to the query page and allow you to view the test or evaluation results.

- Next, open the project data source and expand the results, as shown in Figure 2-15.

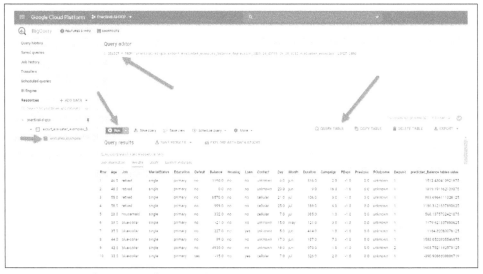

*Figure 2-15. Evaluating results in BigQuery*

- Click Query Table, shown on the far right in Figure 2-15. This button will not show until you select the dataset. You should see the SQL query generate in the Query editor window.

- Type an * symbol after SELECT, again shown in Figure 2-15. This is the same as asking for all columns in SQL. If you are unfamiliar with SQL queries, you can get help with that by consulting any good texts on relational databases.

- Click the Run button, noted in Figure 2-15, and view the results.

- You can also explore the data with Google Data Studio by clicking the Explore with Data Studio link in the middle of the page. Data Studio is a great product for building cool visualizations you can share anywhere.

AutoML Tables is a great tool that you can use to quickly evaluate deep learning models on tabular data. If you are a data scientist or someone who needs to make sense of tabular data, it may very well be the tool you need. However, it is not without expense, and although that expense may be justified, it still will depend on your experience and your available resources. AutoML is a big tool in Google's arsenal, and as we will see, all the main building blocks provide some AutoML variation.

While this chapter is meant as an introduction to the AI Hub and AI Platform, it is also intended to prepare you for working through the examples in the rest of this book. As such, in the next section we cover the Google Cloud Shell, a tool we will use frequently later.

# The Cloud Shell

If you have any significant experience with the GCP, you likely already know your way around the shell and may want to skip this section. For those other readers, the shell will be an essential tool we use later for more complex exercises. Understanding how, why, and when to use the shell will only make you a stronger AI GCP developer.

As a way of introducing the shell and the power it can provide, we are going to create a simple website on the shell—well, perhaps not an entire site, but a page should do the trick. This is a technique we will use later in the book to make actual full working sites featuring AI components we build. For now, open a browser and follow Example 2-13.

*Example 2-13. Opening the cloud shell*

- Open the Google Cloud Platform (*https://console.cloud.google.com*) and log in. Choose your current project if you need to do so.
- Click the > icon at the top right of the window. The tool tip text reads "Activate Cloud Shell."
- A shell window will open at the bottom of the browser. You should see your user email and the project you are currently working on.
- Enter the following command into the console window:
  `$ cloudshell edit`
- This will open a blank editor window, as shown in Figure 2-16.
- From the menu, select File → New to create a new file and name it *index.html*.
- Enter the following HTML text shown in Figure 2-16. Save the file afterward with File → Save:
  ```
  <html>
    <body>Hello World!</body>
  </html>
  ```
- Now start up a self-hosted web server on the console with the following:
  `python -m SimpleHTTPServer 8080`
- That will launch a SimpleHTTPServer on the server running the console on port 8080.
- Go to the web page by clicking the Web Preview button at the top right of the window, as denoted in Figure 2-16.

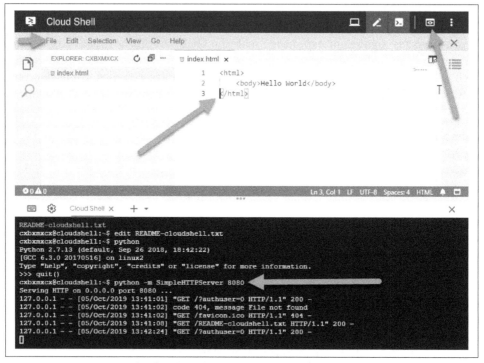

*Figure 2-16. Creating* index.html *and launching a web server*

- This will open a web page with your Hello World! message, or whatever you put in the *index.html* page you created earlier.

You have to admit that being able to edit and run code through a console window in a web browser is quite cool. But we can actually do better than that and install a Visual Studio Code server and run Visual Studio Code in the browser, including any additional modules or installation packages (Example 2-14).

 Visual Studio Code is an open source project from Microsoft. It is quickly becoming a standard in Python development and other languages. The instructions for this example were modified from a blog post (*https://oreil.ly/ty6tQ*) by Christiaan Hees.

*Example 2-14. Installing a Visual Studio Code server*

- From the console, use the right-side menu (the three dots) to enable Boost Mode. This will require you to restart the instance and perform an authorization.

- Install the code server with the following commands:
```
export VERSION=`curl -s https://api.github.com/repos/cdr/code-
server/releases/latest | grep -oP '"tag_name": "\K(.*)(?=")'`

wget https://github.com/cdr/code-server/releases/download/$VERSION/code-
server$VERSION-linux-x64.tar.gz

tar -xvzf code-server$VERSION-linux-x64.tar.gz

cd code-server$VERSION-linux-x64
```

- The first command searches for the latest version of the code server using `curl` and `grep` and saves it to `VERSION`. Then `wget` is used to download this version. Next, `tar` is used to unpack the package, and finally we change directories to the installation folder.

- From the installation folder, launch the server with the following command:
```
./code-server --no-auth --port 8080
```

- Then use the Web Preview feature again to launch the page in a new browser tab. You likely will receive a 404 error, and if you do, just remove the ending ? `authuser=0` from the URL as shown below:
```
https://8080-dot-YOURID-dot-devshell.appspot.com/?authuser=0
change to
https://8080-dot-YOURID-dot-devshell.appspot.com/
```

- Refresh the page again, and you will see the Visual Studio Code IDE running in your browser, as shown in Figure 2-17.

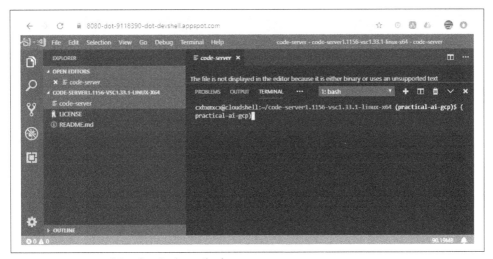

*Figure 2-17. Visual Studio Code in the browser*

Running a console session boosted—that is, enabling a session to use boosted mode—is the same as instantiating a VM instance to run a self-contained console. Running a VM instance uses credits, and therefore you will be billed time for using this method.

One of the great things about the shell is that the session will remain on and active so that you can return to it, which in turn allows for a fully disconnected and cloud-based development environment. Developing on and in the cloud also assures us that our environment is as close to production as possible. No more deploying from pre-configured development machines, only to find you missed some archaic dependency. Instead, we are going to set up our development machine on the Google Console. To do that, we need to install the required Python extensions in Example 2-15.

*Example 2-15. Installing extensions to VS Code*

- VS Code supports a number of extensions for development in many languages, as well as general helper tools like linters or search tools. Installing an extension is accomplished through the interface.

 A *linter* is a programming tool that analyzes code for syntax and style issues. It is always helpful to have a good standard linter for your chosen language.

- From the menu, select View → Extensions.
- This will open the extensions menu, and you can see all the available extensions for VS Code. Unfortunately, the Python extensions don't work, but that is okay because we don't really want to be developing Python code that way anyway. Instead, we will use the VS Code server platform only when we need to diagnose special issues or inspect services we developed.
- You can search for any extension you need in the search bar at the top. Type in a search term such as *data*, *cloud*, or *python*, and the appropriate extensions will be listed.
- Type *rest* into the search box and hit Enter.
- A number of entries will come up, but we likely want the first one, which is called REST Client. This extension will allow us to use REST APIs from the cloud shell, which in turn will ease our development efforts later.

- Select the REST Client extension and then click the Install button. This will install the extension.
- We can test the extension by creating a new file with File → New File from the menu. Name the file *rest.txt*, just as a test file.
- Enter the following text anywhere on the blank document:
  ```
  GET https://example.com/comments
  ```
- Keep your cursor on the line of text and type F1 to open the command window at the top.
- In the command window, and as shown in Figure 2-18, enter the following text to issue the command:
  ```
  Rest Client: Send Request
  ```
- You don't even have to finish typing the text and you can select the command from the filtered list, again as shown in Figure 2-18.

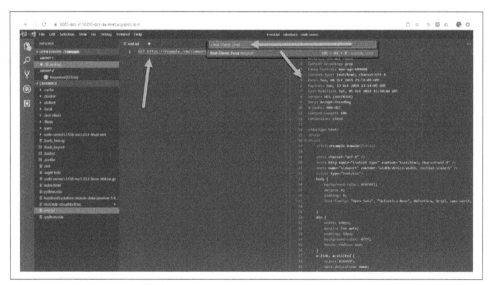

*Figure 2-18. Getting a REST request*

- After the request is made, the response will open in a new pane beside your request window. This can be very useful for diagnosing issues and developing services.

There are indeed many variations of REST clients you can use to test HTTP requests. We will use the one shown here both online and offline in order to test our APIs later. If you have a preference for using another REST client such as Postman, then by all means use it, provided you can replicate the same procedures we will see later.

From running a code server to making REST requests, the Google Cloud Shell has many uses. The shell can be used to manage your data as well as upload and download files, and that is what we will cover in the next section.

# Managing Cloud Data

Up until now we have used the data made available on the GCP by various public sources or by Google itself. However, our goal is to develop AI that can process our own data. To do that, we will need to move and manage data on the GCP. In this section, we introduce a collection of exercises/recipes you can use to move data for later projects in this book. Moving data around will be a common task, and you will likely memorize these recipes quickly.

If you have already worked on the GCP for any amount of time, you likely already know how to move and transfer files around. Consider this section optional or a refresher.

The first exercise we need to perform is to build a bucket or storage container on the GCP (Example 2-16). This will be a place for us to move data around. By default you are provided with 5 GB of free storage. In all of these exercises, we will show you how to use the console, but Google also provides an interface for doing many of the same things.

*Example 2-16. Creating/managing a cloud bucket*

- Open your Google Console Shell (*https://console.cloud.google.com*).
- Enter the following command:
  ```
  gsutil mb gs://practicalai/
  ```
- This will create a new bucket called *practicalai* in your storage account.
- Next, we want to list the buckets in our project with the following:
  ```
  gsutil ls
  ```
- You should see the new bucket in this list. Note the URL starting with *gs*, for Google storage.

- Now we can upload a file into a bucket using the following template:
  ```
  gsutil cp [OBJECT_LOCATION] gs://[DESTINATION_BUCKET_NAME]/
  ```

- You can also use the Google Cloud Storage (GCS) interface (*https://console.cloud.google.com/storage*) to easily upload files to your bucket.

- Open the storage interface in a browser. You can upload files to your bucket using the Upload files button, as shown in Figure 2-19.

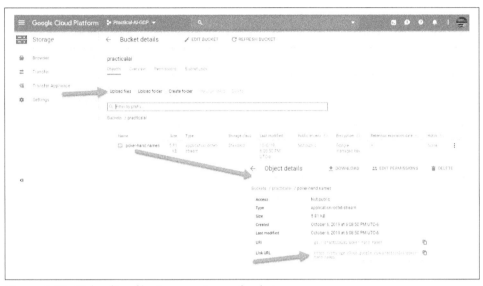

*Figure 2-19. Uploading files to your storage bucket*

- Upload any file from your local computer to the GCS bucket. After you do, you will see the file listed in the bucket. You can also list bucket contents from the console with the following command:
  ```
  gsutil ls -r gs://[BUCKET_NAME]/**
  ```

- Once the file is in a GCS bucket, it can be moved to the console or a notebook in a number of ways. One simple way we can transfer files is with wget, using the following template:
  ```
  wget url
  ```

- You can simply insert the URL to your GCS file and wget will download it into your console session.

We will explore variations on these methods for managing data in GCS buckets in the various exercises later in the book. The important concept to grasp here is that all of our data needs to be processed through GCS buckets before we can process it for AI—at least for the majority of training tasks. When we get to applications that use inference or an actual trained model, we will look at managing data requests through a REST API.

## Conclusion

Google has invested a considerable amount of resources into building an elite AI platform. Google boasts many of the top professionals working in various research and development groups across the globe. On top of all this, the company has been very generous in providing free online resources like Google Colab along with plenty of free credits to spend on the entire GCP for building or learning about AI. While we just briefly touched on what is possible with AI on the GCP, we have the remainder of this book to explore the rest.

While we are still making our way through the complex AI landscape, in the next chapter we finally jump in and start using our first Google AI building block, Vision.

# CHAPTER 3

# Image Analysis and Recognition on the Cloud

The entire landscape of machine learning changed in 2012 when Dr. Geoffrey Hinton from the University of Toronto supervised a team to victory in the ImageNet challenge. Hinton did this with a sleeper machine learning technology called deep learning, paired with his own enhancement called a *convolutional neural network*, or CNN. His CNNs would go on to beat what was considered standard at the time on the ImageNet challenge by several percent, a feat not even thought possible. Since then, deep learning and CNNs have been used to surpass human ability in image recognition and other image- or vision-related tasks. However, these models are still not trivial to build and often require substantial experience, knowledge, and computing power. Fortunately, Google is able to provide a number of pretrained Vision AI services that we can use to our great benefit, as we will learn in this chapter.

In this chapter, we will learn how deep learning is now able to classify images or perform other vision-related tasks better than humans. Then we will construct a simple image classifier to see how the underlying technology works to do object recognition and then construct the Google Vision AI Building Block, where we will explore the API and perform various tasks like product search. We will finish off the chapter by looking at the AutoML Vision service and how it can be used to automatically build vision models.

The following is a summary of the main topics we will discuss in this chapter:

- Deep Learning with Images
- Image Classification
- Transfer Learning Images

- Object Detection and the Object Detection API
- Generating Images with GANs

Only 10 years ago, we believed that being able to replicate human vision was something well beyond our capabilities. It is also a current belief that any advanced AI would need human-level vision. Given that our goal is to produce advanced AI services, we certainly want to explore how vision works, starting in the next section.

## Deep Learning with Images

Deep learning has long been used to classify images and handwritten digits with reasonably good success. The process for doing this is to break apart the image into its pixel values and then feed those into a deep learning network, as shown in Figure 3-1. The problem with this approach is that the image is flattened into a single row of pixel values; thus any representation of features—clusters of pixels that represent something—is lost.

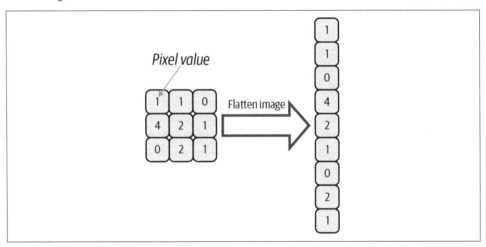

*Figure 3-1. Example of flattening an image*

For instance, consider a picture of a dog. In the picture, there may be features like the nose, eyes, and ears that are distinctly doglike. By flattening the image into a vector of pixels, all information about those features is lost. The data is essentially flattened into a single row of pixels. In fact, this inability to learn features in a flattened image with deep learning was an argument for why neural networks would only ever be a novelty.

There is an old story that used to be told by instructors teaching about neural networks. The story was more a cautionary tale for data science as a whole, but it was often cited as a key danger in neural networks. The tale begins with the United States military teaching neural networks to recognize the difference between US tanks and enemy tanks using images of said tanks. While this tale was told as far back as the '90s, it is believed the Americans performed this experiment in the late '80s—yes, that long ago. They received amazing results and rolled the networks into production. Unfortunately, on the first day of the first real training exercise, the network failed miserably. No enemy tanks were recognized successfully, and in fact, the system recognized friendly tanks as enemies. The problem? A savvy engineer noticed the network had been trained to recognize the difference between cloudy days and clear days, rather than learning to distinguish between US tanks and non-US tanks.

In fact, it would have been impossible for that network to recognize a slight difference in tanks, because the images were flattened before inputting them into a neural network. That flattening of images destroyed any features or elements any network could use to extract features. This understanding squashed any serious research on neural networks for almost 20 years—that is, until Hinton and his team introduced CNNs to the world in 2012 and forever changed deep learning as we know it.

## Enter Convolution Neural Networks

Deep learning and the concept of connected network learning was inspired by biology. We often refer back to biology when we get stuck developing AI or systems comparable to their biological counterparts. This is no different from our work on vision and the discovery of how we see. As it turns out, the eye breaks an image into features using various filters. Hinton surmised that the same thing could be done by convolving, or filtering an image with successive convolutions. To understand how this can be accomplished, let us look at Figure 3-2 and see how various filters can be applied to an image.

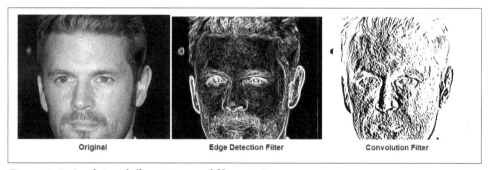

Original          Edge Detection Filter          Convolution Filter

*Figure 3-2. Applying different types of filters to images*

In Figure 3-2, we see an original photo beside versions with different filters applied. The middle image uses a standard edge detection filter, and the image on the right is filtered by a custom convolution filter. The important thing to realize here is that a filter is nothing more than a matrix of numbers that is applied across an image in a step-wise fashion. In each step, the matrix of numbers is multiplied across the image values and summed to a single value and then output as a new pixel value. The results allow us to extract features from an image, and in the case of edge detection, it extracts an edge feature, as shown in Figure 3-3.

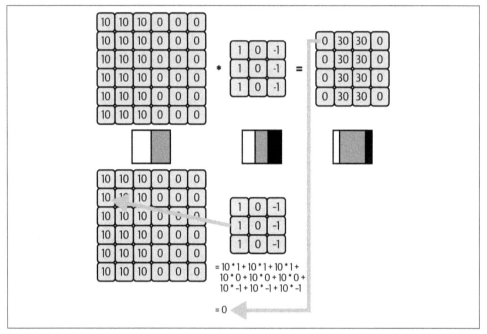

*Figure 3-3. Examples of different filters*

The image of the man in Figure 3-2 is not real, but rather a composite generated by adversarially trained networks. While the result isn't real, the output would not have been possible without the discovery of CNN.

Figure 3-3 shows a 3 × 3 filter being applied using a step size of one, and this results in the reduction of the resulting output image by one pixel. Hinton and his team discovered that you can apply multiple filters, or convolution, across an image, collect the results of those feature extractions, and then flatten all those features into a regular network. The result allows a network to recognize and detect features on a scale previously never thought possible. This all likely still sounds somewhat abstract, so let's perform a simple visualization exercise to show how convolution works (Example 3-1).

*Example 3-1. Understanding convolution*

- Open the TensorSpace.js Playground page (*https://tensorspace.org/html/play ground/index.html*) in your web browser.

- On this page, you will see various examples of CNNs working and being inspected. This page will also provide you with instructions on how to inspect models. Be sure to review the instructions before continuing.

- On the left-side navigation bar, click on the AlexNet entry. AlexNet is the network that was used to beat the AI challenge back in 2012. The network is quite large and may take a few minutes to load.

- After the network has loaded, use the controls to move around and inspect the elements. Click on the first yellow box, which should expand to show the outputs of the first layer of convolution. Figure 3-4 shows the interface zoomed in on the image as it is first being separated into channels and then passed through a first layer of convolution. The resulting yellow images show the output of a single convolution filter applied to the source image.

*Figure 3-4. TensorSpace Playground showing convolution output*

- Each layer can contain multiple filters with different values that extract different features. So for each convolution layer in yellow, one filter is applied to each resulting output image.

- Shrink a yellow layer and expand a blue layer. The blue layers represent *pooling*, an operation performed on convolution as a way of collecting results. This essentially collects all similar features into pools that are then flattened.

- Pan or zoom across until you can expand a green layer. A green layer represents a typical layer of perceptrons that is fully connected to any successive layers. This is the layer that the pools need to be flattened to and passed through.

A CNN layer learns similarly to other layers in a network, with the key difference being where the weights are learned. In a convolution layer, each filter element has a weight. Thus, a filter with size 3 × 3, as we saw in our earlier edge detection example, would have nine weights plus one for a bias. A CNN layer learns by adjusting those weights in order to extract the features it needs to learn to classify the thing it is learning to classify. The whole thing sounds recursive, and it is, hence the beauty of this method. It's even more interesting when you realize that the yellow output filtered image of a dog in Figure 3-4 was learned by AlexNet. In other words, AlexNet learned to extract that image we characterize as a dog because we asked it to learn what a dog looked like. This recursive relationship in learning is a testament to the fact that real AI is indeed here.

You can learn a lot about how convolution learns by playing in the TensorSpace Playground. However, seeing how this comes together in code on top of what we have already learned about building deep learning models will be more helpful. Next, we look at how to build image classification models with CNN.

# Image Classification

You may think that building image classification networks would be extremely complex, and that was true just a few short years ago. Now, however, building an image classifier is almost easier than setting up a simple web page. Indeed, the amount of code is almost the same for simple problems. Of course, much like web pages, there are very complex as well as very trivial examples. For now we will stick to the most basic of samples to get your proverbial feet wet.

In this exercise, we are going to look at the typical starting MNIST classification problem. The basic MNIST dataset consists of handwritten digits totaling 60,000 samples. This is often the first problem you will tackle in image classification because it is a baseline established years ago by researchers tackling the problem of image analysis.

 We use important baselines in deep learning and data science to qualify our results to ourselves and others. If you have never trained on the MNIST, then you most certainly should at least once. For our purposes, however, we are going to look at an MNIST advanced dataset, the MNIST Fashion dataset.

To get started, jump on Google Colab and open the *Chapter_3_fashion.ipynb* example.

---

# Set Up and Load Data

The first thing we need to do for any notebook or application we run is make sure that our environment has the correct dependencies installed. Then, you will often pull in data and prepare that data in some form. Example 3-2 demonstrates how to set imports and load and prepare data.

*Example 3-2. Image classification setup*

- First, create a new code cell and enter the following imports:

```
from __future__ import absolute_import, division, print_function,
                        unicode_literals

import tensorflow as tf
keras = tf.keras
from tensorflow.keras import datasets, layers, models
import matplotlib.pyplot as plt
import numpy as np
```

- Run the cell, which will set the needed imports.
- Create another new code cell and enter the following code to load the dataset:

```
fashion_mnist = keras.datasets.fashion_mnist

(train_images, train_labels), (test_images, test_labels) =
    fashion_mnist.load_data()
```

- Run that cell, which will load the Fashion MNIST dataset and split it into a training dataset and test dataset. There are 60,000 training images/labels with 10,000 test images/labels.
- The Fashion dataset is labeled in 10 classes, but the labels are classes in integer form. To translate those classes into something readable, we will set up appropriate mappings using an array of names in a new cell:

```
class_names = ['T-shirt/top', 'Trouser', 'Pullover', 'Dress', 'Coat',
               'Sandal', 'Shirt', 'Sneaker', 'Bag', 'Ankle boot']
```

- With the data loaded, let's do a quick inspection on the data itself by running the following code in a new cell:

```
train_images[0]
```

- This will output the byte values of the image. Unfortunately, byte values (numbers 0–255) are difficult to work with. We want to instead normalize the data by running the following code in a new cell:

```
train_images = train_images / 255.0
test_images = test_images / 255.0
```

- Normalizing the data allows our networks to learn better. Run the cell where you output the `train_images[0]` image again, and confirm the values are now all in a range from 0 to 1.

 A good rule of thumb in data handling and normalization is to remember that data always works better when it is centered around and close to zero. Keeping numbers close to zero helps you avoid handling large numbers, which can be computationally costly and cause other issues. It is often ideal to center your data from −1 to +1.

With the data loaded, we can move on to inspecting the data so that we can understand what we are working with.

## Inspecting Image Data

Understanding your data and how it looks is essential to data science and deep learning. That means we want to be able to see those images and understand what we are looking at in Example 3-3.

*Example 3-3. Inspecting image data*

- Before we get into viewing individual images, let us first understand the data itself by running the following code in a new cell:

```
print(train_images.shape)
print(len(train_labels))
print(train_labels)
print(len(test_labels))
```

- That code will output the following values:

```
(60000, 28, 28)
60000
array([9, 0, 0, ..., 3, 0, 5], dtype=uint8)
10000
```

- The first value shows us the shape of `train_images`, which represents 60,000 images at 28 × 28 pixel values. Next is the number of `train_labels`, and lastly the number of `test_labels`.

- In order to inspect the images themselves, we are going to construct a helper function. We do this by entering the following code in a new cell and running it:

```
import math
def plot_data(num_images):
grid = math.ceil(math.sqrt(num_images))
plt.figure(figsize=(grid*2,grid*2))
for i in range(num_images):
```

```
    plt.subplot(grid,grid,i+1)
    plt.xticks([])
    plt.yticks([])
    plt.grid(False)
    plt.imshow(train_images[i])
    plt.xlabel(class_names[train_labels[i]])
  plt.show()
```

- The function plt_data takes the number of images we want to show as input and then generates a grid of those images in the notebook. Enter the following code in a new cell:

```
plot_data(25)
```

- Executing the cell will generate the output shown in Figure 3-5. The figure shows a sample set of images in their normalized state values. Don't worry about the color shading; the network will only see these as grayscale.

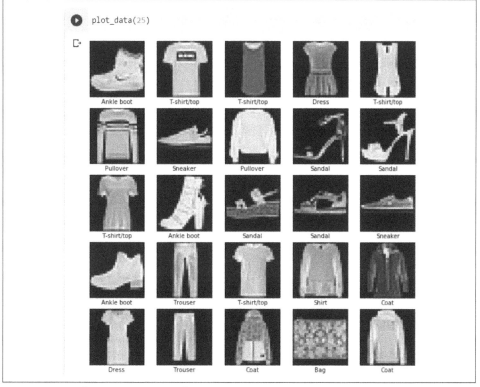

*Figure 3-5. Fashion MNIST sample images*

We can now see what our data looks like and understand the important or descriptive features. You want to pay attention to things that make a class like shoe unique as compared to a sweater. Understanding what features make an image unique can help us characterize CNN. Image features are just one aspect of extracting attributes over an image. Another important consideration is the image channels or colors, which we will cover in the next section.

## Channels and CNN

2D CNN are designed to work exclusively with images and as such are intended to work with colors and channels. An image channel represents a particular frequency, often color, of that data. In a previous exercise, we saw how using AlexNet broke the images into respective red, blue, and green color channels.

Most of us don't see the individual color channels in images. However, color is important to the features we extract in an image. Breaking an image into respective color channels allows the AI to also process color. However, our current image dataset is missing channel information that we will need to add.

 The channels we extract in a typical image are colors: red, green, and blue. However, channels may represent any latent image features, from infrared temperature even to X-rays. While most current cameras only support color, other information may be captured in the near future.

Since our current dataset has no image channels, we need to correct for this. In Example 3-4, we look at how we can add a single channel to allow for processing the data through a CNN layer.

*Example 3-4. Correcting image channels*

- When working with image data or other data types, it is important to understand the shape. A tensor shape can help us identify the structure of the data and make sure it aligns with what our network requires as input. We inspect the shape executing the following code in a new cell:
  ```
  train_images.shape

  #outputs
  (60000, 28, 28)
  ```
- In the shape, the first number represents the number of images, 60,000. The pair of 28s represents the image size (width × height). What we are missing here are the channels, a fourth dimension, since our image is only a single channel, grayscale. We just need to affirm that in the tensor by entering and running the following:
  ```
  train_images = np.expand_dims(train_images, 3)
  test_images = np.expand_dims(test_images, 3)
  ```

- We are adding another axis to our image data to represent the color channel by using the expand_dims function and inputting the current length. The reason we need to do this is to make sure our tensor is of the correct input shape.

- You can confirm the shape was updated by running the following:
  ```
  train_images.shape
  ```

  ```
  #outputs
  (60000, 28, 28, 1)
  ```

- A new single channel has been added to the end of the tensor.

 NumPy (np) provides a number of ways of manipulating tensors that you most certainly will want or need to learn as you master deep learning.

Our data should be in good shape now, and so it is time to move on to building our network.

## Building the Model

At this point we are ready to build a comprehensive CNN model in order to understand how these layers work and interact (Example 3-5). In most cases, though, we will generally look to use predeveloped and pretrained models, which we will cover in the last two major sections of this chapter.

*Example 3-5. Building the CNN model*

- We will start by building just the CNN portion of the network to highlight the new layers shown in the following code:
  ```
  model = models.Sequential()
  model.add(layers.Conv2D(32, (3, 3), activation='relu',
          input_shape=(28, 28, 1)))
  model.add(layers.MaxPooling2D((2, 2)))
  model.add(layers.Dropout(.5))
  model.add(layers.Conv2D(64, (3, 3), activation='relu'))
  model.add(layers.MaxPooling2D((2, 2)))
  model.add(layers.Dropout(.5))
  model.add(layers.Conv2D(64, (3, 3), activation='relu'))
  ```

- Starting with a Sequential model, we add our first Conv2D layer. This layer denotes 32 filters of size 3 × 3 with a default stride of 1. The output of that layer is then pooled, or collected, using MaxPooling2D layers. Output from that layer then goes through a Dropout layer. Dropout layers randomly turn off a percentage of neurons in that layer in every training batch to prevent overfitting and to better generalize the model. After that, you can see that the cycle repeats with more layers configured just a little differently. Make sure to run the cell before continuing.

- You can inspect the model by running the following:

```
model.summary()
```

```
#outputs
Model: "sequential..."
```

| Layer (type)                    | Output Shape        | Param # |
|---------------------------------|---------------------|---------|
| conv2d (Conv2D)                 | (None, 26, 26, 32)  | 320     |
| max_pooling2d (MaxPooling2      | (None, 13, 13, 32)  | 0       |
| dropout (Dropout)               | (None, 13, 13, 32)  | 0       |
| conv2d (Conv2D)                 | (None, 11, 11, 64)  | 18496   |
| max_pooling2d (MaxPooling2      | (None, 5, 5, 64)    | 0       |
| dropout (Dropout)               | (None, 5, 5, 64)    | 0       |
| conv2d (Conv2D)                 | (None, 3, 3, 64)    | 36928   |

```
Total params: 55,744
Trainable params: 55,744
Non-trainable params: 0
```

- Notice that the number of training parameters, or weights, that need to be balanced has increased substantially from our earlier examples.

- Anytime you are training more than 50,000 parameters, you really want to use a GPU over a CPU. Fortunately, Colab allows you to easily swap runtimes. You can change the runtime type from the menu using the menu Runtime → Change runtime type.

- To use the above convolutional layers, we need to funnel them back down into regularly connected layers. We can do this by adding a couple of dense layers like so:

```
model.add(layers.Flatten())
model.add(layers.Dense(64, activation='relu'))
model.add(layers.Dense(10, activation='softmax'))

model.summary()
```

- The first new layer flattens the output from the last convolutional layer from 2D to a flat 1D vector. That vector is then fed into a new dense layer of 64 neurons, followed by an output layer of 10 neurons.

With the model built, it is time to start training it.

## Training the AI Fashionista to Discern Fashions

Once we have everything set up, getting the model compiled and training is fairly simple in Keras. We will next look at how to train and then inspect the results in Example 3-6.

*Example 3-6. Compiling and training a model*

- We start by entering the following code to compile and then train/fit the model:
```
model.compile(optimizer='adam',
              loss='sparse_categorical_crossentropy',
              metrics=['accuracy'])

history = model.fit(train_images, train_labels, epochs=10,
                    validation_data=(test_images, test_labels))
```
- The first line of code compiles the model for training using an Adam optimizer with a loss function that uses sparse_categorical_crossentropy. The categorical cross entropy function allows us to convert our 10-neuron output to an integer class value from 0 to 9 and back. It is a common function and one we will revisit over and over again. Make sure to execute the code before continuing.

- If you switched the notebook's runtime to GPU, the training should take only a few minutes.

- After or even during training, we will often want to inspect performance. We can do this with the following code:
```
plt.plot(history.history['acc'], label='accuracy')
plt.plot(history.history['val_acc'], label = 'val_accuracy')
plt.xlabel('Epoch')
plt.ylabel('Accuracy')
plt.ylim([0.5, 1])
plt.legend(loc='lower right')

test_loss, test_acc = model.evaluate(test_images, test_labels, verbose=2)
```
- Running that code will generate the plot shown in Figure 3-6, which shows the accuracy and validation, or test accuracy. Using high values of dropout with the Dropout layers will ensure that our model generalizes well.

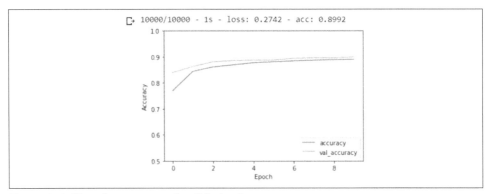

*Figure 3-6. Plot of accuracy and validation/test accuracy*

Dropout layers were recently patented by Google as a measure to avoid patent trolls. Google has stated that many of its patents are intended for this purpose. Patent trolls are companies that create patents on general inventions like Dropout and then pursue companies for infringement. This could have certainly been the case with such a simple concept like dropout.

With a score of 89% accuracy, our fashionista AI is more than capable of picking out several types of fashions. However, we should always strive for better accuracy. Our current AI gives us an 89% confidence of selecting the right fashion type, but is that good enough? If that accuracy is better than a human, then the answer is almost always yes, at least for now. In the future, as more AI systems become the standard, new standards for vision accuracy and other tasks will need to be set. Therefore, in the next exercise we look at how we can improve on the model.

## Improving Fashionista AI 2.0

CNNs are still very much in their infancy as a technology, and we are very much still learning how to use them. Architectural patterns in CNN layers are still evolving, and what extracts the best features will change over time. You may encounter differences of opinion on which structures work well for your data. It can also be difficult to find analogs that match your circumstances exactly. Fortunately, developing your own unique model architectures is getting easier. There are a number of ways to improve our last example, and we will look at improving the feature extraction first.

One problem many newcomers face is understanding the actual CNN process and what effect this has on the data. For the most part, using tools like *TensorSpace.js* goes a long way in helping with that. However, there is one critical element most newcomers and experts alike miss. This is not really an issue with CNN, but rather with the operation we tend to want to do afterward: pooling.

The pooling function we often perform after CNN can obfuscate important feature extraction. Pooling is meant to collect similar features from previous CNN layers and essentially reduce the number of training parameters in the model. However, the pooling operation also removes any form of spatial relevancy in data because it just grabs all similar-looking features no matter where they are in the image. This can be good for general image-recognition tasks like identifying cats or dogs, but if images encapsulate spatial features, they will be lost. So for models that need to work with maps, games, and apparently fashion, we'll want to avoid any use of pooling.

 If you are unsure whether your image data is spatially sensitive, an easy way to test this is to remove a few lower pooling layers. Removing these layers should reduce training performance; if they improve it, your data is contextually spatial.

In Example 3-7, we look at one of many possible techniques to improve the architecture of a CNN model.

*Example 3-7. Improving model architecture*

- For this exercise we will continue in the same notebook. Scroll down farther and look at the improved model shown below:

```
model = models.Sequential()
model.add(layers.Conv2D(32, (3, 3), activation='relu',
        input_shape=(28, 28, 1)))
model.add(layers.MaxPooling2D((2, 2)))
model.add(layers.SpatialDropout2D(.5))
model.add(layers.Conv2D(64, (3, 3), activation='relu'))
model.add(layers.SpatialDropout2D(.5))
model.add(layers.Conv2D(64, (3, 3), activation='relu'))
model.add(layers.SpatialDropout2D(.5))
model.add(layers.Flatten())
model.add(layers.Dense(64, activation='relu'))
model.add(layers.Dense(10, activation='softmax'))
model.summary()
```

- This rewrites the model and removes the lower pooling layers. We still leave in that top pooling layer to account for some image symmetry. Then notice that we convert our Dropout layers to use SpatialDropout2D layers. These special layers account for spatial artifacts. This time we also add the flatten and dense layers in the same block of code and finish by outputting the model summary.

- We can then recompile and train the new model with the following code:

```
model.compile(optimizer='adam',
            loss='sparse_categorical_crossentropy',
            metrics=['accuracy'])
```

```
history = model.fit(train_images, train_labels, epochs=25,
                    validation_data=(test_images, test_labels))
```

- Execute the training code and wait for the model to train. Notice how this model has over three hundred thousand training parameters. This is the result of removing pooling. In order to account for more parameters, we increased the epochs from 10 to 25. Expect this sample to take two to three times longer to train as well.

- Copy the plotting code we used previously to show the history and paste it into a new cell and execute it. The output is shown in Figure 3-7.

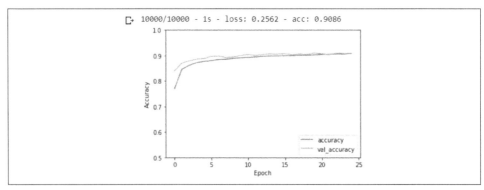

*Figure 3-7. Plot of improved CNN*

- From the results in Figure 3-7, you can see that training and test accuracy continuously increase at the same rate. In fact, the values appear to converge, which is generally the optimum training scenario.

 Remember to always evaluate the training and value or test accuracy as a model trains. If you see the accuracy of the training and test diverge greatly, then you know that the training was overfitting.

Fumbling with CNN architectures and best practices certainly has its novelty, but if you are in a hurry to get something working, it may not be the best first choice. Instead, we can use prebuilt and robust models trained on far more complex datasets. This method is called *transfer learning*, an alternative to image classification we will explore in the next section.

# Transfer Learning Images

Developing your own network models is all well and good, but if you need a state-of-the-art solution up and running quickly, it likely is not your best choice. CNN image classifying networks are expensive to develop and can take countless hours of training. Fortunately, prebuilt and pretrained CNNs abound freely. We can also embed these models either in part or wholly in the networks we develop and train for our own custom solutions.

In the next set of exercises, we look at how to use a pretrained CNN as a base for a new trainable network.

## Identifying Cats or Dogs

As we work through the chapters in this book, we will make the assumption that you need and want less hand-holding. Therefore, we will often just refer to code sections in the downloaded sample notebook rather than showing them in the text. You can either refer back to an earlier exercise or consult the notebook as required.

In this exercise, we are going build a model that can classify an animal as a cat or a dog. The data required to train a robust model from scratch would need to be substantial and/or augmented. The more complex the image, the bigger the network has to be to train on it. Larger networks in turn require more unique data to generalize training on. We can sometimes alleviate this with data augmentation.

Augmenting image data is a process in which you flip, transpose, or perform some other transformation to pictures. This results in additional images, albeit ones very much skewed by the previous data. By using pretrained networks, we can use those previous learnings as a base for extracting features from new sources of images. This allows us to retrain robust models on more specific sets of data more quickly and with fewer images.

Open up the sample exercise *Chapter_3_transfer.ipynb* and follow along with Example 3-8.

*Example 3-8. Looking at cats and dogs*

- The first section of imports is standard, so we can ignore them. There is one new import shown in the following code:
  ```
  import tensorflow_datasets as tfds

  (raw_train, raw_validation, raw_test), metadata = tfds.load(
      'cats_vs_dogs', split=['train[:80%]', 'train[80%:90%]', 'train[90%:]'],
      with_info=True, as_supervised=True)
  ```

- This code loads a new import tfds, a placeholder for additional interesting data-sets. We then use `tdfs.load` to split the data into sets of 80%, 10%, and 10% (`raw_train`, `raw_validation`, and `raw_test`, respectively).

- Next, we are going to update our previous `plot_data` function so that it now takes a dataset and the number of images with this code:

```
get_label_name = metadata.features['label'].int2str
import math
def plot_data(data, num_images):
  grid = math.ceil(math.sqrt(num_images))
  plt.figure(figsize=(grid*2,grid*2))
  i = 0
  for image, label in data.take(num_images):
    i+=1
    plt.subplot(grid,grid,i)
    plt.xticks([])
    plt.yticks([])
    plt.grid(False)
    plt.imshow(image)
    plt.xlabel(get_label_name(label))
  plt.show()

plot_data(raw_train, 20)
```

- The results of running this block of code will output Figure 3-8.

- As you can see in Figure 3-8, the images are different sizes and have slightly different color variations. We need to fix this by normalizing and resizing the images with the following code:

```
IMG_SIZE = 160
def format_example(image, label):
  image = tf.cast(image, tf.float32)
  image = (image/127.5) - 1
  image = tf.image.resize(image, (IMG_SIZE, IMG_SIZE))
  return image, label
```

- This creates a function that takes an image as input. It casts and then rescales data to a float tensor with data normalized to –1 to + 1. Remember that data is best when it is centered on zero. Then the image data is resized to 160 × 160. This is also the size our base model will need.

*Figure 3-8. Sample training images of cats and dogs*

- We can then execute this function across the three datasets (train, validate, and test) using the following code:

```
train = raw_train.map(format_example)
validation = raw_validation.map(format_example)
test = raw_test.map(format_example)

plot_data(train, 25)
```

- The map function maps the `format_example` function to each image within each dataset. Of course, a `for loop` is another option for doing the same thing, but the method just discussed is far more Pythonic.

 "Being Pythonic" is a way of writing code that adheres to best practices for and with Python. Some of these may be coding standards. Others are things like list comprehensions and map functions.

- After the last block of code executes, it will generate the output in Figure 3-9. You can now see the normalized and resized dataset. The skewing of data that happens when the image is resized is nothing to worry about. Cat and dog images are very feature-rich and not so dependent on spatial context. Skewing these images should not have a significant effect on performance. However, for reasons mentioned previously, we would not skew any image data that did depend on spatial importance.

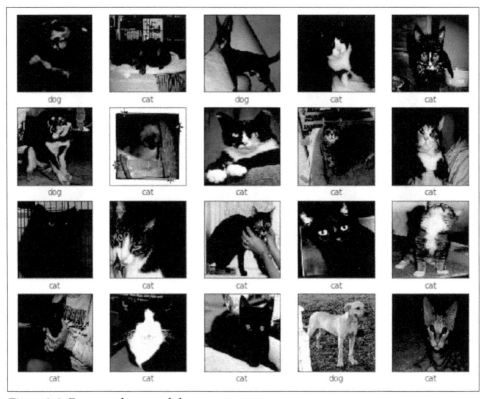

*Figure 3-9. Formatted cats and dogs*

- The last part we want to accomplish is shuffling and batching the data. We do this in a separate step to make sure our data is sufficiently randomized. The following code randomly shuffles and batches the data:

```
BATCH_SIZE = 32
SHUFFLE_BUFFER_SIZE = 1000

train_batches = train.shuffle(SHUFFLE_BUFFER_SIZE).batch(BATCH_SIZE)
validation_batches = validation.batch(BATCH_SIZE)
test_batches = test.batch(BATCH_SIZE)
```

```
for image_batch, label_batch in train_batches.take(1):
    pass

image_batch.shape

#outputs
TensorShape([Dimension(32), Dimension(160), Dimension(160), Dimension(3)])
```

- The last line of code defines the shape of a batch tensor (32, 160, 160, 3). The first number denotes the batch size, and it is followed by two numbers that denote image size (160 × 160) and the last number, 3, which is the number of channels. The images we are using for this example are full color and therefore need to be broken down into red, green, and blue color channels.

 The data in this section is already configured to use three channels. You will likely need to use other tools on raw images to break the image into respective channels before training on images.

With the data loaded, inspected, and normalized, we can move on to building and training the model.

## Transfer Learning a Keras Application Model

As mentioned previously, the concept of reusing training and then extending it to another application is called transfer learning. Transfer learning is a tool you will likely use over and over again. Keras has around 20 CNN application models that have previously been trained on millions of images. These models are useful out of the box if you want to replicate the same model, but we can also work some deep learning magic and partially retrain those models for extended applications.

In Example 3-9, we load a previously trained model and use it to transfer the prelearned feature extraction capabilities, and then train it to recognize cats or dogs.

*Example 3-9. Transfer learning a CNN application*

- The first thing we need to do is import our base model. We are using an existing application model called VGG19. You can find more information on the wide variety of available models by consulting the Keras/TensorFlow docs. Importing this model and setting it up for our input is shown in the following code:
```
IMG_SHAPE = (IMG_SIZE, IMG_SIZE, 3)

base_model = tf.keras.applications.VGG19(input_shape=IMG_SHAPE,
                                         include_top=False,
                                         weights='imagenet')
```

- We load the network into `base_model` with a pretrained set of weights called imagenet, meaning the model was trained on the ImageNet dataset of 50 million images of 1,000 classes.

 ImageNet is a database of millions of images in a thousand different categories. This dataset continually grows and even has its own website (*http://imagenet.org*).

- Next, we want to look at some information about this new model using the following code:
```
feature_batch = base_model(image_batch)
print(feature_batch.shape)
## (32, 5, 5, 512)
base_model.trainable = False
base_model.summary()

#outputs
Model: "vgg19"
...
block5_pool (MaxPooling2D)  (None, 5, 5, 512)    0
=================================================================
Total params: 20,024,384
Trainable params: 0
Non-trainable params: 20,024,384
```

- The model output was cut, but the entire model consists of 22 layers, hence the name. Notice how after setting `base_model.trainable` to False, all of the model's more than 20 million—yep, 20 million—parameters will be frozen and untrainable. One other thing to note is the output shape from the base model (32, 5, 5, 512). This is the output that we push through a couple more layers that we will use to train for our purposes.

- Before we add more layers, we want to construct them so the outputs constrain to our needed outputs. We will do this by first adding a new global average pooling layer with the following code:
```
global_average_layer = tf.keras.layers.GlobalAveragePooling2D()
feature_batch_average = global_average_layer(feature_batch)
print(feature_batch_average.shape)
## (32, 512)

prediction_layer = keras.layers.Dense(1)
prediction_batch = prediction_layer(feature_batch_average)
```

```
print(prediction_batch.shape)
## (32,1)
```

- Then we create a new prediction layer, Dense, of size 1, as shown in the code. We then combine the entire model with the following code:

```
model = tf.keras.Sequential([
  base_model,
  global_average_layer,
  prediction_layer
])

base_learning_rate = 0.0001
model.compile(optimizer=tf.keras.optimizers.RMSprop(lr=base_learning_rate),
              loss='binary_crossentropy',
              metrics=['accuracy'])

model.summary()

#outputs
Model: "sequential"
```

| Layer (type) | Output Shape | Param # |
|---|---|---|
| vgg19 (Model) | (None, 5, 5, 512) | 20024384 |
| global_average_pooling2d (Gl | (None, 512) | 0 |
| dense (Dense) | (None, 1) | 513 |

```
Total params: 20,024,897
Trainable params: 513
Non-trainable params: 20,024,384
```

- Our combined model now has 513 trainable parameters that define our extended model. These additional parameters will learn how to recognize the difference between cats and dogs.

With the extra layers added, we can now jump into training the model using our own specialized data.

# Training Transfer Learning

There are a number of variations you can apply when retraining or transferring knowledge from model to model. The method we use here works primarily when you know the base model or transferred model is already partially trained on your data. We can do this in this case because ImageNet encapsulates 1,000 classes and even subclasses to the breed of cat and/or dog. Therefore, for our current purposes, this method will work great. Keep this in mind when applying transfer learning as it could be highly relevant when training specialized datasets. For example, if you were building an application to recognize license plates, would using a model pretrained on ImageNet be effective? Likely not, but using a model trained on image text would.

In Example 3-10, we look at how to train a combined model on our dataset.

*Example 3-10. Training transfer learning*

- Our first step in transfer learning a model is to set up some hyperparameters for training. Then we will quickly evaluate the model:

```
initial_epochs = 10
validation_steps = 20

loss0,accuracy0 = model.evaluate(validation_batches,
                                 steps = validation_steps)
# outputs
20/20 [==============================] - 2s 115ms/step
                                        - loss: 5.2356
                                        - acc: 0.4938
```

- We evaluate the model initially for 20 iterations. This provides us with a starting baseline for training that we can also review by executing the following code:

```
print("initial loss: {:.2f}".format(loss0))
print("initial accuracy: {:.2f}".format(accuracy0))
# outputs
initial loss: 5.24
initial accuracy: 0.49
```

- We can see that the model starts with an expected accuracy or confidence of 50%, which is what we would expect. In other words, we would expect a random guess that any image is be a cat or dog would be correct 50% of the time.

- Training the model is done simply by executing the fit function as shown below:

```
history = model.fit(train_batches,
                    epochs=initial_epochs,
                    validation_data=validation_batches)
# summary output
Epoch 1/10
582/582 [==============================] - 95s 163ms/step
                                        - loss: 1.0034
                                        - acc: 0.6671
                                        - val_loss: 0.0000e+00
                                        - val_acc: 0.0000e+00
...
Epoch 10/10
582/582 [==============================] - 92s 158ms/step
                                        - loss: 0.2173
                                        - acc: 0.9242
```

```
                          - val_loss: 0.2069
                          - val_acc: 0.9246
```

- Going from 50% to 92% in a relatively short amount of training is impressive.
  Let's look at how the results history plots with the following code:

```
def plot_history():
  acc = history.history['accuracy']
  val_acc = history.history['val_accuracy']

  loss = history.history['loss']
  val_loss = history.history['val_loss']

  plt.figure(figsize=(8, 8))
  plt.subplot(2, 1, 1)
  plt.plot(acc, label='Training Accuracy')
  plt.plot(val_acc, label='Validation Accuracy')
  plt.legend(loc='lower right')
  plt.ylabel('Accuracy')
  plt.ylim([min(plt.ylim()),1])
  plt.title('Training and Validation Accuracy')

  plt.subplot(2, 1, 2)
  plt.plot(loss, label='Training Loss')
  plt.plot(val_loss, label='Validation Loss')
  plt.legend(loc='upper right')
  plt.ylabel('Cross Entropy')
  plt.ylim([0,1.0])
  plt.title('Training and Validation Loss')
  plt.xlabel('epoch')
  plt.show()

plot_history()
```

- The last section of code generates Figure 3-10. We can see that the training and
  test performance are almost perfect, but perhaps we can do better.

Our results should be quite impressive considering the amount of training time and
complexity/quality of the dataset. Fortunately, we can do much better than just
adding some new trainable layers and actually look at retraining some of the base
model itself in the next section.

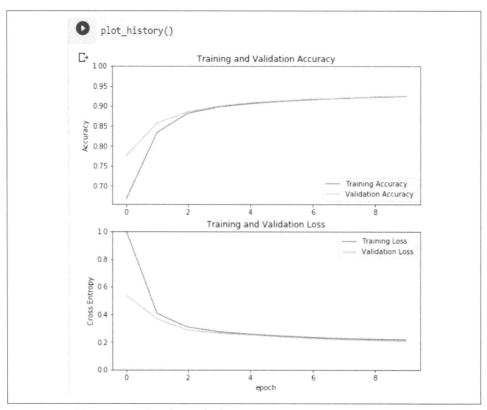

*Figure 3-10. Training results of transfer learning*

## Retraining a Better Base Model

In our previous effort, we avoided interfering with the base model entirely. This allowed us to train the new classification layers we would need to use to learn to differentiate a cat from a dog. Now we can do better by allowing our base model to also learn, or rather improve its learning of cat's and dog's feature extraction. Tuning a model by allowing it to retrain allows us to specialize a generalized model like one trained on ImageNet and apply it to specialized applications. In Example 3-11, we will retrain parts of our base model to further improve inference.

*Example 3-11. Retraining the base model*

- The first thing we need to do is make our base model trainable by executing the following:

```
base_model.trainable = True
```

- After the base model is set to trainable, we want to select only specific layers for training. That way, we can adjust the depth at which we retune the model. In most cases, we want to retune only the last layers of a model.

- We can inspect the number of layers in a model and then set a point in those layers to start training again using the following code:

```
print("Number of layers in the base model: ", len(base_model.layers))
# outputs
Number of layers in the base model: 22

fine_tune_at = 15
for layer in base_model.layers[:fine_tune_at]:
  layer.trainable = False
```

- The code freezes the layers at the fine_tune_at point. After the layers are frozen, we can then compile the model and do a summary output with this code:

```
model.compile(loss='binary_crossentropy',
    optimizer = tf.keras.optimizers.RMSprop(lr=base_learning_rate/10),
    metrics=['accuracy'])
model.summary()
# outputs
Model: "sequential_1"
```

| Layer (type) | Output Shape | Param # |
|---|---|---|
| vgg19 (Model) | (None, 5, 5, 512) | 20024384 |
| global_average_pooling2d_1 ( | (None, 512) | 0 |
| dense_1 (Dense) | (None, 1) | 513 |

```
Total params: 20,024,897
Trainable params: 11,799,553
Non-trainable params: 8,225,344
```

- Notice the huge increase in training parameters. We are essentially retraining more than half of the model, but notice that we are modifying the learning_rate. In the last block of code, we divide the learning rate by 10, scaling it down. We do this so that our model trains more slowly, with fewer but finer changes.

- Enter and execute the following code to retrain the model for an additional 10 epochs:

```
fine_tune_epochs = 10
total_epochs = initial_epochs + fine_tune_epochs

history_fine = model.fit(train_batches,
                        epochs=total_epochs,
```

```
                              initial_epoch = history.epoch[-1],
                              validation_data=validation_batches)

# outputs
Epoch 20/20
582/582 [==============================] - 112s 193ms/step
                                         - loss: 0.0472
                                         - acc: 0.9958
                                         - val_loss: 0.3179
                                         - val_acc: 0.9668
```

- We can see that with an additional 10 training epochs finely adjusting more than half of the model, we can optimize training to over 96%, which is quite impressive. Notice that we always measure real or valid accuracy from the test/validation set and not the training set.

- Execute the `plot_history` function as shown in Figure 3-11. The training and validation history on the plot is a good representation of excellent training.

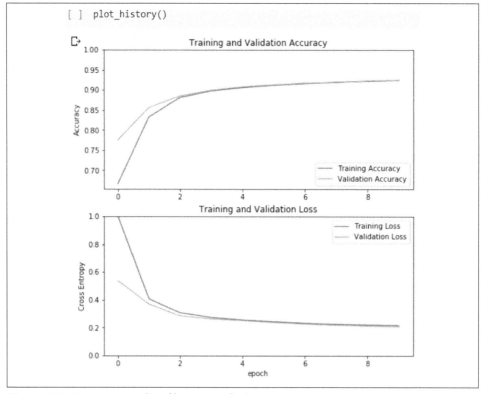

*Figure 3-11. Training results of base transfer learning*

Transfer learning for image classification can be a great boost for most related tasks. However, if you are using spatial data, be sure your base model is a spatially contextual model as well.

You can apply these steps to any other specialized dataset, provided it is similar to the source model's training data. ImageNet is a very comprehensive dataset, so it is likely this will work for most cases.

In the next section, we move beyond mere image classification and look at detecting objects in images.

# Object Detection and the Object Detection Hub API

being able to recognize the contents of an entire photo is all well and good, but what about photos with multiple subjects or objects? What if we wanted to recognize a cat and a dog in the same photo, as well as perhaps identify their position? Doing this with our current model would be impossible, but fortunately Google has exposed an object detection API that can do just that. Google Colab provides a framework called TF Hub that exposes many interesting and advanced APIs. Before we get to working with that API in Example 3-12, let's discuss what object detection is.

## YOLO for Object Detection

YOLO, or "You only look once," is the phrase we use to describe the technique of extracting objects from a single view of an image. Previous methods required multiple observations/viewpoints of the same objects, which was less than ideal. With YOLO, we use a single image to capture any number of objects in an image. In addition, the object detection model can further identify a bounding box to denote what it identifies. Building and running such a model is no easy task—well, it wasn't, until Google introduced the TF Hub and a collection of pregenerated specialized models like the object detection one we will look at now.

*Example 3-12. Using the object detection API*

- Open up example *Chapter_3_objects_tpu.ipynb*.
- This sample uses an extensive amount of import and helper code to set up the sample and identify objects in images. This helper code is general image manipulation code. We won't worry about reviewing this code here, but if you are interested, feel free to examine the code on your own.

- Run the import and helper function code in the first two cells. Then run the block of code that takes the image URL as input. Figure 3-12 shows the result of this image: a couple of chefs working in a New York City kitchen.

*Figure 3-12. The base image for object detection*

- Next, we want to load the object detection model we will use for inference with the following block of code:

```
module_handle =
  "https://tfhub.dev/google/faster_rcnn/openimages_v4/inception_resnet_v2/1"
  #@param ["https://tfhub.dev/google/openimages_v4/ssd/mobilenet_v2/1",
  "https://tfhub.dev/google/faster_rcnn/openimages_v4/inception_resnet_v2/1"]

detector = hub.load(module_handle).signatures['default']
```

- Notice in the code that you can change the model you use fairly easily just by altering the URL. If you are interested, be sure to check the TF Hub for more documentation on various API models.

- Next, we want to create two more functions we will use later to execute the object detection, shown in the code here:

```
def load_img(path):
  img = tf.io.read_file(path)
  img = tf.image.decode_jpeg(img, channels=3)
```

```
    return img

def run_detector(detector, path):
  img = load_img(path)

  converted_img = tf.image.convert_image_dtype(img,
                                    tf.float32)[tf.newaxis, ...]
  start_time = time.time()
  result = detector(converted_img)
  end_time = time.time()

  result = {key:value.numpy() for key,value in result.items()}

  print("Found %d objects." % len(result["detection_scores"]))
  print("Inference time: ", end_time-start_time)

  image_with_boxes = draw_boxes(
    img.numpy(), result["detection_boxes"],
    result["detection_class_entities"], result["detection_scores"])

  display_image(image_with_boxes)
```

- This code sets up two functions: load_img to load the image, and run_detector to execute the detection process. There are plenty of calls to the previous helper functions we omitted inside the second function. Again, if you need to understand how those helper functions work, be sure to explore the code on your own.

- With all the code set up, we can now use the model to perform inference and visualize the output, as shown in Figure 3-13. This figure shows the most confidently detected objects in the image. You can run the detector by calling run_detector, also shown in the figure.

- You can perform the same inference on any image you like, and the code to do this over multiple images is shown here:

```
image_urls = ["https://live.staticflickr.com/52/145575457_a2e799ddb2_b.jpg",
        "https://live.staticflickr.com/141/361586876_095f93b84c_z.jpg",
        "https://live.staticflickr.com/6191/6036522556_dc09b57433_b.jpg"]

for image_url in image_urls:
  start_time = time.time()
  image_path = download_and_resize_image(image_url, 640, 480)
  run_detector(detector, image_path)
  end_time = time.time()
  print("Inference time:")
```

*Figure 3-13. Object with bounding boxes identifying objects*

- Running the last cell will import a number of new images and perform object detection on them as well. Note how the detector is capable of selecting up to 100 objects but shows only a maximum of the most confident.

 Finding the right image source can be tricky. The previous example works best with JPG or JPEG images. Other samples may not work as well for image formatting and the way color channels need to be extracted.

We avoided going into detail on the bounding box drawing code. Most of that code is relatively straightforward, and you can likely just copy this code to another sample without issue. There are also plenty of other resources and examples that use similar code online.

In the next section we look at another image example where we use CNN networks to artificially generate images using GANs.

# Generating Images with GANs

Deep learning researchers have been exploring the use of networks to not only recognize image data, but also generate it as well. This all started back with Google Deep Dream but has since been greatly refined with a class of training we generally refer to as adversarial. There are a number of more specific types of adversarial training we will explore throughout this book. In this section we will look at the powerful GAN.

 Google Deep Dream was a method used to extract the convolutional outputs as they were getting processed through a CNN network. The method allowed us to visualize abstract images of collections of features that were described as dreamlike, when in reality the images were representative of the features the network had learned to extract.

GANs are a powerful technique whereby we train two networks in tandem. One network, the discriminator or inspector, identifies correct-looking images from a batch of correct images, while the other network—we'll call it the generator or forger—tries to trick the inspector network with images it makes up from random data. As the discriminator network gets better at identifying what is real versus what is fake, the forger network likewise also has to improve. Both networks gradually learn, and in tandem they get to be a better discriminator and generator. With sufficient training, a very capable forger can even fool us humans. Figure 3-14 shows the basic architecture of this system. In the figure, "real data" could denote any form of data, including tabular data. For most demonstrations, image data is used in order to best represent not only the power of this technology, but also how it works.

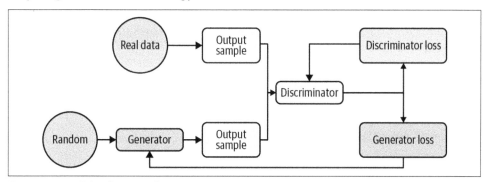

*Figure 3-14. GAN basic architecture*

A GAN, along with other forms of similar architectures we may generalize as adversarial training, is quite sensitive to tuning. It requires careful consideration to understand how data flows through both networks in tandem. Essentially, we need to train both networks in tandem and at the same time. This allows both networks to maintain a balance where they check each other. We will learn more about training GANs and generative architecture in Chapter 7. For now, though, we will see how GANs can learn from images with convolution in the next exercise.

Open the *Chapter_3_GAN.ipynb* in Colab and follow along with Example 3-13.

*Example 3-13. Exploring a GAN from TF Hub*

- Google with TF Hub provides plenty of advanced models you can play with or enhance on your own. The GAN in this exercise is called the BigGAN, so named because it was training on the ImageNet database.

- At the top of the notebook, you will see several sections of comments and an uncommented line. The uncommented line sets the `module_path` variable we will use for this example. The code is shown here:

```
# BigGAN-deep models
# module_path = 'https://tfhub.dev/deepmind/biggan-deep-128/1'
# 128x128 BigGAN-deep
module_path = 'https://tfhub.dev/deepmind/biggan-deep-256/1'
# 256x256 BigGAN-deep
# module_path = 'https://tfhub.dev/deepmind/biggan-deep-512/1'
# 512x512 BigGAN-deep

# BigGAN (original) models
# module_path = 'https://tfhub.dev/deepmind/biggan-128/2' # 128x128 BigGAN
# module_path = 'https://tfhub.dev/deepmind/biggan-256/2' # 256x256 BigGAN
# module_path = 'https://tfhub.dev/deepmind/biggan-512/2' # 512x512 BigGAN
```

- You can easily comment/uncomment out a different BigGAN depending on the different resolutions needed. For our purposes, $256 \times 256$ will work just fine.

- Scrolling down past the imports, we come to the first block of code that loads the TF Hub module:

```
tf.reset_default_graph()
print('Loading BigGAN module from:', module_path)
module = hub.Module(module_path)
inputs = {k: tf.placeholder(v.dtype, v.get_shape().as_list(), k)
          for k, v in module.get_input_info_dict().items()}
output = module(inputs)

print()
print('Inputs:\n', '\n'.join(
  ' {}: {}'.format(*kv) for kv in inputs.items()))
print()
print('Output:', output)
#outputs
Inputs:
```

```
z: Tensor("z:0", shape=(?, 128), dtype=float32)
truncation: Tensor("truncation:0", shape=(), dtype=float32)
y: Tensor("y:0", shape=(?, 1000), dtype=float32)

Output: Tensor("module_apply_default/G_trunc_output:0",
               shape=(?, 256,   256, 3),
               dtype=float32)
```

- This block of code loads the TF Hub module and defines the inputs and outputs. It then outputs the shape of each in order to remind us what image shape and output to handle.

- The next big section of code is taken directly from the source TF Hub example and is a set of utility functions. These functions allow the sample to run the model and handle the output. They are quite standard in these examples, and we will show you how to adapt them in later chapters.

- Just below the large block is a smaller block that initializes the model. It does this by first creating a TensorFlow session and then initializing it, as shown here:

```
initializer = tf.global_variables_initializer()
sess = tf.Session()
sess.run(initializer)
```

- The last block of code is where the action happens. This code defines the inputs used to run the BigGAN module. There are special comment definitions we can use in Colab to denote form input parameters, as shown in the inputs of the cell in Figure 3-15.

- Double-click on the cell block to open the code shown here:

```
#@title Category-conditional sampling { display-mode: "form", run: "auto" }

num_samples = 10 #@param {type:"slider", min:1, max:20, step:1}
truncation = 0.5 #@param {type:"slider", min:0.02, max:1, step:0.02}
noise_seed = 50 #@param {type:"slider", min:0, max:100, step:1}
batch_size = 8 #@param {type:"slider", min:8, max:256, step:2}
category = "162) beagle"
 #@param ["0) tench, Tinca tinca", "1) goldfish, Carassius a...
 # trimmed long, very long line

z = truncated_z_sample(num_samples, truncation, noise_seed)
y = int(category.split(')')[0])

ims = sample(sess, z, y, truncation=truncation, batch_size=batch_size)
imshow(imgrid(ims, cols=min(num_samples, 5)))
```

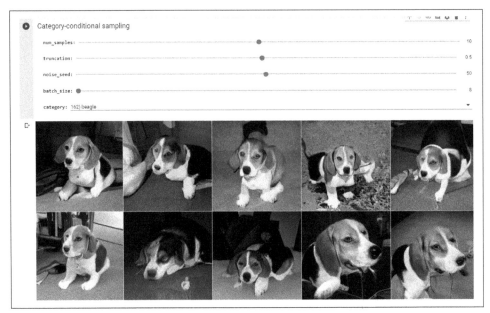

*Figure 3-15. BigGAN inputs and results*

- The top section of code defines the input parameters for the hub module. After that, we can see z defined by a call to `truncated_z_sample` with the inputs from the section above. Y defines the label, extracted again from the category selected input. This GAN was trained on 1,000 categories, and this is the reason that input line is shortened. Z, y, truncation, and session are all input into the sample function to generate a set of sample images.

- From the menu, select Runtime → Run All to observe the notebook run and confirm that the output matches, as shown in Figure 3-15. Feel free to play with this example to generate some new images based on the various categories.

- Truncation determines the amount of cutoff. Adjust it and see what effect it has on image generation.

After running the example, the output you are visualizing is generated from the GAN. It is not pulled from a database of images. There is no database, at least not in the GAN. Remember, the GAN is generating the image based on the category. This is a particular specialization of GANs called a *conditioned GAN*. Conditioning a GAN allows the GAN to generate images/data based on a set of conditions or attributes. We will explore this in Chapter 7.

The BigGAN we are using here was trained on 1,000 classes or conditions. There are many varieties of GANs, but this one is especially powerful because it allows you to partially map across the space between data, or the latent space. A *latent space* refers to the gaps in data we may not have any values for. GANs allow us to map across this latent space and thus generate images in the gaps. We will talk more about latent spaces as we progress through this book.

# Conclusion

Deep learning is currently expanding the AI field, and part of that success has been brought about by image-based tasks. Vision-based AI has been attempted for many years but has often failed to do implementation. Now, with recent advances in CNN, we see AI doing better than humans in most standard vision-based tasks. Consider that in a few years humans could be considered obsolete as visual inspectors and perhaps even as generators. This will likely alter our perception of vision and how we use it in the future. With AI now capable of generating convincing fake images, this has real implications for human culture, information, and media that will continue to resonate for several more years.

Now that we understand vision and images, we can move on to exploring moving images, or video, which we will do later in Chapter 5. In the next chapter, though, we will look at understanding language. Working with and understanding language is fundamental to many AI applications.

# CHAPTER 4

# Understanding Language on the Cloud

We have fantasized about using natural language to control computers since the original *Star Trek* TV series aired in the early '60s. Characters would often interface with the computer by saying "Computer." Since then, we have struggled to use language as an interface to computers and instead have relied entirely on symbolic languages like Python. That is, until fairly recently, with the inception of natural language systems giving us new interfaces like Siri and Alexa.

In this chapter we will discuss language and how advances in deep learning have accelerated our understanding of language. We will first look at natural language processing, or NLP, and talk about why we need it. Then we will move on to the art and science of processing language, from decimating language into numbers and vectors to processing those vectors with deep learning. After that we will discuss word context with recurrent neural networks, or RNN, and then move on to generating text with RNN layers. We will then use RNN to build sequences to sequence learning, which is at the heart of understanding machine translation. We will end with an advanced example that attempts to understand language itself using neural transformations.

Here is a high-level overview of the main topics we will cover in this chapter:

- Natural Language Processing, with Embeddings
- Recurrent Networks for NLP
- Neural Translation and the Translation API
- Natural Language API
- BERT: Bidirectional Encoder Representations from Transformers

This chapter assumes you have completed the contents of the previous chapters and have worked through a couple of the exercises. The samples in this chapter are intended to be introductory and deal with the broad concept of understanding language. To take these concepts further, you may want to explore more fundamentals of NLP later. In the next section, we look at a new, special type of layer that allows us to understand language context.

# Natural Language Processing, with Embeddings

The art and science of natural language processing, NLP, has been around since 1972. Since that time it has evolved from holistic new-age science into defining, cutting-edge research. However, NLP didn't really become known and admired until deep learning helped prop it up.

Deep learning is advancing in many areas of technology, but among all areas, NLP is likely the one that has most benefited. Ten years ago NLP was a tedious and little-understood practice. That all quickly changed when people found ways of combining it with deep learning.

In order to understand language, we need to process huge amounts of data. Deep learning brought about a revolution in NLP because of its ability to process huge amounts of data. Deep learning has also introduced new concepts that allow us to extract understanding from language. Before we get to that, though, let's first discuss the basics of processing language.

## Understanding One-Hot Encoding

Language, or what we can refer to as *text*, is used in documents, books, and, of course, speech. We understand language by interpreting sounds and written words, but that won't work for a computer. Instead, we need to translate the words or characters into numbers. Many techniques have been used to do this, but the current best method is referred to as *one-hot encoding*.

One-hot encoding is used for a number of areas in deep learning and data science, so we will describe it generally here. Whenever we have more than two classes, instead of denoting a class with a single numeric value, we represent it as a sparse vector. We use the term *sparse* because the vector is all zeros except for the spot that contains the class. Figure 4-1 shows how we can break down a block of text into a one-hot encoded sequence. Each word in the block of text is represented as a 1 in the table, with each row in the table denoting the encoding for that word. So the encoding for *Bunny* would be [1,0,0,0,0,0,0]. Notice that the length of the vector needs to account for every word in the whole text. We call the entire collection of text the *vocabulary* or *corpus*. In Figure 4-1, the corpus represents only seven words.

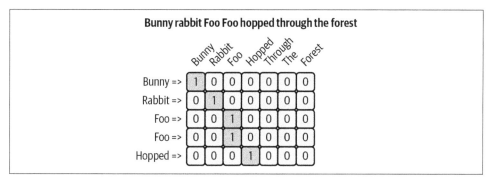

*Figure 4-1. One-hot encoding explained*

As for the words and other punctuation in a corpus, even those can and need to be broken down further. For instance, the word *hopped* from our example is derived from *hop*. We intuitively know this because of our understanding of language. The word *hopped* could also be derived from *hope*, but that would give our example an entirely different meaning. Needless to say, this process of breaking text down into tokens, or *tokenizing* them, is very complex and uses several different approaches for different applications. The process of tokenizing words, or what NLPers refer to as *grams*, is outside the scope of this book, but it is essential knowledge and something you should delve into further if you are building any type of serious NLP system.

One-hot encoding is used heavily on text but also on any data that requires multi-class classification. In the next section, we get back to NLP with word embeddings.

## Vocabulary and Bag-of-Words

When we break text down into tokens, we are in essence creating a vocabulary or list of tokens. From this list we can count how frequently each token appears in the document. We can then embed those counts into a document vector called a *bag-of-words*. Let's look at a simple example of how this works.

Consider the text:

the cat sat on the hat

Our vocabulary and counts for this text may look something like:

the - 2
cat - 1
sat - 1
hat - 1
on - 1

The bag-of-words vector representing this document would then be:

2,1,1,1,1

Notice that the order is irrelevant. We are only interested in how frequently each word appears. Now, say we want to create another bag-of-words vector for a second document, shown below:

the cat sat

The bag-of-words vector for this document would be:

1,1,1,0,0

Notice that the vector contains 0s because those tokens don't appear in the document. Let's consider a third document:

the cat ran away

When we tokenize this document, we need to add two tokens to the vocabulary. In turn, this means that the bag-of-words for the first two documents needs to change. The bag-of-words for our three documents may look something like:

2,1,1,1,1,0,0
1,1,1,0,0,0,0
1,1,0,0,0,1,1

If you look at the shape of the bag-of-words vectors, you can infer that there may be different meanings in the text. Being able to infer meaning from bag-of-words vectors has been successful in classifying everything from spam to movie reviews.

 Bag-of-words vectors are a precursor to building another form of encoding called *term frequency over inverse document frequency*, or TF-IDF. In TF-IDF encoding, we take the frequency of the token and divide it by how frequently the token appears in all documents. This allows you to identify more relevant tokens like *ran* and *away* in the previous example.

## Word Embeddings

From bag-of-words encodings of text into vectors of numbers, NLP researchers moved on to making sense of and recognizing patterns in the numbers. However, a bag of numbers or words wasn't much value without some relation or context. What NLP needed to understand is how words or grams relate to others words or grams.

Understanding the similarity or difference between tokens requires us to measure some form of distance. To understand that distance, we need to break our tokens down into vector representations, where the size of the vector represents the number of dimensions we want our words broken into.

Consider our previous example, with the following three documents:

the cat sat on the hat
the cat sat
the cat ran away

With bag-of-words vectors resembling:

2,1,1,1,1,0,0
1,1,1,0,0,0,0
1,1,0,0,0,1,1

We can find the similarity between documents by taking the cosine distance between any of the two vectors. Cosine distance is the dot product of any two vectors divided by the product of the lengths. We can use the SciPy library spatial module to do the calculation like so:

```
from scipy import spatial

vector1 = [2,1,1,1,1,0,0]
vector2 = [1,1,0,0,0,1,1]

cosine_similarity = 1 - spatial.distance.cosine(vector1, vector2)
print(cosine_similarity)
OUTPUT
0.5303300858899106
```

When using cosine similarity, the value returned will be from –1 to +1, measuring the similarity or distance between vectors. For our code example, we measure the distance between the first and third example documents. The output of .53 means the documents are similar but not exact. You can use this method to determine document similarity using bag-of-words or TF-IDF vectors.

We can also use this method of similarity testing for the tokens themselves. However, this means that we need to learn what those individual token vectors may look like. To do that, we use a special layer type called an *embeddings layer*.

Embeddings learn by using a single deep learning layer that learns the weights associated with random word pairings over a number of dimensions. Let's see how this works by running Example 4-1, where we see how to embed and visualize embeddings.

*Example 4-1. Creating word embeddings*

- Open a new Colab notebook or the example *Chapter_4_Embedding.ipynb*.
- We start with the typical imports as shown here:

```
from __future__ import absolute_import, division, print_function,
                       unicode_literals
import tensorflow as tf

from tensorflow import keras
from tensorflow.keras import layers
import tensorflow_datasets as tfds
```

- Next, we will load the data we will use for this example. The dataset we are using here is from the TensorFlow Datasets library, which is a great source to work with. The code to load this dataset is shown here:

```
(train_data, test_data), info = tfds.load(
    'imdb_reviews/subwords8k',
    split = (tfds.Split.TRAIN, tfds.Split.TEST),
    with_info=True, as_supervised=True)
```

- Running the cell will load the TensorFlow dataset for IMDb Reviews. This dataset was previously tokenized to a vocabulary of 8,000 tokens. The code also splits this dataset into a train and test split, the defaults for a TF project. We use two other options: one for loading info, with_info=True, and the other, as_supervised=True, for supervised learning.
- After the dataset is loaded, we can also explore some information about how the data was encoded (tokenized) using the following code:

```
encoder = info.features['text'].encoder
encoder.subwords[2000:2010]
#outputs
['Cha',
 'sco',
 'represent',
 'portrayed_',
 'outs',
 'dri',
 'crap_',
 'Oh',
 'word_',
 'open_']
```

- The encoder object we return here is of type SubwordTextEncoder, which is an encoder provided with TensorFlow that breaks text down into grams or tokens. We can use this encoder to understand what the vocabulary of words looks like. The second line extracts and outputs the tokens/grams from the encoder. Notice how the tokens may represent full or partial words. Each of the tokens represented has a vector representation of how/when it appears in the sample text.

---

- We can take a look at what these encoded vectors look like with the following new block of code:

```
padded_shapes = ([None],())
train_batches = train_data.shuffle(1000).padded_batch(10,
        padded_shapes = padded_shapes)
test_batches = test_data.shuffle(1000).padded_batch(10,
        padded_shapes = padded_shapes)

train_batch, train_labels = next(iter(train_batches))
train_batch.numpy()
#outputs
array([[ 133, 1032,    6, ...,    0,    0,    0],
       [  19, 1535,   31, ...,    0,    0,    0],
       [ 750, 2585, 4257, ...,    0,    0,    0],
       ...,
       [  62,   66,    2, ...,   17, 2688, 8029],
       [ 734,   37,  279, ...,    0,    0,    0],
       [  12,  118,  284, ...,    0,    0,    0]])
```

- Before we take a look at the data, we first use the top three lines to pad, shuffle, and batch the data into train and test batches. We do this to make sure that the length of each document/review is the same. Then we extract the data and display the list of vectors for each review. The value at each position in the various lists denotes the words/tokens index in the vocabulary.

 There is an important difference here in the encoding vectors. These are not bag-of-words vectors; rather, they ordered vectors of an index into a vocabulary. The key difference is that each index represents a word in that position of text. This is more efficient than bag-of-words encodings because it preserves the context order of words, which is often just as important as the words themselves.

- With the encoded movie reviews downloaded, we can move on to building our embeddings model, shown here:

```
embedding_dim=16

model = keras.Sequential([
  layers.Embedding(encoder.vocab_size, embedding_dim),
  layers.GlobalAveragePooling1D(),
  layers.Dense(16, activation='relu'),
  layers.Dense(1, activation='sigmoid')
])

model.summary()
#outputs
Model: "sequential"
```

```
Layer (type)                  Output Shape           Param #
=================================================================
embedding_1 (Embedding)       (None, None, 16)        130960
_____
global_average_pooling1d (Gl  (None, 16)                   0
_____
dense (Dense)                 (None, 16)                 272
_____
dense_1 (Dense)               (None, 1)                   17
=================================================================
Total params: 131,249
Trainable params: 131,249
Non-trainable params: 0
```

- This model introduces a couple of new layers. The first, the `Embedding` layer, is the layer that will train the weights to determine how similar tokens are in a document. After this layer, we push things into a `GlobalAveragePooling1D` layer. This layer is the same as the pooling layers in CNN, but in this case it is only one-dimensional. We don't need two dimensions for this data since text is only one-dimensional. From the pooling layer, we then move into a `Dense` layer of 16 neurons, which finally outputs to a single `Dense` output layer that uses a sigmoid activation function. Remember, the sigmoid, or squishification, function squishes the output into a range of 0 to 1.

- Then we move from building to training the model with the following code:

```
model.compile(optimizer='adam',
              loss='binary_crossentropy',
              metrics=['accuracy'])

history = model.fit(
    train_batches,
    epochs=10,
    validation_data=test_batches, validation_steps=20)
```

- As we know, the `compile` function compiles the model, and the `fit` function trains it. Notice the choice of optimizer, loss, and metrics in the call to compile. Then in fit, we pass in the training data (`train_batches`), the number of epochs, the validation data (`test_batches`), and the number of validation steps. As you run the cell, watch the output and see how the model trains.

- Next, we can look at the results of training by running the final cell, found in the notebook example. We have seen this code before, so we won't review it again. The output produces Figure 4-2, and we can see how the model trains and validates.

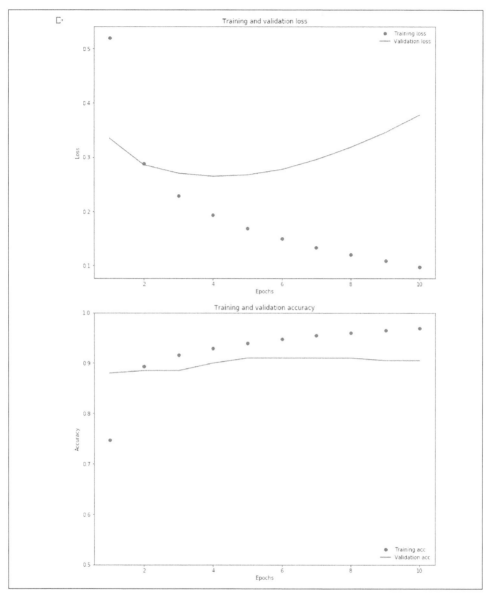

*Figure 4-2. Training the embedding model*

Now that we have the reviews embedded, what does that mean? Well, embedding (the part learned by that first layer) extracts the similarity between words/tokens/grams in our vocabulary. In the next section, we look at why knowing word similarity matters.

# Understanding and Visualizing Embeddings

NLP researchers found that by understanding the relevance of words in documents with respect to other words, we can ascertain the topic or thoughts those documents represent. This is a powerful concept we will explore in more detail in this chapter. Before we do that, however, let's see how word similarity can be visualized and used for further investigation in Example 4-2.

*Example 4-2. Visualize embeddings*

- Embeddings are essentially encoded vectors that represent the similarity between tokens. The representation of that is embedded in a vector of learned weights. We can use those weights to further plot how similar words are using various distance functions like cosine distance. Before that, let's see how we pull the weights out of the model and write them to a file with the following code:

```
e = model.layers[0]
weights = e.get_weights()[0]

import io

encoder = info.features['text'].encoder

out_v = io.open('vecs.tsv', 'w', encoding='utf-8')
out_m = io.open('meta.tsv', 'w', encoding='utf-8')

for num, word in enumerate(encoder.subwords):
  vec = weights[num+1] # skip 0, it's padding.
  out_m.write(word + "\n")
  out_v.write('\t'.join([str(x) for x in vec]) + "\n")
out_v.close()
out_m.close()
```

- This code extracts the weights from the first layer, layer 0, and then, using the encoder again, it enumerates through every word in the vocabulary and outputs the weights for that word. We write the words into the *.meta* file and the actual values into the *.v* file:

```
try:
  from google.colab import files
except ImportError:
  pass
else:
  files.download('vecs.tsv')
  files.download('meta.tsv')
```

- Use this code to download the files we just generated. We need to use those files in an Embeddings viewer or projector. If you encounter issues downloading the files, be sure to follow any prompts. If you have an error with cookies, you need to allow third-party cookies in your browser.

- After the files are downloaded, open a new browser window to the Embedding Projector page (*http://projector.tensorflow.org*). This page will allow us to upload our saved embeddings and view them.

- Click the Load button and load the *meta.tsv* and *vec.tsv* files as suggested by the dialog prompt. When you are done uploading, click off the window to close it.

- Click the Sphereize Data checkbox to view the data more spread out. Type the word *confe* in the search box.

- Make sure the default analysis or distance method is set to PCA. Distance between vectors determines how similar words are over different spaces. There are a number of ways to determine distance. Figure 4-3 shows the sphereized data and the search set for the token *confe*. Notice in the figure how similar words are shown on the right side. We can see in the plot how dissimilar the words are to each other, at least in terms of our document corpus.

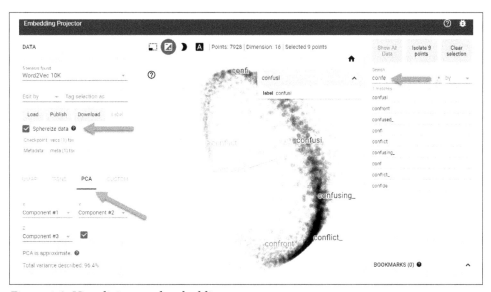

*Figure 4-3. Visualizing word embeddings*

PCA and t-SNE are methods used to visualize word embeddings or vector distances. They are similar to cosine distance but output values in 3D, hence the visualization.

- You are encouraged to continue playing with the embeddings projector to understand how words are similar depending on distance calculation or function.

A key element in our ability to train deep learning models is to understand how similar or dissimilar they are given a corpus of documents. In our last example, each word/token embedding was represented by 16 dimensions. One way to think about these 16 dimensions is as topics, thoughts, or categories. You may often hear these types of vectors referred to as *topic* or *thought vectors* in NLP. The interesting thing to note here is that these topics or thought vectors are learned by the network on its own. By determining the distance between these vectors, we can determine how similar the words are in the context of our corpus (collection of documents).

To represent those topic or thought vectors in space, we can use a variety of visualization techniques. The default technique is principle component analysis, or PCA. PCA is the method by which we take the 16 dimensional vectors and reduce them to a 3D vector we can visualize in space. The project also supports t-SNE and UMAP as other ways to visualize this data. You can also visualize the distance between words using a variety of distance methods. The common method we use to measure distance is cosine or dot project distance. The other methods are euclidean and taxicab distances. Play with the embeddings projector from the last exercise to learn more.

Now that we have a basic understanding of NLP and how data is encoded and embedded, we can move on to making sense of the text in the next section.

## Recurrent Networks for NLP

Being able to understand the similarity between words in a corpus has extensive applications to searching, sorting, and indexing data. However, our goal has always been to have a machine understand language. In order to do that, we also need to further understand the context of language. While our current NLP model provides us with some context between words, it ignores other more important contexts, such as token order. Consider the following two sentences:

- The cow jumps over the moon
- The moon jumps over the cow

There is no difference between the sentences if we just look at the words/vocabulary [cow, jumps, over, the, moon]. If we looked at the bag-of-words or TF-IDF vectors, tokens like *moon* and *cow* would likely show similar values. So how do we as humans understand the difference? It all comes down to the order in which we hear or see the words. If we teach this ordering importance to a network, it likely will understand more about the language and text. Fortunately, another form of layer type was developed called *recurrent networks*, which we will unfold in the next section.

# Recurrent Networks for Memory

Recurrent network layers are a type of layer used to extract features, not unlike CNN, although, unlike CNN, RNN extracts features by sequence or closeness. These layers extract features through order or learning sequences. Recurrent networks don't convolve but rather transpose. Each neuron in a recurrent network transposes its answer to the next neuron. It does this transposition for every element it exposes down the chain at the network. Figure 4-4 demonstrates how the network accepts an input and transposes it. So an RNN layer composed of four neurons would accept an input of up to four in size. You can think of these four inputs as a moving window through the document.

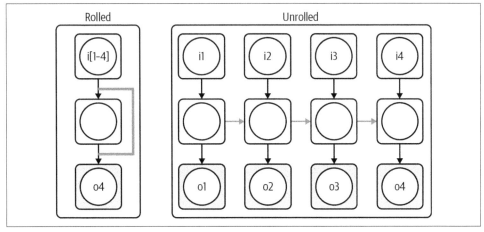

*Figure 4-4. Recurrent neural networks visualized*

In Figure 4-4 we can see how the layer is rolled up to represent the forward and backward pass through the network. Each move of the window over the document inputs the words or tokens at those positions. Since the output from the previous token is fed into the next token, the network learns to associate the order of tokens in the document. It also learns that things like "cow jumps" and "moon jumps" can represent entirely different meanings. The unrolled network in Figure 4-4 shows how the network backpropagates the error through the network weights. Let's see what difference adding a recurrent layer to our last example can make in doing text classification in Example 4-3.

*Example 4-3. Training sentiment with RNN*

- Open the example *Chapter_4_LSTM.ipynb* and follow along.
- This exercise uses several blocks of code from Example 4-1. As such, we will not revisit those here. Instead, we will start by rolling up our data into bigger batches with this code:

```
BUFFER_SIZE = 10000
BATCH_SIZE = 64

train_dataset = train_data.shuffle(BUFFER_SIZE)
train_dataset = train_data.padded_batch(BATCH_SIZE, train_data.output_shapes)

test_dataset = test_data.padded_batch(BATCH_SIZE, test_data.output_shapes)

train_batch, train_labels = next(iter(train_dataset))
train_batch.numpy()
#outputs
array([[ 249,    4,  277, ...,    0,    0,    0],
       [2080, 4956,   90, ...,    0,    0,    0],
       [  12,  284,   14, ...,    0,    0,    0],
       ...,
       [ 893, 7029,  302, ...,    0,    0,    0],
       [1646, 1271,    6, ...,    0,    0,    0],
       [ 147, 3219,   34, ...,    0,    0,    0]])
```

- Notice the difference here. We are increasing the size of our batches to 10,000.
- Now, on to building the model. This time we add a new recurrent layer called an LSTM, for long short-term memory. LSTMs are a specialized form of recurrent layer that work better at preserving memory and avoiding other issues. We will look at many other types of recurrent layers later in the chapter. The revised code to build that model is shown here:

```
model = tf.keras.Sequential([
    tf.keras.layers.Embedding(encoder.vocab_size, 64),
    tf.keras.layers.Bidirectional(tf.keras.layers.LSTM(64)),
    tf.keras.layers.Dense(64, activation='relu'),
    tf.keras.layers.Dense(1, activation='sigmoid')
])

model.summary()
#outputs
Model: "sequential"
```

| Layer (type) | Output Shape | Param # |
|---|---|---|
| embedding (Embedding) | (None, None, 64) | 523840 |

```
bidirectional (Bidirectional (None, 128)              66048
_____
dense (Dense)              (None, 64)                  8256
_____
dense_1 (Dense)            (None, 1)                   65
===============================================================
Total params: 598,209
Trainable params: 598,209
Non-trainable params: 0
```

- The increase in embedding dimensions is now 64, from 16. It is these vectors that are fed into a bidirectional LSTM layer. Bidirectional layers allow for context/ sequence to be learned forward or backward. Notice how the model output shows that the number of trainable parameters has increased dramatically. This will in turn greatly increase the amount of time this sample takes to train, so make sure these notebooks are set to use GPUs when training. The code to compile and fit the model, shown here, is quite similar to the last exercise:

```
model.compile(loss='binary_crossentropy',
              optimizer=tf.keras.optimizers.Adam(1e-4),
              metrics=['accuracy'])

history = model.fit(train_dataset, epochs=10,
                    validation_data=test_dataset,
                    validation_steps=30)
```

- Nothing new here. This block of code will take a significant amount of time to run. It will take several hours without a GPU, so grab a beverage and pause for a break, or work ahead and come back later. It's up to you.

- After training, we can again run our typical training and validation accuracy scores from the history using the standard plotting code. Figure 4-5 shows the output from this sample's training.

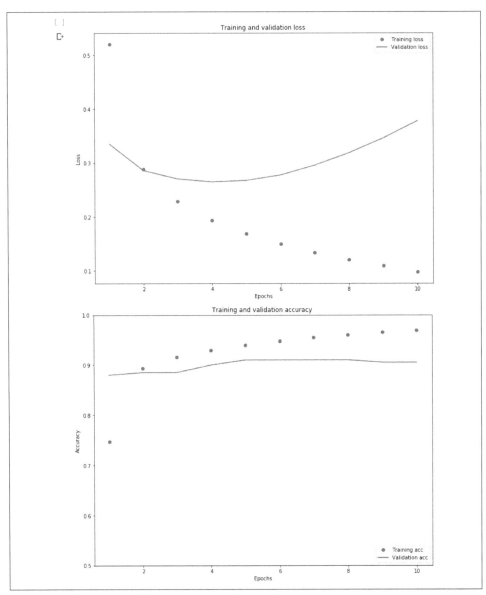

*Figure 4-5. Training/validation accuracy for sample*

With the model trained, we can now use it to understand text. The IMDb dataset is classified by sentiment. Our networks have been training to identify the sentiment, either good or bad, of movie reviews. This is the reason our model outputs a single binary class. In the next section, we will see how we can use this model to predict whether text about a movie is positive or negative.

# Classifying Movie Reviews

Now that we have a model trained on movie review sentiment, we can use that to test whether our own reviews are read as positive or negative by our machine model. Being able to predict text sentiment, whether good or bad, has broad applications. Any industry that acknowledges and responds to feedback will benefit from auto-processing reviewer feedback using AI. If the model is effectively trained, it can provide useful insights and information even outside sentiment. Consider a model trained to identify not just sentiment but perhaps also quality, style, or other factors. The possibilities are endless, provided you can label your training data effectively.

 Google provides a data-labeling service that will label your data per your specifications at a reasonable cost. Labeling a large corpus of text in this manner may be ideal for your needs.

In Example 4-4, we turn our model into a review classifier.

*Example 4-4. Classifying sentiment with RNN*

- This exercise continues from the last exercise that trained the model. Refer to sample *Chapter_4_LSTM.ipynb* and follow along.

- With the model trained, we can now enter some helper functions that will allow us to predict new text the model has never seen before. The helper code is shown here:

```
def pad_to_size(vec, size):
  zeros = [0] * (size - len(vec))
  vec.extend(zeros)
  return vec

def sample_predict(sentence, pad):
  encoded_sample_pred_text = encoder.encode(sample_pred_text)

  if pad:
    encoded_sample_pred_text = pad_to_size(encoded_sample_pred_text, 64)
  encoded_sample_pred_text = tf.cast(encoded_sample_pred_text, tf.float32)
  predictions = model.predict(tf.expand_dims(encoded_sample_pred_text, 0))

  return (predictions)
```

- These methods allow us to predict text with or without padding. Text padding can be important in some applications, so it is something we will want to test.

The importance of padding document vectors is typically related to the size of documents.

 You will likely notice that the validation accuracy does not keep up with the accuracy of model training. Remember that this is a sign of overfitting, and recall the techniques we can use to fix it. Hint: Dropping out is always an option...

- Next, we can run the prediction on a new unseen movie review by running the following code:

```
sample_pred_text = ('The movie was outrageous. The story was cool but
                     graphics needed work. I would recommend this movie.')
predictions = sample_predict(sample_pred_text, pad=False)
print (predictions)
```

- Feel free to enter your own review text and run the cell to see the model's prediction.

 If you find the examples keep disconnecting before training finishes, you can use this hack to keep the session connected. Type F12 to open the developer tools in your browser. Locate the console and enter the following JavaScript:

```
function reconnect(){
    console.log("Reconnecting");
    document.querySelector("colab-toolbar-button#connect").click()
}
setInterval(reconnect,60000)
```

The setInterval function calls the reconnect function every 60,000 milliseconds, or once a minute. The reconnect function returns the connect button from the notebook and clicks it.

You may notice that the sentiment detection is a bit weak or just wrong in some cases. There may be a host of reasons for this, including the size of the LSTM layers, the amount of training, and other factors. In order to improve on this example, we need to look at using more or different recurrent layers.

## RNN Variations

There are plenty of variations to recurrent networks, as we began to see in the last example. Each type of recurrent layer has its strength and weaknesses and may or may not work for your NLP application. The following list summarizes the major types and subtypes of recurrent networks:

*Simple RNN*

The simple model we defined earlier, and considered the base unit. It works well for simpler examples and certain edge cases, as we will see.

*LSTM (long short-term memory)*

A recurrent network layer/cell that attempts to solve vanishing gradients by introducing a gate at the end.

*GRU (Gated Recurrent Unit)*

Addresses the same problem as LSTM, vanishing gradients, but does so without the gate. The GRU tends to have better performance on smaller datasets compared to LSTM.

*Bidirectional RNNs*

A subtype of recurrent network that allows it to process forward and backward, which is useful for text classification, generation, and understanding.

*Nested inputs/outputs*

This is another subtype that allows for the definition of custom networks down to the cell level. It's not something you will likely want to use right away.

Let's take a look at how we can improve on our last example by changing out the layers on our model and retraining our movie-text sentiment classifier in Example 4-5.

*Example 4-5. Going deeper with RNN*

- This sample uses Example 4-4 as the base for all the code. The only part of this example that is different is the construction of the model.

- Open up the sample *Chapter_4_GRU.ipynb* and review the code. Scroll down to where the model is built, as the code is shown below:

```
model = tf.keras.Sequential([
    tf.keras.layers.Embedding(encoder.vocab_size, 64),
    tf.keras.layers.Bidirectional(tf.keras.layers.GRU(32,
            return_sequences=True)),
    tf.keras.layers.Bidirectional(tf.keras.layers.SimpleRNN(16)),
    tf.keras.layers.Dense(16, activation='relu'),
    tf.keras.layers.Dense(1, activation='sigmoid')
])

model.summary()
#outputs
Model: "sequential_3"
```

| Layer (type) | Output Shape | Param # |
| --- | --- | --- |
| embedding_3 (Embedding) | (None, None, 64) | 523840 |

```
bidirectional_3 (Bidirection  (None, None, 64)          18624
────────────────────────────────────────────────────────────────
bidirectional_4 (Bidirection  (None, 32)                2592
────────────────────────────────────────────────────────────────
dense_6 (Dense)               (None, 16)                528
────────────────────────────────────────────────────────────────
dense_7 (Dense)               (None, 1)                 17
================================================================
Total params: 545,601
Trainable params: 545,601
Non-trainable params: 0
```

- Notice that the model has fewer parameters and the structure is quite different. We use two recurrent layers, both with bidirection, in this example. The first layer is a new GRU, which is followed by a second recurrent SimpleRNN layer. The simple layer takes the output from the GRU layer and trims it down so it fits into the first Dense layer. Notice that we use lower counts of input neurons in both RNN layers.

- We can then compile and run the model with the following code:

```
model.compile(loss='binary_crossentropy',
              optimizer=tf.keras.optimizers.Adam(1e-4),
              metrics=['accuracy'])

history = model.fit(train_dataset, epochs=10,
                    validation_data=test_dataset,
                    validation_steps=30)
```

- The model compilation and fit function calls are identical for this example. This example can take several hours to run even if set to GPU mode.

Now that you understand the basics of NLP with embeddings and recurrent networks, we can move on to using the Google API. In the next section, we look at how to use the Translation API to translate text.

# Neural Translation and the Translation API

There are a variety of reasons why we would want to understand or need to process text. One obvious use of this technology is translation between languages. We don't yet have the universal translator from *Star Trek*, but deep learning is getting us closer to that goal every day. The process of translation is a subset of NLP that learns by learning sequences with recurrent networks. However, instead of having a sequence of review text, we learn transformations from one language to another.

This process of learning transformation from one language or set of text to another is based on sequence-to-sequence learning. In the next section, we introduce sequence-to-sequence learning and look at how to build a simple machine translation model.

# Sequence-to-Sequence Learning

We have already learned that RNNs can learn sequences or word association and context. What if we could teach a model or models to encode sequences of one type and decode them as another type? This encoding/decoding model is the basis for something called an *autoencoder*. Autoencoders can be used to extract features from complex data to generate new data, not unlike a GAN. The embedding layers we looked at earlier are based on an autoencoder architecture. We'll learn more about autoencoders and GANs in Chapter 7.

For this application, though, we want our model to encode and remember one sequence, or context of tokens. Then we will build a decoder that can learn to transform those sequences to other sequences. There are many applications for this type of learning, and the one we focus on here is for machine translation. This encoder/decoder concept is shown in Figure 4-6. You can see in the diagram how text from one sequence is converted to another sequence.

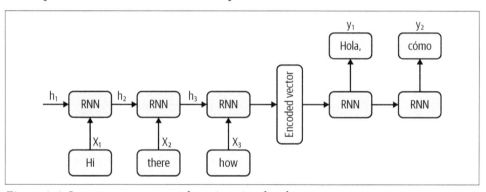

*Figure 4-6. Sequence-to-sequence learning visualized*

In the figure, the text is translated from English ("Hi there, how are you?") into Spanish ("Hola, cómo estás?"). This example text was converted with Google, and it is quite unlikely we could produce similar results building our own model. As we will see later, though, we can borrow the models Google has developed. Instead, it will be helpful for us to review the code or the standard Keras version of sequence-to-sequence learning that follows:

```
from keras.models import Model
from keras.layers import Input, LSTM, Dense

# Define an input sequence and process it.
encoder_inputs = Input(shape=(None, num_encoder_tokens))
encoder = LSTM(latent_dim, return_state=True)
encoder_outputs, state_h, state_c = encoder(encoder_inputs)
# We discard `encoder_outputs` and only keep the states.
encoder_states = [state_h, state_c]
```

```
# Set up the decoder, using `encoder_states` as initial state.
decoder_inputs = Input(shape=(None, num_decoder_tokens))
# We set up our decoder to return full output sequences,
# and to return internal states as well. We don't use the
# return states in the training model, but we will use them in inference.
decoder_lstm = LSTM(latent_dim, return_sequences=True, return_state=True)
decoder_outputs, _, _ = decoder_lstm(decoder_inputs,
                                    initial_state=encoder_states)
decoder_dense = Dense(num_decoder_tokens, activation='softmax')
decoder_outputs = decoder_dense(decoder_outputs)

# Define the model that will turn
# `encoder_input_data` & `decoder_input_data` into `decoder_target_data`
model = Model([encoder_inputs, decoder_inputs], decoder_outputs)
```

That block of code was extracted right from the Keras website's section on sequence-to-sequence learning. It demonstrates the construction of the encoder model and the decoder model. Both encoding/decoding models are constructed from an LSTM layer. These submodels, if you will, are combined into a larger single model. Keep in mind that this is just one part of the code and doesn't include other things like tokenization, embedding, and understanding.

 There are plenty of online materials that can help you understand sequence-to-sequence learning in more detail. Be sure to check out those resources if you want to build your own sequencer.

Getting sequence-to-sequence learning to actually process understandably translated text is outside the scope of this book. Instead, in the next section we will look at how to use the Translation API to do the same thing but more effectively and more easily.

## Translation API

If anyone can build a universal translator, it is most certainly Google. Being the go-to archivist for all human media has distinct advantages. Google has been doing raw translation the longest of any search or other platforms, and it is very much a part of its current business model. Therefore, unless you need to translate some rare language (Klingon is not currently supported), then building your own sequence-to-sequence translator isn't practical.

Fortunately, Google provides the AutoML Translation engine for building custom models on your own pair translations. We will look at that engine shortly. Before that, though, let's look at how to use the Translation API in Example 4-6.

The next couple of exercises require you to have billing enabled on your Google account. As long as you use these services reasonably, you can get away with no charges or just minimal charges. That said, be careful, as experiments can go awry. Be sure to shut down notebooks when you are done with them. We would hate to see you get a huge bill because your Klingon translator repeated translations, or some other silly bug.

*Example 4-6. Translating with the Translation API*

- Open sample *Chapter_4_Translate.ipynb* and follow along.
- The first thing we need to do is acquire a developer key to authorize ourselves on the sample. Click the link in the text for the API developer console (*http://console.cloud.google.com/apis*). From there you will need to create a new API key and authorize it for development.
- Create a new developer API key or use an existing one.
- Run the code in the first code block, with the following code:

```
import getpass

APIKEY = getpass.getpass()
```

- Running that block of code will generate a key pass text box. The box is waiting for you to enter the newly generated developer API key.
- Copy and paste the key from the developer console into the key pass text box. There won't be much fanfare, but if there are no errors, you are in.
- Next, we enter the code that grabs the translation service and translates the text, as shown here:

```
from googleapiclient.discovery import build
service = build('translate', 'v2', developerKey=APIKEY)

# use the service
inputs = ['hello there, how are you',
          'little rabbit foo foo hopped through the forest',
          'picking up all the field mice']
outputs = service.translations().list(source='en', target='es',
# print outputs
for input, output in zip(inputs, outputs['translations']):
  print(u"{0} -> {1}".format(input, output['translatedText']))
  #outputs
hello there, how are you -> Hola cómo estás
little rabbit foo foo hopped through the forest -> pequeño conejo foo foo
              esperaba a través del bosque
picking up all the field mice -> recogiendo todos los ratones de campo
```

- This code first takes the developer API key we previously set and authorizes the service. Then it sets up the text we want to translate and does the translation. In this case, we use the Spanish *es*, but many languages are available. After that, we output the results of the translated text. Yep, so easy.

That service is just so easy to use it begs the question: why would you ever need to use a different translation method? Well, as it turns out, translation is important for things other than languages. Machine translation has been shown to translate program code, domain knowledge, and terms to recipes. With that in mind, we look at how to use AutoML Translation in the next section.

## AutoML Translation

In order to be complete, we will demonstrate how to use the AutoML translation engine, which will allow you to upload and train your own language pairings. This API is not a generic sequence-to-sequence learner, and you are limited to working with languages. The API further limits you to translating from one recognized language to another. You cannot, for instance, do an English-to-English model since the sequencer is trained on languages. This can limit your ability to do any specialized domain-specific language translation, if that is your interest. However, if you just need to do specialized language translation, AutoML is probably the place for you.

 AutoML services from Google are paid services that charge a premium for use. That means any use of these services will incur a charge.

In Example 4-7, we walk through the workflow for setting up and using the AutoML Translation service to create a new model.

*Example 4-7. Using AutoML for translation*

- Point your browser at the AutoML translation page (*https://console.cloud.google.com/translation/dashboard*).
- After the page loads, click on the Datasets menu item on the left side.
- Click Create Dataset to create a new dataset.
- A wizard-type dialog will open, directing you to name the dataset and choose your source and translation languages. Again, these languages cannot be the same, unfortunately.

- After selecting the languages, click Continue to go to the Import tab, as shown in Figure 4-6. From here you can upload tab-separated data pairs. The following is an example of how this data may look in text:

```
hello there, how are you\tqavan pa' chay'
can you understand this language\tlaH Hol Dayaj'a'
what language is this?\tnuq Hol?
```

- You have the option of uploading any language pairings. In the above example, one side of the tab character (\t) is English, and the other side is Klingon. The data you upload will be broken out into test, training, and validation. For this reason, you need a minimum of 100 items for test and validation. The default split is 80% training, 10% testing, and 10% validation, which means you will want a minimum of 1,000 unique training pairs.

- When you have uploaded all your data, click Continue to process the data. As the data is processed into training pairs, it will identify sentences.

- From here you can click on the Train tab to start training the model. Remember that auto machine learning is not only training models but also iteratively searching for optimum model hyperparameters. As such, training times can be substantial.

- When your model has completed training, you can access predictions from the Predict tab, as shown in Figure 4-7.

You now have enough knowledge to decide on what solution to use, either the Translation API, AutoML Translate, or you can build your own sequence-to-sequence learner. Keep in mind, though, that all these fields are still exploding in research and development, and unless you are one of those researchers, you may want to stick with the Translate API or AutoML solutions. They are much easier to use, and in most cases, they are more practical than building and training your own translation models—that is, unless you need to do some form of custom or unsupported translation. In the next section, we change gears from translation to understanding text.

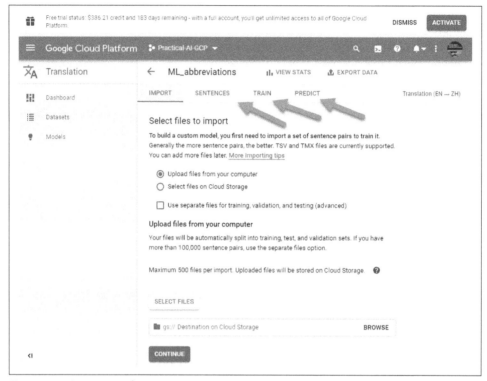

*Figure 4-7. Importing datasets into AutoML*

# Natural Language API

The real goal of any AI agent or application is to be able to naturally interface with us humans. Of course, the best way to do that is with natural language understanding, or NLU. While NLP is designed for the bare processing of text, NLU works to understand the concepts behind the text and even read between the lines. However, sarcasm and other emotionally latent responses are still a mystery. Our ability to give a machine understanding of text through deep learning is improving every day.

We already performed sentiment analysis on movie reviews with good success. Now we will apply sentiment analysis on text to determine if it is either positive or negative. This would require a substantial corpus for training, but fortunately Google has already done that with the Natural Language API. Realize that building our own custom model can take extensive effort to improve on, so we will look at using the Natural Language API in Example 4-8.

*Example 4-8. Natural Language for sentiment analysis*

- Open *Chapter_4_NL_Sentiment.ipynb* and run the first code cell. This will prompt you to enter your developer API key, which is the same key you acquired from the developer console credentials section in the last exercise.

- The first block of code we need to run, shown here, just sets up the sample:
```
from googleapiclient.discovery import build
lservice = build('language', 'v1beta1', developerKey=APIKEY)

quotes = [
    'I'm afraid that the following syllogism may be used by some in the future.
    Turing believes machines think, Turing lies with men Therefore
    machines do not think', # Alan Turing
    'The question of whether a computer can think is no more interesting
    than the question of whether a submarine can swim.', # Edsger W. Dijkstra
    'By far the greatest danger of Artificial Intelligence is that people
    conclude too early that they understand it.', # Eliezer Yudkowsky
    'What use was time to those who'd soon achieve Digital Immortality?',
    # Clyde Dsouza
    'Primary aim of quantum artificial intelligence is to improve human
    freedom, dignity, equality, security, and total well-being.',
    # Amit Ray
    'AI winters were not due to imagination traps, but due to lack of
    imaginations. Imaginations bring order out of chaos. Deep learning
    with deep imagination is the road map to AI springs and AI autumns.'
    # Amit Ray
]
```

- The service is constructed from the call to build, which we import in the first line. We pass in the language and model type. Then we create a list of quotes about AI and thinking machines. We will use these quotes to understand the sentiment.

- With setup complete, we'll move to the next block of code. This block loops through the quotes and sends them to the Natural Language service. The service responds with the analyzed sentiment. After that, the sentiment statistics are output, as shown in the following code:
```
for quote in quotes:
  response = lservice.documents().analyzeSentiment(
    body={
      'document': {
        'type': 'PLAIN_TEXT',
        'content': quote
      }
    }).execute()
  print(response)
  polarity = response['documentSentiment']['polarity']
```

```
magnitude = response['documentSentiment']['magnitude']
print('POLARITY=%s MAGNITUDE=%s for %s' % (polarity, magnitude, quote))
```

- Notice in the code that we construct the request body in JSON. JSON, or Java-Script Object Notation, is a format we commonly use to describe objects. If you are unfamiliar with JSON, check out Google for some resources. JSON will be a key element in how we make and receive these requests/responses.

- You can view the sentiment of each quote by looking at the score and magnitude values for each quote and each sentence in a quote. For instance, we can see that the first quote by Turing is negative, with a score of –0.2 and magnitude of 0.7, while the last quote by Ray has a positive sentiment of 0.2 and magnitude of 1.0. You may get slightly different results.

Analyzing sentiment is just one capability of the Natural Language API. Natural Language also allows you to do a wide variety of applications, from entity extraction to syntax checking. The following is a full list outlining each application:

*Sentiment*
Sentiment analysis allows us to determine if a message is good or bad.

*Entities*
Extracting and identifying entities, things, or objects in a sentence is nontrivial. Entity extraction allows you to identify key entities in text and documents. You can then use this information to augment a search, classify documents, or understand a discussion subject.

*Syntax*
This allows you to inspect the grammar of a sentence. You can determine the voice used and the tense (past, present, or future) for every token. It is not as powerful as Grammarly or the Hemingway app, but it's a start.

*Syntax and entities*
This process allows you to extract both sentiment and entities from a document. This one is quite powerful for the right application.

*Classify content*
Classifying content is similar to entity extraction, with a slight twist. It classifies content based on multiple tokens or words.

Each of these methods is documented more thoroughly on the Google AI Hub for Natural Language API. From here we can move on to another example where we extract entities. Entity analysis and extraction from text has broad applications, from optimizing search to helping a chatbot respond better. This method can be combined with semantic analysis or run in parallel with other analysis types. Imagine being able to identify the semantics, entities, and syntax of any text message or document. We will look at extracting the entities from text in Example 4-9.

---

*Example 4-9. Natural Language for entity analysis*

- Open example *Chapter_4_NL_Entities.ipynb*. The first code cell again needs to be run to set up security. Be sure to copy your API key from the developer console to your key pass text box and type `return`.

- Next, we do the standard import, as seen in the code here:
```
from googleapiclient.discovery import build
lservice = build('language', 'v1beta1', developerKey=APIKEY)
```

- Next, we set up the same list of quotes. We won't show those here. You can also use your own phrases or quotes if you like.

- The code to run the service and output just basic results is shown here:
```
for quote in quotes:
  response = lservice.documents().analyzeEntities(
    body={
      'document': {
        'type': 'PLAIN_TEXT',
        'content': quote
      }
    }).execute()
print(response)
#outputs - shortened
{'entities': [{'name': 'syllogism' ...
{'entities': [{'name': 'question' ...
{'entities': [{'name': 'people' ...
{'entities': [{'name': 'use' ...
{'entities': [{'name': 'aim' ...
{'entities': [{'name': 'learning' ...
```

- If you look through the entities output, you can see some interesting results. You will note the entry for Turing also associates a Wikipedia article about him, possibly pointing to a source of the quote itself.

Natural language analysis used to be done primarily with regex expressions looking for preset rule matches. Companies would build rules engines that allowed them to correlate and qualify their data. With the Natural Language API, regex rules engines are quickly becoming a thing of the past. We will revisit the Natural Language API in future chapters. For now, we move on to exploring the top model in NLP and NLU: BERT.

# BERT: Bidirectional Encoder Representations from Transformers

Bidirectional Encoder Representations from Transformers, or BERT, is the state of the art in NLP and NLU. It was so state-of-the-art that Google considered it a global security threat. Researchers at Google feared that BERT could be used to generate fake news, or worse, fake commands or orders. Imagine an AI capable of tweeting believable yet fake content to the world!

 We use the term *state of the art* (SOA) to refer to the latest peak in model research for a given task. SOA for a model will then be the baseline for all future models built to handle similar tasks.

The fear of BERT being used for nefarious purposes has subsided, likely because, while the model is good and is closing the gap, it is still far off from actual human communication. Now, Google and other vendors have released BERT and other variations to the public as open source.

Through that release, NLP researchers could see how much the landscape of NLP has changed in just a few short years. BERT introduces a number of new concepts to NLP and refines some old ones as well, as we will see. Likewise, the NLP techniques it introduces are now considered state of the art and are worth our focus in this section.

BERT works by applying the concept of bidirectional encoding/decoding to an attention model called a *Transformer*. The Transformer learns contextual relations in words without the use of RNN or CNN but with an attention-masking technique. Instead of reading a sequence of text like we have seen before, BERT consumes the entire text all at once. It uses a masking technique called *Masked LM* (MLM) that randomly masks words in the input and then tries to predict them. This provides a bidirectional view of the context around a word. The following is a summary of the main techniques used by BERT:

*Masking (Masked LM)*
Masking adds a classification layer on top of the encoded input. This classifier is used to extract the probability of pairwise matching of words, essentially providing the context of a word/token in the entire input. This removes the need to extract context using RNN or even CNN. However, it does require the input to be positionally encoded to preserve spatial context. With BERT, this masking technique provides bidirectionality. This is unique to Google's BERT, whereas the OpenAI GPT model, similar to BERT, uses a like mechanism that is not bidirectional.

*Positional encodings*

MLM requires PE to be encoded in a number of ways:

- By encoding the position of the word in the sentence.

- By learning not only the pairing of words, but also how they combine to create sentences. This is called *segment* or *sentence embedding*.

- By using a *word embeddings* layer to encapsulate the importance of the word in the input.

*Next sentence prediction*

BERT provides the ability to predict large parts or segments of a document using MLM. However, it was also trained on sentence pairings, making it even more capable of predicting the next sentence or segment. This ability opened up further interesting pairings, such as giving BERT an answer and expecting the question. This fed the speculation that BERT could be used to develop believable fake news or other communication for nefarious purposes.

With these advances, BERT has completely reformulated NLP overnight. The recurrent network layers we covered earlier are now being replaced by attention transformative networks. We will cover the details of this change in Chapter 5, where we take a far more in-depth look at how to build a BERT model. For the rest of this chapter, we will look at how to train a BERT model to do inference on various tasks. In the next section, we'll discuss the first task of building a semantic model with BERT.

## Semantic Analysis with BERT

We have already built a semantic analysis network model to classify the sentiment of IMDb-style movie reviews. This model worked relatively well but may have lacked some finesse. For instance, our previous model would likely miss sarcastic movie reviews like "His performance was great, if he was playing a rock." Sarcasm and other language idioms are difficult to capture semantically. BERT is able to learn these difficult idioms more capably and quickly than recurrent networks. Recurrent networks, by definition of learning sequences by passing state into deeper layers, are computationally expensive. This is in contrast to BERT, which uses the bidirectional attention transformation mechanism that is much more performant. That performance increase will become very apparent when we train BERT to learn sentiment.

TF Hub provides a service for BERT, but we won't use that here. Instead, we will use a module called *ktrain*. ktrain is a Python module built on top of Keras/TensorFlow that provides a number of helpful trainers for image and text recognition. We will use more of ktrain later for image analysis in video, but for now we will look at using it for text in Example 4-10.

*Example 4-10. BERT sentiment analysis*

- Open up *Chapter_4_BERT_IMDB.ipynb* and follow the code. Since this model is not provided by TF Hub, we can skip the security step in earlier examples.

- We will start by installing the ktrain module into Colab with the following command:

```
!pip3 install ktrain
```

- Next, we import ktrain and the text module, as shown in the following code:

```
import ktrain
from ktrain import text

ktrain.__version__
```

- ktrain encapsulates all the modules needed for processing and training models, so you only need to import it. This greatly simplifies developing and training complex models, which in turn will greatly ease our development of higher-functioning applications.

- The bulk of the code we need for this example is for loading the data itself, shown here:

```
import tensorflow as tf
dataset = tf.keras.utils.get_file(
    fname="aclImdb.tar.gz",
    origin="http://ai.stanford.edu/~amaas/data/sentiment/aclImdb_v1.tar.gz",
    extract=True,
)

# set path to dataset
import os.path
#dataset = '/root/.keras/datasets/aclImdb'
IMDB_DATADIR = os.path.join(os.path.dirname(dataset), 'aclImdb')
print(IMDB_DATADIR)
```

- Running that block of code downloads the IMDb movie review dataset to a local path. ktrain works by being fed the source path of the test and training data, so that's all we need to do.

- Next, we load the data and preprocessor. We assign it the mode, in this case BERT, names, and classes, as shown in the code here:

```
(x_train, y_train), (x_test, y_test), preproc =
    text.texts_from_folder(IMDB_DATADIR,
        maxlen=500,
        preprocess_mode='bert',
        train_test_names=['train','test'],
        classes=['pos', 'neg'])
```

- With data loaded, the model is built and a learner is constructed. Notice that we limit the length of input to 500 characters. This will simplify our model and make it quicker to train. Next, we create a learner that sets the model up for training and then performs the training/validation fit, as shown in the following code:

```
model = text.text_classifier('bert', (x_train, y_train), preproc=preproc)
learner = ktrain.get_learner(model,train_data=(x_train, y_train),
                             val_data=(x_test, y_test), batch_size=6)

learner.lr_find()
learner.lr_plot()
```

- At the end of the block, the learner first finds the appropriate learning rate and then plots out the loss of this search.

- From there, we need to train the model using a given threshold and number of epochs. These samples can take a while, so take note that training times might be longer. The code to autofit the model is shown here:

```
learner.autofit(2e-5, 1)
```

- The last block of code will take over an hour to run on a CPU notebook and slightly less on a GPU notebook. This is significantly better than our previous semantic analysis example by an order of magnitude. Our previous examples could take hours with a GPU. You may want to use our previous reconnection hack from the end of Example 4-7 to keep the Colab session running without disconnecting.

- Finally, we review the plot of the training output and then do a sample prediction with the following code:

```
learner.lr_plot()

predictor = ktrain.get_predictor(learner.model, preproc)

data = [
  'I am glad the popcorn was good, but my seat was still uncomfortable.',
  'That actor was fantastic, if he were a rock.',
  'Graphics were amazing but the story lacked character.',
  'This movie made me think why do things matter?',
    ]

predictor.predict(data)
#outputs
['neg', 'pos', 'neg', 'pos']
```

- Retraining the BERT model for a longer time would likely improve the results.

- Figure 4-8 shows how well the BERT model is able to adapt to our new task, movie-review sentiment analysis.

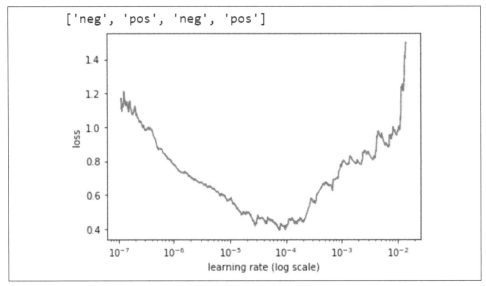

*Figure 4-8. Output of training loss from BERT model*

You can see from the output of the last exercise that the model does a surprisingly good job learning to distinguish language nuances. Keep in mind that the model we are using is a BERT-trained model that we are applying transfer learning to. The amount of training we did for this example is about the minimum, and you should expect your results to improve with more training. This is the same process used with transfer learning, where we retrained a previously trained model to recognize cats and dogs. For the sake of keeping things simple, we used ktrain, a nice, compact helper library, to download and set up the BERT model for us. We will continue to use ktrain in the next section to build a documentation system.

## Document Matching with BERT

After looking at sentiment, we can move on to determining document similarity with BERT. We've already seen how we could use bag-of-words and TF-IDF vectors to compare document similarity. This allows you to find similar content more easily in things like search or document matching. In Example 4-11, we retrain BERT to classify documents into topics or categories.

*Example 4-11. BERT document analysis*

- For this exercise, we are going to retrain BERT to identify similar documents defined from previously set categories. The dataset we are using in this exercise, 20newsgroups_dataset, is from the scikit-learn tutorial series.

- Open the example *Chapter_4_BERT_DOCs.ipynb* and make sure the runtime type is set to GPU.

- The first code block defines the basic environment setup and install of `ktrain`. We won't review that here, but be sure to take a look at it.

- Jumping to the next block of code, we can see that the categories are getting selected. In this example, we use only four categories provided by the sample dataset. This will greatly reduce our training times. From there, we load the data using `sklearn`. `sklearn` has become a standard for various machine learning exercises like this one. The complete code is shown here. The last lines show how the training and test data is set to the various lists:

```
categories = ['comp.graphics', 'misc.forsale',
              'sci.space', 'rec.sport.hockey']
from sklearn.datasets import fetch_20newsgroups
train_b = fetch_20newsgroups(subset='train',
   categories=categories, shuffle=True, random_state=42)
test_b = fetch_20newsgroups(subset='test',
   categories=categories, shuffle=True, random_state=42)

print('size of training set: %s' % (len(train_b['data'])))
print('size of validation set: %s' % (len(test_b['data'])))
print('classes: %s' % (train_b.target_names))

x_train = train_b.data
y_train = train_b.target
x_test = test_b.data
y_test = test_b.target
#outputs
size of training set: 2362
size of validation set: 1572
classes: ['comp.graphics', 'misc.forsale', 'rec.sport.hockey', 'sci.space']
```

- With the data loaded, we can move on to building the training and testing datasets with the following code:

```
import ktrain
from ktrain import text

(x_train,  y_train), (x_test, y_test),
preproc = text.texts_from_array(x_train=x_train, y_train=y_train,
                     x_test=x_test, y_test=y_test,
                     class_names=train_b.target_names,
                     preprocess_mode='bert',
                     ngram_range=1,
                     maxlen=350,
                     max_features=35000)
```

- Then we build, train, and plot the model losses with the following code:

```
model = text.text_classifier('bert', train_data=(x_train, y_train),
                    preproc=preproc)
```

```
learner = ktrain.get_learner(model, train_data=(x_train, y_train),
                             batch_size=6)

learner.lr_find()
learner.lr_plot()
```

- The last section of code finds the learning rates, but the next section of code optimizes the learning:

```
learner.autofit(2e-5, 5)
```

- After the model has been autofit, we move on to extracting a predictor and then confirming our classes with the following code:

```
predictor = ktrain.get_predictor(learner.model, preproc)
predictor.get_classes()
#outputs
['comp.graphics', 'rec.sport.hockey', 'sci.electronics', 'sci.space']
```

- With the predictor object, we can then run a prediction of some text of interest using the code here:

```
predictor.predict('Deep learning is to science as humor is to laughter.')
```

- The output class will depend on the amount of time you trained the model for. With more training, the class may make more or less sense. Keep in mind that we have limited the number of topics in our trainer, which in turn limits our ability to recognize document types.

 You can also switch your Colab notebook to use an offline (local notebook) by running Jupyter on your local computer. To switch your runtime connection, click the runtime info dropdown, located at top right, and select the connection type. The dialog will also guide you through setting up and configuring this further.

These examples can take a considerable amount of time, so it usually helps to be particularly careful with your setup. Of course, after you fumble your first 12- or 24-hour training session, you begin to learn very quickly. Regardless of our simplistic results, it should be apparent how accessible it is to train NLP with BERT and ktrain. In the next section, we look at a more custom example that illustrates how to source and load data.

## BERT for General Text Analysis

We have seen how to use BERT a couple of different ways on prepared datasets. Prepared datasets are excellent for learning, but they're not practical in the real world. Therefore, in Example 4-12 we look at how to use BERT to do some general text analysis.

*Example 4-12. BERT text analysis*

- In this exercise we are going to use jokes as our text analysis source. Jokes and humor can be difficult to determine for us humans, so this will be a great demonstration of BERT. The jokes we will use are from a GitHub repository (*https:// github.com/taivop/joke-dataset*). We'll be looking at the *stupidstuff.org* joke list in particular. Note: Some of these jokes should be considered NSFW.

- Open the example *Chapter_4_BERT_Jokes.ipynb*. The first cell starts by installing ktrain and wget. We will use wget for pulling down the JSON document of joke text.

- Then we jump down to downloading and saving the raw JSON joke text using wget with the following code:

```
import wget

jokes_path = "stupidsuff.json"
url = 'https://raw.githubusercontent.com/taivop/joke-dataset/master/
stupidstuff.json'
wget.download(url, jokes_path)
```

- With the file downloaded, we can open the file and parse the JSON into our jokes and humor lists. The humor list will hold the funny class 0 if the joke is not funny and 1 if it is. In the code block, we set the fun_limit variable to 4. This value will set the rating at which we decide a joke is funny. The ratings for this dataset go from 1 to 5, so 4 is about 80%. The following is the code to load and parse the JSON into the needed data lists:

```
import json

jokes = []
humor = []
fun_limit = 4
fun_total = 0
not_total = 0
with open(jokes_path) as json_file:
    data = json.load(json_file)
    for d in data:
      joke = d['body']
      jokes.append(joke)
      if d['rating'] > fun_limit:
        humour.append(1)
        fun_total += 1
      else:
        humor.append(0)
        not_total += 1
print(jokes[244], humor[244])
print(fun_total, not_total)
```

- You can adjust the fun limit to any value you want, but be sure you get a good split of data. The last line in the last code block will output the ratio of funny to not funny. Ideally we would want the data split about 50/50. This is often quite difficult to do, however, so we will just use a value that doesn't create too large a difference.

- We load the joke data into the X set of inputs. Then the Y set is defined by the humor list. We now need to break these sets up into training and test sets using the following code:

```
cut = int(len(jokes) * 0.8)
x_train = jokes[:cut]
x_test = jokes[cut:]
y_train = humor[:cut]
y_test = humor[cut:]
```

- The value we use to determine the cut value (.8) determines the split percentage in our dataset. With .8, we are using 80% of the data for training and therefore 20% for testing.

- Then we prep the model with the following code:

```
import ktrain
from ktrain import text

(x_train,  y_train), (x_test, y_test),
preproc = text.texts_from_array(x_train=x_train, y_train=y_train,
                                x_test=x_test, y_test=y_test,
                                class_names=['not','funny'],
                                preprocess_mode='bert',
                                ngram_range=1,
                                maxlen=500,
                                max_features=35000)
```

- This is similar to the code we saw prepping the data. This helper preps our raw text input as defined by the options. Notice the changes we use here for ngram_range, maxlen, and max_features.

- Next, we retrain the model with the following single line of code:

```
learner.autofit(2e-5, 1)
```

- After that we extract the predictor and get the classes again with this code:

```
predictor = ktrain.get_predictor(learner.model, preproc)
predictor.get_classes()
```

- With the predictor, we can cast a prediction with the following code:

```
predictor.predict('A man walked into a bar. The bartender yelled back,
                  get out, we're closed.')
#outputs
'not'
```

- You can of course try other humorous statements, questions, or whatever and determine if it finds the text funny.

Of course, training the last example for more epochs or on a larger corpus would provide much better results, generally. The same repository we used for the source of this example also provides a Reddit source of almost 200,000 jokes. Training on that source would likely be more interesting but would certainly require much more time and resources.

While training BERT is more efficient than recurrent network NLP systems, it does require a large corpus in order to learn since it still encapsulates a large model of parameters. However, with tools like ktrain, we can retrain BERT in a relatively short time on more specialized tasks. This should allow for the development of more robust custom models tackling real-world problems in the near future.

## Conclusion

As a society we have been on a rigorous path to making our interface with computers more natural, and being able to understand language and text is a big part of that. NLP has started to reshape the world in many ways, and this in turn has shaped our ability to interface with complex systems. We can now read and process the reviews of thousands or millions of users almost instantly, giving businesses the ability to understand how people are using or consuming a commercial service instantly. Google has given us the ability to open services that can process text in a number of ways, from translation to just understanding the entities or syntax of a document. Google further enhanced NLP by open sourcing its controversial BERT model, with pre-trained BERT models now able to be retrained on everything from sentiment to document similarity, and perhaps even jokes.

In the next chapter we take NLP a step further and introduce you to building chatbots. Chatbots come in all flavors, from assistants like Siri or Alexa to fictional conversational models like the one featured in the movie *Her*. We will use chatbots as a way to build an interface into a new ML assistant framework.

# CHAPTER 5

# Chatbots and Conversational AI

Understanding language and text, the semantics, subjects, and even syntax, is powerful. Ultimately our goal has always been to create a natural language interface between humans and machines. To do that, our NLP system needs to not only understand text, but also be able to generate new responses as well. The common term we use for such interfaces now is *chatbot* or *conversational AI*.

You have likely already interfaced with chatbots many times in your life. Chatbots come in all forms, from the powerful assistants we see in Siri and Alexa to the common support chatbots you may see on a product website. In most cases they provide a more natural interface to a computing device, like your phone. However, conversational AI may play a part in future human companionship.

Conversational AI is a form of chatbot that allows for free-flowing speech and is not goal oriented. Goal-oriented chatbots like Siri and Alexa are task-specific; they respond to individual tasks or goals. Conversational bots are still very much in their infancy, but that is expected to change in the near future.

 A great example of one possible future conversational AI is featured in the 2013 movie *Her*, starring Joaquin Phoenix and Amy Adams. In the movie, the protagonist falls in love with the AI, only to realize the AI is incapable of falling in love with him.

In this chapter we look at what role chatbots have played in interfacing with computers. We look at the history of the chatbot and how one is typically built. Then we move on to the types of chatbots and explore Dialogflow from Google to create a goal-oriented chatbot. From there we move on to understanding text generation in more depth. We'll use that knowledge to build a conversational chatbot users can interact with and learn from.

Here is a summary of the main topics we will cover in this chapter:

- Building Chatbots with Python
- Developing Goal-Oriented Chatbots with Dialogflow
- Building Text Transformers
- Training Conversational Chatbots
- Using Transformer for Conversational Chatbots

The later sections in this chapter will require that you understand all the material in Chapter 4 thoroughly. We will also take a closer look at BERT transformer and how it works in more detail.

# Building Chatbots with Python

Chatbots have been around for more than 40 years. In that time these bots have gone from simple code using rules in the form of if/else statements to deep learning networks. What you also may not realize is that the current wave of bots like Alexa, Siri, and Google have more in common with the if/else bots of old than the new ones we will develop in this chapter.

Chatbots can be divided into two primary types: goal oriented and conversational. Goal-oriented chatbots are task oriented and provide no artificial or generated feedback, while conversational chatbots provide responses that are almost entirely artificially generated, or the intention is that they be perceived that way.

Chatbots were originally developed using very low-tech methods based on rules-based engines coded as if/else statements to define responses. Over time, this matured to using regular expression statements to match and extract patterns in text, not unlike the NLP work we did in Chapter 4. Most chatbots use some form of NLP to break down text and feed it to a rules-based engine. The current wave of goal-oriented chatbots (Alexa, Siri, and Google) are built primarily on top of rules-based engines.

It is likely that goal-oriented chatbots like Siri will continue to use rule engines for some time to come. Early versions of goal-oriented bots tried to inflect some conversational banter, but this was poorly received, more than likely because the banter consisted of canned and repetitive responses. It is likely that as conversational AI becomes stronger, we will see the likes of Siri becoming conversational.

The type of chatbot we want to focus on in this chapter is the deep learning variety. These bots don't use rules but learn inference/responses from training against large volumes of text. Text generation and conversational AI is still difficult to develop since it requires developing a machine to understand and respond to language. We will look at building conversational AI later in this chapter.

For now, though, let's jump back to a rules-based chatbot engine that can provide conversational AI. In Example 5-1, we build a rules-based conversational chatbot using the ChatterBot Python library. This will give us an overview of what type of components compose a chatbot and how they interact.

*Example 5-1. Building a conversational ChatterBot bot*

- Open example *Chapter_5_ChatterBot_bot.ipynb* and run the first block of code to install chatterbot and the chatterbot_corpus as shown here:

```
!pip install chatterbot
!pip install chatterbot_corpus
```

- Next, we want to do some imports and then set up the ChatBot object with the following code:

```
from chatterbot import ChatBot
from chatterbot.trainers import ChatterBotCorpusTrainer
import logging

logging.basicConfig(level=logging.INFO)
chatbot = ChatBot('Convo Bot')
```

- We first enable logging so we can see the chatbot's thought/rules processing. Then we build a new chatbot from ChatBot.

- From there we build a trainer using a corpus trainer and then set the corpus to use English, as shown in the following code:

```
trainer = ChatterBotCorpusTrainer(chatbot)

trainer.train(
    'chatterbot.corpus.english'
)
```

- After the bot is trained, notice how much faster this rules-based training is compared to deep learning. We then can test the bot on a simple question using the code here:

```
response = chatbot.get_response('Hi there, how are you?')
print(response)
#outputs
INFO:chatterbot.chatterbot:Beginning search for close text match
INFO:chatterbot.chatterbot:Processing search results
INFO:chatterbot.chatterbot:Similar text found: Hi there, how are you? 1.0
INFO:chatterbot.chatterbot:Using "Hi there, how are you?" as a close match
   to "Hi there, how are you?" with a confidence of 1.0
INFO:chatterbot.chatterbot:0. Excluding recent repeated response
   of "Hi there, how are you?"
INFO:chatterbot.chatterbot:No responses found. Generating alternate response
   list.
INFO:chatterbot.chatterbot:No known response to the input was found.
```

```
Selecting a random response.
INFO:chatterbot.chatterbot:BestMatch selected "What do you get when you cross
    finals and a chicken? Eggs-ams." as a response with a confidence of 0
INFO:chatterbot.chatterbot:Adding "Hi there, how are you?" as a response to
                "Hi there, how are you?"
What do you get when you cross finals and a chicken? Eggs-ams.
```

It is quite interesting to follow the output and see how the bot follows through the thought/rules-based process.

These type of conversational bots are educational and entertaining, more so to those who make them. They still lack any interesting character. As we humans can tell, they are nothing more than regurgitated text. What we really want is an AI that can devise new phrases, which we will look at building later.

Before that, though, let's look at another example where we can use a rules-based chatbot to build a goal-oriented bot. For Example 5-2, we look again to ChatterBot to build a goal-oriented chatbot. These are the types of bots that are dedicated to completing simple or not-so-simple tasks. We do not expect good conversation from a goal-oriented chatbot.

*Example 5-2. Building a goal-oriented ChatterBot*

- Open sample *Chapter_4_ChatterBot_goal.ipynb* and run the first cell to install ChatterBot and the required corpus, like we did in the last exercise.

- Next, we can lump all the familiar code together with some new code that loads a modified corpus and introduces a new concept called a *logic adapter*. Logic adapters allow us to modify the intent or logic of the bot. This is shown in the code here:

```
from chatterbot import ChatBot
from chatterbot.trainers import ChatterBotCorpusTrainer
import logging

logging.basicConfig(level=logging.INFO)
bot = ChatBot(
    'Math & Time Bot',
    logic_adapters=[
        'chatterbot.logic.MathematicalEvaluation',
        'chatterbot.logic.TimeLogicAdapter'
    ]
)
```

- By adding these new logic adapters, we have adapted the ChatterBot's default conversational behavior to resemble a more goal-oriented bot.

- We can then test this bot with the following code:

```
    response = bot.get_response('What is 4 + 9?')
    print(response)
    )
```

- Notice that the response has now been formulated as the input math equation plus the answer.

- This bot also has a time function we can text running the following code:
```
    response = bot.get_response('What time is it?')
    print(response)
    )
```

- Note that the response will be in universal (UTC) or Greenwich Mean Time (GMT).

Whether you want a conversational or goal-oriented chatbot, ChatterBot has you covered, for basic applications anyway. ChatterBot does support a number of other types of training workflows, from a corpus of lists to statements or other training input. Be sure to check out the ChatterBot repository (*https://github.com/gunthercox/ChatterBot*) if you want to learn more.

If we really want a robust goal-oriented chatbot, the best place to look is Google. Google has developed a goal-oriented chatbot framework called Dialogflow, which we will learn about next.

# Developing Goal-Oriented Chatbots with Dialogflow

Goal-oriented chatbots became essential with the development of bots like Siri, Alexa, and Google. These bots opened up a whole interface to our computing resources that we depend on in our daily lives. At-home assistant devices are now becoming more common in homes all over the world, but at work we still depend on antiquated computers and systems to interface.

So why do we have so many powerful home-use devices but none that can help us be more productive at work? That all comes down to marketing. The vendors of these devices thought it would be easier to sell them to home users first. As it turns out, they were right. Building home-use chatbots is far easier than developing more specialized work bots. Google has considered this problem and developed Dialogflow as a way for businesses to develop powerful, integrated goal-oriented chatbots.

Dialogflow is a rules-based chatbot that uses more natural language idioms to construct, not rules, but intents. Intents in Dialogflow don't define rules but instead define the intended action of the chat user using the bot. So instead of thinking of a text conversation as a workflow of rules, we think of it as intended actions.

In a typical rules-based chatbot, you define rules based on speech idioms or key phrases. Then you build up these rules to define some task. Consider an example where you may want to order a pizza or other food for delivery. A traditional rules bot may first ask for your name, then your order, and finally where you live. With intents, all we need to define is an intended action to order pizza.

By thinking of a conversation this way, an agent or chatbot can identify parts of conversation that may match intended actions. After the chatbot identifies the intended action, it can then continue pursuing all information relevant to that action until it has enough to proceed with the task. In a more symbolic or rules-based system, we would need to define the rules each element requires. With actions, we work the opposite way, first identifying the goal of the talker and then finding the required info to complete said goal. Dialogflow is still technically a rules-based bot, but by using intentions, it requires the bot to understand the actions first.

Figure 5-1 demonstrates how the typical intent/action workflow transpires when a user interacts with Dialogflow. In the figure, a bot may first ask the user what they want, much like Siri or Alexa. For instance, a user may make a request for an Uber. Internally, the chatbot has been pretrained on a few intents using various training phrases. It is the bot's role to determine the intent of the user by interpreting the user's spoken text. In Figure 5-1, the user calls for an Uber, which in turn triggers the intent: "call for Uber."

The intent, call for Uber, also requires some additional information set in the intent. In the example request, the user never specified a name, a destination, a pickup, or the ride type. Since the bot understands what the user wants—to enact the call-for-Uber intent—it can also make sure to ask the user for the other information in further questions. Then when the bot has the required information, it can make the call, or what we call *fulfill the task.*

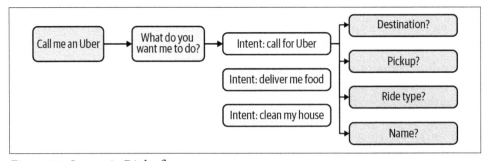

*Figure 5-1. Intents in Dialogflow*

We are going to build a very simple chatbot with Dialogflow. While Example 5-3 is a simple example, it can help you appreciate the elegance and power of this way of describing tasks/goals.

*Example 5-3. Simple Dialogflow chatbot*

- We don't have a code example for this exercise, so just open up the Dialogflow page (*https://dialogflow.cloud.google.com*). You may be required to sign in, but this is just a formality. Dialogflow is currently a free service due to quickly changing API.

- After you sign in, select the option Create New Agent. A dialog will pop up asking you to name the agent. Call it *PersonalAssistant* for now. We will use this agent as a personal assistant. Next, set the language, time zone, and project to your preferences.

- Click on the Intents menu option on the left side, and then click the Create Intent button at the top right. Name the intent `call_for_uber` and click Save to save the intent.

- There are many ways to define and use an intent in Dialogflow. The following list breaks down the various elements that may compose an intent:

*Context*
> You can define not only what text or training text matches an intent but also the contexts. A context could be a user's geographic location or some other preference. Using contexts allows you to create nonlinear conversations as well.

*Events*
> Events allow you to trigger intents using nonverbal signals. This could be a simple button click or another trigger, like an external service.

*Training phrases*
> Training input defines how the chatbot recognizes what intent the user wants to execute. Dialogflow uses a hybrid of rules and ML-based learning to determine the intent. You can adjust these settings as needed. We will cover more details about training shortly.

*Actions and parameters*
> The intent needs to know what information, in the form of parameters, is needed for it to complete its action/task. With intents, we can enforce the requirement of some parameter, thus requiring the bot to request this information from the user. If the user never completes all the information, the bot never attempts to fulfill the task.

*Responses*
> An intent may have a number of default responses as well as predefined responses to extract some parameter or inform the user of some other

information. Responses can also help direct the user to provide the correct information in the future.

*Fulfillment*

After the bot identifies the intended intent and then extracts the required parameters from the user, it can then look to fulfill the task. Fulfillment defines how the task is fulfilled, provided the given parameters.

- Currently all we want is to enter some training phrases, so select the Add Training Phrase option. A text box will appear, allowing you to enter the following text phrases. Hit return after each entry:

```
call me an Uber
get me an Uber from my house to work
get me an Uber from my house to the mall
I am Micheal, please call me an Uber XL from my house at 123 main street to
  my work at 456 side street
```

- Notice that as you entered the last phrase, the text *Micheal* was identified as an entity of type `Person`. It also identified the addresses as location entities. Figure 5-2 shows how the last training phrase identified the entities. Dialogflow will automatically recognize entities in training phrases. This is useful because we conjugate false training phrases, like the last statement, to determine the perfect request. From that perfect request we can determine the parameters/entities that we need to extract for relevance. But notice that it didn't understand the ride type *XL* as an entity. We will have to fix that later.

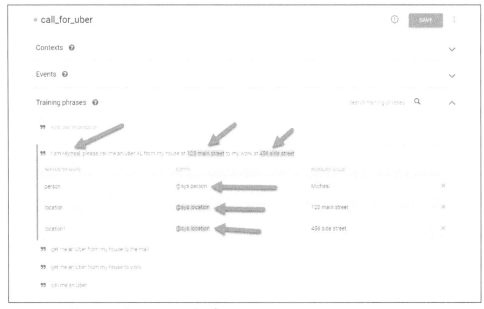

*Figure 5-2. Training phrases in Dialogflow*

- Scroll down to the Action and Parameters section and note that the entities have been extracted already. The default extraction for each of these entities is fine, but we do want to make them required. Click on the Required box for each parameter, as we need these for the bot to complete the task. After you click Required, you will notice that you can now define prompts in the Prompts columns. We will use the defaults for now. Make sure and click Save after doing any edits.

- Go back to the Training Phrases section and highlight and select the *Uber XL* text, as shown in Figure 5-3. Click Create New Link at the bottom of the page to create a new entity type.

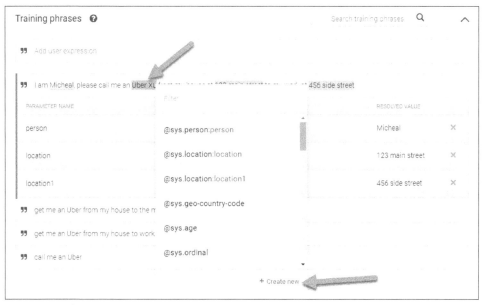

*Figure 5-3. Creating a new entity type*

- You will be taken to a new dialog page. Name the entity type *ubertype*. Next, we want to define some synonyms. Enter the text for the Uber ride types *UberX*, *Uber Comfort*, and *Uber XL*, and then add a synonym for the ride type you want to default to Uber. For our example, shown in Figure 5-4, we added the synonym *Uber* to *Uber X*, which is the cheapest. Now we can add the ubertype entity to our intent. Be sure to save your edits.

*Figure 5-4. Defining a new entity*

- Go back to the `call_for_uber` intent and select the *Uber XL* text. You will be prompted with a dropdown for selecting the entity type. Our new custom type will be at the bottom. Scroll down and select it. When you do, the color will change, as shown in Figure 5-5.

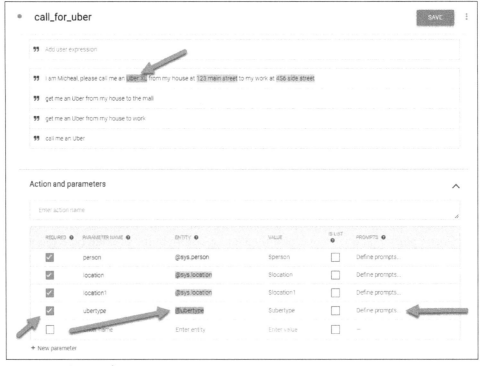

*Figure 5-5. Setting the entity*

- Scroll down to the Action and Parameters section and make sure the Required box is selected for the ubertype entity, as shown in Figure 5-5.

- Next, click the Define Prompts link beside the ubertype, as shown in Figure 5-5. This will open a dialog and allow you to define some additional prompts. Since ubertype is a custom entity, we will want to create our own user prompts. This will make our bot more natural and helpful to the user. Enter the following text as three separate prompts:

```
What type of Uber?
Please provide the Uber ride type?
Uber has 3 ride types, Uber X, Uber Comfort and Uber XL. Please select one.
```

- The prompts are currently selected at random, but ideally we would want prompts provided in the order given. If the user failed to understand the first prompt, the bot would progress to the next one, and so on. This allows you to increase the detail on each successive response.

- Make sure to save all your work. Now we are ready to deploy and test. Yes, it was that easy.

- Click the Integrations panel on the left menu, and then select the Dialogflow Phone Gateway option. This will allow us to test our chatbot using a phone call. Some long-distance charges may apply.

> There are plenty of other integration options available to test your chatbot. Using the phone option is just the coolest because you can use natural language and talk to the bot, so be sure to try it at least once.

- Follow the default options on the dialog to select a number that is closest to you. After you are finished setting up the number, call the service.

- Make a call to the chatbot and try and request an Uber. How does the bot do? What needs to be improved on?

From this point, you can automate the bot to perform the intent/action/task the user requested. This is called *fulfillment*. Dialogflow provides a whole section to develop those automations.

Dialogflow was designed to be easy to use, but it also exposes the developer to working with a better NLU model. At the time of writing, Dialogflow was not 100% ML/DL but rather used a hybrid of rules and ML. This will likely change as NLU models like BERT become more robust. By using an intents/action-based model, Dialogflow can adapt to a pure ML model seamlessly in the future.

Upgrading Dialogflow to a full deep learning architecture may not be far off. While this likely won't change the current workflow and use of intents, it may open up and provide for more conversational elements, like general discussions about weather or geography, for instance.

Dialogflow is a great tool that will likely accommodate most of your needs. However, if you need to customize elements or add other workflows, being able to adapt or develop your own preprocessor or post processor is essential. Therefore, in the next section we look at how the latest NLP approaches can be used to generate novel text.

# Building Text Transformers

In Chapter 4, we looked at how to use NLP with deep learning to process text for a number of applications. We covered how basic NLP is accomplished with embedding layers, recurrent networks, and sequence-to-sequence learning. Then we explored BERT at a superficial level, looking at a few examples of how it was used.

BERT was successful because of a new Transformer model that didn't need to use recurrent networks for contextualizing tokens. Recurrent networks, as we have seen, are performance intensive. This in turn required expensive training resources to develop models. The Transformer model could train on the same data corpus far more efficiently and with much better results. As such, recurrent networks are quickly becoming history when we talk about developing applications for NLP.

 Development of AI has seen many cases like the RNN. RNNs will likely continue to work for analyzing time series or other forms of time data. While RNN is losing favor for NLP currently, that doesn't mean it won't be reinvented for some other task. Reinvention is a common theme in AI, and a great example of that is the perceptron itself. The perceptron went in and out of favor for 50 years before becoming the hero it is today.

In order to understand the full workflow of these new models, we will break down building a full chatbot into a number of exercises. Each exercise and section will define in more detail what is needed to work. The outline for these sections is listed here:

- Loading and Preparing Data
- Understanding Attention
- Masking and the Transformer
- Encoding and Decoding the Sequence

The code for the full chatbot is provided in the example *Chapter_5_Transformer_Chatbot.ipynb*. Before jumping to the end, try following the exercises in order.

As with most data science and machine learning tasks, we always start with the data.

# Loading and Preparing Data

Loading data is the most frequent task you will need to perform when building your own models. Most real-world problems don't provide helpful tools to load datasets. You will often need and want to develop your own.

In this section, we take a detailed look at the steps you need to take when processing raw data for NLP/NLU. You can use a number of these techniques to load the data you need to process for your particular custom model.

In Example 5-4, we show you how to download and process data for input into the model.

*Example 5-4. Loading and preparing NLP data*

- Open the *Chapter_5_Tranformer_Chatbot.ipynb* example. Run the first code cell, as shown here:

```
from __future__ import absolute_import, division, print_function,
                       unicode_literals

import tensorflow as tf
tf.random.set_seed(1234)

!pip install tensorflow-datasets
import tensorflow_datasets as tfds

import os
import re
import numpy as np

import matplotlib.pyplot as plt
```

- The first code block loads all the required imports and preps the sample.
- The first step is to load data. The dataset we are using here is the Cornell Movie-Dialogs Corpus. This is an interesting and fun corpus to train conversational AI on if you like movies. It provides a full set of movie dialog that we will define as questions and answers. Following is the code to load the data from the server at Cornell:

```
path_to_zip = tf.keras.utils.get_file(
  'cornell_movie_dialogs.zip',
  origin=
  'http://www.cs.cornell.edu/~cristian/data/
  cornell_movie_dialogs_corpus.zip',
  extract=True)

path_to_dataset = os.path.join(
    os.path.dirname(path_to_zip), "cornell movie-dialogs corpus")

path_to_movie_lines = os.path.join(path_to_dataset, 'movie_lines.txt')
path_to_movie_conversations = os.path.join(path_to_dataset,
                                    'movie_conversations.txt')
```

- After the data is loaded, we need to process the data for input into our model. The steps we will take as part of a typical NLP are as follows:

  1. First, we want to extract rows or sentences, typically just a subset, from the training data. This extracted data may further be broken up into training, test, and validation as well. Using only a subset has a couple of advantages, the main one being the ability to reuse the corpus for many other models.

  2. Next, raw text needs to be preprocessed and cleaned. We typically break text down into sentences and then process those sentences into words by splitting on white space, like spaces. We remove numeric or other special characters as well. The preprocess_sentence function will clean and process the test for us.

  3. The next step is to tokenize the text, which is the process of breaking down text into its component words or grams. The process of tokenizing content is a complex rules-based process. For our purpose, we are going to use Subword-TextEncoder to tokenize and encode the content.

  4. Next, we will filter content. In many cases, we may want to filter out certain training phrases or content from our corpus. In this example, we will filter content by sentence length.

  5. Next, we need to encode the text based on the vocabulary and generate text vectors of questions and answers.

  6. Finally, the input into our model needs to be a consistent length. So the last step in our processing will be to pad the inputs, much like we did in the previous NLP exercises in Chapter 4.

- With our preprocessing workflow outlined, let's look at the first block of code that parses the sentences into questions and answers:

```
MAX_SAMPLES = 50000

def preprocess_sentence(sentence):
  sentence = sentence.lower().strip()
  sentence = re.sub(r"([?.!,])", r" \1 ", sentence)
```

```
    sentence = re.sub(r'[" "]+', " ", sentence)
    sentence = re.sub(r"[^a-zA-Z?.!,]+", " ", sentence)
    sentence = sentence.strip()
    return sentence

def load_conversations():
  id2line = {}
  with open(path_to_movie_lines, errors='ignore') as file:
    lines = file.readlines()
  for line in lines:
    parts = line.replace('\n', '').split(' +++$+++ ')
    id2line[parts[0]] = parts[4]

  inputs, outputs = [], []
  with open(path_to_movie_conversations, 'r') as file:
    lines = file.readlines()
  for line in lines:
    parts = line.replace('\n', '').split(' +++$+++ ')
    conversation = [line[1:-1] for line in parts[3][1:-1].split(', ')]
    for i in range(len(conversation) - 1):
      inputs.append(preprocess_sentence(id2line[conversation[i]]))
      outputs.append(preprocess_sentence(id2line[conversation[i + 1]]))
      if len(inputs) >= MAX_SAMPLES:
        return inputs, outputs
  return inputs, outputs

questions, answers = load_conversations()

print('Sample question: {}'.format(questions[75]))
print('Sample answer: {}'.format(answers[75]))
#outputs
Sample question: bianca , i need to talk to you i need to tell you
Sample answer: i really don t think i need any social advice from you right
        now .
```

- The last block of code loads the movie lines as question-and-answer conversations. It splits out the actors' conversations into a question-and-answer. Then it preprocesses and cleans the sentences with the `preprocess_sentence` function. The function lowercases, removes symbols, and strips out ending punctuation from the sentences.

- With the text preprocessed into question-and-answer text, we can move onto tokenizing it with SubwordTextEncoder. This class both tokenizes the corpus and identifies the vocabulary. The code to build the tokenizer and do the encoding is shown here:

```
tokenizer = tfds.features.text.SubwordTextEncoder.build_from_corpus(
    questions + answers, target_vocab_size=2**13)

START_TOKEN, END_TOKEN = [tokenizer.vocab_size], [tokenizer.vocab_size + 1]
```

```
VOCAB_SIZE = tokenizer.vocab_size + 2

print('Vocab size: {}'.format(VOCAB_SIZE))
print('Number of samples: {}'.format(len(questions)))
print('Tokenized sample question: {}'.format(
    tokenizer.encode(questions[75])))
#outputs
Vocab size: 8333
Number of samples: 50000
Tokenized sample question: [5374, 3, 4, 137, 9, 182,
                            9, 5, 4, 137, 9, 87, 29]
```

- The tokenized output shows how the word at each index in the sentence is identified by its index into the vocabulary. In the code you can also see how there is a Start_Token and End_Token defined. These are extracted from the vocabulary. Also note that we have just constructed a tokenizer and encoder here and have not yet used it to encode the sentences.

- With the tokenizer/encoder built, we can move on to using it on all our question-and-answer raw text strings. Remember, we cannot feed raw text into our models. This text needs to be tokenized and encoded with the following code:

```
MAX_LENGTH = 40

def tokenize_and_filter(inputs, outputs):
  tokenized_inputs, tokenized_outputs = [], []

  for (sentence1, sentence2) in zip(inputs, outputs):
    sentence1 = START_TOKEN + tokenizer.encode(sentence1) + END_TOKEN
    sentence2 = START_TOKEN + tokenizer.encode(sentence2) + END_TOKEN
    if len(sentence1) <= MAX_LENGTH and len(sentence2) <= MAX_LENGTH:
      tokenized_inputs.append(sentence1)
      tokenized_outputs.append(sentence2)

  tokenized_inputs = tf.keras.preprocessing.sequence.pad_sequences(
      tokenized_inputs, maxlen=MAX_LENGTH, padding='post')
  tokenized_outputs = tf.keras.preprocessing.sequence.pad_sequences(
      tokenized_outputs, maxlen=MAX_LENGTH, padding='post')
  return tokenized_inputs, tokenized_outputs

questions, answers = tokenize_and_filter(questions, answers)
```

- MAX_LENGTH will limit the size of the question/answer sentences we use for training. This will reduce our training size and our time to train.

- Finally, we want to prepare the data into the proper tensors our model can consume. This, as you have seen in previous chapters, can be messy code, but fortunately TensorFlow has a helper called the *Dataset API*. The Dataset API also allows for the data to be pipelined into the model. Pipelining allows the data to be fed into the tensor using prefetching and caching. This makes feeding the model more efficient as it uses less memory. All of this functionality is encapsulated in the final code section here:

```
BATCH_SIZE = 64
BUFFER_SIZE = 20000

# decoder inputs use the previous target as input
# remove START_TOKEN from targets
dataset = tf.data.Dataset.from_tensor_slices((
    {
        'inputs': questions,
        'dec_inputs': answers[:, :-1]
    },
    {
        'outputs': answers[:, 1:]
    },
))

dataset = dataset.cache()
dataset = dataset.shuffle(BUFFER_SIZE)
dataset = dataset.batch(BATCH_SIZE)
dataset = dataset.prefetch(tf.data.experimental.AUTOTUNE)
```

- The Dataset API will also allow us to set the Buffer_Size when we shuffle the data. Set the Batch_Size to determine our training set size. Finish by setting up prefetching with the Autotune setting.

With the data loaded, we can move to the next phase, understanding how attention works.

## Understanding Attention

One of the major problems we face in any data science or deep learning scenario is understanding attention, or correlation between features. We often want or need to understand how a model attends or correlates key areas of an image or sentence. Consider Figure 5-6, which shows how areas of a sentence attend or correlate well with other areas. In data science we can prepare our data to compensate for these strong correlations, but in deep learning, that is far more difficult. We often need to handle these strong correlations after the fact using various techniques.

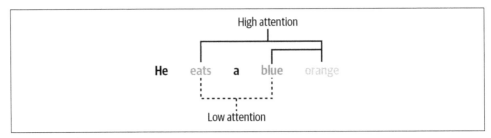

*Figure 5-6. Attention in a sentence*

For the example in Figure 5-6, we want our network to learn to recognize the association with the words shown. We want the network to learn the attention/correlation. Understanding word context or sequences worked well and is why we used recurrent networks like LSTM. While this works well for simple classification analysis of text for entities, syntax, or sentiment, it does not work so well for longer sections of text.

Recall when we learned how to translate text with the sequence-to-sequence (Seq2Seq) model. In a Seq2Seq model, we teach the model by feeding it pairs of text. The model is then able to translate text by using the learned context of words and how they relate to other words. However, we are still limited to fixed-length text pairings. Because of this shortcoming, a new method of understanding word correlation or attention was founded.

From the need to translate larger and larger documents came a new way to understand document context and attention. What was needed was an attention mechanism that could identify word pairings over large documents. We now use the term *attention* to define building a context vector of word pairings. A number of attention mechanisms have been developed. The following is a brief summary:

- Content-base attention—Graves [2014]
- Additive—Bahdanau [2015]
- Location-Base—Luong [2015]
- General—Luong [2015]
- Dot Product—Luong [2015]
- Scaled Dot-Product—Vaswani [2017]
- Self-Attention—Cheng [2016]
- Global/soft—Xu [2015]
- Local/hard—Xu [2015]; Luong [2015]

The last three items define broader aspects of how attention mechanisms can be applied as a whole. Each of these broader-attention mechanisms are further defined here:

*Self-Attention*

We, in fact, already understand this mechanism. This is what a recurrent network does now in that it relates the strength of a word in a sequence to other words in the sequence.

*Soft versus hard attention*

Soft attention allows some gradual overlap of the attending function. This allows partial words or short grams to also be absorbed. Hard attention locks the focus to just that word or token with no overlap.

*Global versus local attention*

A global attention mechanism can be broadly defined as a soft attention mechanism; that is, a global attender tries to include all overlap words that may require focus or attention. In some cases, these may be words outside the source sentence. A local attender, on the other hand, just focuses on the words around it.

In the seminal paper "Attention Is All You Need" (Vaswani et al., 2017), the authors introduced *Transformer*, a new model that used soft attention to extract word context without using recurrent networks. What's more, this new architecture allowed for the model to include self-attention, again replacing the need for recurrent networks.

Transformer uses a multihead self-attention component, as pictured in Figure 5-7. The source for the figure is the paper by Vaswani et al. mentioned earlier. As we can see from the figure, the main inputs are Q (query), K (key), and V (value). Each input represents a head, or input network layer. These inputs then have a scaled dot-product attention function applied across them. We saw how the dot product function can be used to measure distance when we looked at word embeddings in Chapter 4. The transformer uses a scaled version of a dot product to measure and apply attention.

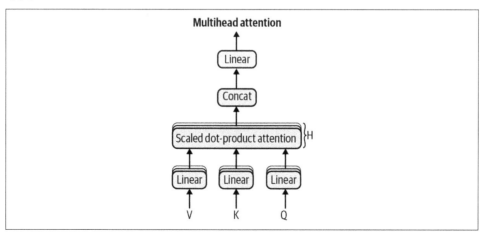

*Figure 5-7. Multihead attention block*

We can examine the code for this function by looking at the *Chapter_5_Trans-former_Chatbot.ipynb* example and scrolling down to the Attention section. The first block of code shows the `scaled_dot_product_attention` function, shown here:

```
def scaled_dot_product_attention(query, key, value, mask):
  matmul_qk = tf.matmul(query, key, transpose_b=True)

  depth = tf.cast(tf.shape(key)[-1], tf.float32)
  logits = matmul_qk / tf.math.sqrt(depth)

  if mask is not None:
    logits += (mask * -1e9)

  attention_weights = tf.nn.softmax(logits, axis=-1)

  output = tf.matmul(attention_weights, value)

  return output
```

This function scales the attention weights by the scaled dot product as it is applied to the query, key, and value. Understanding the math in detail is outside the scope of this book and would require further study in NLP. The main thing to realize here is that this attention mechanism replaces recurrent networks. Next, we can look at how this is combined into a multihead attention block with the following code:

```
class MultiHeadAttention(tf.keras.layers.Layer):
  def __init__(self, d_model, num_heads, name="multi_head_attention"):
    super(MultiHeadAttention, self).__init__(name=name)
    self.num_heads = num_heads
    self.d_model = d_model
    assert d_model % self.num_heads == 0

    self.depth = d_model // self.num_heads

    self.query_dense = tf.keras.layers.Dense(units=d_model)
    self.key_dense = tf.keras.layers.Dense(units=d_model)
    self.value_dense = tf.keras.layers.Dense(units=d_model)

    self.dense = tf.keras.layers.Dense(units=d_model)

  def split_heads(self, inputs, batch_size):
    inputs = tf.reshape(
        inputs, shape=(batch_size, -1, self.num_heads, self.depth))
    return tf.transpose(inputs, perm=[0, 2, 1, 3])

  def call(self, inputs):
    query, key, value, mask = inputs['query'], inputs['key'], inputs[
        'value'], inputs['mask']
    batch_size = tf.shape(query)[0]

    query = self.query_dense(query)
    key = self.key_dense(key)
```

```
    value = self.value_dense(value)

    query = self.split_heads(query, batch_size)
    key = self.split_heads(key, batch_size)
    value = self.split_heads(value, batch_size)

    scaled_attention = scaled_dot_product_attention(query, key, value, mask)

    scaled_attention = tf.transpose(scaled_attention, perm=[0, 2, 1, 3])

    concat_attention = tf.reshape(scaled_attention,
                                   (batch_size, -1, self.d_model))

    outputs = self.dense(concat_attention)
    return outputs
```

That code block defines a class called `MultiHeadAttention`. You can think of this class as an attention block or super layer, if you will. In the `init` function, we can see the construction of three input top layers defined by query `query_dense`, key `key_dense` and value `value_dense`, as an output layer of dense, called dense. The `call` function, which infers the forward pass, is where all the action happens. Inside the call function, we can see that the layers are first split. Then the layers are all scaled into a `scaled_attention` tensor, which is then transposed. The output of this is then concatenated into a final output layer.

Now that we understand how attention is used to find context between tokens, we can move to further understanding the Transformer and masking.

## Masking and the Transformer

Think back to our discussion of BERT and masking. Masking with lookahead allows BERT to understand input bidirectionally. It does this by randomly trying to match pairs of inputs that have been masked or filtered. By doing this lookahead, a Transformer learns to understand token sequence or context going forward or backward. Consider the following text:

> He looked around the room for his friend Ernie. What would Bert do without Ernie?

As a person, you can infer that the first word in the first sentence, *He*, is referencing the subject in the second sentence, *Bert*. However, a machine trained to only understand text in a single direction could never infer that same context from only looking forward. A machine would try and reference previous text for what *He* was referencing. In our example, though, there is no previous text, which is the origin of the problem.

Masking is not especially difficult, but it does require some nuances with tensors. The first block of code we will look at is how we need to pad the mask with the `create_padding_mask` function, as shown here:

```
def create_padding_mask(x):
  mask = tf.cast(tf.math.equal(x, 0), tf.float32)
  return mask[:, tf.newaxis, tf.newaxis, :]

print(create_padding_mask(tf.constant([[1, 2, 0, 3, 0], [0, 0, 0, 4, 5]])))
```

Then we can create the lookahead mask with the function create_look_ahead_mask, as follows:

```
def create_look_ahead_mask(x):
  seq_len = tf.shape(x)[1]
  look_ahead_mask = 1 - tf.linalg.band_part(tf.ones((seq_len, seq_len)), -1, 0)
  padding_mask = create_padding_mask(x)
  return tf.maximum(look_ahead_mask, padding_mask)

print(create_look_ahead_mask(tf.constant([[1, 2, 0, 4, 5]])))
```

The benefit of using recurrent or convolutional networks for contextualizing inputs is being able to determine relative token positioning. This is a problem with a Transformer model. A transformer learns the broader context of a token/word and ignores position. Of course, position can still be quite important in many ways. Therefore, as a way of remembering position, we encode this into a new layer/weights. The code to do this is shown here, encapsulated in the PositionalEncoding class:

```
class PositionalEncoding(tf.keras.layers.Layer):
  def __init__(self, position, d_model):
    super(PositionalEncoding, self).__init__()
    self.pos_encoding = self.positional_encoding(position, d_model)

  def get_angles(self, position, i, d_model):
    angles = 1 / tf.pow(10000, (2 * (i // 2)) / tf.cast(d_model, tf.float32))
    return position * angles

  def positional_encoding(self, position, d_model):
    angle_rads = self.get_angles(
        position=tf.range(position, dtype=tf.float32)[:, tf.newaxis],
        i=tf.range(d_model, dtype=tf.float32)[tf.newaxis, :],
        d_model=d_model)
    sines = tf.math.sin(angle_rads[:, 0::2])
    cosines = tf.math.cos(angle_rads[:, 1::2])

    pos_encoding = tf.concat([sines, cosines], axis=-1)
    pos_encoding = pos_encoding[tf.newaxis, ...]
    return tf.cast(pos_encoding, tf.float32)

  def call(self, inputs):
    return inputs + self.pos_encoding[:, :tf.shape(inputs)[1], :]

sample_pos_encoding = PositionalEncoding(50, 512)

plt.pcolormesh(sample_pos_encoding.pos_encoding.numpy()[0], cmap='RdBu')
plt.xlabel('Depth')
```

```
plt.xlim((0, 512))
plt.ylabel('Position')
plt.colorbar()
plt.show()
```

Again, the math here requires a bit better understanding of NLP, one that could fill a book itself. For our purposes, realize that this code just measures the distances using sine/cosine functions and encodes that as word position. That encoded word position is then used as another feature into our model.

Okay, so we understand a bit more about the Transformer. The last part of the transformation process we need to understand is how the model actually transforms data, which we will cover in the next section.

## Encoding and Decoding the Sequence

The whole structure of a Transformer model was discovered by trying to optimize translation with a sequence-to-sequence learning model. We already briefly looked at Seq2Seq learning in Chapter 4. In a Seq2Seq model, there is a set of encoder and decoder layers (submodels). For machine translation, these models remember a sequence of text in one language and then learn to translate it to another language. In essence, the text is transformed by the model into a learned response. For translation, that learned response would be the transformation to another language. However, it is important to realize that learned response could be any transformation, hence the name of the model—*Transformer*.

Figure 5-8, sourced from the paper "Attention Is All You Need," shows the entire architecture of the Transformer model. Inputs are fed into the encoder layer and then pass through the multihead attention block and out via a forward pass that is combined and normalized. The output from this is fed into another multihead attention block. The output of this block is combined with the output of another block that has taken the output of the previous step. This combined output is fed through another layer, then added and normalized again to output the probabilities.

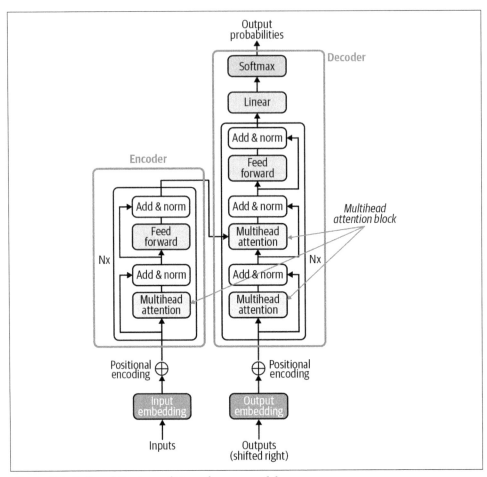

*Figure 5-8. Full architecture of Transformer model*

There is a lot going on in Figure 5-8, so we will break it down further by the internal components, the encoder and the decoder. The encoder and decoder models here serve the same function as we saw in the Seq2Seq models from Chapter 4. We will start with the encoding layer. The code to build the encoding layer is in a function called encoder_layer, shown here:

```
def encoder_layer(units, d_model, num_heads, dropout, name="encoder_layer"):
    inputs = tf.keras.Input(shape=(None, d_model), name="inputs")
    padding_mask = tf.keras.Input(shape=(1, 1, None), name="padding_mask")

    attention = MultiHeadAttention(
        d_model, num_heads, name="attention")({
            'query': inputs,
            'key': inputs,
            'value': inputs,
```

```
            'mask': padding_mask
        })
    attention = tf.keras.layers.Dropout(rate=dropout)(attention)
    attention = tf.keras.layers.LayerNormalization(
        epsilon=1e-6)(inputs + attention)

    outputs = tf.keras.layers.Dense(units=units, activation='relu')(attention)
    outputs = tf.keras.layers.Dense(units=d_model)(outputs)
    outputs = tf.keras.layers.Dropout(rate=dropout)(outputs)
    outputs = tf.keras.layers.LayerNormalization(
        epsilon=1e-6)(attention + outputs)

    return tf.keras.Model(
        inputs=[inputs, padding_mask], outputs=outputs, name=name)

sample_encoder_layer = encoder_layer(
    units=512,
    d_model=128,
    num_heads=4,
    dropout=0.3,
    name="sample_encoder_layer")

tf.keras.utils.plot_model(
    sample_encoder_layer, to_file='encoder_layer.png', show_shapes=True)
```

The last line in that code block will output a very helpful plot of the model or layer
for encoding. It is very helpful to review and visually identify the main elements in
this submodel. It is quite large, so you will need to scroll up and down through the
model to see it all. With an encoder layer defined, we can now build the encoder itself
with the following code:

```
def encoder(vocab_size,
            num_layers,
            units,
            d_model,
            num_heads,
            dropout,
            name="encoder"):
    inputs = tf.keras.Input(shape=(None,), name="inputs")
    padding_mask = tf.keras.Input(shape=(1, 1, None), name="padding_mask")

    embeddings = tf.keras.layers.Embedding(vocab_size, d_model)(inputs)
    embeddings *= tf.math.sqrt(tf.cast(d_model, tf.float32))
    embeddings = PositionalEncoding(vocab_size, d_model)(embeddings)

    outputs = tf.keras.layers.Dropout(rate=dropout)(embeddings)

    for i in range(num_layers):
        outputs = encoder_layer(
            units=units,
            d_model=d_model,
            num_heads=num_heads,
```

```
            dropout=dropout,
            name="encoder_layer_{}".format(i),
        )([outputs, padding_mask])

    return tf.keras.Model(
        inputs=[inputs, padding_mask], outputs=outputs, name=name)

sample_encoder = encoder(
    vocab_size=8192,
    num_layers=2,
    units=512,
    d_model=128,
    num_heads=4,
    dropout=0.3,
    name="sample_encoder")

tf.keras.utils.plot_model(
    sample_encoder, to_file='encoder.png', show_shapes=True)
```

The second-to-last line in the preceding code block creates an encoder sample object. In this sample, it creates two encoder layers using a vocabulary size of 8,192, plus 512 units, 4 heads, and 128 dimensions for the embedding layers and finally a dropout rate of 0.3. The last line of code will output the architecture of the encoder model. Again, it's helpful to review and understand how this structure works. It is too large to show here, so be sure to load up the example and run the code blocks to see the model.

From the encoder, we can move on to the decoder, or the lookahead. The decoder layer is comprised of the masked multiple multiheaded attention components. The attention mechanism receives input from the encoder. The other output from the last full pass of input works as a lookahead. We use the mask to mask out tokens during the attention pass as a way of better contextualizing tokens. The full code for the decoder layer is in a function called decoder_layer, shown here:

```
def decoder_layer(units, d_model, num_heads, dropout, name="decoder_layer"):
    inputs = tf.keras.Input(shape=(None, d_model), name="inputs")
    enc_outputs = tf.keras.Input(shape=(None, d_model), name="encoder_outputs")
    look_ahead_mask = tf.keras.Input(
        shape=(1, None, None), name="look_ahead_mask")
    padding_mask = tf.keras.Input(shape=(1, 1, None), name='padding_mask')

    attention1 = MultiHeadAttention(
        d_model, num_heads, name="attention_1")(inputs={
            'query': inputs,
            'key': inputs,
            'value': inputs,
            'mask': look_ahead_mask
        })
    attention1 = tf.keras.layers.LayerNormalization(
        epsilon=1e-6)(attention1 + inputs)
```

```
attention2 = MultiHeadAttention(
    d_model, num_heads, name="attention_2")(inputs={
        'query': attention1,
        'key': enc_outputs,
        'value': enc_outputs,
        'mask': padding_mask
    })
attention2 = tf.keras.layers.Dropout(rate=dropout)(attention2)
attention2 = tf.keras.layers.LayerNormalization(
    epsilon=1e-6)(attention2 + attention1)

outputs = tf.keras.layers.Dense(units=units, activation='relu')(attention2)
outputs = tf.keras.layers.Dense(units=d_model)(outputs)
outputs = tf.keras.layers.Dropout(rate=dropout)(outputs)
outputs = tf.keras.layers.LayerNormalization(
    epsilon=1e-6)(outputs + attention2)

return tf.keras.Model(
    inputs=[inputs, enc_outputs, look_ahead_mask, padding_mask],
    outputs=outputs,
    name=name)

sample_decoder_layer = decoder_layer(
    units=512,
    d_model=128,
    num_heads=4,
    dropout=0.3,
    name="sample_decoder_layer")

tf.keras.utils.plot_model(
    sample_decoder_layer, to_file='decoder_layer.png', show_shapes=True)
```

The last two lines in the last code block create a decoder layer and output the model. You can see that the architecture of this model gets complex quite quickly. Understanding all elements of this model can take a while, so walk through it slowly. Use the architecture plot of the model to show how the flow of this submodel comes together. Now we can construct the full decoder model with the following code:

```
def decoder(vocab_size,
            num_layers,
            units,
            d_model,
            num_heads,
            dropout,
            name='decoder'):
    inputs = tf.keras.Input(shape=(None,), name='inputs')
    enc_outputs = tf.keras.Input(shape=(None, d_model), name='encoder_outputs')
    look_ahead_mask = tf.keras.Input(
        shape=(1, None, None), name='look_ahead_mask')
    padding_mask = tf.keras.Input(shape=(1, 1, None), name='padding_mask')
```

```python
    embeddings = tf.keras.layers.Embedding(vocab_size, d_model)(inputs)
    embeddings *= tf.math.sqrt(tf.cast(d_model, tf.float32))
    embeddings = PositionalEncoding(vocab_size, d_model)(embeddings)

    outputs = tf.keras.layers.Dropout(rate=dropout)(embeddings)

    for i in range(num_layers):
        outputs = decoder_layer(
            units=units,
            d_model=d_model,
            num_heads=num_heads,
            dropout=dropout,
            name='decoder_layer_{}'.format(i),
        )(inputs=[outputs, enc_outputs, look_ahead_mask, padding_mask])

    return tf.keras.Model(
        inputs=[inputs, enc_outputs, look_ahead_mask, padding_mask],
        outputs=outputs,
        name=name)

sample_decoder = decoder(
    vocab_size=8192,
    num_layers=2,
    units=512,
    d_model=128,
    num_heads=4,
    dropout=0.3,
    name="sample_decoder")

tf.keras.utils.plot_model(
    sample_decoder, to_file='decoder.png', show_shapes=True)
```

The construction of the decoder is almost a clone of the encoder, with a few subtle differences, as mentioned previously. You can again review the model that gets generated from the last line of code. While the code for the encoder and the decoder is similar, the models that are generated end up being quite different. Be sure to again note those differences.

With the encoder and decoder built, we can move on to constructing the full Transformer class, as shown in the following code:

```python
def transformer(vocab_size,
                num_layers,
                units,
                d_model,
                num_heads,
                dropout,
                name="transformer"):
    inputs = tf.keras.Input(shape=(None,), name="inputs")
    dec_inputs = tf.keras.Input(shape=(None,), name="dec_inputs")

    enc_padding_mask = tf.keras.layers.Lambda(
```

```
        create_padding_mask, output_shape=(1, 1, None),
        name='enc_padding_mask')(inputs)

    look_ahead_mask = tf.keras.layers.Lambda(
        create_look_ahead_mask,
        output_shape=(1, None, None),
        name='look_ahead_mask')(dec_inputs)

    dec_padding_mask = tf.keras.layers.Lambda(
        create_padding_mask, output_shape=(1, 1, None),
        name='dec_padding_mask')(inputs)

    enc_outputs = encoder(
        vocab_size=vocab_size,
        num_layers=num_layers,
        units=units,
        d_model=d_model,
        num_heads=num_heads,
        dropout=dropout,
    )(inputs=[inputs, enc_padding_mask])

    dec_outputs = decoder(
        vocab_size=vocab_size,
        num_layers=num_layers,
        units=units,
        d_model=d_model,
        num_heads=num_heads,
        dropout=dropout,
    )(inputs=[dec_inputs, enc_outputs, look_ahead_mask, dec_padding_mask])

    outputs = tf.keras.layers.Dense(units=vocab_size, name="outputs")(dec_outputs)

    return tf.keras.Model(inputs=[inputs, dec_inputs], outputs=outputs, name=name)

sample_transformer = transformer(
    vocab_size=8192,
    num_layers=4,
    units=512,
    d_model=128,
    num_heads=4,
    dropout=0.3,
    name="sample_transformer")

tf.keras.utils.plot_model(
    sample_transformer, to_file='transformer.png', show_shapes=True)
```

The Transformer class combines all the components. You can review the architecture of the full model that is output from the last lines of code. Notice how the inputs are broken up and padded with a padding mask and lookahead mask with the encoded inputs. All of this is pushed through the decoder, which decodes the inputs into a single dense layer and outputs the results. It is important to note the use of dropout and normalization as well throughout the entire model. Dropout and normalization are used to prevent both overfitting and vanishing/exploding gradient problems. Both of these issues can happen quickly when training models have many layers, as this Transformer model does.

With the model built, we can move on to training it.

## Training Conversational Chatbots

We have a Transformer model built, and now we want to train it. The automatic process of training the model is more or less the same as we have done for previous projects. Our goal here, again, is making the AI or model as conversational as possible. That means that you should be able to feed the model text and get realistic responses.

This means we need/want to customize the loss calculation and the learning rate for a conversational bot. Let's open back up the *Chapter_5_Transformer_Chatbot.ipynb* and scroll down to the training section and the code shown:

```
def loss_function(y_true, y_pred):
  y_true = tf.reshape(y_true, shape=(-1, MAX_LENGTH - 1))

  loss = tf.keras.losses.SparseCategoricalCrossentropy(
      from_logits=True, reduction='none')(y_true, y_pred)

  mask = tf.cast(tf.not_equal(y_true, 0), tf.float32)
  loss = tf.multiply(loss, mask)

  return tf.reduce_mean(loss)
```

Normally we would just use the default loss from the `SparseCategoricalCrossen tropy` function. However, we need to modify the output due to the padding. We account for this in the loss by adding/multiplying the mask back in.

Staying in the same area and scrolling to the next block of code, you can see where we define a `CustomSchedule` class. This class schedules the learning rate in a manner suggested in the paper "Attention Is All You Need." In the original paper, the authors suggested a customized learning over the period of training. The rate starts out large and then quickly trails off to some minimum value using geometric scaling.

We can see the code for that block here:

```
class CustomSchedule(tf.keras.optimizers.schedules.LearningRateSchedule):

  def __init__(self, d_model, warmup_steps=4000):
    super(CustomSchedule, self).__init__()

    self.d_model = d_model
    self.d_model = tf.cast(self.d_model, tf.float32)
```

```
    self.warmup_steps = warmup_steps

  def __call__(self, step):
    arg1 = tf.math.rsqrt(step)
    arg2 = step * (self.warmup_steps**-1.5)

    return tf.math.rsqrt(self.d_model) * tf.math.minimum(arg1, arg2)

sample_learning_rate = CustomSchedule(d_model=128)

plt.plot(sample_learning_rate(tf.range(200000, dtype=tf.float32)))
plt.ylabel("Learning Rate")
plt.xlabel("Train Step")
```

Run the code block, and note the plot of the learning rate from the sample `Custom Schedule` object.

We are now ready to compile the model in the next section.

## Compiling and Training the Model

With custom loss and learning rate functions in hand, we can start training the model. First, we will revisit the last section of code that builds the model, as follows:

```
tf.keras.backend.clear_session()

# Hyper-parameters
NUM_LAYERS = 2
D_MODEL = 256
NUM_HEADS = 8
UNITS = 512
DROPOUT = 0.1

model = transformer(
    vocab_size=VOCAB_SIZE,
    num_layers=NUM_LAYERS,
    units=UNITS,
    d_model=D_MODEL,
    num_heads=NUM_HEADS,
    dropout=DROPOUT)
```

The last block builds the Transformer. Now we can move on to compiling the model in the next block of code:

```
learning_rate = CustomSchedule(D_MODEL)

optimizer = tf.keras.optimizers.Adam(
    learning_rate, beta_1=0.9, beta_2=0.98, epsilon=1e-9)

def accuracy(y_true, y_pred):
  y_true = tf.reshape(y_true, shape=(-1, MAX_LENGTH - 1))
```

```
        return tf.keras.metrics.sparse_categorical_accuracy(y_true, y_pred)

    model.compile(optimizer=optimizer, loss=loss_function, metrics=[accuracy])
```

Notice how we use the `CustomSchedule` class to build the `learning_rate` function used in the optimizer. We also define a `custom accuracy` function in order to measure the corrected accuracy. This needs to be done since we are using a custom loss function. Finally, we compile the model, and it is ready for training.

Training times for this example are fairly quick compared to some of the other NLP examples. Be sure that your runtime is set to GPU before doing training on this model. The difference between GPU and CPU with this model can be staggering. As usual, the code to actually train the model is typically the simplest bit, as shown:

```
EPOCHS = 20

model.fit(dataset, epochs=EPOCHS)
```

 You can train this model in batches to gradually build a model to the level that you want or need. This works by training the model for 20 epochs and then testing and evaluating it. Then you can go back and train the same model for another 20 epochs or more. Just remember that your model will be gone if the runtime is reset.

On a GPU, this example can train in about 30–45 minutes. The original Transformer model described in the paper was trained for 3.5 days with 8 GPUs to attain state-of-the-art NLP accuracy. You likely won't be able to expect any state-of-the-art results with this training size; you will need a much larger corpus. You can of course train this model to your heart's content. Before that, though, you may want to look at the next section, where we evaluate the model.

## Evaluation and Prediction

Evaluating a model is really what any AI development comes down to. Understanding how well your algorithm or AI agent performs is critical for creating the best AI. As such, we typically want to do our best when evaluating our models.

Since the Transformer model uses so many customizations, we also need to take those into account when performing our model evaluation. To do the model evaluation, we have to apply the same process across the test inputs. This means we have to go through the same workflow we did when we prepared the training text:

1. Preprocess the inputs as we did before.

2. Tokenize the input sentence the same as before, as well as add `Start_Token` and `End_Token` flags.

---

3. Encode the documents into vectors.

4. Add the padding masks and lookahead masks.

5. Perform the transformation of the model on the data. However, we need to pass the input through the decoder first, then take the output from that transformation, and the input, and feed it back into the model. In this way, the model predicts based on previous words it has seen.

The code to do this evaluation and prediction can be found in *Chapter_5_Transformer_Chatbot.ipynb*, in the "Evaluation and Prediction" section:

```python
def evaluate(sentence):
    sentence = preprocess_sentence(sentence)

    sentence = tf.expand_dims(
        START_TOKEN + tokenizer.encode(sentence) + END_TOKEN, axis=0)

    output = tf.expand_dims(START_TOKEN, 0)

    for i in range(MAX_LENGTH):
        predictions = model(inputs=[sentence, output], training=False)

        predictions = predictions[:, -1:, :]
        predicted_id = tf.cast(tf.argmax(predictions, axis=-1), tf.int32)

        if tf.equal(predicted_id, END_TOKEN[0]):
            break

        output = tf.concat([output, predicted_id], axis=-1)

    return tf.squeeze(output, axis=0)

def predict(sentence):
    prediction = evaluate(sentence)

    predicted_sentence = tokenizer.decode(
        [i for i in prediction if i < tokenizer.vocab_size])

    print('Input: {}'.format(sentence))
    print('Output: {}'.format(predicted_sentence))

    return predicted_sentence
```

We can test the model by using the code in the next code block, as shown here:

```python
output = predict('Where have you been?')
output = predict("It's a trap")
#outputs
Input: Where have you been?
Output: a week ? a year ?
Input: It's a trap
Output: come on , keep it . tell it . tell me where the sit down is .
```

Note that the output from the model will depend on the amount of training you spend on the model. More training will provide you with better answers. Constructing a full working chatbot or AI assistant is outside the scope of this book and requires many other parts and services. For now, let's look at an alternative method for creating a conversational chatbot using BERT.

# Using Transformer for Conversational Chatbots

BERT is the encapsulation of a Transformer model that has been trained on an extensive corpus. We've seen how we can use BERT in a few different ways in Chapter 4 using ktrain. We want to be able to use our model as a full chatbot using the example we just trained. To do that, however, we are going to have to add save checkpoints to our model. That way we can retrieve our model later for use in our chatbot.

In the next exercise, we learn how to apply known training checkpoints to our model. That way we can extract the model at any point in time later on for any epoch that was of interest. This is not just useful for chatbots, but also has many uses in building deep learning apps. We will see the steps outlined in Example 5-5 applied in future exercises as well.

*Example 5-5. Saving and restoring models*

- Open the modified example *Chapter_5_Transformer_Chatbot_save.ipynb*. We will refer to the lines in the code that have been added to allow this example to save.
- The first new line we see added is at the top and installs some new dependencies, as shown in the following command:
```
!pip install h5py pyyaml

from google.colab import drive
drive.mount('/content/drive')
```
- The second bit of code maps your Google drive as a local drive. This will allow us to save the weights to that drive so we don't have to worry about training getting lost. After that block runs, you will be prompted to follow a URL to get an authorization code. Follow the link, and copy and paste the code in the required text box.
- Next, we are going to scroll all the way down to the training code section. We need to add a callback that will allow the `fit` function to save the model to a known location. Notice how the training call to the `fit` function has been modified:
```
checkpoint_path = "/content/drive/My Drive/training_tt/cp.ckpt"
checkpoint_dir = os.path.dirname(checkpoint_path)

# Create checkpoint callback
```

```
cp_callback = tf.keras.callbacks.ModelCheckpoint(checkpoint_path,
                save_weights_only=True,verbose=1)

EPOCHS = 100

model.fit(dataset, epochs=EPOCHS, callbacks=[cp_callback])

!ls {checkpoint_dir}
```

- This code now saves the model after every epoch in the `checkpoint_path` direc-tory. Notice how the callback is passed into the `fit` function. We can restore the model using the following code:
  ```
  model.load_weights(checkpoint_path)
  ```

- That single line will load the weights for the last trained epoch. You can then use the model to respond to chat messages in a conversational manner.

Our Transformer code now saves a model we can use in a simple conversational chat-bot. In Example 5-6, the final exercise of this chapter, we show you how to load the model back and use it as a conversational chatbot.

*Example 5-6. A conversational chatbot*

- In this exercise we load the Transformer model we trained earlier and use it as a conversational chatbot. Note that you must run the *Chapter_5_Trans-former_Chatbot_save.ipynb* example before running this exercise.

- Open example *Chapter_5_AI_Chatbot.ipynb* and run the first couple of cells to do the setup. We won't review those cells here as you should be familiar with the content.

- The first new block of code lists the contents of our Transformer training folder, shown here:
  ```
  checkpoint_path = "/content/drive/'My Drive'/training_tt/"
  checkpoint_dir = os.path.dirname(checkpoint_path)

  !ls {checkpoint_dir}
  ```

- You will want to make sure and run this block of code first to confirm you have weights saved.

- Most of the rest of the code is the same as our previous Transformer chatbot, except in this case we don't load and preprocess any data for training. The code in this example just supports loading a saved version of the tokenizer and build-ing the model. We need the same exact model and tokenizer to load weights from and use as a chatbot.

- The next new block of code loads the tokenizer we saved with pickle and can be found at the start of the "Evaluation and Prediction" section.

 Pickle is a helpful Python library for serializing objects to disk. Then you can reload the objects for use in Python.

- We need to use the same tokenizer in order to decode our model predictions correctly. If we used any tokenizer, the responses would likely not make sense since the tokenization and encoding process order may change. The code to load the tokenizer and reset the Start_Token and End_Token is shown:

```
import pickle

with open('/content/drive/My Drive/training_tt/tokenizer.pickle',
        'rb') as handle:
    tokenizer = pickle.load(handle)

START_TOKEN, END_TOKEN = [tokenizer.vocab_size], [tokenizer.vocab_size + 1]
VOCAB_SIZE = tokenizer.vocab_size + 2
MAX_LENGTH = 40
```

- Then we reload the model and the weights with the following code:

```
checkpoint_path = "/content/drive/My Drive/training_tt/cp.ckpt"
model.load_weights(checkpoint_path)
```

- That code loads the weights from the saved location on your Google Drive. This allows you to rerun this example later or in tandem with the previous notebook. We can then encapsulate our chatbot into a Colab form using the following code:

```
#@title AI Conversational ChatBot { run: "auto" }
input = 'how big are you?' #@param {type:"string"}

response = predict(input)
```

- The tag {run:'auto'} will force the sheet to rerun every time you enter text. Responses will be output below the cell.

How well this chatbot works will depend on how much effort you put into training it. This model could take days to train to an accuracy that provides novel and interesting results. The great aspect of this demo is that you can be extensively training and still chatting with a constantly updated conversational AI.

# Conclusion

Chatbots are the ultimate culmination of our need to naturally interface with machines using natural language. While we typically identify chatbots as either functional goal oriented or conversational, the lines are blurring. Dialogflow, a goal-oriented bot, includes conversational queues that will likely be expanded upon. Imagine in the future calling an AI bot to book a flight and then getting off track making simple conversation, as you may do with a regular human operator.

This chapter was special in that we introduced a new form of deep learning, the Transformer model, for determining context, correlation, or attention. Whatever term you use, this new model has turned NLP upside down and has almost replaced recurrent networks overnight. The Attention mechanism that powers the Transformer is now making its way to other ML areas of DL. Attention is now being used for image analysis with convolution, potentially upending image analysis in the next year, or sooner. Being able to understand the basics of the Transformer model for building chatbots or other apps will be essential.

For the next chapter, we jump back into the area of image analysis but this time in the context of moving images or video. Video provides an excellent canvas for learning not only what's in the image but also the actions or context, not unlike our journey into NLP with Transformers.

# CHAPTER 6

# Video Analysis on the Cloud

With the improved developments in image analysis, it was only a matter of time before we would be using the same techniques to analyze video. If we ignore the audio, video is for the most part just a stack of pictures—pictures that are in a given sequence that describes some order of events or context. As we learned from NLP, context can matter, and in video it certainly matters.

In this chapter we look at the process of analyzing video for a variety of applications, ranging from video indexing for capturing or tagging content in videos, to using the event sequence itself to capture the activity. Video indexing, while just an extension of image analysis, has wide-ranging use cases, from security to streaming. Indexing video is like asking the question "Who are they?" while identifying motion or action in video can answer the question "What are they doing?"

In this chapter we will first look at how to load and analyze video with Python on Colab. Then, we look at applications of AI with respect to video, in particular the task of automatic video indexing. From video indexing, we will move on to using a webcam to detect faces. Finally, we finish on a practical example in which we use a TF Hub human-motion detector to identify human activity in videos.

The following is a list of the main topics we will cover in this chapter:

- Downloading Video with Python
- Video AI and Video Indexing
- Building a Webcam Face Detector
- Recognizing Actions with TF Hub
- Exploring the Video Intelligence API

Video analysis is a complex task and typically requires an exponential amount of training time and/or computational resources. This may be something to keep in mind when working with the exercises in this chapter and in any real-world development you pursue later. In the next section, we look at the basics of handling and managing video with Python.

# Downloading Video with Python

Ignoring audio, video analysis is the process of analyzing a sequence of images defined in an order or context. If we ignore context in video, then the frames can be treated just like images, and we can use some of the same techniques we used to analyze images. Therefore, our first step is to understand how to download videos and render them as images.

YouTube is arguably the best source of video content for any serious AI analysis. However, YouTube doesn't necessarily make it easy to download videos. Fortunately, Python provides an updated library called *youtube_dl* that we can use to address this problem. We will look at how to use this library to download and process a video from YouTube in Example 6-1.

*Example 6-1. Downloading YouTube videos*

- Start with a new Colab notebook or open the *Chapter_6_youtube.ipynb* example. The first thing we will need to do is download the most recent version of the *youtube_dl* library by entering and executing the code into a new cell:
  ```
  !pip install --upgrade youtube_dl
  ```

- YouTube and downloaders are in a constant downloading arms race. YouTube spends considerable effort making it difficult to download its videos. Conversely, the authors of *youtube_dl* update their code to work with the most recent preventions. That means we always need to download and use the most recent version.

- Next we will run a few imports needed for this task, as shown here:
  ```
  from google.colab.patches import cv2_imshow
  import cv2
  import numpy as np
  import youtube_dl
  ```

- OpenCV is an image processing library that is already installed on Colab. You cannot render images in a notebook directly, and we need to use a helper function called cv2_imshow from a patch in Colab to show images.

- Then, in another new cell, we set up the source video URL and use the *youtube_dl* library to pull the information dictionary from YouTube, as shown in the following code:

```
video_url = 'https://www.youtube.com/watch?v=t8tjT9MA7yU'

download_options = {}
download = youtube_dl.YoutubeDL(download_options)
info_dict = download.extract_info(video_url, download=False)
formats = info_dict.get('formats',None)

for format in formats:
  for k in format:
    print("Key : {} , Value : {}".format(k,format[k]))
```

- The video_url points to video on YouTube that will be our source. We then use the *youtube_dl* module's YouTubeDL function passing in blank options to download the video's information dictionary in *info_dict*. We then extract the formats and display the list in output below the cell. Run the cell, and note how much information and detail is displayed about each format.

- With the formats identified, we can now loop through the list and select a video to download and render as images. The code here shows how simply this can be done:

```
for f in formats:
  if f.get('format_note',None) == '144p':
    url = f.get('url',None)
    capture = cv2.VideoCapture(url)
    if not capture.isOpened():
        print('video not opened')
        exit(-1)

    while True:
        ret, frame = capture.read()
        if not ret:
            break

        cv2_imshow(frame)

    capture.release()
```

- This code loops through the formats and selects the lowest-resolution format. Then it captures the video and reads/renders the frames to the notebook. Running the cell will produce the output shown in Figure 6-1.

 If you don't want to have the whole video render, just stop execution of the cell.

*Figure 6-1. Rendering a video to Colab notebook*

 The ability to pull down any YouTube video for analysis is very powerful, but realize it may not always work. It is not in the best interest of YouTube to allow this since it can bypass their advertising.

Now that we can process any public video on YouTube, we can move on to understanding how to use AI on video.

# Video AI and Video Indexing

Video presents a new set of information that we can extract and begin to understand on a larger scale. Video analysis has been done extensively with movement detection for many years, but with new advances in AI, it opens up even further. Now, any AI application that works with images can be relatively easily extended to video. We will look at just such an example of this by extending the object detection sample from Chapter 3 as a form of video indexer.

Video indexing is a relatively new process made possible with ML/AI technologies. There are plenty of ways in which you may want to index video for all manner of purposes. From security videos that detect intruders to videos that just count inventory, the possibilities are endless. In Example 6-2, we look at how to build a video indexer that detects objects in the video.

*Example 6-2. Detecting objects in video*

- Open the notebook *Chapter_6_vididx.ipynb*. In this exercise we are going to combine the code from two previous exercises, Examples 5-1 and 3-12. Example 3-12 used the object detection API in Colab to detect and count images.

- We will again start by importing *youtube_dl* and then doing the needed imports, shown here:

```
!pip install --upgrade youtube_dl

import cv2
import numpy as np
import youtube_dl
from google.colab.patches import cv2_imshow
import time
```

- We set the video_url and download the formats. This time we also set some other parameters for controlling the size of the images. Remember, image size and channels are important when we feed those into a deep learning network. The following code shows how this comes together:

```
vid_id = 't8tjT9MA7yU'
video_url = 'https://www.youtube.com/watch?v=' + vid_id

download_options = {}
download = youtube_dl.YoutubeDL(download_options)
info_dict = download.extract_info(video_url, download=False)
formats = info_dict.get('formats',None)
cnt = 0
```

```
new_width = 512
new_height = 512
```

- We have seen most of this code before. The difference this time is we prepare to format the images and save them instead of rendering them. Then, in the next block of code, we loop through the formats and save the images to the local folder:

```
for f in formats:
    if f.get('format_note',None) == '144p':
        url = f.get('url',None)
        capture = cv2.VideoCapture(url)
        if not capture.isOpened():
            print('video not opened')
            exit(-1)

        while True:
            ret, frame = capture.read()
            if not ret:
                break
            cnt += 1
            filename = vid_id + "_" + str(cnt) + ".jpg"
            frame = cv2.resize(frame, (new_width, new_height))
            cv2.imwrite(filename, frame)

    capture.release()
print("total frames", cnt)
#outputs
36208
```

- Let that code run to completion. It may take a few minutes to render and save the whole video. If you change the YouTube ID (vid_id) to a longer video, expect many more frames to process.

- With the video saved as image frames, we will enter some test code in order to view image frames. The following code creates a function to render a specific frame and shows a form that allows you to switch frames automatically:

```
#@title Video Render by Frame { display-mode: "form", run: "auto" }

def load_render_image(filename):
    img = cv2.imread(filename)
    img = cv2.cvtColor(img, cv2.COLOR_BGR2RGB)
    cv2_imshow(img)
    return img

frame_num = 911 #@param {type:"slider", min:1, max:36328, step:1}
filename = vid_id + "_" + str(frame_num) + ".jpg"
load_render_image(filename)
print(filename)
```

- You can use the slider shown on the form in Figure 6-2 to move through and render the frames. Note that you may need to change the max number from 36,328 to whatever your total frame count is.

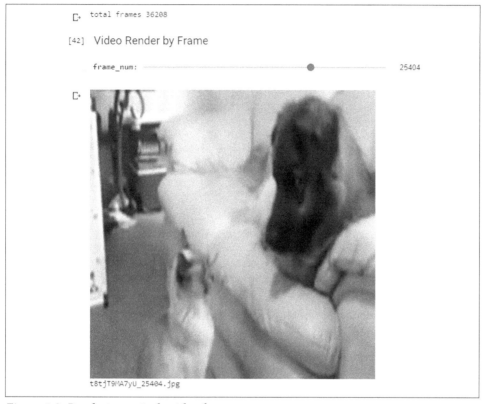

Figure 6-2. Rendering a single video frame

- With the video loaded and frames rendered to disk, we can now load the object detection module with the following code:

```
!pip install --upgrade tensorflow-hub

import tensorflow as tf
import tensorflow_hub as hub

module_handle =
    "https://tfhub.dev/google/faster_rcnn/openimages_v4/inception_resnet_v2/1"
    #@param ["https://tfhub.dev/google/openimages_v4/ssd/mobilenet_v2/1",
    "https://tfhub.dev/google/faster_rcnn/openimages_v4/inception_resnet_v2/1"]

detector = hub.load(module_handle).signatures['default']
```

- The process for loading the object detection module is the same as in Example 3-12.

- Then we need a couple of helper functions to run the detection and render results. Code for both functions is shown here:

```
def render_results(results, top_items = 5):
  ents = results["detection_class_entities"][:top_items]
  scores = results["detection_scores"][:top_items]
  for i in range(len(ents)):
    print(ents[i], scores[i])


def run_detector(objects, detector, path):
  img = load_render_image(path)

  converted_img  = tf.image.convert_image_dtype(
    img, tf.float32)[tf.newaxis, ...]
  start_time = time.time()
  result = detector(converted_img)
  end_time = time.time()

  result = {key:value.numpy() for key,value in result.items()}

  print("Found %d objects." % len(result["detection_scores"]))
  print("Inference time: ", end_time-start_time)
  render_results(result, top_items=objects)
```

- Most of this code is from Example 3-12. Its purpose is just to detect objects and display the top *n* results.

- Everything is now prepared, and we will build another simple form to scroll through the images and detect the top number of objects. The code to do that is shown here:

```
#@title Count Objects in Frame { display-mode: "form", run: "auto" }

frame_num = 9470 #@param {type:"slider", min:1, max:36328, step:1}
objects = 5 #@param {type:"slider", min:1, max:100, step:1}
filename = vid_id + "_" + str(frame_num) + ".jpg"
run_detector(objects, detector, filename)
```

- Adjusting the sliders will set the frame and number of objects you want to detect in the image.

- Be sure to set the notebook to run with a GPU. Notice the difference this makes in the inference time.

Consider how impressive this last exercise was. We just loaded a video from YouTube and arbitrarily scanned a video frame for the objects in that frame. Note that we could just as easily use any classification network on video for the same or better results. Furthermore, being able to use video frames as training input alleviates many problems with having enough data. Having just a few videos of classification subjects can provide huge amounts of classification data.

 Because it can take 45 seconds to infer objects, we won't write a full video indexer here. Therefore, extending the last example to index full videos is left up to the reader. It also may not be practical to index every frame, but every 5, 10, or 20 frames instead.

How you decide to index each frame of a video is up to you and may depend on many factors. You will most certainly want to index content to a backend database as well as be able to analyze statistics from indexed results.

Aside from just image frames, we can also consider the context or sequence of frames in a video, essentially which frames or actions come before other actions, telling us what the subject in the video is doing. We will work on understanding context later in this chapter. Before that, let's revisit the indexing video process and look at capturing faces.

# Building a Webcam Face Detector

In this section we are going to look at ways of capturing video from your webcam for AI processing. We will first grab the webcam feed from a Colab notebook and then use that video to both identify and recognize faces. For the first exercise, we will create a webcam face detector.

Before that, though, we will go through a step to make sure we have access to a GPU. When you set a notebook to use a GPU, it may not always force Colab to give you one, which can be a tad annoying. Many libraries you use for building AI may require a GPU to work.

In Example 6-3, we use a single block of code to determine what available GPUs you have. Colab may restrict your GPU usage, especially if you use a lot of GPU training. Examples 6-4 and 6-5 require a GPU runtime, and this code will test that.

*Example 6-3. Determining GPUs available*

- Open example *Chapter_6_GPU.ipynb* to see the code we can use for checking for available GPU instances:

```
from __future__ import absolute_import, division, print_function,
                      unicode_literals

import tensorflow as tf
print("Num GPUs Available: ",
    len(tf.config.experimental.list_physical_devices('GPU')))
```

- If you find you have no GPU instances available, you can try the exercise with a CPU. However, many exercises in this book perform better with a GPU, and the next two exercises require it.

Be sure you have a GPU instance available before attempting the next exercise. You will be able to record video, but the face recognition component requires a GPU. If you have a GPU available, then proceed to the next exercise.

For Example 6-4, we look at how to connect your webcam through a Google Colab notebook. We will then use the output of the video to detect faces.

*Example 6-4. Building a webcam face detector*

- Open example *Chapter_6_Webcam_face.ipynb* and make sure the notebook is set to GPU runtime. Then run the first cell. The bulk of the contents of this first cell are sourced from a blog post (*https://oreil.ly/fKTz3*) by Offer Sadey.
- We will show some snippets of that first block to highlight some important concepts in the following code:

```
!pip install ffmpeg-python
!pip install face_recognition

from IPython.display import HTML, JavaScript, display
from google.colab.output import eval_js
from base64 import b64decode
import numpy as np
import io
import ffmpeg

webcam_file = 'webcam.mp4'

VIDEO_HTML = """
<script>
...
</script>
"""

def start_webcam():
  js = JavaScript('''
    async function startWebcam() {
      const div = document.createElement('div');

      const video = document.createElement('video');
      video.style.display = 'block';
      const stream =
        await navigator.mediaDevices.getUserMedia({video: true});

      document.body.appendChild(div);
```

```
        div.appendChild(video);
        video.srcObject = stream;
        await video.play();

        // Resize the output to fit the video element.
        google.colab.output.setIframeHeight(
          document.documentElement.scrollHeight, true);

        return;

      }
      ''')

  display(js)
  data = eval_js('startWebcam()')

start_webcam()

def get_video():
  display(HTML(VIDEO_HTML))
  data = eval_js("data")
  binary = b64decode(data.split(',')[1])

  return binary
```

- In order for us to capture webcam video in a Colab notebook, we need to run some JavaScript in the browser. IPython provides a number of hooks into the browser, including the ability to run JavaScript. This allows us to hook up the browser's webcam recorder to render and record video. One other thing to note is the couple of pip installs at the start of the file. The first package, ffmpeg-python, allows us to work with video files, while the second installs a package that will help us more easily do face recognition, the face_recognition package.

- The next block of code reads the webcam video and saves it to the local drive, as shown here:

```
webcam = get_video()

with open(webcam_file, 'wb') as f:
  f.write(webcam)
```

- When you run the last block of code, it will start recording the video. A button will show, allowing you to stop recording when you have enough video.

- Next, we are going to run some more imports with the following block of code:

```
%pylab inline
import face_recognition
import cv2
import matplotlib.patches as patches
from IPython.display import clear_output
```

```
from matplotlib.pyplot import imshow
import matplotlib.pylab as plt
```

- If you don't have a GPU runtime, this last block of code will fail. The `face_recog
  nition` module requires a GPU instance.

- The last block of code opens the video and extracts the frames to do face recognition on, as shown here:

```
video_capture = cv2.VideoCapture(webcam_file)
frame_count = 0
while video_capture.isOpened():
    ret, frame = video_capture.read()
    if not ret:
        video_capture.release()
        break

    frame_count += 1
    if frame_count % 3 == 0:
        frame = cv2.cvtColor(frame, cv2.COLOR_BGR2RGB)
        title("Webcam")
        plt.imshow(frame)
        rgb_frame = frame[:, :, ::-1]
        face_locations = face_recognition.face_locations(rgb_frame)

        for face_location in face_locations:
            plt.plot(face_location[1], face_location[0], 'bo')
            plt.plot(face_location[1], face_location[2], 'bo')
            plt.plot(face_location[3], face_location[2], 'bo')
            plt.plot(face_location[3], face_location[0], 'bo')
        plt.show()
        clear_output(wait=True)
```

- The last block of code extracts a frame from the video and does face recognition
  analysis with the libraries' CNN pretrained package. If it recognizes a face, it
  places four blue dots around it. Most of the work in this sample is being done by
  a library called OpenCV. OpenCV is a powerful image analysis framework that
  uses a combination of techniques to extract image information. The OpenCV
  library can be difficult to install, especially on Windows. Colab provides it by
  default.

That last exercise showed us how to capture webcam video and use it to detect faces
using the OpenCV API. In order for the library to recognize specific faces, we need to
create face embeddings. Face embeddings are much like the other embeddings we
created with words in the sections on NLP (Chapters 4 and 5). We will cover building
face embeddings in the next section.

# Understanding Face Embeddings

Face detection, analysis, and recognition have been around since the late 1990s without the use of deep learning. The method used to identify faces is reasonably low tech and just uses facial features as input features. The OpenCV library is equipped with algorithms for extracting these facial features. Typically, the features extracted from an image would include attributes like:

- Height of the face (cm)
- Width of the face (cm)
- Average color of face (R, G, B)
- Width of lips (cm)
- Width between eyes (cm)

We can then encode those features into a vector that represent values for each feature. For example, let's say that our face had the following features:

| Face Height | Face Width | Face Color | Lip Width | Eye Width |
|---|---|---|---|---|
| 24.2 | 16.2 | (255,224,189) | 5.4 | 2.6 |

This data would be converted to an input vector that looks like:

```
[24.2, 16.2, 255, 224, 189, 5.4, 2.6]
```

With an input vector, we can then create a face embedding of this information not unlike the word embeddings we constructed for NLP in Chapters 4 and 5. Face embeddings allow us to take the representation of a face and learn to recognize it with a deep learning network. The *face_recognition* library uses these embeddings to recognize faces with high accuracy.

For Example 6-5, we are going to look at how to recognize faces, particularly celebrity faces in video. We are going to automate our face extraction so that we can download the top 100 images for a celebrity we want to recognize. Then we will use the YouTube downloader to download a celebrity video and see if we can recognize the faces in them. To make things interesting, we are going to do facial recognition of Will Ferrell and Will's celebrity clone, Chad Smith. Both men are quite famous, Will more so, and look remarkably alike.

*Example 6-5. Recognizing faces in video*

- Open example *Chapter_6_Face_rec.ipynb* and run the first cell. This exercise requires a GPU instance, so make sure that you have one and that it is enabled.

- Next we will do our required additional library installs with the following commands:

```
!pip install face_recognition
!pip install --upgrade youtube_dl
```

- With the dependencies installed, it's time to download the video with the next block of code:

```
from __future__ import unicode_literals
import youtube_dl

video_url = 'https://www.youtube.com/watch?v=DHdkpSAteG0'

download_options = {}
download = youtube_dl.YoutubeDL(download_options)
info_dict = download.extract_info(video_url, download=False)
formats = info_dict.get('formats',None)

for f in formats:
  if f.get('format_note',None) == '144p':
    url = f.get('url',None)

print(url)
```

- We have already seen this code, and this is just an abridged version that downloads the appropriate URL format. OpenCV can process the video directly from this URL.

- After getting the URL of the video, we then want to do more imports and determine the length of the video with the following code:

```
import face_recognition
import cv2

input_movie = cv2.VideoCapture(url)
length = int(input_movie.get(cv2.CAP_PROP_FRAME_COUNT))
print(length)
```

- With video set, we can now move on to finding face images to set up for our face embeddings. Since Will is a well-known celebrity, we can use another helpful module, *bing_image_downloader*, to automatically download an image search for *will ferrell*. The following code does the image search for keywords (*will ferrell*), saves the images, and then processes them as face embeddings:

```
git clone https://github.com/gurugaurav/bing_image_downloader
cd bing_image_downloader
pip install .

from bing_image_downloader import downloader
import os

keywords = "will ferrell"
```

```
from bing_image_downloader import downloader
downloader.download(keywords, limit=100, adult_filter_off=False,
                    force_replace=True)
```

- Running that last block of code will generate a lot of output. It will download the 100 images found by searching Bing. You should first see the images being downloaded.

 This example was originally developed with the Google image downloader. However, this code broke due to API changes from Google, and one of the consequences of this ongoing issue was to prevent YouTube videos from being downloaded.

- Next, we need to encode the images based on the face detected in them. We will store all the embeddings in a vector called encoded_faces.

```
path = '/content/dataset/bing/will ferrell'
from os import listdir
from os.path import isfile, join
files = [path + '/' + f for f in listdir(path) if isfile(join(path, f))]
print(files)

encoded_faces = []
for file in files:
  if os.path.isfile(file):
    print('Encoding image - ' + file)
    img = face_recognition.load_image_file(file)
    img_enc = face_recognition.face_encodings(img)[0]
    encoded_faces.append(img_enc)

print(encoded_faces)
```

- Code in that cell first loads the images from the location we downloaded them to with the Bing downloader. Then we loop through the files and encode them with the face_recognition module. The last line prints the embedding/encoding vectors so you can see what they look like.

- The last block of code again does the heavy lifting. This is where we loop through the video and process each frame to recognize a face. If a face is recognized, a red rectangle is drawn around it and it is labeled. Code for that block is shown here:

```
from google.colab.patches import cv2_imshow

face_locations = []
face_encodings = []
face_names = []
frame_number = 0
```

```
while True:
    ret, frame = input_movie.read()
    frame_number += 1

    if not ret:
        break

    OpenCV uses) to RGB color (which face_recognition uses)
    rgb_frame = frame[:, :, ::-1]

    face_locations = face_recognition.face_locations(rgb_frame)
    face_encodings = face_recognition.face_encodings(rgb_frame,
        face_locations)

    face_names = []
    for face_encoding in face_encodings:
        match = face_recognition.compare_faces(encoded_faces,
            face_encoding, tolerance=0.50)
        face_names.append(keywords)

    for (top, right, bottom, left), name in zip(face_locations,
                                                face_names):
        if not name:
            continue

        cv2.rectangle(frame, (left, top), (right, bottom),
                    (0, 0, 255), 2)

        cv2.rectangle(frame, (left, bottom - 25), (right, bottom),
                    (0, 0, 255), cv2.FILLED)
        font = cv2.FONT_HERSHEY_DUPLEX
        cv2.putText(frame, name, (left + 6, bottom - 6), font, 0.5,
                    (255, 255, 255), 1)

    cv2_imshow(frame)
input_movie.release()
cv2.destroyAllWindows()
```

- Figure 6-3 shows the partial output of a series of frames. We can see in the images that the algorithm is correctly identifying Will Ferrell, but in many of the frames, it also incorrectly identifies Chad Smith as Will. We could likely correct this misinterpretation by feeding the face_recognition classifier images of Chad as well. However, if we did that, then we would also need to change our logic when a face was recognized. This would require inspecting the match object output from the compare_faces function call.

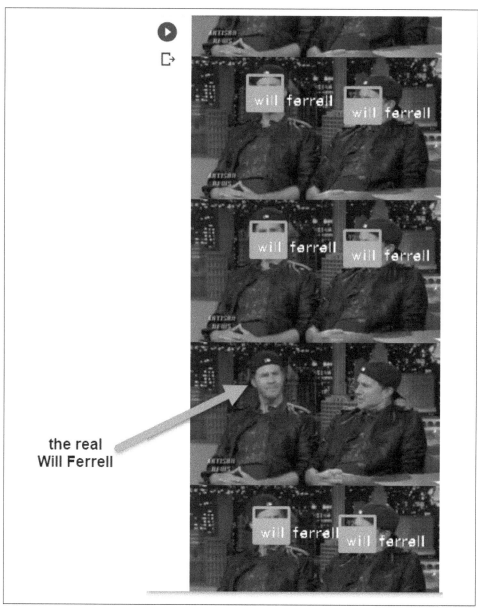

*Figure 6-3. Recognizing faces in a video*

Of course, the possibilities with this example are endless. Not only can you automatically feed in video to recognize if a face is present, but you can also recognize who it is and at what frame or instant it appears. This could allow you to detect not only when someone is in video but also who it is, provided you know that information. The results from this facial recognition system may not be for high-security scenarios, since it misidentified Chad as Will. But if you are just looking to index who is in a video, this system will likely work well enough for that. Keep in mind that we just blindly used any images for this recognition. We did not go through the images we automatically downloaded from Bing and make sure that they were all Will and were good images for encoding. If we were developing a more robust system, we would probably use a variety of facial images of various subjects with better labeling.

In the next section, we jump back to working with TF Hub. We have used TF Hub previously for a few tasks. The hub can be a great resource to test fully working models. We will use a model from this hub to look at action recognition.

## Recognizing Actions with TF Hub

TF Hub provides us with plenty of pretrained models we can use as is or modify in some form of transfer learning scenario. A majority of these models have been developed for image classification and NLP/NLU. However, as we have already seen, there are plenty of other application models, like the BigGAN. Another such application model variant has been trained to recognize actions in video. This model functions not unlike other image classification models. In this case, though, we use the importance of sequence/context as a new dimension in learning.

In video, we still consider an individual frame as being in two dimensions (width and height), but with video we add a third dimension for time. Figure 6-4 shows how we can build a network architecture to capture this context with various layer types. By introducing the dimension of time to vision, we create another opportunity to understand context on that dimension. We previously used convolutional networks to scan across an image's two dimensions in order to better capture contextual features. Likewise, when we first worked with NLP, we saw how recurrent networks could capture the sequence of words in a sentence.

For video, we will use convolutional layers for capturing the context in frames, and then recurrent layers for capturing context in frame order again, as shown in Figure 6-4. Just realize that we are using both types of network layers to extract the context within the frame and where the frame is in time.

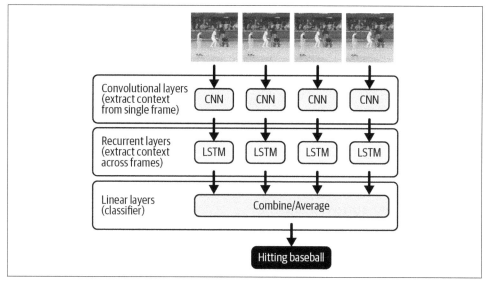

*Figure 6-4. An action recognition model*

Fortunately, Google has already constructed a few models using the CNN/RNN architecture with the purpose of recognizing actions. RNN layers allow the model to differentiate between action sequences, with the model previously trained on action demonstrations.

For Example 6-6, we are going to use another model form, the TF Hub. This model has been trained on action demonstrations captured with Kinect. Kinect is the Microsoft interface that captures your action as input into an Xbox system. The model we are using here can identify 400 forms of actions. There is a 600-actions model as well, and there will likely be larger ones in the future.

*Example 6-6. Recognizing actions in video*

- Open example *Chapter_6_Action_Recognition.ipynb* and run the first cell. This first cell installs a later version of TensorFlow and the *youtube_dl* library.

- The next cell after that includes all the imports for this exercise. You will notice we use logging in this example as well. We won't show this block of code as it is self-explanatory.

- After the imports, we revisit our standard YouTube code block, as shown here:

```
video_url = 'https://www.youtube.com/watch?v=lUVlSwQ9tSU'

download_options = {}
download = youtube_dl.YoutubeDL(download_options)
info_dict = download.extract_info(video_url, download=False)
```

```
formats = info_dict.get('formats',None)

for f in formats:
  if f.get('format_note',None) == '144p':
    url = f.get('url',None)

print(url)
```

- This code is the same as what we used in the previous exercise. It just identifies the link to the proper format of video we want to download and saves that into a variable URL.

- Next, we need some helper code to load the video and extract the contents. This code is courtesy of the TensorFlow authors and is shown here:

```
def crop_center_square(frame):
  y, x = frame.shape[0:2]
  min_dim = min(y, x)
  start_x = (x // 2) - (min_dim // 2)
  start_y = (y // 2) - (min_dim // 2)
  return frame[start_y:start_y+min_dim,start_x:start_x+min_dim]

def load_video(path, max_frames=0, resize=(224, 224)):
  cap = cv2.VideoCapture(path)
  frames = []
  try:
    while True:
      ret, frame = cap.read()
      if not ret:
        break
      frame = crop_center_square(frame)
      frame = cv2.resize(frame, resize)
      frame = frame[:, :, [2, 1, 0]]
      frames.append(frame)

      if len(frames) == max_frames:
        break
  finally:
    cap.release()
  return np.array(frames) / 255.0

def animate(images):
  converted_images = np.clip(images * 255, 0, 255).astype(np.uint8)
  imageio.mimsave('./animation.gif', converted_images, fps=25)
  with open('./animation.gif','rb') as f:
      display.display(display.Image(data=f.read(), height=300))
```

- All of this code heavily relies on cv2 (OpenCV) to process and manipulate the video. The first function, crop_center_square, is used to extract the center part of the frame. The load_video function processes each frame of the video.

`Animate`, the last function, animates the frames in the notebook as if it were a video.

- Along with the model, we also want the labels the model is trained to. This will help us generate a friendly name rather than some number. The code to download and save the labels is shown here:

```
KINETICS_URL =
    "https://raw.githubusercontent.com/deepmind/kinetics-i3d/master/data/
    label_map.txt"
with request.urlopen(KINETICS_URL) as obj:
    labels = [line.decode("utf-8").strip() for line in obj.readlines()]
print("Found %d labels." % len(labels))
```

- Running this cell will download the 400 labels for the action model.

- The next block of code uses the previous helper functions to load the video and output the shape of the data:

```
sample_video = load_video(url, max_frames=250)

print("sample_video is a numpy array of shape %s." % str(sample_video.shape))
animate(sample_video)
```

- The output of this cell is shown in Figure 6-5. You can see the shape of the data and then the animated frames of the video. It may be obvious to you as a human just looking at the single frame what the action is, but let's continue. Notice how the shape of the data represents the frames (250) first, then the frame size (224 × 224), and then the channels (3).

*Figure 6-5. Example output of baseball batter*

- At the end of the notebook is our code to determine the action in the video, as shown here:

```
model_input = np.expand_dims(sample_video, axis=0)

with tf.Graph().as_default():
  i3d = hub.Module("https://tfhub.dev/deepmind/i3d-kinetics-400/1")
  input_placeholder = tf.placeholder(shape=(None, None, 224, 224, 3),
                                      dtype=tf.float32)
  logits = i3d(input_placeholder)
  probabilities = tf.nn.softmax(logits)
  with tf.train.MonitoredSession() as session:
    [ps] = session.run(probabilities,
                       feed_dict={input_placeholder: model_input})

print("Top 5 actions:")
for i in np.argsort(ps)[::-1][:5]:
  print("%-22s %.2f%%" % (labels[i], ps[i] * 100))
#outputs
...
Top 5 actions:
hitting baseball          96.65%
catching or throwing baseball 1.74%
playing cricket           1.60%
catching or throwing softball 0.01%
playing kickball          0.00%
```

- The code loads the model TensorFlow graph with the hub.Module function. After that, an input_placeholder variable is created to hold the frames being fed into the graph. A TensorFlow graph is the raw executable form of the model. We have already been constructing such models, but TensorFlow 2.0 allows us to avoid those details. We can now build models with abstractions called *layers*, which are much easier to use and manipulate.

This placeholder is then fed into the module as a variable placeholder. Placeholders are a way of setting up a network graph. After that, the output logits denote the output of the model. Note that the model is not running yet. Logits are then turned into probabilities by applying a softmax function. This whole model can then be started by obtaining a session and then running it with session.run. The output of this code shows the top 5 actions and their inferred probability. From the output, you can see the model has correctly identified the action as *hitting baseball*.

The video in the last example shows the final home run in the Oakland Athletics' 20-game winning streak. This event was further made famous and found a place in the data science hall of fame because of its portrayal in the 2009 movie *Moneyball*. The movie stars Brad Pitt and Jonah Hill and portrays the first use of data science in sports. In the film, data science has come to the rescue of a failing ball club. In the movie, data science is credited for the team being the first in history to win 20 straight games.

As you can see, our ability to analyze video has become quite powerful in a very short time. Let's revisit what we are able to do. We can now index video for objects, faces, and actions. This is all quite powerful, but Google has taken this a step further. Google has developed a new Video Intelligence API that can do all that and more. We will cover this new API in the next section.

# Exploring the Video Intelligence API

Google has developed a new service called the *Video Intelligence API* (VIAPI) that is capable of indexing video in many areas. The API currently has several features, outlined in the following list:

*Label detection*
Attempts to label the scene.

*Shot detection*
Detects when the camera shot has changed.

*Explicit content detection*
Detects if content is not suitable for work (NSFW).

*Speech transcription*
Transcribes the speech in the video.

*Object tracking*
Detects the objects in a scene.

*Text detection*
Detects and reads the text. You will need to consult the documentation to learn what languages it can transcribe.

*Logo detection*
Detects the presence of logos or symbols.

*Celebrity detection*
Can identify the faces of celebrities in many different areas.

The Video Intelligence API and services are all available through a GUI interface. This can be very useful if you are just doing one-off tests or need to process a small number of videos. If you need to develop a full workflow, you will need the API portion, which we will cover shortly.

The really great thing about this is that Google provides 1,000 free minutes of these services per month. That may seem like a lot, but keep in mind there are 1,440 minutes in a day. One thousand minutes a month equates to roughly 33 minutes a day. If you used all of the features in the API service, you would be looking at spending $0.70/minute, which equates to $30,000 a month for full-time video analysis on all services for a single video. Keep in mind that those prices reflect computational use and expenditures.

You could always instantiate a powerful GPU server on the GCP capable of doing the same workload for cheaper. However, if you need a full-time video indexer, this Video Intelligence API is likely not what you want. But if you just need something for one-offs or for short corporate training videos, for instance, then it is perfect.

The other great thing about the VIAPI is that it is accessible from the Google Cloud command line and infrastructure. For Example 6-7, we are going to look at using the VIAPI. This service is paid and does require that you have billing enabled on your account. As well, there is some credential setup that may seem awkward. At the time of writing, this product was still in early beta testing, and some of the workflow for setting up credentials will hopefully be simplified in the future.

*Example 6-7. Using the Video Intelligence Hub*

- Open the sample *Chapter_6_VIAPI.ipynb* and run the first cell. The commands in the first cell, shown here, install the Google Cloud tools and set up the environment:
```
!pip install google-cloud
!pip install google-cloud-videointelligence
!gcloud init
```
- Running that cell will install the dependencies and may require you to restart the runtime. After the install, the init will run, and the interface will question you on how you want to set up your account. We will continue to use the practical-ai-gcp project we set up earlier for various exercises. If you skipped that step, just create a new project with that ID.
- Next, we will go to the documentation page (*https://cloud.google.com/video-intelligence/docs/quickstart*) and set up the correct API permissions and credentials. This step requires some attention to detail, so you may need to work through this step a few times to get it right. Be patient.

- After setting up the credentials, you will be prompted to download a JSON credential file to your PC. We now need to upload that file with the following code:
  ```
  from google.colab import files
  uploaded = files.upload()
  ```

- Select the file you downloaded earlier and upload it to your Colab notebook by running the cell.

- With the service file credentials uploaded, we can now move on to configuring the environment to use them with the following code:
  ```
  !export GOOGLE_APPLICATION_CREDENTIALS='{UPLOADED CREDENTIALS FILE}.json'
  ```

- You can copy the filename from the cell output that uploaded the file earlier. Then paste the name into the spot labeled *Uploaded Credentials File.*

- Now we can move to the last cell and the very simple code to analyze a video with VIAPI, shown here:
  ```
  !gcloud ml video detect-labels gs://cloud-ml-sandbox/video/chicago.mp4
  ```

- The output of that simple call is a JSON file. An abridged version is shown here:
  ```
  {
    "name": "us-west1.104032612573769453",
    "metadata": {
      "@type": "type.googleapis.com/google.cloud.videointelligence.v1...",
      ...
    "done": true,
    "response": {
      "@type": "type.googleapis.com/google.cloud.videointelligence.v1...",
      "annotationResults": [
        {
          ...
        }
      ]
    }
  }
  ```

- The annotation results from the output provide more details about what is identified in the video. If you run this video, you will see results such as roads, cities, and geographical features.

The VIAPI also allows you to call the service using REST requests. The Google docs provide more information on how to access the service endpoints.

Hopefully, you can appreciate how easy it is to analyze a video to extract information. Video provides another way for our AI to contextualize information in terms of time. This has been used to recognize actions more effectively, but it also works for other forms of context like language. While the current VIAPI is primarily vision-based, meaning it consumes only image frames, audio and action processing is emerging. Over the coming weeks and months, we can expect more use of time context for things like action recognition and even understanding the sound or speech in video.

While it remains to be seen how popular the VIAPI will be, it certainly will influence many aspects of our lives. We will talk about those impacts and more in the last section of this chapter.

## Conclusion

Understanding the content of video has many applications, including security, safety, health, sports, and so on. Continuing with the world's infatuation with video, video indexing of content will likely be one of the fastest-growing AI trends in the next decade. In this chapter, we saw how relatively easy it is to build powerful models to determine content automatically.

In the chapter exercises, we were able to extract objects, recognize faces, and understand actions. This is only the start of what will be possible in the near future. We could then potentially take those actions, in addition to voice, as input into our AI systems, allowing AI to understand not just voice and language but also body and gesture communication. We often forget the importance of our body language and gestures when communicating.

Google is already investing a lot in video AI applications. Through this investment, services like the VIAPI and TF Hub can provide powerful out-of-the-box applications to companies looking for video AI solutions. This investment has also made these services relatively easy to consume, and this is a strong indication that Google expects broad appeal in the future.

From video analysis, we now move on to generating new content. AI generation of content has broad appeal across many, many applications and services, from creating fake news and artwork to faux celebrity faces. Generating content with AI is exploding and is the focus of our next chapter.

# CHAPTER 7

# Generators in the Cloud

Creativity and the generation of new content were once the litmus test for true intelligence and what we thought consciousness may resemble. As it turns out, we were wrong. Creating "new" content isn't that hard. In fact, we have created new content many times in previous chapters either as an effect or intent. Deep learning itself has made it possible to create new content across a wide variety of domains, from generating fake text from a chatbot to posting fake news on the web.

The explosion of deep learning has manifested many forms of content generation. Ironically, content generation systems are rarely the work of a single network and are often system trained in pairs or adversarially. We have already seen this with encoder/decoder architectures used for Seq2Seq learning. As we will see in this chapter, there are many other forms of adversarial learning to generate content.

It may seem that creating new content just for the purpose of creating new content would have a narrow appeal. Indeed, the ability to understand how content is created provides many insights into the domain problem itself, allowing us to tune new inputs and features in our models and ultimately how we understand data. As we will see, these types of insights have given us the ability to create things we've only dreamed of.

Generating content with AI is currently seen as the fastest-growing area of deep learning, an area we will focus on in this chapter. We will start by looking at content creation with generators, or what is typically coined *adversarial learning*. This type of learning falls under a broader category of unsupervised learning.

We will begin our discussion of what unsupervised and adversarial learning is by building an autoencoder and a variational autoencoder (VAE). From there we move back to the GAN, where we learn how to train a GAN on images. From there we build on our understanding of GANs and move on to examples of Pix2Pix and

CycleGAN, GAN variations that provide powerful content generators. Finally, we revisit the concept of attention and see how it can be used in the Self-Attention GAN.

Here is a brief summary of the main concepts we will cover in this chapter:

- Unsupervised Learning with Autoencoders
- Generative Adversarial Network
- Exploring the World of Generators
- Attention and the Self-Attention GAN

# Unsupervised Learning with Autoencoders

Our journey thus far has been centered on supervised learning, that is, training networks to learn on labeled data. The real fun begins when we train on data with no labels. Training on data that isn't labeled is called *unsupervised learning*. You may think that training on data with no labels would be very hard. Indeed, that was the perception for many years. It was a perception that demanded that anything worth learning be labeled/classified first. Unsupervised learning flips this perception on its head by first learning the representation or latent space in data.

We often refer to the *latent space* in data when talking about generations. The latent space is the space between data points and/or features. The great strength of deep learning networks is the ability to map the latent space in data. Thus, if we have two data points labeled X and Z but no other data, the latent space in this example might be denoted Y, the area between X and Z.

If this is still fuzzy, consider a historical example: the explorer and evolutionist Charles Darwin, who first discovered and detailed the concept of biological species in his work *On the Origin of Species* (1859). Darwin would go on to explain that various animals, while visually similar, may still be quite different species. He developed this idea by learning the specific traits of each animal and then using those learned traits to classify animals more effectively.

From Darwin's research, we could then work backward, concluding that animals evolved into their species. Understanding a species' evolution is like understanding or mapping the latent space in its evolution. We have been able to archaeologically discover some of those gaps or missing links in humans, allowing us to fill in more gaps in the knowledge of our evolution.

In unsupervised learning, your network/AI is just like Darwin. Instead of using some assumed label, the student tries to learn the representation or how key traits may map across the latent space. Then, based on that knowledge, it can use that mapping to define its own classes. The model or network can then learn to categorize data based on those classes and from that even learn to generate like representations. It is that ability to generate like representations that empowers our ability to generate new content with deep learning networks.

Supervised learning is now often used to teach deep learning to newcomers. It just seems to be a more natural way to teach and learn the subject. Before that, though, it used to be standard to teach deep learning through autoencoders first. Autoencoders use a very simple form of unsupervised learning. Now that you have, or should have, a comfortable understanding of deep learning, we can focus more on how it can be applied to deep learning with autoencoders.

Autoencoders use unsupervised learning to learn representation of an input into a lower dimensional space, or what we call an embedding or encoding.. We have already worked with autoencoders in three forms: first, in NLP when we looked at the encoder/decoder architecture; second, when we used embedding layers to understand word similarity; and third, when we discovered transformers like BERT that use encoder/decoder architectures.

Autoencoders learn to rebuild the original representation from that learned lower form. This is illustrated in Figure 7-1. In the figure, we can see that the input is fed into an encoder section of the network. This encoder reduces the input into a concise lower form. For example, we may take an input image of 28 × 28 pixels or 784 input dimensions down to 128 or fewer intermediary dimensions. From that lower space, the network then uses its decoder portion to rebuild the representation back to the original, or at least it tries to. Based on that generated image, we can then determine an amount of error or loss. This is the same loss we can push back and use to train the network. The network thus learns to build a better representation of the original. It is that learned lower intermediary form or latent representation that we can use to denote the object itself.

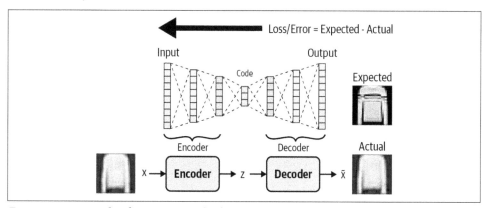

*Figure 7-1. Example of an autoencoder learning*

In the next collection of exercises, we look at the progression from plain and simple autoencoders to variational autoencoders. Variational autoencoders learn not only the latent representation but also a distribution that describes that space. Then we will finish with GANs.

All of these techniques fall under unsupervised learning, which can be further sub-classed to the area called *adversarial learning* and sometimes *self-supervised learning*. The term *adversarial* was coined from the practice of using two competing sides of a network or entire networks. For Example 7-1, we look at the vanilla autoencoder and basic unsupervised/adversarial learning.

*Example 7-1. Understanding autoencoders*

- Open *Chapter_7_AE_VAE_GAN.ipynb* and run the code blocks up to and including the Constants code block, shown here:
  ```
  TRAIN_BUF=60000
  BATCH_SIZE=512
  TEST_BUF=10000
  DIMS = (28,28,1)
  N_TRAIN_BATCHES =int(TRAIN_BUF/BATCH_SIZE)
  N_TEST_BATCHES = int(TEST_BUF/BATCH_SIZE)
  ```

- The top blocks of code just do the typical imports and other setup. Most of this should be familiar to you by now.

- Next we will start by importing our sample dataset. We will be using the MNIST Fashion dataset. While it can be fun to try and train on diverse sets of data, it is better to learn by training on the same set. The code to load, normalize, and batch the fashion dataset is shown here:
  ```
  (train_images, train_labels), (test_images, test_labels) =
    tf.keras.datasets.fashion_mnist.load_data()

  train_images = train_images.reshape(
    train_images.shape[0], 28, 28, 1).astype("float32") / 255.0
  test_images = test_images.reshape(
    test_images.shape[0], 28,     28, 1).astype("float32") / 255.0

  train_dataset = (
      tf.data.Dataset.from_tensor_slices(train_images)
      .shuffle(TRAIN_BUF)
      .batch(BATCH_SIZE)
  )
  test_dataset = (
      tf.data.Dataset.from_tensor_slices(test_images)
      .shuffle(TEST_BUF)
      .batch(BATCH_SIZE)
  )
  ```

- There are a couple of things to note about the last code section. The first is the way in which we reshape the data to 28 × 28 × 1 instead of 28 × 28. We are doing this to support convolutional input. Second, we can see that the data is getting shuffled and batched according to our previous constant settings. That means that 60,000 images will be used for training and 10,000 images for testing.

- The next couple of code blocks create the classnames and output examples from the class. We have seen this code before, so we won't need to revisit it here. Figure 7-2 shows the output from these cells before we add noise.

*Figure 7-2. Raw fashion dataset without noise*

- It can be difficult to visualize the learning experience, so to better demonstrate this, we are going to add noise to the input images. Remember, our ultimate goal is for the network to learn the original representations and generate them. We add the noise and output the results as shown in Figure 7-2 with the following code:

```
noise = augmenters.SaltAndPepper(0.1)
seq_object = augmenters.Sequential([noise])

train_x_n = seq_object.augment_images(train_images * 255) / 255
test_x_n = seq_object.augment_images(test_images * 255) / 255

plot_data(25, train_x_n, train_labels)
plot_data(25, test_x_n, test_labels)
```

- That last step may take a few minutes. We are, after all, adding random noise to 70,000 images. The result is shown in Figure 7-3.

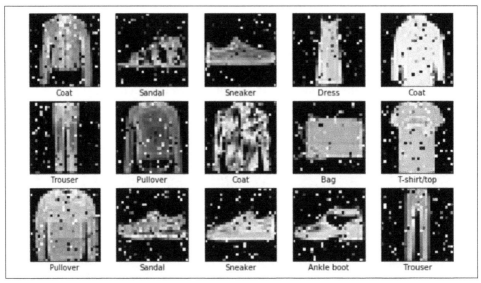

*Figure 7-3. Raw fashion dataset with noise*

- Now we need to create the two sides to our adversarial encoder/decoder network. The first side we create is the encoder, and it is quite similar to a typical classifier/regressor network. Instead of outputting a single classification, however, this network only narrows to some middle or latent representation. In a supervised problem, we may narrow the output to 10, one for each class. But our output size of 10 is based on a simplistic label we used to define classes. In an encoder, we allow the network to learn some middle representation and then use that to rebuild the original. From the latent view, the network's second side, the decoder, is constructed. The decoder generates what it thinks should be the original. The full code for this is shown here:

```
input_layer = Input(shape=(28, 28, 1))

encoded_layer1 = layers.Conv2D(64, (3, 3), activation='relu',
                               padding='same')(input_layer)
encoded_layer1 = layers.MaxPool2D( (2, 2), padding='same')(encoded_layer1)
encoded_layer2 = layers.Conv2D(32, (3, 3), activation='relu',
                               padding='same')(encoded_layer1)
encoded_layer2 = layers.MaxPool2D( (2, 2), padding='same')(encoded_layer2)
encoded_layer3 = layers.Conv2D(16, (3, 3), activation='relu',
                               padding='same')(encoded_layer2)
latent_view    = layers.MaxPool2D( (2, 2), padding='same')(encoded_layer3)

decoded_layer1 = layers.Conv2D(16, (3, 3), activation='relu',
```

```
                    padding='same')(latent_view)
decoded_layer1 = layers.UpSampling2D((2, 2))(decoded_layer1)
decoded_layer2 = layers.Conv2D(32, (3, 3), activation='relu',
                    padding='same')(decoded_layer1)
decoded_layer2 = layers.UpSampling2D((2, 2))(decoded_layer2)
decoded_layer3 = layers.Conv2D(64, (3, 3),
                                activation='relu')(decoded_layer2)
decoded_layer3 = layers.UpSampling2D((2, 2))(decoded_layer3)
#output layer
output_layer   = layers.Conv2D(1, (3, 3), padding='same')(decoded_layer3)
```

- Notice that in the decoder, we need to upsample the data after convolution. Normally, when breaking down an image for classification, we downsample pool data after convolution, but in this case we do the reverse.

- After the model sides and layers are constructed, we can move on to building the model and compiling it, as shown in the following code:

```
model = Model(input_layer, output_layer)
model.compile(optimizer='adam', loss='mse')
model.summary()
#--- Output ---
Model: "model"
```

| Layer (type) | Output Shape | Param # |
|---|---|---|
| input_1 (InputLayer) | [(None, 28, 28, 1)] | 0 |
| conv2d (Conv2D) | (None, 28, 28, 64) | 640 |
| max_pooling2d (MaxPooling2D) | (None, 14, 14, 64) | 0 |
| conv2d_1 (Conv2D) | (None, 14, 14, 32) | 18464 |
| max_pooling2d_1 (MaxPooling2 | (None, 7, 7, 32) | 0 |
| conv2d_2 (Conv2D) | (None, 7, 7, 16) | 4624 |
| max_pooling2d_2 (MaxPooling2 | (None, 4, 4, 16) | 0 |
| #END ENCODER | | |
| #START DECODER conv2d_3 (Conv2D) | (None, 4, 4, 16) | 2320 |
| up_sampling2d (UpSampling2D) | (None, 8, 8, 16) | 0 |
| conv2d_4 (Conv2D) | (None, 8, 8, 32) | 4640 |
| up_sampling2d_1 (UpSampling2 | (None, 16, 16, 32) | 0 |

| conv2d_5 (Conv2D) | (None, 14, 14, 64) | 18496 |
|---|---|---|
| up_sampling2d_2 (UpSampling2 | (None, 28, 28, 64) | 0 |
| conv2d_6 (Conv2D) | (None, 28, 28, 1) | 577 |

```
=================================================================
Total params: 49,761
Trainable params: 49,761
Nontrainable params: 0
```

- You can see the model summary has been split where the encoder and decoder architectures meet. Notice at this point how big the representation of the latent or middle view is (4 × 4 × 16).

- Training this example can be broken down into two lines of simple code—deceptively simple code. We will go over each line in detail to highlight their importance. The first line of code is shown below:

```
early_stopping = EarlyStopping(monitor='val_loss', min_delta=0, patience=10,
                               verbose=5, mode='auto')
```

- In that single line, we set up an early stopping monitor that watches the validation/test loss. If the test loss becomes stable, the training quits.

- The second line of code is where the model is trained, but there are several parameters we need to understand in detail. Shown here is the model training code:

```
history = model.fit(train_x_n, train_images, epochs=20, batch_size=2048,
                    validation_data=(test_x_n, test_images),
                    callbacks=[early_stopping])
```

- The key thing to notice here is that the model is fed the training images that have been noised train_x_n as the X, with the Y or expected output to be the raw training images themselves. In essence, we still treat the model as supervised, except the expected labeled output is the raw images we first loaded. Therefore, our model learns not only what the expected representation should look like, but also what to do when it doesn't.

- Let the sample train for the 20 epochs, and after it is complete, run the last cell block to test and show some sample output:

```
n = np.random.randint(0,len(test_images)-25)
preds = model.predict(test_x_n[n:n+25])

preds = preds.reshape(-1, 28, 28, 1)
plot_data(25, preds, test_labels[n:n+25])
```

- Running this cell will generate output similar to Figure 7-4. A couple of things to note are that we are feeding into noised test images `test_x_n` and that the output of those images needs to be slightly reshaped for our modified `plot_data` function.

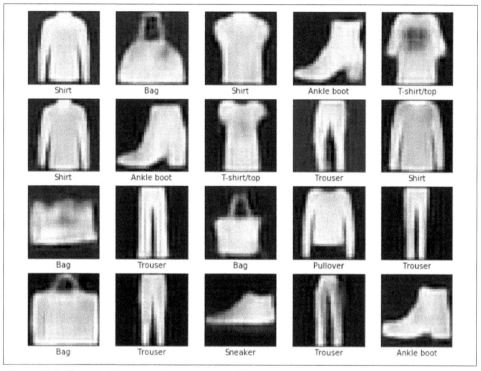

*Figure 7-4. Denoised output from autoencoder*

Notice that in the sample generated output, the network was able to reconstruct the fashions without the noise even though the network was being tested on images with the noise. This shows that the network learned what the images should look like without the noise. Now, we added the noise to make this demonstration more visual, but it is important to realize the noise doesn't have to be there. What's more, the noise can be interpreted as noise or perhaps as another signal of data entirely. While latent signal noise isn't something we often associate with images, it may be more helpful to think of it as noise in sound or music. For example, a single instrument played in an orchestra could be defined as a specific signal. Could we then use the same autoencoder procedure to remove that single instrument from a final track? We likely could.

There are a number of examples of research being done with autoencoders and GANs to generate or modify music/sound. While the research has been promising, it often fails due to poor representations of music. Music is, after all, not just a single representation in a single point in time like an image. Music and sound are representations across time, which means most music models are fun to play with but are nowhere near as powerful as the image equivalents. This single added dimension of time seems to complicate problems immensely. Of course, we are working on that, but the pace is considerably slower than other research.

The autoencoding process we just looked at works well for all manner of data and applications. It can be used to map and reduce large feature sets into categories, not unlike the embeddings we used in NLP. Autoencoders have become a backbone for how we understand embeddings. They have also become an essential part in dimensionality reduction and feature extraction for larger data problems. While raw autoencoders, ones that compare raw pixel values for differences, are effective, they lack the ability to capture the essence of something. We will look at how we can do that with variational autoencoders in the next section.

## Mapping the Latent Space with VAE

Raw autoencoders learn by capturing the differences in pixel values between the input or test and generated images. While this system is effective, as we saw, it lacks the finesse to understand the true essence or latent representation of the data. How we describe the essence of anything depends on our field of study. For our purposes, let's consider one of the purest fields, math. In math, we often refer to the essence of something as a *data distribution*. In Figure 7-5, the image shown is a probability density distribution that was captured from a sample of data.

Generating a probability distribution from data allows us to map across the data representation and understand those latent spaces. In Figure 7-5, we can see two distributions, one defined for the shoe and the other for the sweater. For this simple example, the distribution are shown in two dimensions, but we often consider much larger dimensions.

Essentially, anything that we define as data can be described as a distribution as well. Therefore, if we can learn the distribution that generated the image, we likely have a better ability to generate a new image. Indeed, that is the case, and this one concept will carry us through the rest of the chapter.

The problem we then face is calculating the error or loss between distributions. As it turns out, mathematicians have already solved this using something called the *Kullback–Leibler* divergence, or just KL divergence. This is also demonstrated in Figure 7-5, where we can see the divergence is getting measured between image distributions. The actual visualization of the KL divergence would look much different. However, you can still appreciate that there is a difference between both, and we can indeed measure that difference.

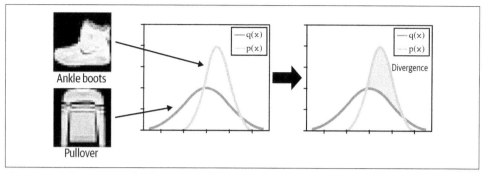

*Figure 7-5. Measuring the divergence between image distributions*

Figure 7-6 shows how the encoder/decoder architecture is updated to reflect that we are now using a distribution as the learned middle representation. Since a distribution is now the middle, we stick with the standard parameters that describe a normal or Gaussian distribution. The normal distribution is generally the most common and often the go-to for us to use. The parameters we use to describe a normal distribution are mu (u) or the mean, and sigma (s) or the standard deviation (variance). You can see that those two parameters are fed into the decoder, along with a new sample (E) generated from the distribution parameters mu and sigma.

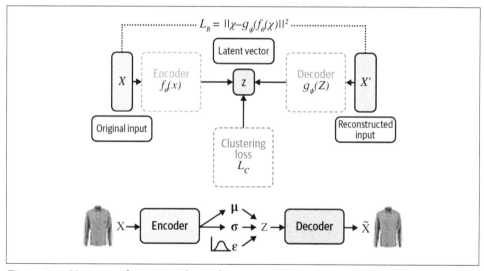

*Figure 7-6. Variational autoencoder architecture explained*

In Example 7-2 we look at how a variational autoencoder (VAE) is constructed and then discuss how that knowledge can be used to understand the latent mappings.

*Example 7-2. Mapping latent spaces with VAE*

- Open *Chapter_7_AE_VAE_GAN.ipynb* and run the code blocks up to and including the VAE class, as shown in the following code:

```python
class VAE(tf.keras.Model):
    def __init__(self, **kwargs):
        super(VAE, self).__init__()
        self.__dict__.update(kwargs)
        self.enc = tf.keras.Sequential(self.enc)
        self.dec = tf.keras.Sequential(self.dec)

    def encode(self, x):
        mu, sigma = tf.split(self.enc(x), num_or_size_splits=2, axis=1)
        return ds.MultivariateNormalDiag(loc=mu, scale_diag=sigma)

    def reparameterize(self, mean, logvar):
        eps = tf.random.normal(shape=mean.shape)
        return eps * tf.exp(logvar * 0.5) + mean

    def reconstruct(self, x):
        mu, _ = tf.split(self.enc(x), num_or_size_splits=2, axis=1)
        return self.decode(mu)

    def decode(self, z):
        return self.dec(z)

    def compute_loss(self, x):
        q_z = self.encode(x)
        z = q_z.sample()
        x_recon = self.decode(z)
        p_z = ds.MultivariateNormalDiag(
          loc=[0.] * z.shape[-1], scale_diag=[1.] * z.shape[-1]
          )
        kl_div = ds.kl_divergence(q_z, p_z)
        latent_loss = tf.reduce_mean(tf.maximum(kl_div, 0))
        recon_loss = tf.reduce_mean(
          tf.reduce_sum(tf.math.square(x - x_recon), axis=0))

        return recon_loss, latent_loss

    def compute_gradients(self, x):
        with tf.GradientTape() as tape:
            loss = self.compute_loss(x)
        return tape.gradient(loss, self.trainable_variables)

    @tf.function
    def train(self, train_x):
        gradients = self.compute_gradients(train_x)
```

```
        self.optimizer.apply_gradients(zip(gradients,
                                    self.trainable_variables))
```

- It may take a few minutes to run the code, so take that time to review the VAE class in detail. Pay particular attention to the `compute_loss` function. Notice that loss is calculated in two parts, the reconstruction loss and the latent loss. The latent loss is essentially the KL divergence. This means our model is now training to reduce the reconstruction and latent losses equally. Notice the `ds.MultivariateNormalDiag` function as well. This function generates the distribution based on the mean (mu) and standard deviation (sigma) parameters.

- The next block of code constructs the encoding and decoding layers, shown here:

```
N_Z = 2
encoder = [
    tf.keras.layers.InputLayer(input_shape=DIMS),
    tf.keras.layers.Conv2D(
        filters=32, kernel_size=3, strides=(2, 2), activation="relu"
    ),
    tf.keras.layers.Conv2D(
        filters=64, kernel_size=3, strides=(2, 2), activation="relu"
    ),
    tf.keras.layers.Flatten(),
    tf.keras.layers.Dense(units=N_Z*2),
]

decoder = [
    tf.keras.layers.Dense(units=7 * 7 * 64, activation="relu"),
    tf.keras.layers.Reshape(target_shape=(7, 7, 64)),
    tf.keras.layers.Conv2DTranspose(
        filters=64, kernel_size=3, strides=(2, 2),
        padding="SAME", activation="relu"
    ),
    tf.keras.layers.Conv2DTranspose(
        filters=32, kernel_size=3, strides=(2, 2),
        padding="SAME", activation="relu"
    ),
    tf.keras.layers.Conv2DTranspose(
        filters=1, kernel_size=3, strides=(1, 1),
        padding="SAME", activation="sigmoid"
    ),
]
```

- Skipping past building the layers, we can see that the VAE model is built with the encoder/decoder and Adam optimizer:

```
optimizer = tf.keras.optimizers.Adam(1e-3)
model = VAE(
    enc = encoder,
    dec = decoder,
```

```
        optimizer = optimizer,
)
```

- We will skip past the next plot reconstruction code for brevity's sake. After that, we come to the training code, as shown here:

```
n_epochs = 20
for epoch in range(n_epochs):
    for batch, train_x in tqdm(
        zip(range(N_TRAIN_BATCHES), train_dataset), total=N_TRAIN_BATCHES
    ):
        model.train(train_x)
    loss = []
    for batch, test_x in tqdm(
        zip(range(N_TEST_BATCHES), test_dataset), total=N_TEST_BATCHES
    ):
        loss.append(model.compute_loss(train_x))
    losses.loc[len(losses)] = np.mean(loss, axis=0)

    display.clear_output()
    print(
        "Epoch: {} | recon_loss: {} | latent_loss: {}".format(
            epoch, losses.recon_loss.values[-1],
            losses.latent_loss.values[-1]
        )
    )
    plot_reconstruction(model, example_data)
```

- The training code runs through the image batches and trains on each batch for the total number of epochs, n_epochs. After each training loop, we can see that a test loop is run and the test losses are recorded.

- As you run the training cell, the output will be generated. The output shows the original data beside the reconstructed data and test samples. The images may appear to line up in some parts but not in others. This is just coincidence.

- While we created a middle layer–simplified representation in our previous raw autoencoder, being able to visualize what that space looked like wasn't practical. With a VAE, however, we can now see what simple changes the distribution parameters make to the output. Figure 7-7 shows a grid of the mapped image distributions across our entire learned space. The code to generate the output in Figure 7-7 is shown here:

```
nx = ny =10
meshgrid = np.meshgrid(np.linspace(-3, 3, nx), np.linspace(-3, 3, ny))
meshgrid = np.array(meshgrid).reshape(2, nx*ny).T
x_grid = model.decode(meshgrid)
x_grid = x_grid.numpy().reshape(nx, ny, 28,28, 1)

canvas = np.zeros((nx*28, ny*28))
for xi in range(nx):
```

```
    for yi in range(ny):
        canvas[xi*28:xi*28+28, yi*28:yi*28+28] = x_grid[xi,
                              yi,:,:,:].squeeze()
fig, ax = plt.subplots(figsize=(10,10))
ax.matshow(canvas, cmap=plt.cm.Greys)
ax.axis('off')
```

- Run the cell and spend some time examining the output. Notice that the bottom line is of a similar visual class, but as you move up the plot, this changes dramatically.

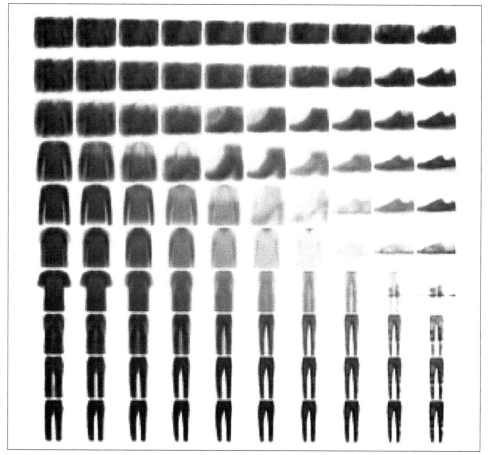

*Figure 7-7. Displaying the latent space in a VAE*

Looking at the latent space of a network brain can give you a whole new understanding of how models learn. Notice in Figure 7-7 that the model gets very dim in areas with major changes across classes. You can see this at the intersection of several classes (shoes, shirts, trousers, and so on) in the middle right of the plot. In simple terms, those gray or lighter areas are suggestions of confusion or indecision. Those are areas for which the model has difficulty outputting a single correct answer. Likely, over time and with much more training, our model would make those gray areas darker.

What makes a VAE so truly exciting is the ability to learn the essence of our data. The VAE is learning the distribution of the data and how to map across that distribution. That gives us the ability to generate not only known data but also never-before-seen data. Being able to map our understanding across the latent space is what gives us the ability to add glasses to a face or swap the face entirely. While this is possible with VAE variations, a better method is the generative adversarial network, which we look at next.

## Generative Adversarial Network

We already looked at the generative adversarial network when we explored image generation in Example 3-11. At that time we learned that a GAN is a generator, or what we called a *forger*. The forger tried to construct a good-enough fake that the critic or discriminator would believe it was real. Hopefully, this structure sounds more familiar now, and the keen among you may realize that a GAN is nothing more than an inverted autoencoder. Figure 7-8 shows the architecture and function of the GAN. Notice that the generator generates images alongside real images and both are presented to the discriminator. In turn the discriminator determines a loss for the error when predicting a real image as well as the loss for predicting a fake. Both networks work in tandem trying to both learn and out predict the other. In so doing, they both get better, and eventually you get a really good discriminator as well as a good generator. That is the general idea, but it's not always so easy to balance.

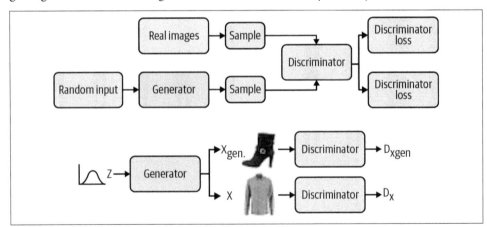

*Figure 7-8. Architecture and flow of the GAN*

We can break down a GAN in terms of an autoencoder to help us understand and familiarize the architecture more quickly. First, the discriminator is really the same as the encoder side of an autoencoder. Both perform the same function, and the added benefit here is that the discriminator also becomes a very good and useful classifier on its own. Second, the generator is the decoder half of an AE. The generator learns to create a passable replica from nothing, not unlike a decoder. It could be argued that a decoder is given more information, but the roles are quite similar.

The mathematics of a GAN really all break down to matching/creating learned distributions. If you are still having some problems visualizing the difference between a distribution and a single value, consider a bag. We can visualize a bag as a distribution of data—not entirely random data, but data that follows some rules. Pulling from the bag, or what we will call *sampling*, produces a single value, a block, a shape, or perhaps an image. You could pull another value from the bag, and a different image may appear, but one that still follows the rules of the distribution. Previously, we defined those rules as mu and sigma parameters in normal distribution. The problem with that is that we assumed a normal distribution. While normal distributions are the most common, they are far from the only distribution. Fortunately, GANs ignore distributional parameters and instead are able to focus on the raw outputs and inputs.

Refer back to Figure 7-8 and notice that the loss is being calculated on the generated output and real image input. This is similar to a VAE but differs in that the sampling itself is from the generator. This is the part that is trying to learn the real distribution and how to generate a sample from it. In a VAE, the decoder, aka the generator, constructed samples from distribution parameters. With a GAN, the generator, aka the decoder, learns how to model the distribution and sample.

For the next exercise, we look at a more or less basic, or vanilla, GAN. A vanilla GAN is supposed to come with no bells and whistles, but our version has just a couple. One of them is the use of CNN layers. We typically denote convolutional GANs with a DCGAN name for dual convolutional GAN, not to be confused with a CGAN or conditional GAN, which we will review later. The GAN we look at in Example 7-3 is a vanilla GAN with convolution.

*Example 7-3. A Fashion GAN with convolution*

- Open *Chapter_7_AE_VAE_GAN.ipynb* and run the code blocks up to and including the GAN class. The GAN class is quite large, so we will just look at the `compute_loss` function code here:

```
def compute_loss(self, x):
        z_samp = tf.random.normal([x.shape[0], 1, 1, self.n_Z])

        x_gen = self.generate(z_samp)
        logits_x = self.discriminate(x)
```

```
logits_x_gen = self.discriminate(x_gen)

# losses of real with label "1"
disc_real_loss = gan_loss(logits=logits_x, is_real=True)
# losses of fake with label "0"
disc_fake_loss = gan_loss(logits=logits_x_gen, is_real=False)
disc_loss = disc_fake_loss + disc_real_loss

# losses of fake with label "1"
gen_loss = gan_loss(logits=logits_x_gen, is_real=True)

return disc_loss, gen_loss
```

- We can see in the `compute_loss` function that three loss functions are run. The first loss calculation determines the discriminator's loss, `disc_real_loss`, when determining a real image. We also need to determine the loss when inferring a fake generated image, `disc_fake_loss`. The third function is the generator loss, `gen_loss`, which measures the error in generated images. All three of these loss calculations use the `gan_loss` function shown here:

```
def gan_loss(logits, is_real=True):
    if is_real:
        labels = tf.ones_like(logits)
    else:
        labels = tf.zeros_like(logits)

    return tf.compat.v1.losses.sigmoid_cross_entropy(
        multi_class_labels=labels, logits=logits
    )
```

- Loss in the GAN, the `gan_loss`, is calculated based on how close the output matches. In a GAN, we use a true/false test: 1 for true and 0 for false or wrong. The `gan_loss` function uses this truth test to return the difference in truth, 0 or 1 and in between.

- With the basic GAN out of the way, we can move on to constructing the discriminator and generator with the following code:

```
N_Z = 64
# resembles a decoder architecture
generator = [
    tf.keras.layers.Dense(units=7 * 7 * 64, activation="relu"),
    tf.keras.layers.Reshape(target_shape=(7, 7, 64)),
    tf.keras.layers.Conv2DTranspose(
        filters=64, kernel_size=3, strides=(2, 2),
        padding="SAME", activation="relu"
    ),
    tf.keras.layers.Conv2DTranspose(
        filters=32, kernel_size=3, strides=(2, 2),
        padding="SAME", activation="relu"
    ),
```

```
        tf.keras.layers.Conv2DTranspose(
            filters=1, kernel_size=3, strides=(1, 1),
            padding="SAME", activation="sigmoid"
        ),
    ]

    # resembles an encoder architecture
    discriminator = [
        tf.keras.layers.InputLayer(input_shape=DIMS),
        tf.keras.layers.Conv2D(
            filters=32, kernel_size=3, strides=(2, 2), activation="relu"
        ),
        tf.keras.layers.Conv2D(
            filters=64, kernel_size=3, strides=(2, 2), activation="relu"
        ),
        tf.keras.layers.Flatten(),
        tf.keras.layers.Dense(units=1, activation=None),
    ]
```

- One thing you may notice is that the architecture for both models is quite different rather than just a mirror of itself in an autoencoder. In a GAN, we break that middle connection that defines an autoencoder. Instead we work with raw output, and thus our models can and in some ways need to be different. Notice that the discriminator is far simpler than the generator. This seems counterintuitive, but the reason for this is that the discriminator model will usually work better. The problem with this is that we need to maintain balance within a GAN and keep the discriminator in check with the generator. If we don't, the discriminator will learn faster than the generator, which in turn will block its ability to learn. A GAN works like climbing a ladder, first one side up and then the other. The process all breaks down when only one side goes up.

- In order to balance the learning, we create different optimizers with different learning rates, as the following code shows:

```
# optimizers
gen_optimizer = tf.keras.optimizers.Adam(0.001, beta_1=0.5)
disc_optimizer = tf.keras.optimizers.RMSprop(0.005)# train the model
model = GAN(
    gen = generator,
    disc = discriminator,
    gen_optimizer = gen_optimizer,
    disc_optimizer = disc_optimizer,
    n_Z = N_Z
)
```

- Notice that the generator optimizer is tuned to learn far more slowly than the discriminator optimizer. This is intentional and balances the GAN's ability to learn. A GAN is notoriously difficult to train, and this aspect of balance is key.

- The plot reconstruction and training code is all that remains. We have covered this code before, and it resembles the VAE, so we won't go over it again here. The output from training is shown in Figure 7-9. Notice that the generation of images is quite different. The image detail is more pronounced but more fuzzy in some localized areas.

*Figure 7-9. Generated output from a GAN*

GANs are really just an extension of a VAE with the ability to learn the essence or source distribution of a sample set. In a VAE, we limit ourselves to a particular distribution, like the normal. With a GAN, however, the generator learns the distribution no matter what it is. There are in fact many different distributions that can describe data that we define, and there are likely many more.

There are many other variations of GANs that use a number of techniques for varying the input, output, and the way content is generated. We will look at some other key variations, starting in the next section with image translation GANs.

# Exploring the World of Generators

Autoencoders and the VAE predate the GAN by many years. However, it wasn't until GANs were shown to be such useful generators with the ability to create such finely nuanced content that the whole art of creating generators became such a big thing. Now, generators like GANs and VAEs make news almost daily with some cool new photo, dance, or even video. While one can't deny how interesting generators are, it really is the flip side of the generator where all the power lies.

Techniques for mapping or understanding the latent space in the domain are wide and varied. There are many ways to learn that space, and the number of GAN variations is almost doubling yearly. With all those variations and approaches, it is difficult to make sense of it all or even know where to start. In the next section, we will try and break down the main generator learning path. From here you can decide what part of the path you need to travel to and perhaps where to get off and do your own thing. This path isn't broken down historically or intended to break up the technology by method/type, etc. The path is more of a suggestion you follow before you decide on your own path.

There are literally thousands of GAN variations for everything from picture to recipe generation. It can seem daunting, but it should also suggest amazing potential. Think of a GAN that you could teach/train to describe/generate some aspect of your job or life. Did you just think of a new use for a GAN?

# A Path for Exploring GANs

The upcoming list of GANs have been broken out by progression of difficulty, novelty, and real-world use. They may not all provide a practical application to everyone. However, keep an open mind, and try to look for alternate uses where possible. In this list, we start with where we have already been as a baseline:

*Autoencoder*
Make sure you understand this model well, especially the loss function. This entire model is becoming the veritable Swiss Army knife of deep learning, so learn it well.

*Variational autoencoder*
Understanding how this model learns gives us a basis for introducing the GAN. It can and has been shown to be just as successful as GANs for applications like aging photos.

*GAN*
The vanilla GAN is the cornerstone of all GANs, so again, learn this one well.

*DCGAN (dual convolutional GAN)*
Again, we already jumped ahead to this example training the Fashion MNIST data earlier. The only big difference here is the use of convolutional layers.

*CGAN (conditional GAN or VAE)*
A conditional GAN allows us to learn and train our generator/discriminator on conditions or attributes of the data. One such attribute, for instance, may be a person's age in photos. By mapping this attribute through the latent space, we can then generate images of different ages.

*WGAN (Wasserstein GAN)*
The main difference with this GAN is the method by which we calculate loss. In this GAN, we use something called Wasserstein distance, which is a better method of calculating distribution distance. The WGAN and DCGAN are quite common in a number of GANs now.

*CoGAN (coupled GANs) and DualGAN*
These models use two generators and two discriminators for paired/coupled learning. Doubling or growing models is a growing trend in deep learning. It seems that the ability to train models in tandem can be a powerful technique.

*StackGAN and ProGAN (progressive GANs)*

A stack GAN, like its name suggests, has GANs stacked one on top of the other. This is not unlike the CoGAN, but the modeling of loss is quite different. Continuing with this progressive growing is the ProGAN. The ProGAN is a GAN that builds itself up by progressively growing more layers.

*CycleGAN and Pix2Pix*

With previous GANs, the training was always trying to model the real image. The advent of the Pix2Pix GAN introduced a new concept of teaching a GAN to learn not only the latent space, but also how to transform from one latent space to another. Being able to transform across latent spaces becomes quite powerful, and we will take a special look at this method later in this chapter.

*SAGAN (Self-Attention GAN)*

This GAN is based more on the Transformer with attention architecture that we looked at with BERT. This form of GAN has been shown to have amazing potential, from conditional generation to transformation. We will take a special look at this type of GAN later in this chapter.

*StyleGAN*

The current state of the art is this form of GAN from Nvidia. One particular model, trained on celebrity photos, has been shown to be almost flawless. Figure 7-10 shows a number of examples generated with StyleGAN from the Nvidia source on the GitHub site (*https://github.com/NVlabs/stylegan*).

*Figure 7-10. StyleGAN-generated faces*

From faces to everything in between, generators enable us not only to create content, but also to understand that content better. Newer forms of GANs go one step further and work to transform that content from one understanding or latent representation to the next. We will explore how to apply those types of transformations in the next section.

## Translating Images with Pix2Pix and CycleGAN

Now that we understand generators, variations, and what is possible, it is time to look at some more practical applications. One such application is the translation of known or learned spaces to different learned spaces. We call this type of translation *paired* because the GAN is trained on target and input pairings. The target image is an image of a cityscape, and the expected input is a labeled version of the same image.

Figure 7-11 shows the input image on top and the target on the bottom. This may sound a bit confusing, so let's review. The input image will be the image that has been colored in blocks over the various regions of the cityscape. In the example, you can see the road is purple, cars are blue, trees and grass are green, and so on. The target image, the image we want the generator to output, is the actual cityscape image itself. The goal of our GAN is to generate that image from that blocky, colored input image.

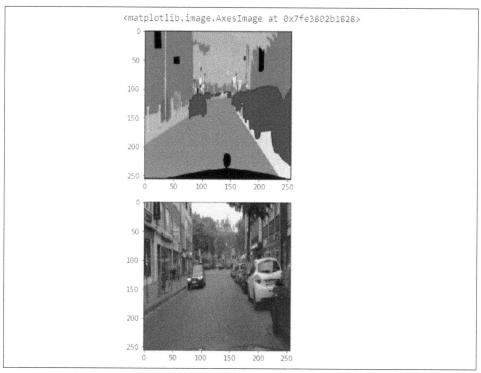

*Figure 7-11. CityScape Pix2Pix sample data*

To accomplish this translation magic, the basic GAN method and architecture will still work. The big change is a slight variation in the way we calculate the loss. The best way to observe this is to look at an example, such as Example 7-4.

*Example 7-4. Pix2Pix image translation*

- Open *Chapter_7_Pix2Pix.ipynb* and run all the code blocks. From the menu, select Runtime → Run All. This GAN can take a while to train, so let it run while you work through the exercise.

- Most of the code in this example is review, and we will cover only the critical parts here. The first part is loading the dataset with the following code:
```
_URL =
 'https://people.eecs.berkeley.edu/~tinghuiz/projects/pix2pix/datasets/
 cityscapes.tar.gz'

path_to_zip = tf.keras.utils.get_file('cityscapes.tar.gz',
                                       origin=_URL,
                                       extract=True)

PATH = os.path.join(os.path.dirname(path_to_zip), 'cityscapes/')
```

- That last block loads the CityScape Pix2Pix dataset from the Berkeley site. This dataset has been carefully constructed for this example, but there are plenty of other examples listed on the sample page.

- One thing we do in this example is a lot of upsampling and downsampling with convolution layers. As a result, we create two helper functions for upsampling and downsampling, shown here:
```
def downsample(filters, size, apply_batchnorm=True):
  initializer = tf.random_normal_initializer(0., 0.02)

  result = tf.keras.Sequential()
  result.add(
      tf.keras.layers.Conv2D(filters, size, strides=2, padding='same',
                             kernel_initializer=initializer,
                             use_bias=False))

  if apply_batchnorm:
    result.add(tf.keras.layers.BatchNormalization())

  result.add(tf.keras.layers.LeakyReLU())

  return result

def upsample(filters, size, apply_dropout=False):
  initializer = tf.random_normal_initializer(0., 0.02)
```

```
result = tf.keras.Sequential()
result.add(
  tf.keras.layers.Conv2DTranspose(filters, size, strides=2,
                                  padding='same',
                                  kernel_initializer=initializer,
                                  use_bias=False))

result.add(tf.keras.layers.BatchNormalization())

if apply_dropout:
    result.add(tf.keras.layers.Dropout(0.5))

result.add(tf.keras.layers.ReLU())

return result
```

- The upsample/downsample functions are used to move the data up and down a U network, or *UNet*. UNets, pictured in Figure 7-12, have been shown to make better generators because they are better able to sample up and down the latent distribution. It is as if the UNet learns to autoencode and rebuild the representation into its own form. We can see the full UNet architecture in the generator code shown here:

```
def Generator():
  inputs = tf.keras.layers.Input(shape=[256,256,3])

  down_stack = [
    downsample(64, 4, apply_batchnorm=False), # (bs, 128, 128, 64)
    downsample(128, 4), # (bs, 64, 64, 128)
    downsample(256, 4), # (bs, 32, 32, 256)
    downsample(512, 4), # (bs, 16, 16, 512)
    downsample(512, 4), # (bs, 8, 8, 512)
    downsample(512, 4), # (bs, 4, 4, 512)
    downsample(512, 4), # (bs, 2, 2, 512)
    downsample(512, 4), # (bs, 1, 1, 512)
  ]

  up_stack = [
    upsample(512, 4, apply_dropout=True), # (bs, 2, 2, 1024)
    upsample(512, 4, apply_dropout=True), # (bs, 4, 4, 1024)
    upsample(512, 4, apply_dropout=True), # (bs, 8, 8, 1024)
    upsample(512, 4), # (bs, 16, 16, 1024)
    upsample(256, 4), # (bs, 32, 32, 512)
    upsample(128, 4), # (bs, 64, 64, 256)
    upsample(64, 4), # (bs, 128, 128, 128)
  ]

  initializer = tf.random_normal_initializer(0., 0.02)
  last = tf.keras.layers.Conv2DTranspose(OUTPUT_CHANNELS, 4,
                                         strides=2,
```

```
                                                   padding='same',
                                                   kernel_initializer=initializer,
                                                   activation='tanh')
    # (bs, 256, 256, 3)

    x = inputs

    # Downsampling through the model
    skips = []
    for down in down_stack:
      x = down(x)
      skips.append(x)

    skips = reversed(skips[:-1])

    # Upsampling and establishing the skip connections
    for up, skip in zip(up_stack, skips):
      x = up(x)
      x = tf.keras.layers.Concatenate()([x, skip])

    x = last(x)

    return tf.keras.Model(inputs=inputs, outputs=x)
```

- All of this code represents a UNet architecture, as shown in Figure 7-12.

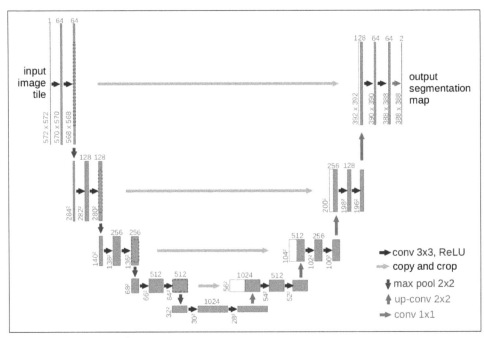

*Figure 7-12. UNet architecture*

- The other major change is the calculation and determination of loss. Figure 7-13 shows the loss calculation flowchart for the generator and discriminator. In the generator, loss is calculated based on the generated image and target image as well as the loss from the discriminator that is fed the input image and generated image. Conversely, with the discriminator, loss is calculated again on the real and fake. This time, however, the paired input image is also fed in as part of its real test. It therefore will learn what a real pairing looks like and what a fake pairing does not look like.

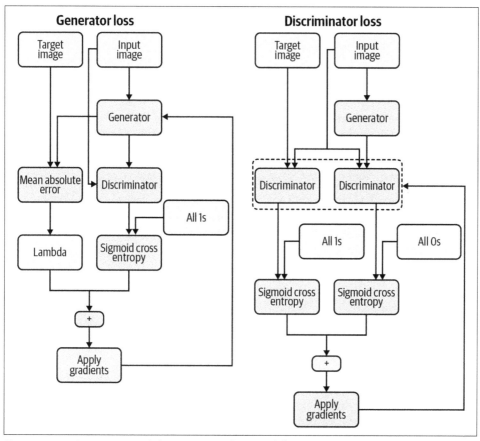

*Figure 7-13. Generator and discriminator loss workflows*

- The code that uses and applies the loss is shown here:

```
@tf.function
def train_step(input_image, target, epoch):
  with tf.GradientTape() as gen_tape, tf.GradientTape() as disc_tape:
    gen_output = generator(input_image, training=True)
```

```
disc_real_output = discriminator([input_image, target], training=True)
disc_generated_output = discriminator([input_image, gen_output],
                                      training=True)

gen_total_loss, gen_gan_loss, gen_l1_loss = generator_loss(
    disc_generated_output, gen_output, target)
disc_loss = discriminator_loss(disc_real_output, disc_generated_output)

generator_gradients = gen_tape.gradient(gen_total_loss,
                                        generator.trainable_variables)
discriminator_gradients = disc_tape.gradient(disc_loss,
                                             discriminator.trainable_variables)

generator_optimizer.apply_gradients(zip(generator_gradients,
                                        generator.trainable_variables))
discriminator_optimizer.apply_gradients(zip(discriminator_gradients,
                                            discriminator.trainable_variables))

with summary_writer.as_default():
    tf.summary.scalar('gen_total_loss', gen_total_loss, step=epoch)
    tf.summary.scalar('gen_gan_loss', gen_gan_loss, step=epoch)
    tf.summary.scalar('gen_l1_loss', gen_l1_loss, step=epoch)
    tf.summary.scalar('disc_loss', disc_loss, step=epoch)
```

- Note the use of `tf.GradientTape()`. Gradient tape is like an old ticker tape of gradients that have been applied or will be applied in backpropagation on the network model. Also note the way we record and track the loss using `tf.sum mary`. This method is used to log output for visualization in TensorBoard. We will look at using TensorBoard in a later example.

- The network can take several hours to train, so be patient. It also can be helpful to just sit and watch the training. Notice that the generated images often add lines to the road where there are none. You will also notice the absence of shadows or lighting, and in some cases you will see added shadows.

Image-to-image paired translation has all manner of practical applications. There have even been examples where a user can draw in real time and the image is fed into a generator. The generator then outputs what it has learned. This example has been shown to quickly render cats or even code HTML. The applications of this technique are likely endless, and we leave it up to you to pursue more on your own.

Now, paired translations are great, but what if we could apply this technique to unpaired data? This is what we will look at in the next section.

## Translating unpaired images with CycleGAN

With paired image learning, we are just extending the learning space the GAN has to learn. Ideally what we would like to do is train a model to do image-to-image or other forms of translation with no pairing. But how do you teach something to create something with no baseline or example? How do you teach a painter to paint a landscape, for instance?

As it turns out, this is something we tackle all the time. If an artist paints a landscape, the painting needs to look like a landscape. When we look at an object and infer what it is, we also understand what it is not. If you look at a dog, you see a dog, but you don't, for instance, see a cat or a giraffe—at least as you define it. Your brain is essentially doing internal classification by translating the image to thought and to speech all the time.

A good example of this internal translation process was suggested by the authors of the CycleGAN paper (*https://oreil.ly/Z3vv0*). They explained the process of translating images or text as being not unlike language translation. Consider translating a word from English to French and then back to English. The back-to-English translation at the end can be used to determine the consistency of the original translation. This back-and-forth translation is known as *cycle consistency* since you perform this procedure in cycles. Hence, we calculate the loss by determining the error in the first and second translation processes. The whole process is detailed more thoroughly in Example 7-5.

*Example 7-5. Image translation with CycleGAN*

- Open *Chapter_7_CycleGAN.ipynb* and run the whole sheet from the menu Runtime → Run All. Training times for this example can take a while.
- We will first load our sample data. For this example, we will use maps. This is a set of aerial map photos/tiles with street map tiles/images. There are a number of other sample datasets you can try (*https://oreil.ly/Dnq7O*). The code to load the data is shown here:

```
dataset, metadata = tfds.load('cycle_gan/maps',
                        with_info=True, as_supervised=True)

train_A, train_B = dataset['trainA'], dataset['trainB']
test_A, test_B = dataset['testA'], dataset['testB']
```

- We load the data into `train_A` and `train_B` datasets. `train_A` contains the aerial photos, and `train_B` contains the map view. Figure 7-14 shows the combined output from the results of the next several cells.

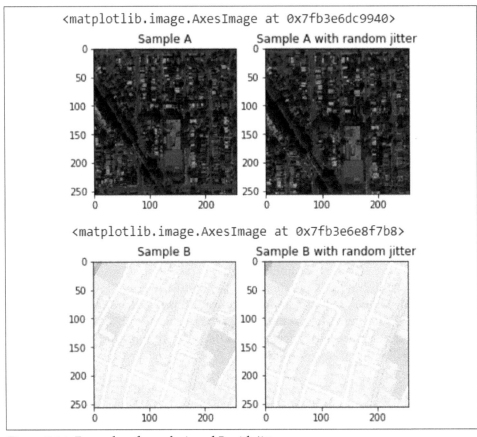

*Figure 7-14. Examples of sample A and B with jitter*

- Scroll down to the next block of code:

```
OUTPUT_CHANNELS = 3

generator_g = pix2pix.unet_generator(OUTPUT_CHANNELS,
                                      norm_type='instancenorm')
generator_f = pix2pix.unet_generator(OUTPUT_CHANNELS,
                                      norm_type='instancenorm')

discriminator_x = pix2pix.discriminator(norm_type='instancenorm',
                                        target=False)
discriminator_y = pix2pix.discriminator(norm_type='instancenorm',
                                        target=False)
```

- That last block of code loads the generator and discriminator models from the previous Pix2Pix examples. Notice that we load `generator_g` and `generator_y` as well as `discriminator_x` and `discriminator_y`. The two pairs are used to determine the forward/backward cycle consistency. This is a bit advanced, so further details may be found on the example itself.

- Continue reading and scrolling down through the code. Pay particular attention to the `train_step` function code, not shown here. `train_step` is used to calculate the loss, and this is where you can see how the forward/backward cycle consistency is calculated.

- Scroll down further to the train function, shown here:

```
def train(epochs, domain_A, domain_B, sample):
  for epoch in range(epochs):
    start = time.time()

    n = 0
    for image_x, image_y in tf.data.Dataset.zip((domain_A, domain_B)):
      train_step(image_x, image_y)
      if n % 10 == 0:
        clear_output(wait=True)
        print(epoch)
        generate_images(generator_g, sample)
      n+=1

    clear_output(wait=True)
    generate_images(generator_g, sample)

    if (epoch + 1) % 5 == 0:
      ckpt_save_path = ckpt_manager.save()
      print ('Saving checkpoint for epoch {} at {}'.format(epoch+1,
                                                ckpt_save_path))

    print ('Time taken for epoch {} is {} sec\n'.format(epoch + 1,
                                                time.time()-start))

train(EPOCHS, train_A, train_B, sample_A)
```

- The last line of code calls the function with the epochs and uses training set A (`train_A`) as the input and training set B (`train_B`) as the targets. We also throw in the sample from set A as our baseline for plotting. Figure 7-15 shows the sample output from training this example with set A as the inputs and set B as the targets, as well as with B as the inputs and A as the targets. The code to run that last example is shown below:

```
train(EPOCHS, train_B, train_A, sample_B)
```

- Notice that all we needed to do is reverse the targets and inputs.

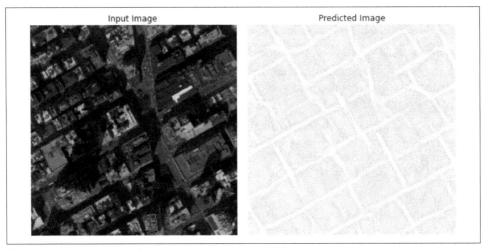

*Figure 7-15. Examples of training output*

Improvements are still being made to the CycleGAN, and it also has its own variations. This particular GAN shows the most promise for general real-world use in many applications, from medical imaging to geology. We use images here, but it is conceivable that other data types could be used. In the next section, we will look at further enhancements to a GAN that allow us to colorize and enhance a picture or video using an attention mechanism.

## Attention and the Self-Attention GAN

The Self-Attention GAN was developed to address issues in capturing global context. Convolutional layers, the ones often used in GANs, are great at isolating local context in images. However, they fail to capture global context or absolute positioning. We saw this in Chapter 3 when we developed the Fashionista AI. In that example, we discovered that the pooling we often do after convolutional layers removes spatial context. As it turns out, that spatial context made a big difference in training our AI. We were able to fix this somewhat by removing pooling, but in reality this is more of a hack. Convolutional layers are designed to work with pooling and can fall apart when removed.

To overcome these issues, the author of the original GAN paper, Ian Goodfellow, contributed to writing "Self-Attention Generative Adversarial Networks" (*https://oreil.ly/ Zxhxj*) with primary author Han Zhang. The paper was written to address the need for better capturing of global context. We saw when we addressed natural language problems that attention could be used to capture token context better. The authors had also read the "Attention Is All You Need" paper and concluded that they could also use the same mechanism in a GAN. They were right, and they found that coupling convolution with attention was far better at learning finer details.

At this point, it may be helpful to return to the CycleGAN and Pix2Pix examples from earlier sections in this chapter. In those examples, we can see the GAN architecture get impressive results. However, pay attention to the finer details in those examples. Be sure to compare those examples with our results in this section.

We didn't go into explicit detail on how attention works in Chapter 5 when we covered Transformers and attention and used BERT. Now that we have moved farther along, we can spend more time on attention itself. While we understand the concept of attention, or why we want to know how something attends to something else, attention mechanisms can be broken down further and used in a variety of forms and applications, as follows:

*Global (soft) versus local (hard) attention*
Global attention focuses on the relation, spatial or temporal, in the raw source. In an image, this would be pixel distance relationship or temporal distance in text. Local attention, on the other hand, is an internal mechanism that attends to the hidden states within the encoder/decoder mechanism. In an autoencoder, we would wrap this attention mechanism around the encoder/decoder translation layer.

*Soft versus hard attention*
Both of these methods refer to local attention and how they attend across the encoder/decoder layer. Soft attention encodes the hidden vector as a weighted sum, while hard attention uses the scores themselves to select a single state. The subtle difference is actually nontrivial, and the hard-attention internal classifier becomes nondifferentiable. That simply means we can't use automatic differentiation to discern the gradients needed for weight updates in backpropagation. Instead we employ complex mathematical techniques to get hard attention working.

*Hierarchical attention*
This was proposed to combine various attention mechanisms from forward to back, or vice versa, through the entire model in a hierarchical fashion.

*Self-Attention (SA)*
The concept here is to relate the input sequence to the embedding itself. Think of this as a combination of soft and hard (global and local) attention mechanisms. Said another way, a pixel in an input image using SA is attended to by the hidden state or intermediate vector. Think of the impact of this for a second. Using SA, we can understand the importance of any pixel relative to the value of the hidden middle state itself. Not only does this allow our network to learn what is more important to its internal representation, but it also gives it more room to learn the finer details.

Think about how you remember something. You may easily recall who was at a meeting, but can you recall what they were wearing? You can think of this as your brain's self-attention mechanism removing those less important details. If fashion is important to you, then you may very well have remembered what they were wearing. This is your brain's SA mechanism picking up that detail as important to your encoding of the meeting. Of course, our brains likely don't encode actual memories like this, but hopefully the analogy gets past your SA.

Training a full Self-Attention GAN model to do anything would take days on a GPU. It's not even practical on a CPU anymore. TensorFlow Processing Units, or TPUs, use performance enhancements in TF/Keras code that give an order-of-magnitude increase. At time of writing, an SAGAN that takes 45 days to train on a GPU may take two days on a TPU. Needless to say, this isn't really practical for us to look at training an example. Instead, like BERT, we will use a trained and customized SAGAN model that can do some powerful things. Before we get to that, though, let's understand in detail how self-attention works.

## Understanding Self-Attention

In this book, we assume you are first a programmer, or are more inclined to learn like one anyway. That means that while you may like math, it isn't your go-to for learning new concepts. Instead, your affinity in learning some new concepts is with code, and that is what we do here. For Example 7-6, we look at how attention works from just a code-first perspective.

*Example 7-6. Understanding Attention*

- Open *Chapter_7_Attention.ipynb* and run just the first cell. This will initialize the basic imports needed for this simple example.
- In this example, we are going to assume three four-vector inputs. You could visualize these as just four pixel (2 × 2) images that have been flattened and the values normalized. The code for this is shown here:
```
x = [
  [1., 0., 1., 0.], # Input 1
  [0., .5, 0., .5], # Input 2
  [.75, .75, .75, .75]  # Input 3
 ]
x = np.array(x)
```
- With self-attention, we assume every input has three latent representations: a key, query, and value. The key and value representations denote the context of the input, and query denotes the context when attended. In a neural network, these

values become the learned weights and often start randomized. For our contrived example, we have set them to predictable values, as shown in the following code:

```
w_key = [
  [1, 1, 1],
  [1, 1, 1],
  [1, 1, 1],
  [1, 1, 1]
]
w_query = [
  [1, 0, 1],
  [1, 0, 0],
  [0, 0, 1],
  [0, 1, 1]
]
w_value = [
  [2, 2, 2],
  [3, 3, 3],
  [4, 4, 4],
  [5, 5, 5]
]

w_key = np.array(w_key)
w_query = np.array(w_query)
w_value = np.array(w_value)
```

- The preceding w denotes that each array is a weight matrix and therefore the parameters that need to be learned. One thing to note is that the size of the weight matrices is set by the input batch size. In this simple example, there are three inputs in one batch.

- Following this, we create the derived keys, querys, and values tensors by applying the dot product (@) against the weight tensors for key, value, and query. The code to do this is shown here:

```
keys = x @ w_key
querys = x @ w_query
values = x @ w_value

print(keys)
print(querys)
print(values)
```

- After applying dot products to generate base element tensors, we can move on to calculating the attention scores using the query tensor dot product with the keys as shown here:

```
attn_scores = (querys @ keys.T)
print(attn_scores)
```

- Those raw scores essentially need to be normalized, and we will use the Softmax function to do that. Softmax is akin to determining the probability of one element occurring within all other elements in a tensor or vector. The code to produce the Softmax output is shown here:

```
attn_scores_softmax = tf.nn.softmax(attn_scores, axis=-1).numpy()
attn_scores_softmax = np.round(attn_scores_softmax, decimals=2)
print(attn_scores_softmax)
```

- After we calculate `attn_scores_softmax`, we use `np.round` to make the values easier to read. These scores denote the attention multiplier that should be used to attend the outputs.

- Before generating the attended outputs, however, we need to adjust the actual weights using the earlier values representation we generated. We can do that by using the following code:

```
weighted_values = values[:,None] * attn_scores_softmax.T[:,:,None]
print(weighted_values)
```

- This generates new value weights that we can apply to the inputs. The difference with these updated weights is that they have been attended. Calculating the outputs is shown here:

```
outputs = np.sum(weighted_values, axis=0)
print(outputs)
```

- The output of this whole operation is the updated outputs of the model with attention applied. You can think of this whole process as an attention layer. In fact, TF/Keras has various implementations of these types of layers. Keep in mind that in our trivial example the weights were just initialized and are the part that needs to be learned.

Self-attention itself is making its way into every form of deep learning networks. While it started out as being strictly for NLP problems, it quickly converted itself to images and then, naturally, to GANs. In our last example, the attention mechanism itself could be used as an added layer to your deep learning network. While training a full SAGAN may be interesting, it would hardly be practical. Instead, we will look at a more practical example of an SAGAN in the next section.

## Self-Attention for Image Colorization—DeOldify

Over the last half dozen years, deep learning has been advancing in apparent leaps and bounds, but nothing practical has arisen—nothing that developers or those so inclined could pick up and run with. For many, this was a testament to how difficult deep learning actually was. Many believed that you needed a PhD to obtain any level of success at all. That obviously isn't true anymore, as we have completed many complex exercises in this book. Now we even have programmers going beyond mere implementation and building novel applications.

One such instance of a programmer going beyond mere implementation is Jason Antic. Jason is the typical self-described average programmer who made it big extending an SAGAN into DeOldify. DeOldify is a customized implementation of an SAGAN that allows you to colorize and enhance old images and videos easier than easy.

Jason, with the assistance of fast.ai, his deep learning alma mater, has surpassed DeOldify. They are now attempting to produce a GAN that is capable of colorizing, removing noise and jitter, and enhancing old images and videos. The project is called NoGAN, and they are calling the process *decrappification*. Jason has also become a renowned GAN collaborator and expert in only a couple of short years.

As we discussed before, the whole process of training an SAGAN on Colab is out of the question. Furthermore, setting up a local desktop environment is outside the scope of this book. Fortunately, DeOldify has become so popular that specialized Colab notebooks have been constructed to facilitate image colorization. We will look at the basics of using one of these notebooks for colorizing your own images in Example 7-7.

*Example 7-7. Using an SAGAN—DeOldify*

- Open *Chapter_7_ImageColorizerColab.ipynb* and run the entire runtime, Runtime → Run All, from the menu. This sheet is based entirely on the original. If you run into problems with this version, check the DeOldify site on GitHub (*https://github.com/jantic/DeOldify*). This is a must-see site for anyone interested in enhancing old photos or videos.

- DeOldify uses PyTorch, a deep learning framework similar to TensorFlow and Keras. It is also installed by default in Colab, as can be seen by the first code cell, shown here:
```
import torch

if not torch.cuda.is_available():
    print('GPU not available.')
```

- The next code block downloads and installs DeOldify and its requirements. No need to focus on this.

- From here we import some other helpers and set the backend further. Note that this example needs to run with a GPU runtime, so be sure that runtime is engaged. The code to import is shown here:
```
import fastai
from deoldify.visualize import *

torch.backends.cudnn.benchmark = True
```

- We will be using a previously saved and trained model, using the following code:

```
!mkdir 'models'
!wget https://www.dropbox.com/s/zkehq1uwahhbc2o/ColorizeArtistic_gen.pth?...
```

- The model download in this case is .pth, a PyTorch saved model. In this example, we use the artistic model. At the time of writing, DeOldify used three different models. More information is available on their GitHub.

- Everything is ready to go, and now we just need to create the colorizer with the following code:

```
colorizer = get_image_colorizer(artistic=True)
```

- With the colorizer created, we can use it with the next code block, shown here:

```
source_url =
 'https://external-preview.redd.it/jkVU0SBAdzjVrwL8yJXzqOjsjCzyeJPPqKbw_E...'
 #@param {type:"string"}
render_factor = 35  #@param {type: "slider", min: 7, max: 45}
watermarked = True #@param {type:"boolean"}

if source_url is not None and source_url !='':
    image_path = colorizer.plot_transformed_image_from_url(url=source_url,
      render_factor=render_factor, compare=True, watermarked=watermarked)
    show_image_in_notebook(image_path)
else:
    print('Provide an image url and try again.')
```

- Figure 7-16 is the result of running the last cell with two different input images. You can easily change the input URL to any image that can be viewed online. Right-click or context menu–click any image in your browser and you should see an option to copy the image address. You can use that as the source for the input image. Dropbox is another option, but you need to set the dl query parameter at the end of the URL equal to 1, with download equals true. The default is false.

- Notice that in the lower-right-corner image of Figure 7-16 a couple of the figures have dark, or what Jason and company describe as "zombie," skin. You can clearly see this dark-gray skin on the gent standing directly in the middle. Yet his feet are a nice skin tone. We can surmise that this may occur because the training data used very few samples of only partial clothing. This makes for an interesting problem, and it should be exciting to see how or if the authors can compensate for this.

*Figure 7-16. Example output of DeOldify*

- The final block of code runs through the generator in the SAGAN and adjusts some rendering parameters. This is where the render_factor comes from in the last cell. You can think of the render factor as a variable for lighting and contrast. Perhaps Jason or others will be able to build other tuning parameters in the future. The code for the final block is shown here:

```
for i in range(10,46,2):
    colorizer.plot_transformed_image('test_images/image.png',
                                     render_factor=i,
                                     display_render_factor=True,
                                     figsize=(8,8))
```

- Running that code generates a series of images with varying render factors. This can give you an idea of how you can vary this parameter to alter your results.

DeOldify is a great example on so many levels of the practicality, power, and endless possibilities we apply with GANs and generator models. This whole area of AI, deep learning, and machine learning is so broad that many newcomers will surely make their mark. The sheer number of endless possibilities of GAN applications also translates to an endless number of applications. Does that mean developers like Jason are going to be the norm? Only time will tell. Jason was the first, but there likely will be many more. Could you be the next Jason Antic about to make your own breakthrough?

 DeOldify has a number of models and notebooks for various colorization applications. Be sure to check out their GitHub repository (*https://github.com/jantic/DeOldify*) for more information and a look at the video colorizer notebook.

That sums up our technical look at generators and in particular the GAN in a few of its forms. In the last section, we conclude with some final thoughts.

# Conclusion

Generators are quickly becoming a primary application of deep learning, particularly AI/machine learning. This is in vast contrast to where we started in Chapter 1 when we looked at supervised problems of regression and classification. The generator, a deep learning model that can generate unique content, is making interesting composite images, but it can do so much more. We ended this chapter using the SAGAN to colorize images, where we saw that the real power of GANs is in understanding the latent space. Being able to understand the latent space, the space between data, provides us direct insights not only into generating new data but also into what happens in those gaps.

Understanding the latent space in GANs has been used to generate fake celebrity faces or faces with glasses and mustaches. Generators provide us direct insight into the latent space of a model, but rest assured that all models have latent spaces. With GANs, though, we can learn latent representations of reduced spaces that make complex data easier to map and understand. We are really only starting to scratch the surface of what is possible here.

In the next chapter, we build more intelligent agents in the cloud with reinforcement learning. Reinforcement and deep reinforcement learning are powerful approaches to powering agents that can continually learn by exploring their environment.

# CHAPTER 8

# Building AI Assistants in the Cloud

As the world plunged into a pandemic in early 2020, the need for smarter AI became clear. Essential workers all over the globe were at high risk of being carriers and sources of contagions. We needed AI that could not only make better decisions but also help buffer those essential workers with smarter AI assistants. Now, we're not talking about incarnating Data, the android from *Star Trek*. It is only 2020 after all. What we are talking about is creating smarter AI assistants that can assist us in physical tasks— AI that can assist us in times of crisis, like we've seen in 2020.

We already have many assistant platforms such as Siri, Alexa, and Google itself. Couldn't they do what we need from smarter assistants? In part, yes, but most of these systems themselves are not real AI. Many are in fact rule-based systems developed by programmers and defined through extensive testing and training. Most of these assistant services are transitioning to real AI, but this takes time. The other main downside of these services is the input mechanism itself. In almost all cases, these services rely on voice- or text-based natural language input. These are great, but what about the old adage "a picture is worth a thousand words"?

In this chapter we explore a new domain of smarter AI that uses reinforcement learning. Reinforcement learning (RL) is a special form of learning that is intended to be dynamic and self-learning. We will explore the basics of what RL is and how it works.

We will break down building the agent and agent brain into the following sections:

- Needing Smarter Agents
- Introducing Reinforcement Learning
- Building an Example Agent with Expected SARSA
- Bringing Deep to Reinforcement Learning

For those of you who already have a background in reinforcement learning, stick around. You may find some material interesting and/or key to the next chapter.

In the following section, we begin by looking at why we need smarter AI "agent" assistants.

# Needing Smarter Agents

Google, Apple, and Microsoft are constantly improving their agent platforms. Since the inception and mainstream use of agents like Siri, the world has become enamored with such systems. Movies and TV shows have featured romantic relationships with this new breed of AI.

However, our current base of agent systems is in most cases rules-based and/or trained using methods like supervised learning. We have used supervised learning plenty in this book. From that experience you likely realize by now how far those systems are from the reality portrayed in movies and TV shows. So what is the answer to building better self-learning AI assistants? Quite simply, it is looking for a new approach to building AI agents, like using reinforcement learning.

The term *agent* in AI generally refers to any model/code that can make decisions on its own. In the past, these were rules-based models developed by coders. Now these models develop rules through training and learning on their own. This training is often in the form of supervised or unsupervised learning. Both methods have been used to train agents, but they lack the ability to dynamically improve on learnings. This is where reinforcement learning will come in. We will use the term *agent* as it pertains to both an RL agent and your typical AI agent like Siri or Alexa. They typically are not interchangeable, and we will learn why they shouldn't be. We use the term in this book to denote a smart system that takes input from a user and provides an action. The action may be as simple as a yes-or-no response or something far more complex.

If we look more closely at the current breed of AI agents, we see further holes in their makeup. In most cases these agents have a poor ability to dynamically improve on knowledge in real time. In most cases these agents do all their learning or training offline. As we will see, reinforcement learning allows us to create agents that can continually learn online and improve upon knowledge, thus giving users the ability to customize their own agents specific to their needs using their own data. This is in stark contrast to how mainstream agents learn now. In almost all cases, huge floods of data from all users are fed into an agent platform. This is great because it creates a nice general agent capable of handling many users. However, it lacks personal feel, and not everyone benefits from being clumped together. It also isn't likely such agents would ever really attract romantic interest. Should that be our goal, to create an agent that users fall in love with? The short answer is probably yes. After all, what better way to engage users?

In an episode of *The Big Bang Theory*, "The Beta Test Initiation," the character Raj falls for Siri. The episode plays on the fact that Raj is unable to talk to women but can talk to his "agent," Siri. While at the time this scenario was perceived as being unlikely, it is now considered a possibility. Think of the possibilities if we could develop a warm and caring agent that could be customized to an individual's needs. While our goal may not be creating love interests, it certainly could be building agents for therapy or comfort. Imagine an agent that is individualized for you and that is always there for you—an agent that can suggest goals or interests designed specifically for you and your needs. While you may not feel obliged to fall in love with such an agent, it may well become a dependency.

Now that we understand the need for smarter agents, we will start by learning how to build them with reinforcement learning.

# Introducing Reinforcement Learning

We have already explored at some length supervised and unsupervised learning as well as GANs. While all of these forms of learning are powerful, they lack the ability to continually learn. In almost all modern AI/ML systems, the model is trained off-line—that is, the model is pretrained with a set of data and then used in the real world. We further build our models on subsets of data using the training and test paradigm. As we have seen, in most cases this works fine until any change is needed. Then when anything changes, we often retrain the whole model again.

Reinforcement learning is intended to move away from supervised learning and allow the agent to learn by exploring its own environment. Instead of us telling the RL AI to do this or that, we instead give the agent rewards when completing tasks. You can think of this exactly as you would training a dog. For instance, if you are training your dog to shake its paw, you show the dog a treat or reward and then show the dog what you want, giving the treat/reward until the dog completes the task. Eventually, through trial and error the dog will learn what you are asking it to do. Giving the reward reinforces the actions the dog took, and the next time you perform the trick, your canine friend should get better at it. This is reinforcement learning.

In order to explicitly understand this, let's look at the flow of the reinforcement learning system, as depicted in Figure 8-1. In the figure, you can see two elements, the agent and the environment. Inside of the environment are the states that the agent can be at. A state can be anything, but it is often helpful to think of it in more basic terms, like eating, sleeping, or studying. So an agent such as yourself may be in the state of sleeping in your home environment. As an agent in that environment, you may do a number of actions. You likely need to first wake up, so that could be your first action.

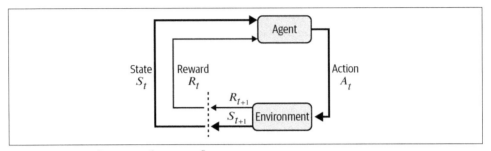

*Figure 8-1. Reinforcement learning flow*

Does that mean you get a reward? It depends on the system and the goals. Rewards may be negative, so if you wake up too early, you could potentially get a negative reward based on waking up too early. That will be your body's way of reinforcing not waking up so early again. Of course, there could be other rewards in future states and tasks. Perhaps you need to get to work or school, where you get more rewards than the negative reward from waking up early. This would mean your day had positive rewards, and assuming you like positive rewards, waking up early is something you would continue doing.

In the early days of RL, negative rewards were almost always used as rules or nudges to help more quickly train/guide the agent. However, this had the effect of placing too much human bias on a system. We were in effect trying to guide the agent into what not to do instead of what to do, though it was a system we wanted to learn completely on its own. Now, we often prefer to minimize negative rewards. This also has the added benefit of creating more novel or emergent behaviors from RL AI.

The basic flow of an RL system can help us understand how an agent learns. Next we want to look at how an agent can manage and learn how to move between the states in the environment. To do that, let's step back and understand the Markov decision process (MDP). The MDP is fundamental to RL and describes how the agent can move across states in an environment.

Figure 8-2 shows an example of an MDP that may describe what your typical morning looks like. In the diagram, we can see that each box represents a state. The darker box state represents the terminal state—attending work or school—which is the goal. The numbers beside each state represent the probability of you going to that state. You would start this process in the start state of sleeping. Each arrow represents an action you can take. If you are sleeping, you can continue to sleep or wake up. As you move to a new state, if there is a reward, you receive it. Rewards are denoted by the word *reward*. You can see that there are negative as well as positive rewards. It would be your goal to complete this MDP by obtaining the highest rewards. Can you find the optimum path?

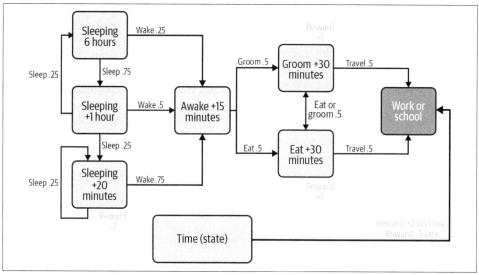

*Figure 8-2. MDP of a person waking up and going to work*

Before trying to solve the MDP, we also need to consider the big state at the bottom of the diagram. This state represents a global state, a state that affects all other states. Time is almost always a global state for any process, but few simple MDPs consider it. We consider it here to introduce the concepts of *state hierarchies* and *global states*.

In this example, it should be mentioned that the global state of time is not discrete. That is, we do not represent it as a series of times but rather as a continuous state. We will explore the difference between discrete and continuous states later in the chapter. For now, just consider the differences in the diagram and what they mean to an agent trying to optimize their trajectory.

Reinforcement learning was actually developed to solve what we refer to as the *credit assignment* and *temporal credit assignment* problems. In the credit assignment problem, we determine how much credit we can assign to an unknown task. In other words, what tasks must you complete in order to complete some bigger tasks? In the sample MDP, we have arbitrarily assigned credit to the grooming and eating tasks with rewards. It's up to the agent to decide how best to learn the optimum way to maximize those rewards. If this is still a little unclear, we are going to look at a code example that applies to a single state environment in the next section.

# Multiarm Bandits and a Single State

In learning RL we often explore a number of toy problems, problems or thought experiments that allow us to grasp simple concepts and then move up from there. We often start with the single state problem. A single state with multiple actions is not unlike the analogy of the multiarmed bandit.

The multiarmed bandit is so named after the Vegas slot machines affectionately referred to as *one-armed bandits*. In this problem, we consider the bandit as a single state with multiple actions. The goal of the agent is to find the arm that provides the maximal rewards. In other words, what is the maximum value that agent can obtain pulling each arm? To demonstrate this, let's look at a simple code example, Example 8-1.

*Example 8-1. The multiarm bandit*

- Open *Chapter_8_Bandit.ipynb* and run the first code block, shown here:
  ```
  import random

  reward = [1.0, 0.5, 0.2, 0.5, 0.6, 0.1, -.5]
  arms = len(reward)
  learning_rate = .1
  episodes = 100
  Value = [0.0] * arms
  print(Value)

  OUTPUT - [0.0, 0.0, 0.0, 0.0, 0.0, 0.0, 0.0]
  ```
- This code does the initial setup for the arms, where each arm has a different value represented by the reward array. We also set up some other training variables for `learning_rate` and episodes. One episode is considered one pull of an arm. We also initialize a starting list of values, Value, for the agent. The agent will update this list of values based on each pull.
- Move to the next code cell and run it as shown below:
  ```
  for i in range(0, episodes):
      action = random.randint(0,arms-1)
      Value[action] = Value[action] + learning_rate * (
          reward[action] - Value[action])

  print(Value)

  OUTPUT - [0.717570463519, 0.39705443395267553, 0.13026431198,
            0.41661409150166717, 0.4888187886688896,
            0.08332281830033345, -0.37290670858355]
  ```
- Based on the output values from Value, we can see the highest value of 0.71 is the first arm, much as we would expect. The rest of this code is not unlike our other

---

previous training code. The difference here is in the equation we use to calculate values. Notice that during each episode iteration the agent selects a random arm and then pulls it. It updates its Value table using the value equation:

*Value[action] = Value[action] + learning_rate × (reward[action] − Value[action])*

The value equation conveniently maps to the code almost perfectly. Notice in this equation that the actions value *Value[action]* is used. We add to *Value[action]* the value from the reward minus the value for the action, but instead of using the whole value, we only take a portion of the value set by the *learning_rate*. The *learning_rate* used in this manner is the same as the application of alpha (learning rate) in deep learning.

Take a look at this example and understand how we use the value equation. However, the equation is only one side of solving RL problems. The other side is understanding how we can get an agent to more efficiently search a state space. After all, our last example was about the agent searching the bandit for the best arm to pull. A random search is less than optimal, and we can improve on this by introducing a couple of tricks in the next section.

## Choosing the greedy action

One of the tenets of reinforcement learning is *trial-and-error learning*. Trial-and-error learning refers to the process in which an agent drops into an environment and tries the various actions in a state or states. Agents explore the various actions, either randomly or using other methods. One approach is to always use the best action according to our table or list of known values. Let's explore another example in Example 8-2 to understand this further.

*Example 8-2. Exploring the multiarm bandit greedily*

- Open *Chapter_8_Bandit_Greedy.ipynb* and run the first code block shown here:

```
import random

reward = [1.0, 0.5, 0.2, 0.5, 0.6, 0.1, -.5]
arms = len(reward)
learning_rate = .1
episodes = 10000
Value = [5.0] * arms
print(Value)

def greedy(values):
    return values.index(max(values))

OUTPUT - [5.0, 5.0, 5.0, 5.0, 5.0, 5.0, 5.0]
```

- The key difference to note in this code section is the introduction of a new function called *greedy*. The greedy function takes the values list and returns the index or action for the maximum value. This will be the action the agent should choose. In order to allow the agent to explore all actions, we also increase the original values from 0.0 to 5.0. A value of 5.0 will force the agent to try all the arms at least once.

- The next code section is again almost identical to the last exercise. In this example, though, we can see the greedy function being used to choose the agent's action, as seen in the following code:

```
for i in range(0, episodes):
    action = greedy(Value)
    Value[action] = Value[action] + learning_rate * (
        reward[action] - Value[action])

print(Value)
OUTPUT - [1.0000000000000009, 0.9923854510918054, 0.9204542494255955,
          0.9923854510918054, 0.9899692772647101,
          0.9171819032836618, 0.8980262055809499]
```

- When the cell finishes running, we can see the values are now cast more like probabilities, providing us better approximations for the best arm to pull. However, notice that not all the values match the corresponding value. This means that while we can determine an optimum action, it does less than picking a second-best action. Note how the arm with a value of 0.6 is generating a value less than the 0.5 arms.

We refer to the method of exploration the agent uses in the last example as *greedy*, just like the name of the function. Greedy exploration always chooses the action with the best value. The values are more explicitly referred to as *action-values*, where each action-value denotes the value to the agent of performing that action. While the value of an action can help us determine how to solve environments of a single state, what we ideally want is a full solution that can handle multiple states and actions. In the next section, we begin to discuss state-action values, or what we refer to as *quality*, and how they are used to solve an MDP.

## Adding Quality and Q Learning

We can now build upon our knowledge of action-values for a single state and start to consider state-action values. State-action values are frequently simplified to *quality*, or often just Q. Quality denotes how valuable an action is at a given state, a state-action value. The results of this combination are thanks to two gentlemen, Richard Bellman and Chris Watkins. Chris is the individual who in 1989 came up with the combined concept of Q Learning, or learning the quality of a state-action. He used tenets developed by Richard Bellman going back to the 1950s that describe how you might consider what future actions could impact your current actions.

Bellman derived the concept of an update equation that could be used to approximate what an agent's future rewards may look like. Before we get into what this equation looks like, let's extend our last sample problem into one with multiple bandits. When an agent pulls an arm, it not only gets a reward, but that also action moves it to a new multiarm bandit. This is the full MDP problem we will tackle in Example 8-3.

*Example 8-3. Contextual bandits and Q Learning*

- Open *Chapter_8_Bandit_Q.ipynb* and run the first code block, shown here:
```
import random

arms = 7
bandits = 7
learning_rate = .1
gamma = .9
episodes = 10000
reward = []
for i in range(bandits):
    reward.append([])
    for j in range(arms):
        reward[i].append(random.uniform(-1,1))
print(reward)
```

- In this example, each bandit has seven arms, and there are seven bandits. This time we randomly initialize the bandits in order to make the problem more unique during each run.

- The next thing we want to do is to create our Q table, or what we might call the agent's *policy*. You may see the symbol π used to denote an agent's policy. The policy will determine how the agents make decisions. The following code creates a blank maximal policy, not unlike our last exercise:
```
Q = []
for i in range(bandits):
    Q.append([])
    for j in range(arms):
        Q[i].append(10.0)
print(Q)

def greedy(values):
    return values.index(max(values))
```

- Next we break out a new Q Learning equation into its own function, shown in the next code cell:
```
def learn(state, action, reward, next_state):
    q = gamma * max(Q[next_state])
```

```
q += reward
q -= Q[state][action]
q *= learning_rate
q += Q[state][action]
Q[state][action] = q
```

- Finally, we set up the agent's training code, as shown here:
```
bandit = random.randint(0,bandits-1)
for i in range(0, episodes):
    last_bandit = bandit
    bandit = random.randint(0,bandits-1)
    action = greedy(Q[bandit])
    r = reward[last_bandit][action]
    learn(last_bandit, action, r, bandit)

print(Q)
```

- In this example we keep things simple and assume that when an agent pulls an arm, it just leads to another random agent. Therefore, the agent again is just learning to maximize its pull based on the agent, but it does not try to optimize a path through those agents. That is an important distinction.

In the last exercise, we used the Q Learning equation. This is the equation that Watkins developed that has become a staple for much of modern reinforcement learning. The learn function from the example purposely breaks down this learning equation to simplify things. The full Q Learning equation looks like the following:

*Q[state, action] = Q[state, action] + learning_rate × (reward + gamma × max(Q[state, action]) – Q[state, action]))*

Where:

gamma = the discount factor of the Bellman equation
max = the maximal action for the next state

The value of gamma denotes the discount factor. We use a discount factor based on the concept Bellman derived that showed how future or expected rewards should be discounted. Thus for each update of the agent's Q values (state-action), we take into account what future rewards may impact the current Q value. This can be hard to visualize by just looking at arrays, so to see this in action, we are going to use a more robust reinforcement learning test platform called *OpenAI Gym* in the next section.

## Playing with OpenAI Gym

OpenAI, the AI company developed by Elon Musk, has produced a framework for testing and building reinforcement learning. The environments featured in this framework are often considered the standards against which to build RL. If you study any amount of RL, you will encounter using the Gym to test your agents against.

---

Gym is also convenient since the core components are installed by default on Google Colab. It's almost like Google wanted us to build RL agents in the cloud.

Gym provides a number of quite complex Atari environments and other toy examples we can learn and explore with. In our next exercise, we are going to look at one of the most basic examples, the FrozenLake environment. Figure 8-3 shows the various states of the FrozenLake environment from the Gym. The *S* denotes the start square, the *F* represents a passable frozen patch of ice, the *H* represents treacherous holes that can kill the agent (negative rewards), and the *G* represents the final goal of the agent, the positive reward square, if you will. The goal is for the agent to start at S and navigate to the G (goal) square as efficiently as possible.

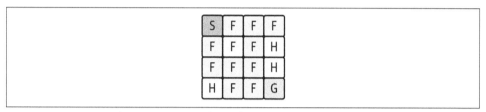

*Figure 8-3. FrozenLake environment from the Gym*

Next we will use FrozenLake as the environment for a Q Learning agent. The goal of our agent will be to find the optimum path to the reward. Jump back into Colab and follow along with Example 8-4.

*Example 8-4. Q Learning on FrozenLake*

- Open *Chapter_8_QLearning.ipynb* and run up to the code block shown here:
  ```
  env = gym.make("FrozenLake-v0")
  ```

- The previous blocks of code are for imports and displaying the collection of Gym environments. We won't need to showcase that here. Instead, look at how simple it is to create an environment like FrozenLake.

- After that, we introduce some training parameters, or hyperparameters, we will use to train our agent:
  ```
  alpha = 0.4  # learning rate
  gamma = 0.9  # discount factor
  total_steps = 10000
  ```

- Alpha again is our learning rate, or how quickly we want our agent to learn. This hyperparameter is almost equivalent to the learning rate we use for deep learning. Gamma is the discount factor. A value of 1.0 represents that all future or past rewards count the same. We often keep this value close to 1.0. A value of 0.9 will work well for this example. The `total_steps` variable will set how long we want our agent to train for.

- Next we again want to initialize our Q table, or policy. This time we want to do this with all 1s, again to promote our agent to search out all actions:
```
Q = np.ones((env.observation_space.n, env.action_space.n))
print(Q)
```

- The observation space denotes the number of states in our environment. The action space represents the number of actions for each state. An agent may move up and down or left and right from each state. If an agent is in an outer square and cannot move, it just stays within that square. Thus an agent in the top row that tries to move up would just continue to be in the same square. By setting our initial Q values to all 1s we will encourage the agent to try all actions from each state at least once.

- The next two cells are shown below and are used to define how the agent acts and learns. The first function, act, takes the state as input and returns the maximal or greedy action. After that we see the learn function, which again encapsulates the Q Learning equation in a slightly updated manner:
```
def act(state):
    return np.argmax(Q[state, :])

def learn(state, state2, reward, action):
    predict = Q[state, action]
    target = reward + gamma * np.max(Q[state2, :])
    Q[state, action] = Q[state, action] + alpha * (target - predict)
```

- The learn function is the same Q Learning equation we used in the last exercise, but it's just defined a little more explicitly.

- From here we see a helper function called render, shown here:
```
def render(t, env):
    clear_output()
    print(f'Rendering Learning Step {t}')
    env.render()
    print(Q)
    if t < 20:
        time.sleep(2)
    elif t % 100 == 0:
        time.sleep(2)
```

- We use the render function to smartly render the environment after each training step. A single training step is a single request for the agent to learn. You may notice that many other examples will feature episodic training, meaning the agent learns from each episode. In this example, we allow the agent to learn online, which means the agent learns as it plays.

- Finally, we come to the last block of code that trains an RL agent.

- Be sure to run all the cells in the notebook, and pay particular attention to the output of the last cell.

As you run the example, you will see the training output being generated. The red dot represents the agent, and you can visualize it moving around the lake. With each move, you will also see the agent's Q table or policy being updated and output. An example of this output is shown in Figure 8-4, which shows the start and end of agent training.

Notice that the top line represents state 1, the starting point on the lake. Each number on a line represents an action, and that action could be up, down, left, or right. The last line in the output table represents the goal. The reason this line contains all 1s is that the agent never moves from this point. When the agent lands on the goal square, the environment resets itself. Likewise, the other lines with all 1s represent the holes in the ice. Thus, when the agent falls in a hole, it receives a negative reward, and the environment again resets.

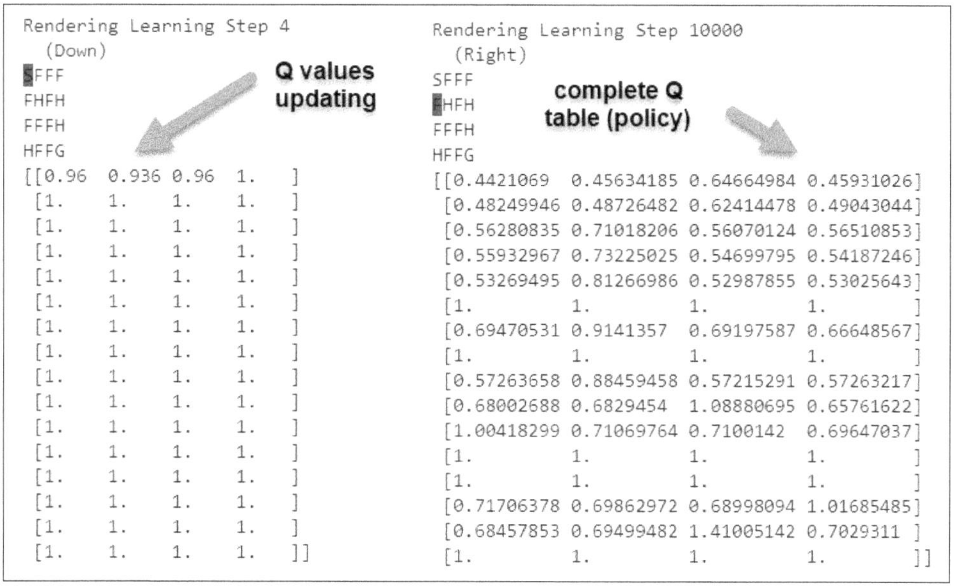

*Figure 8-4. Sample training output for FrozenLake*

See if you can follow the Q values/state-action values on the last line of the Q table back to the first line. Remember, each number represents an action-value. In our current example, the agent is acting greedy and always chooses the maximum value. Of course, choosing the best action may not always be the best course of action.

Imagine always picking your favorite food to eat, regardless of the consequences. While you may get short-term satisfaction/rewards, long-term results could be less beneficial, not to mention that by always choosing the best option, you may miss other long-term benefits. Imagine never discovering the favorite food to begin with. After all, how did you find that favorite in the first place? As it turns out, this is a problem we constantly wrestle with in RL. It is called the Exploration/Exploitation Dilemma (EE). EE is fundamental to RL and is the subject of our next section.

## Exploration Versus Exploitation

Exploration versus exploitation is something we face daily. When you go for lunch, for example, do you pick your favorite place down the street or try a new place? You know your favorite place is consistent, and you won't be disappointed. However, what if that new place is better? What if it is worse? If it is worse, you could waste money and time, and perhaps risk indigestion. But if it is better, what if it is *a lot* better, like life-changing better? How do you balance when to take risks (explore) and when to just use your previous knowledge (exploit)? That challenge is the same posed to RL when we try to balance an agent's need to explore with using its gained knowledge to exploit.

Balancing the EE is something we can do in RL in a number of ways. The most common method is to use a rate of exploration we will call *epsilon*. By using a simple rate like epsilon, we can balance an agent's tendency to explore new actions. Let's look at Example 8-5.

*Example 8-5. Q Learning with epsilon*

- Open *Chapter_8_QLearning_EE.ipynb*. This example is almost identical to the last exercise, with just a couple of differences. Run the notebook up to the code block shown here:
  ```
  epsilon = .5  #exploration rate

  alpha = 0.4  # learning rate
  gamma = 0.9  # discount factor
  total_steps = 10000
  ```

- Notice the addition of our new term *epsilon*. We use epsilon to denote how much an agent explores during each step.

- Keep running code blocks until you come to the block with the act function, shown here:
  ```
  def act(state):
    if np.random.uniform(0, 1) < epsilon:
      action = env.action_space.sample()
    else:
      action = np.argmax(Q[state, :])
    return action
  ```

- The act function has now changed to accommodate the agent randomly exploring at a rate of epsilon. Recall that epsilon was earlier set to 0.5, or 50% of the time. That means the agent will decide to explore about half the time.

- Run the rest of the entire notebook and observe the results. Are they what you expected?

What you may hopefully come to realize is that the agent continues to explore when it likely shouldn't. After all, in this limited example, the lake is only so big, and there is only one correct path. So our agent is no longer choosing the optimum path all the time, which is good. It unfortunately doesn't know when to stop. We will cover how to correct this in the next section.

## Balancing exploration and exploitation

The EE dilemma in RL is by no means recent, and many ways have been derived to tackle this problem. While some are more successful than others, often the simplest approach works best, which is what we will cover here. So instead of using a static value for epsilon, we can use a method that degrades epsilon over time. Decreasing epsilon over time allows the agent to explore early when it should and then rely on knowledge exploitation later. There are a number of ways to implement this as well, but we will stick with a simple method called *linear epsilon decay*. To understand how this works, let's dive into Example 8-6.

*Example 8-6. Q Learning with EGreedy*

- Open *Chapter_8_QLearning_EGreedy.ipynb*. Again, this example is almost identical to the last. Run the notebook up to the code block:
  ```
  epsilon = 1.0
  min_epsilon = 0.01
  max_epsilon = 1.0
  decay_rate = 0.001

  alpha = 0.4  # learning rate
  gamma = 0.9  # discount factor
  total_steps = 10000
  ```
- This time we can see that the value for epsilon is 1.0, which means 100% exploration. That is the value epsilon will start at. The terms below this represent the minimum, maximum, and decay rate. The min_epsilon term represents the lowest value we want exploration to go to. At 0.01, that equals a 1% chance. The term max_epsilon represents the starting value. The decay_rate term represents the amount epsilon should decay over each step. In this example we use an exponential decay over time, but keep in mind that you could use any function to decay epsilon.
- Next we will jump down and look at the function used to decay epsilon over time. Scroll down to the following section of code:

```
learning_steps = 0
while learning_steps < total_steps:
  state = env.reset()
  while True:
    render(learning_steps, env, epsilon)

    action = act(state)
    state2, reward, done, info = env.step(action)
    learn(state, state2, reward, action)
    state = state2

    learning_steps += 1
    epsilon = min_epsilon + (max_epsilon - min_epsilon) *
                      np.exp(-decay_rate * learning_steps) ❶

    if done:
        break

env.close()
```

❶ This shows the function used to decay epsilon. We use the `np.exp` function to decay epsilon exponentially. This works well for this environment since it is small and the agent can learn it quickly. You could just as easily use a linear function to decay epsilon, and for larger environments this may be a better option.

- Run all the code in the notebook and observe the training of the agent.

Notice that as the agent trains this time, it appears quite erratic to start. Then as training continues, it quickly becomes less erratic and starts to make consistently good decisions. This is a result of that exponential decay of the epsilon or exploration rate of the agent. While decaying exploration rate can help solve decision-making, it still lacks forward- or backward-thinking knowledge. That is, our agent thinks only one step ahead when it could do much better. We will start to explore how an agent can use that forward or backward knowledge in the next section.

## Understanding Temporal Difference Learning

Reinforcement learning is the combination of three distinct threads intended to solve an MDP:

- The first thread is known as Monte Carlo, so named after the trial-and-error method we use in exploration.
- This, combined with a second thread called *Dynamic Programming* (DP), derived from Bellman, is essentially a basis for the Q table or policy.

- The third thread is the application of *temporal difference* (TD) *learning*. TD learning is about adding the concept of time or passing of events to our learning methods. Dr. Richard Sutton, considered the father of RL, is often considered responsible for pulling these three threads together.

 If you have read anything about RL over the last few years, you've likely encountered the name David Silver. David was a student of Sutton's at the University of Alberta and has been responsible for some of the most major advances in RL to date!

We have already considered time in our previous example and equations. TD one step or TD(0) very closely resembles our multiarmed bandit problems. Figure 8-5 shows what we refer to as backup diagrams of TD(0), SARSA, Q Learning, and Expected SARSA. Each large circle in the diagram represents a state in which the dots identify actions or state-actions. With TD(0), we consider only the current action for a given state. Consider this an example of our first exercise with a single multiarmed bandit.

Next, we see SARSA, an acronym for "state-action-reward, state-action." In this diagram, we first consider the state-action as it leads to a given state, denoted s'. From that we can see the best action being identified. The Q Learning diagram comes next. Again, we start with a state-action pair that leads to a new state, but now we consider all actions from that state. This is represented by the sweep lines on the diagram. If you refer back to the Q Learning equation, you will note that we always use the max state-action value.

Finally, in the last diagram, Expected SARSA, we see a slight difference. The max state-action is not used to predict the next action. Instead, we take another virtual step and determine the best action from that new state. In essence we let our agent time-travel one step into the future.

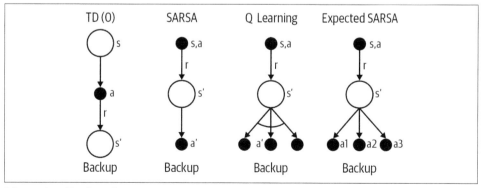

*Figure 8-5. Backup diagrams*

Backup diagrams like the ones in Figure 8-5 are a good way to understand the key differences between various RL methods. The examples we look at here are sufficient for our needs, but there are deeper diagrams that show other families of RL methods.

Figure 8-6 demonstrates the differences between those three threads that combined to create modern RL. With the Monte Carlo method, an agent moves through a complete episode or game before applying an update. The red denotes the update or learning trail of the agent. DP, on the other hand, does a sweep of all state-actions and then updates. We often refer to DP as a *planning method*. The middle thread, temporal difference, is the family of methods we will use in this book.

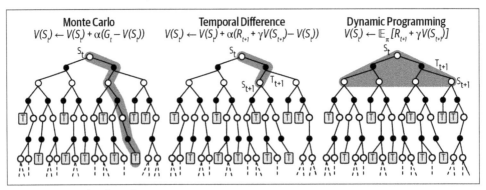

*Figure 8-6. RL backup diagrams*

David Silver used the Monte Carlo method with an algorithm called *Monte Carlo Tree Search* to develop AlphaGo. AlphaGo was the first AI/RL agent to defeat a human player in the game of Go. David would go on to develop a more advanced agent called *AlphaGo Zero*. The key difference between the original and Zero was the use of training input. In the original agent, Silver used human examples as input. The improvement with Zero was derived by letting the agent completely learn on its own, with no human examples. This led not just to a much better agent but to an agent orders of magnitude better. Whereas the original agent beat Lee Sedol—regarded as the best human player—two out of three games, Zero actually made Sedol quit playing Go professionally when it was released a couple of years later.

Each foundational RL method/thread has its weaknesses and strengths. Some methods are better suited for playing games of Go, while others are better at planning large simulations. For our purposes, we will stick to TD learning as it provides the following benefits:

- It can update the policy (Q table) after every step.
- It can be used to learn online while the agent is playing.
- It works well for continuous environments; it's nonepisodic.

- It is typically more efficient than full MC.
- It is more concise in training; other methods require a full search of the entire state space, which is often not practical.
- It works well for discrete actions and environments.

However, TD is not without flaws and is problematic for the following reasons:

- It can become biased early, which is problematic for large environments or state spaces.
- It is more sensitive to the initial value estimates, which is why we have been using a value/quality of 1.0 as our initial values.

To help us understand RL, we'll address some key terms in the next sections.

### Episodic versus continuous learning

We have already used the term *episodic learning* when discussing the Monte Carlo method. Episodic learning is where an agent updates its policy only after completing an episode. Refer back to Figure 8-6 and the MC backup diagram as a prime example of episodic learning. The problem with this type of learning is that an agent has to complete a full episode in the environment before it learns and updates the policy. This results in our agent learning off policy. An agent that can learn continuously is able to update its policy with each step, thus allowing it to continually learn. A continuous learning agent is more robust because it can immediately update its decisions based on new information.

### On policy versus off policy

Policy, often denoted by the symbol $\pi$, represents the agent's decision matrix, or brain. An agent makes decisions against the policy. In our examples, we use a Q table to both reflect and encapsulate the agent's policy and help it understand environment. Be careful to note that we simplify these concepts for our examples. While it may seem that on policy would always be the best choice, there are a number of reason for using off-policy agents. In deep reinforcement learning, the deep Q network, or DQN, algorithm is an off-policy agent. The agent does not update its policy until after a certain number of steps or the completion of a reward. As it turns out, off-policy agents are often easier to implement if the agent has no model. We will cover more about what a model is in the next section.

### Model-based versus model-free

In our examples, our agent uses a Q table that functions as a policy and understanding of the environment. Thus our agent is on policy, but the policy is not the model. Q Learning is intended to be off policy and generally model-free. A full model of the environment requires us to understand and map the entire state space, understanding all actions and possible outcomes or values.

Model-based learning is where the agent has a complete model of the environment, meaning it can look up any state-action quality values as needed. Conversely, model-free agents do not capture all state-action pairs but rather key state-action pairs in their policies. If the agent encounters a new state-action pair, it can interpolate over previously observed states to predict a next action. Model-free agents are typically employed for massive state spaces, state spaces so big they outnumber the number of atoms in the observable universe. Yes, you read that correctly. An example of such a massive environment is the Atari games featured in the OpenAI Gym and the game of Go.

 If you want to try your hand testing the classic Atari games in Gym, it's best to do that with RL powered by deep learning, otherwise known as *deep reinforcement learning*.

### Discrete versus continuous actions or states

We have kept our samples to discrete action and state spaces. Discrete actions are examples of an agent choosing to move left or right. Continuous actions are a refinement of discrete actions. Instead of just providing a direction, a continuous action also outputs an amount. So a continuous action may look like "turn left 0.5 for 50%," meaning the agent turns only 50% left.

Likewise, the FrozenLake environment uses discrete states, one state per block. We can also easily represent individual discrete states in our Q table, whereas continuous states will be represented by value ranges. In the LunarLander environment, for instance, states are represented by $x$ and $y$ coordinates where the values are continuous over some range. While we could still discretize those values into categories, in practice this works poorly. Instead, we now use deep learning to consume those continuous state spaces. Deep reinforcement learning is the area of RL you will want to pursue for agents that use continuous actions or state spaces.

The attributes of policy, model, and continuity are important factors to consider when building RL for your sample environment. In this book, we want our agents to learn quickly and consistently over a small-to-medium-state space. That means, we want to keep our agent discrete for both action and state spaces. As well, the agent should be on policy, allowing it to learn dynamically and continuously. Last, we want our agent to be model-based. This will allow us to review instances of an agent's model later. In the next section, we use all of this new knowledge to understand an improved method, Expected SARSA.

# Building an Example Agent with Expected SARSA

We have already seen in the last section how Expected SARSA differs from Q Learning. SARSA itself only slightly differs from Q in that it is intended to be an online (on-policy) continuous learning algorithm that can be used with discrete or continuous environments with a model or model-free approach. It is such a flexible and powerful method that it is the basis for many similar and powerful methods, like proximal policy optimization (PPO) and soft actor critic (SAC). We call these methods *policy improvement methods* since they continually work to update a continuous policy.

 PPO and SAC are based on a family of RL methods called *policy gradient improvement*. These methods improve the policy by working to understand how to maximize the action value in each state.

Next, we will use SARSA as our training algorithm again on the FrozenLake Gym environment. While the algorithm is similar to Q, it has some key differences, so we will review the key sections in Example 8-7.

*Example 8-7. FrozenLake with Expected SARSA*

- Open *Chapter_8_SARSA_FrozenLake.ipynb*. Again, this example is almost identical to the last. Run the notebook up to the code block shown here:
  ```
  def learn(state, state2, reward, action, action2):
          predict = Q[state, action]
          target = reward + gamma * Q[state2, action2]
          Q[state, action] = Q[state, action] + alpha * (target - predict)
  ```

- This time the major changes are in the `learn` function. To start with, we added another parameter as input, an `action2` term. `action2` input represents the next action the agent will take after taking a virtual step forward. Then notice that the target value calculation has changed. Now, instead of taking the maximal action over the next state, we take the agent's action2 Q value. There is a subtle difference here, so as a comparison, let's list the Q Learning `learn` function again here:
  ```
  def learn(state, state2, reward, action):
    predict = Q[state, action]
    target = reward + gamma * np.max(Q[state2, :])  ❶
    Q[state, action] = Q[state, action] + alpha * (target - predict)
  ```

  ❶ The key difference between Q and SARSA is identified here in the code example. You can go back and review the various backup diagrams to help you understand the change.

- Scroll down to the bottom training cell block as shown here:

```
learning_steps = 0

while learning_steps < total_steps:
  state = env.reset()
  while True:
    render(learning_steps, env, epsilon)

    action = act(state)
    state2, reward, done, info = env.step(action)

    action2 = act(state2) ❶
    learn(state, state2, reward, action, action2)
    state = state2
    action = action2

    learning_steps += 1
    epsilon = min_epsilon + (max_epsilon - min_epsilon) *
                       np.exp(-decay_rate * learning_steps)
```

❶ The learning code is again similar to Q, but notice some key changes. Notice that after taking a step (env.step), the agent again calls learn, but this time passing in state2. The action from this virtual move is then fed into our learn function to perform an update. When the code runs another loop, the act function is called again with the updated state, but keep in mind that this new action could be different from what we used in the last call to learn.

- Run all the code cells and watch the output of the agent.

This example will train about 10 times faster than our previous Q Learning examples, which is quite impressive considering the minor change. However, it is not a good test of the algorithm itself. So in the next section, we will look at running SARSA over a substantially harder environment.

## Using SARSA to Drive a Taxi

The OpenAI Gym has thousands of environments and variations you can use to test your RL algorithms. Most of those environments use continuous states and/or actions, which makes it difficult but not impossible to use discrete methods. In most cases, progressing to the more difficult environments will require the augmentation of deep learning. Fortunately, there is another discrete environment called *Taxi* that will give our SARSA algorithm a better test.

The Taxi environment shown in Figure 8-7 demonstrates the layout. In the figure, the solid lines denote walls or impassable areas. The four letters indicate pickup and drop-off locations for passengers. It is the agent's goal to pick up and drop off passengers to and from those squares. The agent receives a –1 reward every time it moves, a

+20 reward for each successful drop-off, and a –10 reward for each incorrect drop-off.

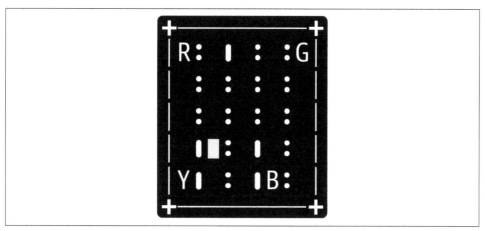

*Figure 8-7. OpenAI Gym Taxi environment*

To get a better sense of how this looks, let's bring up a new code example in Example 8-8.

*Example 8-8. Taxi Driver with Expected SARSA*

- Open *Chapter_8_SARSA_Taxi.ipynb*. This example is similar to the last one, but this has more changes near the end of the notebook. Run the notebook up to the code block shown here:

```
def render_game(env):
    clear_output()
    env.render()
    time.sleep(.5)
```

- We see here a new render_game function with the sole purpose of rendering the game output and pausing the execution for .5 seconds. This example can take considerably more time. Therefore, we only want to output an agent playing the game every few episodes. We need to use episodes in this example in order to limit an agent's steps. The state space is much larger, and we need to make sure our agent doesn't end up in an endless loop.

- Scroll down to the next cell, shown here:

```
def play_game(env,ep, max):
    d = False
    s = env.reset()
    st = 0
    while not d and st < max:
        a = act(state)
```

```
s2, r, d, i = env.step(a)
print(f'Episode:{ep} Step{st} reward:{r}')
render_game(env)
st += 1
```

- This code shows a new function, `play_game`. We input into `play_game` the current environment, the number of the episode, and an action or step limit called *max*. The max value will limit the agent's steps. You can see from the code that the agent is just playing the game with its current policy.

- Next, we will scroll down to the last cell, as shown here:

```
step = 0
max_steps = 100

total_episodes = 10000

learning_steps = 0
rewards = 0
total_rewards = 0

for episode in range(total_episodes):
  step = 0
  state = env.reset()
  action = act(state)

  while step < max_steps:
    #env.render()

    state2, reward, done, info = env.step(action)
    action2 = act(state2)
    learn(state, state2, reward, action, action2)

    state = state2
    action = action2

    step += 1
    rewards+=reward
    epsilon = min_epsilon + (max_epsilon - min_epsilon) * np.exp(
      -decay_rate * learning_steps)

    if done:
      break

  if episode > 100 and episode % 50 == 0:
    play_game(env, episode, max_steps)

env.close()
```

- While most of this code should look familiar, there are a number of differences. First, we are playing the agent in episodes with a maximum step limit. This is again to prevent the agent from endlessly wandering. We set the number of steps an agent can take in the max_steps term. While we are making the agent episodic, this is not episodic learning. In episodic learning, the agent learns only after a full complete episode. In this case, the agent is continually learning. The last major change is the bottom of the code, where we can see that after every 50 episodes after the first 100, the agent plays a sample game. The agent won't learn anything by playing this game, and the purpose of this is just for us to monitor output.

• Run all the cells in the notebook, and observe the agent training.

As the agent learns how to drive the taxi, you will see it get better and better at this task. Eventually, it will learn to pick up and drop off passengers in a timely fashion. On the surface of this example, it appears that the agent is working in just a bit larger state than our FrozenLake example. The FrozenLake had a 4 × 4 play area, making 16 squares, which equated nicely to 16 states. You would think that the Taxi environment with a 5 × 5 play area would equate to 25 squares and thus 25 states. However, there are in fact 500 states in the Taxi environment. In order to understand why that is, let's look at some more code in Example 8-9.

*Example 8-9. Understanding the Taxi state space*

• The code for OpenAI Gym is all open source, which allows us to look in depth at how the environments work. You can find a link to the *taxi.py* source on GitHub (*https://github.com/openai/gym/blob/master/gym/envs/toy_text/taxi.py*).

• If you open up that code, at the very top is a description of how the state space is calculated:

```
class TaxiEnv(discrete.DiscreteEnv):
    """
    The Taxi Problem
    from "Hierarchical Reinforcement Learning with the MAXQ Value Function
     Decomposition"
    by Tom Dietterich
    Description:
    There are four designated locations in the grid world indicated by R(ed),
    G(reen), Y(ellow), and B(lue). When the episode starts, the taxi
    starts off at a random square and the passenger is at a random location.
    The taxi drives to the passenger's location, picks up the passenger,
    drives to the passenger's destination (another one of the four
    specified locations), and then drops off the passenger. Once the
    passenger is dropped off, the episode ends.
    Observations:
    There are 500 discrete states since there are 25 taxi positions, 5
    possible locations of the passenger (including the case when the
    passenger is in the taxi), and 4 destination locations.
```

```
Passenger locations:
- 0: R(ed)
- 1: G(reen)
- 2: Y(ellow)
- 3: B(lue)
- 4: in taxi

Destinations:
- 0: R(ed)
- 1: G(reen)
- 2: Y(ellow)
- 3: B(lue)

Actions:
There are 6 discrete deterministic actions:
- 0: move south
- 1: move north
- 2: move east
- 3: move west
- 4: pickup passenger
- 5: dropoff passenger

Rewards:
There is a reward of -1 for each action and an additional reward of +20
for delivering the passenger. There is a reward of -10 for executing
actions "pickup" and "dropoff" illegally.
"""
```

- If you scroll down the code further, you can see how this state space is initialized, as follows:

```python
def encode(self, taxi_row, taxi_col, pass_loc, dest_idx):
    # (5) 5, 5, 4
    i = taxi_row
    i *= 5
    i += taxi_col
    i *= 5
    i += pass_loc
    i *= 4
    i += dest_idx
    return i

def decode(self, i):
    out = []
    out.append(i % 4)
    i = i // 4
    out.append(i % 5)
    i = i // 5
    out.append(i % 5)
    i = i // 5
```

```
out.append(i)
assert 0 <= i < 5
return reversed(out)
```

- The encode and decode functions are what translate the state from a hierarchy into a single value number. This translation is the way in which we layer states in a hierarchical fashion.

At the top of the code listing, you will see mention of hierarchical reinforcement learning (HRL). HRL is a technique we can use to encapsulate environment state and is something we will elaborate on further in the next section.

## Understanding hierarchical states

One thing that often confuses newcomers is how we can or may perceive state in RL. A simple example of state in an environment is the FrozenLake. For Lake, this is a simple matter of taking $4 \times 4$ squares, which equals 16 locations or states to move. This same analogy works for Taxi to give us the base states.

In Figure 8-8, we have shown how the Taxi states are laid out in layers, or in a hierarchy, if you will. One way to think about this is that when the agent first starts, it is at the top layer. At the top layer there are only 25 states for navigation. Now, if an agent manages to find and pick up a passenger, then the state elevates to the next layer group. In the next layer group there are five distinct navigation layers. That means at this level, there are 125 states, or $5 \times 25$. Finally, when it's time to drop the agent off, it needs to pick the correct drop-off location. There are four drop-off locations, which means we need to multiply that by our last layer of states. Thus, in the final layer, we have a total of 500 states calculated as follows:

- First layer (navigation) = 25
- Second layer (pickup) = $25 \times 5 = 125$
- Third layer (drop-off) = 125 (second layer) $\times$ 4 (3rd layer) = 500 total states.

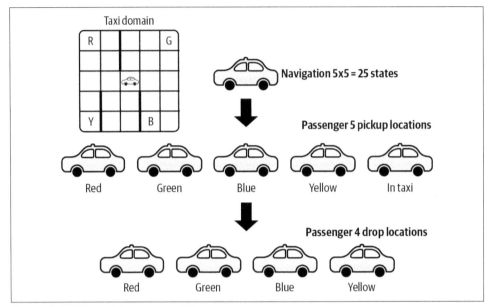

*Figure 8-8. Hierarchical states of Taxi*

If you refer back to Figure 8-8 and think for a second, you can start to appreciate that perhaps 500 states is overkill. After all, if the taxi picks up a passenger at the red location, it likely doesn't need to drop it off there as well. Likewise, do we need to allow the agent to have actions for pickup or drop-off at any locations other than those designated? By reducing the necessary actions and/or states, we give the agent a smaller search space and thus speed up training. For this example, those changes could potentially be significant. You could reduce the search space from 3,000 state-action values (500 states × 6 actions/state = 3,000) to around 2,000. To do that, you would need to drop actions and states when the agent is not on a drop-off or pickup point. While this would allow the agent to train 30% faster, it does limit flexibility. We can, of course, do better, and in the next section we introduce Hierarchical Reinforcement Learning.

## Learning State Hierarchies with Hierarchical Reinforcement Learning

Teaching the agent to drive a taxi can be a lot of fun using Q Learning or Expected SARSA. As we have seen, the training times take longer because the agent has more states to explore. But the agent doesn't really have more area to explore, just the states the agent may be in when it is exploring the same area. We can think of this as an *agent state*, or what some (like Sutton) refer to as *options*. You can think of options as being any state that affects the agent.

Think back to our figure that described an MDP, represented in Figure 8-9. In this figure, we can see the wake-up MDP described, and then at the bottom, we have a global or agent state as a semi-MDP. *Semi-MDPs* refer to MDPs that have a global set of agent states where the agent may need to do something differently based on that agent state. So in the case of our wake-up semi-MDP, an agent could awaken in three different agent states. Each of these states or options (early, on time, or late) would define a subset of MDPs that should be solved differently. If you wake up late, for instance, you likely have to skip eating or grooming in order to receive a positive reward.

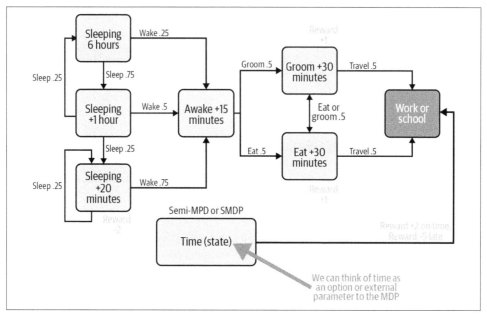

*Figure 8-9. MDP and semi-MDP defined*

The Taxi environment is an excellent example of a semi-MDP. In that environment, the agent has a couple of options: carrying a passenger or not carrying a passenger. Based on those options, the agent may also have various suboptions, or hierarchies. Figure 8-10 shows the base taxi domain as well as a description of the option hierarchies an agent may explore or be in.

In this diagram, we expand the options to include the actions or tasks an agent may need to perform to change an option. Looking back at the diagram, we can perceive the Get option acquires a passenger, while Put drops the passenger off. Then, if the agent needs a passenger, it can use the Get option. From Get we can see two subsets of options, Pickup and Navigate. Since Pickup is also a leaf node, or what we refer to as *terminal*, it also should map to an action. Likewise, we break Navigate down to the four movement options or actions/tasks: Up, Right, Down, and Left. Exposing the states through a hierarchy of options also allows us to see the learning hierarchy itself.

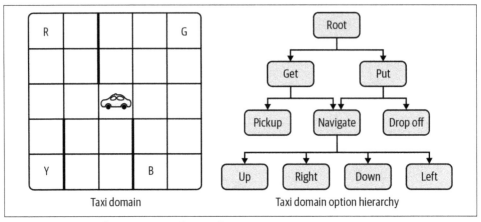

*Figure 8-10. Taxi domain option hierarchy*

Hierarchical Reinforcement Learning (HRL) is how we train an agent to learn a state hierarchy more efficiently. Thomas G. Dieterich was the first to really explore this field, and it has since expanded to include many related aspects of state hierarchies and abstractions. As you may have noticed looking at the taxi.py source, Thomas was instrumental in building that environment.

The allure of learning hierarchies is that we can break down the state hierarchies into agent tasks with the hope that if we can train an agent to tackle a particular task, then that task could be used as a subset in a harder problem. RL has many roots in animal behavior, and we believe this is fundamental to how we learn. When you go outside for a walk, for instance, you may focus on where you want to walk, but do you really need to worry about how you tie your shoes beforehand? No, because the tie-shoe task is already a task that you have mastered. This subtask now becomes part of your go-outside-and-walk task, but you certainly don't need to relearn how to tie your shoes every time. Essentially, this is our same goal when we abstract state hierarchies. We break down smaller, concise tasks that can be reused as part of larger tasks.

HRL is not something that has received as much hype as deep reinforcement learning. DRL is more visually impressive and has been shown to solve very complex tasks, while HRL and state abstractions are more about reuse and solving bigger problems. HRL has recently seen traction with the inclusion of deep learning, but this only makes things far more complicated. For our purposes, we are going to stick with some basic forms of HRL.

Given your knowledge of deep learning, you may be prepared to tackle deep HRL. If you are more serious about this type of AI, you can search for HRL or state abstractions in RL. You should be aware though that HRL and state abstractions are quite math and programming intensive.

We are going to look at a simple early form of HRL that should explain the base concepts further in the next section.

### Functional decomposition with MAXQ

To solve a hierarchy of states, we can assume that any state in that hierarchy has an optimum reward/goal. Thus it follows that if we decompose each substate in that hierarchy and solve for it, we could derive an entire solution. If you think back to our earlier Q Learning examples, this is simply finding the maximum Q value over each state in the hierarchy.

This functional decomposition of states is known as *MAXQ-0*. The zero on the end denotes no abstractions, that is, we need to solve the problem directly. MAXQ-Q is the higher form of this process, and is known as *MAXQ with state abstractions*. Let's look at a simple in code in order to understand how this works and what it looks like in Example 8-10.

*Example 8-10. Taxi with MAXQ-0*

- Open the example *Chapter_8_Taxi_MAXQ.ipynb* and look to the second code cell after the imports. The start of the code block is shown here:
```
class Agent:
    def __init__(self, env, alpha, gamma):
        self.env = env
```

- In this example we start by creating a new class called Agent. We can see this class is initialized with the environment env, learning rate alpha, and the discount factor gamma.

- The next block of code sets up the option hierarchy or states. We need to do this manually in MAXQ-0:
```
not_pr_acts = 2 + 1 + 1 + 1
  # gotoS,D + put + get +        root (non primitive actions)
nA = env.action_space.n + not_pr_acts
nS = env.observation_space.n
self.V = np.ones((nA, nS))
self.C = np.ones((nA, nS, nA))
self.V_copy = self.V.copy()

s = self.south = 0    ❶
```

```
n = self.north = 1
e = self.east = 2
w = self.west = 3
pickup = self.pickup = 4
dropoff = self.dropoff = 5
gotoS = self.gotoS = 6
gotoD = self.gotoD = 7
get = self.get = 8
put = self.put = 9
root = self.root = 10

self.graph = [
    set(),  # south
    set(),  # north
    set(),  # east
    set(),  # west
    set(),  # pickup
    set(),  # dropoff
    {s, n, e, w},  # gotoSource
    {s, n, e, w},  # gotoDestination
    {pickup, gotoS},  # get -> pickup, gotoSource
    {dropoff, gotoD},  # put -> dropoff, gotoDestination
    {put, get},  # root -> put, get
]

self.alpha = alpha
self.gamma = gamma
self.r_sum = 0
self.new_s = copy.copy(self.env.s)
self.done = False
self.num_of_ac = 0
```

❶  We numerically identify each state in the option hierarchy, starting with 0 for
   south or down. This allows us to identify each option in the hierarchy we will
   need to explore. It may also be helpful to think of executing an option as a
   task. Looking back to Figure 8-10, we can also see that the lower levels in the
   hierarchy are defined with lower option numbers. This is not by accident but
   is a helpful way for us to distinguish between primitive and terminal node-
   based options. A terminal node represents the end, or termination, of a state.
   What we are doing here is essentially creating an option graph.

   If you are unfamiliar with graph theory, it may be useful to explore
   that further as a way of understanding this example better. Graph
   theory is a mathematical way of associating elements or nodes in a
   hierarchy or other manner. The concept has been applied to many
   areas of computer science and machine learning.

- Remember, our goal is to decompose the hierarchy, so we also need some code to help identify primitive and terminal options. The code to do that is shown here:

```
def is_primitive(self, act):
  if act <= 5:
    return True
  else:
    return False

def is_terminal(self, a, done):
  RGBY = [(0, 0), (0, 4), (4, 0), (4, 3)]
  taxirow, taxicol, passidx, destidx = list(self.env.decode(self.env.s))
  taxiloc = (taxirow, taxicol)
  if done:
      return True
  elif a == self.root:
      return done
  elif a == self.put:
      return passidx < 4
  elif a == self.get:
      return passidx >= 4
  elif a == self.gotoD:
      return passidx >= 4 and taxiloc == RGBY[destidx]
  elif a == self.gotoS:
      return passidx < 4 and taxiloc == RGBY[passidx]
  elif self.is_primitive(a):
      # just else
      return True
```

- In this example, a primitive option is a movement option, and terminal options are higher up. Again, refer to Figure 8-10 to see this.

- Next we will jump into the learning code itself to see how we evaluate and explore each level:

```
def evaluate(self, act, s):
  if self.is_primitive(act):
    return self.V_copy[act, s]
  else:
    for j in self.graph[act]:
        self.V_copy[j, s] = self.evaluate(j, s)
    Q = np.arange(0)
    for a2 in self.graph[act]:
        Q = np.concatenate((Q, [self.V_copy[a2, s]]))
    max_arg = np.argmax(Q)
    return self.V_copy[max_arg, s]

# e-Greedy Approach with eps=0.001
def greed_act(self, act, s):
  e = 0.001
  Q = np.arange(0)
```

```
    possible_a = np.arange(0)
    for act2 in self.graph[act]:
        if self.is_primitive(act2) or (not self.is_terminal(act2, self.done)):
            Q = np.concatenate((Q, [self.V[act2, s] + self.C[act, s, act2]]))
            possible_a = np.concatenate((possible_a, [act2]))
    max_arg = np.argmax(Q)
    if np.random.rand(1) < e:
        return np.random.choice(possible_a)
    else:
        return possible_a[max_arg]
```

- The function greed_act is where exploration takes place. Notice how it loops through each of the primitive actions. It then totals the value for those actions into a Q table called Q. We can see in the evaluate function how each level is evaluated based on whether it is a primitive state or higher. If it is primitive, the function returns the current value for that option/task/action. If the action is not primitive, then we recursively call evaluate on lower-level actions/tasks.

- We bring this all together in a function called *MAXQ_0*, shown here:
```
def MAXQ_0(self, i, s):  # i is action number
    if self.done:
        i = 11                      # to end recursion
    self.done = False
    if self.is_primitive(i):
        self.new_s, r, self.done, _ = copy.copy(self.env.step(i))
        self.r_sum += r
        self.num_of_ac += 1
        self.V[i, s] += self.alpha * (r - self.V[i, s])
        return 1
    elif i <= self.root:
        count = 0
        while not self.is_terminal(i, self.done): # a is new action num
            a = self.greed_act(i, s)
            N = self.MAXQ_0(a, s)
            self.V_copy = self.V.copy()
            evaluate_res = self.evaluate(i, self.new_s)
            self.C[i, s, a] += self.alpha * (
                self.gamma ** N * evaluate_res -    self.C[i, s, a])    ❶
            count += N
            s = self.new_s
        return count

def reset(self):
    self.env.reset()
    self.r_sum = 0
    self.num_of_ac = 0
    self.done = False
    self.new_s = copy.copy(self.env.s)
```

**❶** MAXQ_0 itself is a function that recursively iterates over the option tree shown in Figure 8-10. In this line we can see the derivation of a $C$ term indexed by $i$ for option, $s$ for state, and $a$ for action. You can think of $C$ as the Choice for each option, where each option represents the functional decomposition of lower options.

- Finally, our training code for this example becomes very simple and is shown here:

```
alpha = 0.15
gamma = .7
env = gym.make('Taxi-v3').env
taxi = Agent(env, alpha, gamma)
episodes = 5501
sum_list = []
for j in tqdm(range(episodes)):
    taxi.reset()
    taxi.MAXQ_0(10, env.s)      # start in root
    if taxi.r_sum > -20:
      sum_list.append(taxi.r_sum)
    if (j % 1000 == 0):
        print('already made', j, 'episodes')

sns.set(style='darkgrid')
sns.set(font_scale=1.5)
plt.figure(figsize=(15, 7.5))
plt.plot(sum_list)
plt.xlabel('episode num')
plt.ylabel('points')
plt.show()
```

- Run the entire code, and watch how quickly the agent is able to solve the problem. We don't demonstrate any output in this example, but the output rewards show well enough that the agent is solving the entire environment, although perhaps not as consistently as we may like.

Using HRL as a way to solve our Taxi environment proved to be very effective in this example. However, HRL itself proved to be too complex to implement in most mainstream research. In our example with MAXQ-0 and no assumption of state abstraction, we needed additional coding to make the example work. Implementing state abstractions can make an approach more generic but way more complex as well. This additional complexity also introduced further nuances that made algorithms less portable to other environments.

Ideally, RL researchers like to create algorithms that can be applied universally across domains. HRL has evolved to define levels of states as state abstractions. You won't see simple examples of these models very often. In almost all cases now, the field of reinforcement learning has moved to include deep learning. We will explore why that is the case in the next section.

# Bringing Deep to Reinforcement Learning

Deep reinforcement learning (DRL) has become the standard by which most mainstream RL is done these days. At its most basic form, DRL is just the augmentation of DL onto RL. The addition of DL allows us to tackle problems with many more states than Taxi but also allows us to reconsider what a state looks like.

In our previous examples, we assumed all states were discrete. That allowed us to consider only 16 discrete states in FrozenLake or 500 in Taxi, while in reality state space is rarely discrete but continuous. We can think of continuous state as any space constrained by upper- and lower-bound variables but not with any defined intermediary discrete states.

Look at Figure 8-11, which shows a cup or ball on a table in both discrete and continuous spaces. While we can say that the cup/ball is in a discrete state of 2,2, we can also say it has a continuous state of 2.2 units right and 2.3 units down. Notice that we could still be rounding those numbers off. To be more precise, our ball/cup may have an exact position of 2.219823,2.34534. The more precise we can be about state, the more precise our learning algorithm can be, thus allowing an agent finer control.

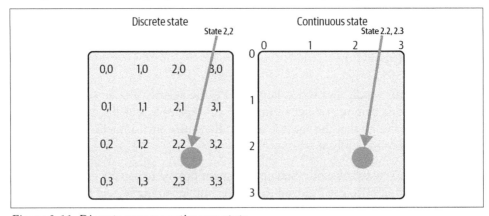

*Figure 8-11. Discrete versus continuous state*

Of course, being more precise impacts the dimensionality of our state space, which in turn forces us to consider much larger state spaces. However, what if we abstracted our perception of state to just what we observed at any point in time? This is not unlike what we humans do and are doing right now. We, for instance, are not able to see infinitely; our sight is limited, often to just what is immediately around us. Our world and state at any point in time are only partially visible, yet we can accomplish many things. If we put this in RL terms, the MDP of our lives at any single point in time is only partially observable. Thus our MDP becomes a partially observable MDP, or POMDP.

POMDP and state abstractions sound very similar. The main difference is that a state abstraction attempts to solve sub- or semi-MDPs, while a POMDP works to solve the entire problem by considering only a partial view. Let's look at a game example with an agent playing the classic 3D game Doom.

When the agent encounters monsters, it should kill them. Yet a monster could be in multiple states on its own. Casting the problem as a hierarchical MDP would require us to model several levels of options or state abstractions. Yet in most cases, if the agent sees a monster, all it needs to understand is what actions will kill it, assuming the monster generates a positive reward. So in effect, the agent needs to understand only the basics of killing a monster and moving through the environment. By adding deep learning to RL, we can move to using continuous states and consider the problem as a POMDP. In the next section, we go over the first deep learning application to RL, called DQN.

# Deep Q Learning

Deep learning applied to RL was first done with straight Q Learning, and the resulting system was called a *deep Q network*, or DQN. The DQN algorithm was first responsible for tackling and besting the classic Atari games like Breakout. In order to understand how we can integrate DL with RL, it is best to look at a quick code example. Fortunately, DQN is not that much more difficult than the other DL systems we have already built, so it hopefully should be more familiar than the previous RL algorithms. Let's jump into the DQN coding example in Example 8-11.

*Example 8-11. DQN on CartPole*

- Open the example *Chapter_8_DQN.ipynb* and run the code up to the following cell:
```
env = wrap_env(gym.make("CartPole-v1"))
```

- There are a number of cells above this cell that work to set up a display wrapper around the environment. This display wrapper allows us to save the output of a run through an environment as an MP4 video. That means any call to env.render() does not render to the notebook output but instead saves a frame of video.

- Scroll down farther and you can see a new section of code that will randomly play the environment, shown here:
```
observation = env.reset()

while True:
  env.render()
  action = env.action_space.sample()
```

```
observation, reward, done, info = env.step(action)

if done:
    break;

env.close() # make sure and close environment before showing video
show_video()
```

- Run the notebook up to and including the last cell, and you will see an example of CartPole running. CartPole is an environment that challenges the agent to balance a pole on top of a cart.

- Scroll down to the top of the next block with the top of the code shown here:
```
import tensorflow.keras as k
import tensorflow.keras.layers as kl
import tqdm.notebook as nb

class DQNAgent():
    def __init__(self, state_size, action_size):
        self.weight_backup      = "cartpole_weight.h5"
        self.state_size         = state_size
        self.action_size        = action_size
        self.memory             = deque(maxlen=2000)
        self.learning_rate      = 0.001
        self.gamma              = 0.95
        self.exploration_rate   = 1.0
        self.exploration_min    = 0.01
        self.exploration_decay  = 0.995
        self.brain              = self._build_model()
```

- In this case, we create a new class called *DQNAgent* that will encapsulate the code for our agent. Most of the terms in this example should be familiar, except for a few. Two new fields have been added for memory and a brain. Brain will hold the agent's internal DL network, and memory holds our training batches of data. Since Q Learning is off policy, we need to batch up training steps in a memory and use those later for training.

- Scroll down further to the next function, build_model:
```
def _build_model(self):
    # Neural Net for Deep-Q learning Model
    model = k.Sequential()
    model.add(kl.Dense(24, input_dim=self.state_size, activation='relu'))
    model.add(kl.Dense(24, activation='relu'))
    model.add(kl.Dense(self.action_size, activation='linear'))
    model.compile(loss='mse',
                optimizer=k.optimizers.Adam(lr=self.learning_rate))

    if os.path.isfile(self.weight_backup):
        model.load_weights(self.weight_backup)
```

```
    self.exploration_rate = self.exploration_min
  return model
```

- This code builds the deep learning model for our agent. You can see this is a simple three-layer network where the inputs are defined by the state size and the output is defined by the action size. Notice that our loss is defined as MSE, or mean squared error, with an Adam optimizer. That makes this model a regressor and not a classifier.

- Move down further, and you will see three more functions. The first function, save_model, just saves the model. The second function, act, is the equivalent of our previous Q Learning examples. Then the third function, remember, is where each previous set of state and actions are put to memory. Those memories will be batched later for training into the network:

```
def save_model(self):
  self.brain.save(self.weight_backup)

def act(self, state):
  if np.random.rand() <= self.exploration_rate:
      return random.randrange(self.action_size)
  act_values = self.brain.predict(state)
  return np.argmax(act_values[0])

def remember(self, state, action, reward, next_state, done):
  self.memory.append((state, action, reward, next_state, done))
```

- Further below is the replay function. Replay is where we replay remembered actions against the network and use those for training. The code for that is shown here:

```
def replay(self, batch_size):
  if len(self.memory) < batch_size:
      return
  sample_batch = random.sample(self.memory, batch_size)
  for state, action, reward, next_state, done in sample_batch:
    target = reward
    if not done:
      target = reward + self.gamma * np.amax(
        self.brain.predict(next_state)[0]) ❶
    target_f = self.brain.predict(state)
    target_f[0][action] = target
    self.brain.fit(state, target_f, epochs=1, verbose=0)
  if self.exploration_rate > self.exploration_min:
    self.exploration_rate *= self.exploration_decay
```

❶ Inside the replay function we can see how batches of remembered events are randomly sampled for input into the network. We then feed each of those events into the network and determine the difference or loss between what we expect the Q should be, calculated here, and what the network is predicting. Notice that this line is equivalent to our previous implementation of the Q equation. The last part of the code is where we decrease the explora tion_rate epsilon.

- Jump to the next block of code, and we can see that this is where the agent is set up and trained:

```
batch_size = 32
episodes = 100

state_size = env.observation_space.shape[0]
action_size = env.action_space.n
agent = DQNAgent(state_size, action_size)

for index_episode in nb.tqdm(range(episodes)):
    state = env.reset()
    state = np.reshape(state, [1, state_size])

    done = False
    index = 0
    while not done:
        action = agent.act(state)
        next_state, reward, done, _ = env.step(action)
        next_state = np.reshape(next_state, [1, state_size])
        agent.remember(state, action, reward, next_state, done)
        state = next_state
    agent.replay(batch_size)
```

- This code loops through a number of training episodes and then lets the agent explore the environment in each episode. We can see the agent learning in the call to agent.replay at the last line of code.

- Finally, after the agent is trained to a specified number of episodes, we can review how well the agent played the game with the following code:

```
state = env.reset()
while not done:
    env.render()
    action = agent.act(state)
    next_state, reward, done, _ = env.step(action)
    state = next_state

env.close()
show_video()
```

- Run the full notebook, and after the agent has finished training, you can visualize the output in the notebook as a video.

The DQN agent in this example will need about 10,000 training episodes/iterations to make the agent solve the environment. This may seem like a lot, but realize that a similar DQN agent used to beat the Atari games required 50–100 million iterations.

While an Atari environment is substantially more complex, it still requires days or even weeks of training. Training times like this have been a constant criticism of DRL. Fortunately, the DQN model is now several years old, and DRL has advanced considerably since then. In the next section, we will look at a mainstream advance in RL and DRL that we will find useful for our purposes.

## Optimizing Policy with Policy Gradient Methods

One of the key downsides to using Q Learning and explicitly DQN agents is their need to work off policy. This off-policy characteristic is what requires the DQN model to use the memory mechanism we saw in the last exercise. To get away from working off-policy and back to working on-policy, we need to consider our old friend SARSA and TD learning.

Remember, Expected SARSA was on policy and allowed the agent to train while using the same policy. The mechanism that uses the concept of TD one-step will allow our agent to work on-policy and is called a *policy gradient* (PG) *method*. PG methods define a whole other area of DRL known as *policy improvement methods*, whereas the basis of DQN and Q Learning define an area of DRL known as *value-based methods*. Now, you would think one method would outperform the other, and that is indeed the case in some areas. For example, value-based methods tend to perform better on discrete environments and action spaces, whereas policy gradient methods perform better on continuous action and state spaces.

 *Generalized policy iteration*, or GPI, is a term we use to denote an algorithm that iteratively improves a policy. GPI is a basis for the TD methods we have covered in this chapter.

In DQN, it was obvious to denote where classic reinforcement methods were used and where deep learning took over. The family of PG methods is much more integrated into the RL method itself. Consequently, the math used to explain these methods is quite intense and requires in-depth knowledge of advanced linear algebra. Rather than getting into the graduate-level math needed to explain PG, we are going to instead look at a simple example. Keep in mind that "simple" is relative here, and if you find some of the following concepts overwhelming, not to worry. We will revisit this model again in the next chapter in more detail. For now, though, let's dig into a code example so we can see how this works and then understand the details later. Example 8-12 introduces a simple PG method augmented with an actor-critic architecture.

*Example 8-12. Policy value on LunarLander*

- Open the example *Chapter_8_A2C_PG_LL.ipynb*. This example uses the same base of code to render the environment. Run the code up to the following cell:

```
env = wrap_env(gym.make("LunarLander-v2"))
```

- In this exercise we are going to tackle the difficult problem of landing a space capsule on the moon. This environment used to be an old video game going back to the 1970s. The object of the game is to land the lander on an identified landing pad. If the lander comes in too fast, it will crash. Likewise, if the lander misses the landing zone, it also will crash. A reward is given for how well the lander safely lands, with an optimum reward of 200 being a perfect landing.

- Continue to the next cell, and you will see the construction of the base brain model. We often use the term *brain* to denote the agent's learned model. The code for the brain is shown here:

```
class PolicyValueBrain(tf.keras.Model):
  def __init__(self, num_actions):
    super().__init__('mlp_policy')

    self.hidden1 = kl.Dense(32, activation='relu')   ❶
    self.hidden2 = kl.Dense(32, activation='relu')
    self.value = kl.Dense(1, name='value')
    # Logits are unnormalized log probabilities.
    self.logits = kl.Dense(num_actions, name='policy_logits')
    self.dist = ProbabilityDistribution()

  def call(self, inputs, **kwargs):
    # Inputs is a numpy array, convert to a tensor.
    x = tf.convert_to_tensor(inputs)

    hidden_logs = self.hidden1(x)
    hidden_vals = self.hidden2(x)
    return self.logits(hidden_logs), self.value(hidden_vals)   ❷

  def action_value(self, obs):
    logits, value = self.predict_on_batch(obs)   ❸
    action = self.dist.predict_on_batch(logits)
    return np.squeeze(action, axis=-1), np.squeeze(value, axis=-1)
```

❶ Here we can see the start of where we define two dense layers. Be careful to note that we do not join these layers; rather, they exist separately and in parallel to each other. Notice how we define two more layers after this: one layer called *value*, which denotes the output or expected value, and another called *logits*, which denotes the agent's best action.

❷   You can see inside the call function where we combine these layers and generate the output of actions and value.

❸   Inside the `action_value` function is where we predict the logits and value. Logits are then converted to an explicit action in the next line.

- We can see that this brain returns an action and a value. This is different from our previous RL examples, and to use this output, we still need to create an agent. However, in this case, our agent needs to be slightly different in order to use these values.

- Scroll down to the next block, and you can see the start of an agent called *A2CAgent*, shown here:

```python
import tensorflow.keras.losses as kls
import tensorflow.keras.optimizers as ko

class A2CAgent:
  def __init__(self, model, lr=7e-3, gamma=0.99, value_c=0.5,
                        entropy_c=1e-4):
    self.gamma = gamma
    # Coefficients are used for the loss terms.
    self.value_c = value_c
    self.entropy_c = entropy_c

    self.model = model
    self.model.compile(
      optimizer=ko.Nadam(learning_rate=lr),
      # Define separate losses for policy logits and value estimate.
      loss=[self._logits_loss, self._value_loss])
```

- An A2C agent, or advantage actor-critic agent, is a method by which we use an online actor to act on a policy in concert with a critic that measures the error of that action. We can see inside this `init` function how the model is composed and the loss is defined.

- The bulk of the A2C code is for the determination of loss, but we will look at one key section, the `train` function, as shown here:

```python
def train(self, env, batch_sz=64, updates=100):
    # Storage helpers for a single batch of data.
    actions = np.empty((batch_sz,), dtype=np.int32)
    rewards, dones, values = np.empty((3, batch_sz))
    observations = np.empty((batch_sz,) + env.observation_space.shape)

    ep_rewards = [0.0]
    next_obs = env.reset()
    for update in nb.tqdm(range(updates)):
      for step in range(batch_sz):
        observations[step] = next_obs.copy()
        actions[step], values[step] = self.model.action_value(
```

```
        next_obs[None, :])
      next_obs, rewards[step], dones[step], _ = env.step(actions[step])

      ep_rewards[-1] += rewards[step]
      if dones[step]:
        ep_rewards.append(0.0)
        next_obs = env.reset()
        tf.summary.scalar('rewards', data=ep_rewards[-2],
                      step=(len(ep_rewards) - 1))

    _, next_value = self.model.action_value(next_obs[None, :])

    returns, advs = self._returns_advantages(rewards, dones,
                                  values, next_value)
    # A trick to input actions and advantages through same API.
    acts_and_advs = np.concatenate([actions[:, None],
                              advs[:, None]], axis=-1) ❶
    losses = self.model.train_on_batch(observations,
                              [acts_and_advs, returns])
    tf.summary.scalar('losses', data=losses[0], step=update)
  return ep_rewards
```

❶ Most of this code should likely feel somewhat familiar now, and it is quite similar to most of the previous training code. The exception is at the bottom; prior to this section, we saw a note that discusses combining the action and advantage. The action and value methods returned from the brain denote the action and advantage output. We denote the value as an advantage to denote the amount by which the agent can do better.

- Be sure to review the rest of the code in the A2CAgent class, but again, we will revisit the calculations in this code during the next chapter. The key takeaway from this code is that our agent is finding not only the best action but also a value that can tell it how much better it may be able to do.

- Jump to the next code block, and you can see where we set up some logging for TensorBoard. Since most RL algorithms can take a substantial amount of training time, we want to be able to monitor the progress in real time. TensorBoard will allow us to do that. Following is the code for setting up TensorBoard:

```
%load_ext tensorboard  #this line at top of the notebook

logdir = os.path.join("logs",
                  datetime.datetime.now().strftime("%Y%m%d-%H%M%S"))
file_writer = tf.summary.create_file_writer(logdir)
file_writer.set_as_default()

%tensorboard --logdir logs
```

- When running this complete example, you will see the TensorBoard output, as shown in Figure 8-12. You can monitor two plots: one for the amount of loss, which we want to see decrease, and one for total episode rewards, which we want to see increase.

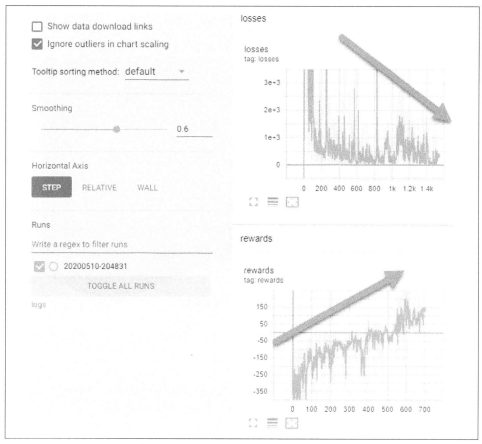

*Figure 8-12. TensorBoard output showing losses and rewards*

- Finally, we can run the training and view the agent playing the game with the following two blocks of code:

```
agent = A2CAgent(model)
rewards_history = agent.train(env, batch_sz=128, updates=2000)
print("Finished training, testing...")
env.close()

agent = A2CAgent(model)
env = wrap_env(gym.make("LunarLander-v2"))
```

```
print("%d out of 200" % agent.test(env)) # 200 out of 200
env.close()
```

- In the first block, the agent is created and trained. Then in the second block, we create a new agent using the pretrained brain (model), create a brand-new wrapped environment, and then test that agent and brain. The results of the last frame of that test are shown in Figure 8-13.

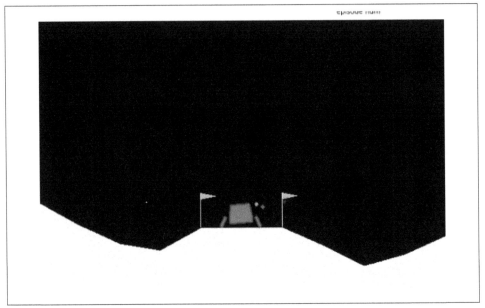

*Figure 8-13. Landing the lunar lander*

- Run all the code in the notebook and go grab a coffee or some lunch. Training typically takes around 20–25 minutes, but your results may vary.

That last exercise demonstrated the power behind what we would consider to be just a vanilla PG method augmented with an actor-critic advantage. This method is quite advanced, but hopefully it shows the power of DRL for solving complex tasks like landing a lunar lander. We will look at using other optimized DRL methods in Chapter 9. For now, let's finish up this chapter with the conclusion.

# Conclusion

In this chapter we looked at methods for improving on AI learning with reinforcement learning. RL is a method that allows for agent AI to learn by trial and error, giving agents the ability not only to explore their environment but also to continually learn on their own.

---

Reinforcement learning is still in its infancy but has shown promise in many aspects of AI learning, from beating humans at the game of Go to besting scores on old Atari games. DRL has shown that AI can indeed be smarter than us and approach problems outside our limited understanding, giving it the ability to better solve known as well as unknown problems.

In the next chapter, we look at applying DRL to an agent platform that can help us better regulate the foods we consume. We will build an app called Eat/No Eat that we can train to help us decide on the foods we should and should not eat.

# CHAPTER 9

# Putting AI Assistants to Work

Throughout this book, we have used a variety of deep learning architectures and systems to do our bidding. Many of the applications we have developed have obvious use cases for commercialization, while some do not. In the previous chapter, we introduced the concept of smarter AI assistants that could be powered by deep reinforcement learning. For the examples in that chapter, we looked at using AI agents to play games and solve puzzles. The purpose of that was to demonstrate how AI was evolving into something beyond rules-based, or supervised, learning. As we learned, reinforcement learning allows us to build constantly learning and evolving agents. In this chapter, we extend that concept to a full agent assistant that can recommend the food you should or shouldn't eat.

In this chapter, we build the Eat/No Eat agent assistant. The purpose of this smart assistant is to monitor your food intake and suggest which dishes you should or shouldn't consume. The agent will be able to do this just by looking at a picture of the food you plan to eat. Building an agent that can consume images of food and decide whether or not the user eats is no easy task. It will require us to revisit many of the things we've learned in this book.

We will start this chapter off by looking at what food datasets may be good candidates for a basis of training the agent. Reinforcement learning is powerful, but it also requires extensive training. In this case, we are going to use elements of pretraining or pre-exploration, where we will first train parts of the agent model against a well-known food dataset. After we train the first section of the model, known as the *nutritionist*, we will move on to preparing the agent itself. As we saw in the previous chapter, there are many RL algorithms that can be applied. For this agent, we will use what is now considered a classic, the DQN.

The DQN agent will consume output from the nutritionist in order to decide if the user can eat or not. To do that, we will use pretraining to train the DQN agent with a set of starting behaviors. When those starting behaviors are trained, we can let the agent loose and allow it to learn on its own. Then we will finish off the chapter talking about next steps for this simple agent—how you, the user, may improve on the Eat/No Eat agent or build your own intelligent agents in the future.

Building our own intelligent agents will take the coordination of several key pieces. We will cover each major element in the following sections:

- Designing an Eat/No Eat AI
- Selecting and Preparing Data for the AI
- Training the Nutritionist Model
- Optimizing Deep Reinforcement Learning
- Building the Eat/No Eat Agent
- Testing the AI Agent
- Commercializing the AI Agent

The project in this chapter was designed to employ several key elements of previous chapters. At the same time, we will take a more practical approach to building the AI in this chapter. Often times, engineering real-world applications requires more finesse and making do with what you have. Building the Eat/No Eat AI will be no exception to that, as we will begin to see in the next section.

# Designing an Eat/No Eat AI

In the coming years, there will likely be an explosion of smarter agents. These agents may be developed on single monolithic platforms like Siri, Alexa, and Google. Alternatively, agent apps may coexist alongside other apps on your phone or whatever future computing device you employ. Either way, AI agents that can help us make better-informed decisions may become the norm. It only stands to reason, then, that an agent assistant that can help people would top that list. This is in part the concept for the Eat/No Eat agent.

The Eat/No Eat agent concept is about helping people make better decisions about the foods they consume. Not all foods are healthy for all people. Not only that, but the foods you consumed when you were younger are likely different from the ones you should eat now. Children have nutritional requirements that are very different from those of their grandparents. Likewise, people who perform different jobs need different diets. A construction worker may need to eat higher amounts of fat as opposed to someone working on a computer all day, not to mention other factors like body type, genetics, stress, and so on. It's no wonder so many of us struggle to eat a healthy diet.

The Eat/No Eat app is not designed by a nutritionist, and the food ratings have been mapped arbitrarily based on the author's direct food knowledge and experience.

Eat/No Eat is about building a smart agent that can identify the foods you should eat and those you shouldn't. First you will show the agent an image of the food you want to eat. In turn the agent will respond with "Eat" or "No Eat." If you eat the food and the agent recommended you eat the food and the food was good for you, the agent is rewarded. Conversely, if you eat the food and the agent didn't recommend it for you and the food is bad for you, the agent is rewarded. Figure 9-1 shows how we may give an agent an immediate reward based on various user actions, to eat or not to eat.

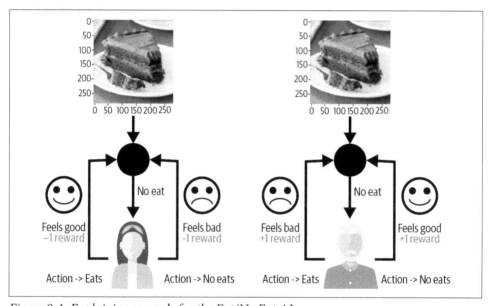

*Figure 9-1. Explaining rewards for the Eat/No Eat AI*

On the left side of Figure 9-1, we can see the user is a young girl. She feeds the agent an image of cake and the agent responds with "No Eat," which seems appropriate. However, because she is a little girl, she can consume the cake with few ill effects and will likely feel good after eating the cake. Perhaps this is because she needs a lot of energy to play with friends. Alternatively, by not eating the cake, she may lack energy and feel lethargic. On the right side of Figure 9-1 is an older man feeding the same cake image into the agent. In this case, though, the agent is correct and is rewarded positively. We can see that if the man eats the cake and feels bad, we reward the agent positively. The same is true if the man doesn't eat the cake and feels good. Again, the agent is rewarded positively.

We train the agent with either positive or negative rewards based on how the user feels and what choice the agent suggested. However, this also requires the agent to understand more about the user. In this example, we would need to feed in the user's age and gender as well as the image. Recall from Chapter 8 our discussion about reinforcement learning. These inputs become the current state of the agent. Figure 9-2 shows what types of state input we could potentially feed an agent.

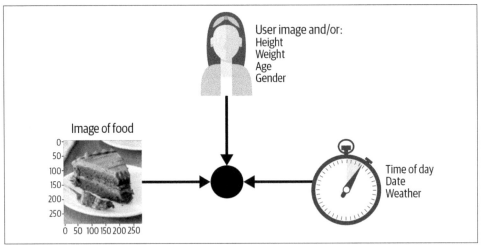

*Figure 9-2. Possible input states into agent*

While we could feed all of these inputs into the agent as the user's state, it isn't practical, at least not as a first attempt. Instead, for our first attempt at building this application, we will look at feeding just the input image into the agent. We will also break our agent up into two parts. The first half will be a nutritionist model that will break down the food images into some nutrition state, as shown in Figure 9-3. From there, the output of the nutritionist model will be fed into a deep reinforcement learning agent we've seen before: DQN.

Figure 9-3 shows version 1.0 of the Eat/No Eat AI and a possible future version. Our first agent will only take output from the nutritionist model, but future versions could be set up to take other attributes to represent state. The state output from the nutritionist represents arbitrary nutrition/health ratings for a category of food, where the output of the model is a regression fit to the arbitrary nutrition ratings in the model.

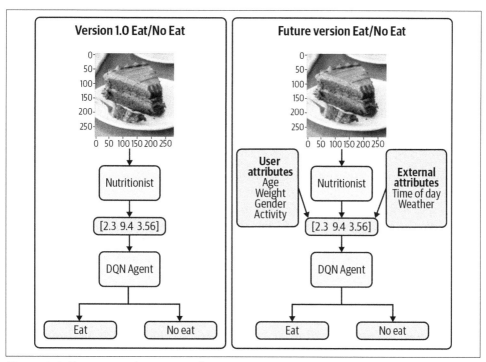

*Figure 9-3. Examining the agent architecture*

What I found by building this app was that trying to ascertain the actual macronutrients in food, essentially trying to estimate protein, carbohydrates, and fat for prepared foods, caused for poor-fitting models. Instead, the method I found that works best was estimating the nutritional quality of foods by category on a more general scale. We will uncover more about training the nutritionist model later in this chapter.

As we will see, by reducing the state of the input from a full 300 × 300 image to just three continuous inputs, we can establish a working agent with less training data. Less training data means we can train the nutritionist model and the DQN agent more quickly, thus allowing us to prove the concept of the Eat/No Eat agent sooner or in fewer iterations.

Having the available data to build a working concept of an AI is a constant issue. Many times projects will fail because companies didn't have what they considered the right data, whereas oftentimes the data isn't the problem, but rather the method itself was flawed. More data does not always mean better data or better models. Over and over again, we see advanced AI models trained in the lab fail when applied to the real world. This is why we also want to emphasize that the Eat/No Eat agent will continually learn from real-world data. Since initial training data is often key to building AI, it will be the focus of our next section.

## Selecting and Preparing Data for the AI

A reinforcement learning agent is often designed by the state it consumes. Many advanced deep reinforcement learning agents will use raw visual state as input. This is the case for agents designed to play the classic Atari games. In those cases, raw images of the game play area were fed into the agent.

Agents were set up to consume images by using convolutional network layers to pre-process the input, essentially by extracting the relevant features from the image. This image input system can work very well in games with a fixed point of view, but it often fails when put into real-world practice. Another issue that arises is the sheer amount of training this takes. For instance, it takes on the order of 3 million–60 million training iterations to train an agent on Atari, which is far from practical when developing our Eat/No Eat app.

Therefore, the simplest way we can make our agent quicker to train is to reduce the state. That means using raw images is out of the question, at least for feeding directly into the agent. Instead, we will make an intermediary model called the *nutritionist*. You can think of the nutritionist as an embedding or encoder. It will encode the food images down to some arbitrary vector that represents nutritional attributes of the food. That small set of attributes, a size 3 vector, then can be fed as state into the RL agent. This will allow us not only to train the agent far more quickly but also to retrain the agent in real time. However, the trick now becomes building an effective nutritionist model.

To train the nutritionist model, we want a set of food images that is categorized in some manner. Fortunately, there are plenty of food image datasets that fit this bill. The Food-101 dataset is similar to other well-known datasets (MNIST, CIFAR) in that it has one thousand images for each category. In Food-101 there are 101 categories of food for a total of 101,000 images. This is quite a nice, comprehensive dataset, but it's a little too big for training on Colab. There is a smaller dataset called Recipes5K, created by Marc Bolaños from the University of Barcelona, that will work better.

Recipes5K are defined the same as Food-101 in that it uses the same food categories. It differs in that it contains far fewer examples per category but also contains recipe information. We will ignore the recipe information for this project. All we need right now is food images labeled by food category. Let's see how we can set up and prepare the Recipe5K dataset for training for our nutritionist in Example 9-1.

*Example 9-1. Loading and preparing data for the nutritionist*

- Open *Chapter_9_Data_Prep.ipynb* and run the first code block that loads all the imports.

- Next, we want to pull down the custom Recipes5K dataset from Dropbox and unpack it, as shown in the following code:

```
data_folder = 'data'
recipes_zip = tf.keras.utils.get_file('recipes.zip',
    origin = 'https://www.dropbox.com/s/i1hvs96mnahozq0/Recipes5k.zip?dl=1',
    extract = True)
print(recipes_zip)
data_folder = os.path.dirname(recipes_zip)
os.remove(recipes_zip)
print(data_folder)
```

- We first use `tf.keras.utils` function `get_file` to pull down and unpack the *Recipes5K.zip* file. The `extract=True` input also tells the function to unzip the folder into a temporary path. After that, we print out some paths to see where things are saved and delete the original downloaded ZIP file, since we no longer need it.

- Next, we create some folder paths, as shown in the code here:

```
!dir /root/.keras/datasets
data_folder = data_folder + '/Recipes5k/'
images_folder = data_folder + 'images/'
print(images_folder)
```

- After setting the folder paths, we will the list the contents of the images folder with the following code:

```
%ls {images_folder}
```

- Run the cell, and the output of the last line should display the 101 food category image folders. Each folder contains the images of food for that category.

- With the food images loaded, we can move on to loading nutritional labels. The nutritional labels that we will train the nutritionist to are set up in *foods.txt*. The code to download *foods.txt* is shown here:

```
foods_txt = tf.keras.utils.get_file('foods.txt',
    origin = 'https://www.dropbox.com/s/6jjje7mhqo9ycyi/foods.txt?dl=1')

print(foods_txt)
```

- *foods.txt* is a list of food categories with arbitrary nutrition information about each category. An example of *foods.txt* is shown here:

```
name,keto,carbs,health
apple_pie,1,10,1
baby_back_ribs,9,3,6
baklava,1,10,4
beef_carpaccio,10,1,8
```

```
beef_tacos,2,4,7
beef_tartare,10,1,8
beet_salad,2,8,10
```

- Each food category is identified by nutritional attributes on a 1–10 scale. The first attribute is keto for keto diet–friendly. The next is for foods high in carbs, and the last is for the overall wholesomeness of the food. These foods were rated somewhat arbitrarily, so feel free to update *foods.txt* if you disagree with any ratings. As stated previously, we first attempted to define food categories by protein, fat, and carbs for each category, but this ended up not being very successful.

 A keto diet is extremely low in carbohydrates and high in protein. It is a form of dieting that has shown to be successful for most ages and activity levels. In fact, this diet works better when an individual's activity level is low. The author of this book used a keto-based diet to lose 180 pounds, going from a weight of around 400 pounds down to a weight of 220 within 18 months.

- The next code cell defines a function for extracting and normalizing the food category information. Remember that we always want to define input data around 0, or close to it. For that reason we take the food attribute data, defined on a scale of 1 to 10, and subtract 5, as shown here:

```
def get_category_array(keto, carbs, health):
  return np.array([float(keto)-5, float(carbs)-5, float(health)-5])
```

- Following this, in the next cell, we define a function that will read the *foods.txt* file and extract the nutrient information into a list, as shown in the following code:

```
import csv

def get_food_nutrients(nutrient_file):
  foods = {}
  with open(foods_txt) as csv_file:
    csv_reader = csv.reader(csv_file, delimiter=',')
    line_count = 0
    for row in csv_reader:
      if line_count == 0:
        print(f'Column names are {", ".join(row)}')
        line_count += 1
      else:
        categories = get_category_array(row[1],row[2],row[3])
        foods[row[0]] = categories
        line_count += 1
    print(f'Processed {line_count} lines.')
  return foods
```

- Run the previous cell and the next one, as shown, to fill the category nutrient list:
```
food_nutrients = get_food_nutrients(foods_txt)
print(food_nutrients)
```

- The next step is to load the images and match them up with the labels so we can train the nutritionist model. Run the next couple of code blocks as shown:
```
from fastprogress.fastprogress import master_bar, progress_bar
from IPython.display import Image
from os import listdir
from pickle import dump

def load_image(image_path):
    img = tf.io.read_file(image_path)
    img = tf.image.decode_jpeg(img, channels=3)
    img = tf.image.resize(img, (299, 299))
    img = tf.keras.applications.inception_v3.preprocess_input(img)
    return img, image_path
```

- The first section of the above code features some new imports. We first import `fastprogress` to render some nicer progress bars for the long-running tasks of loading and labeling images. After that, the `load_image` function is defined to read the image from the path. From reading the image, it decodes, resizes, and processes it with the various helper functions. For the nutritionist, we are going to use a pretrained Inception model with transfer learning. Therefore, we need to process the image using an Inception preprocessor.

- Next we define the `load_images` function for loading and pairing the images, as shown in the following code:
```
def load_images(food_w_nutrients, directory):
    X = []
    Y = []
    mb = master_bar(listdir(directory))
    for food_group in mb:
      try:
        for pic in progress_bar(listdir(directory + food_group),
              parent=mb, comment='food = ' + food_group):
          filename = directory + food_group + '/' + pic
          image, img_path = load_image(filename)
          Y.append(food_w_nutrients[food_group])
          X.append(image)
      except:
        continue
    return X,Y
```

- All this function does is iterate over the food category folders and load each of the images. It then labels the images per the food category nutrients that we extracted from *foods.txt* earlier.

- Finally, we put the pieces together and load everything into X and Y datasets, as shown here:

```
X, Y = load_images(food_nutrients, images_folder)
print(len(X), len(Y))
```

At the end of the last exercise, we will have a training set of data ready to be trained on the nutritionist model. We will look at how to build and train the nutritionist encoder in the next section.

## Training the Nutritionist Model

The nutritionist model we need to build next is really just an encoder. Remember that we covered autoencoders in Chapter 7 when we discussed GANs. In this case, the nutritionist model is going to learn a useful and user-defined encoding. For our Eat/No Eat app, we are going to encode a food to some arbitrary nutrition values. The encoding could be anything but really should be meaningful to the data and the expected result.

 You could use this image encoding method for a variety of other applications outside of eating food. Some possible ideas include house or real estate pricing, vacation rentals, equipment inspection, and so on. Images are also just one possible input method. Encoders could be developed for text using NLP networks or transformers, with the possibility of making a Read/No Read app. This could be extended further to guide students through learning. Imagine a smart agent that could guide your learning process over complex material like deep learning.

For the next exercise, we are going to set up and build the nutritionist model/encoder. We will base this agent on an established classification model called InceptionResNet2. This model uses convolutional and residual networks for better feature extraction from images. It was found to be the best model to use for this particular application. We will use transfer learning to convert this model from a classifier to a regressor. The model is currently built to classify the ImageNet dataset to one thousand classes. Instead, we are going to retrain the model to generate three linear outputs that match the foods' nutrients. Let's see how this all works by jumping into Example 9-2.

*Example 9-2. Building the nutritionist encoder*

- Open *Chapter_9_Build_Nutritionist.ipynb*. The first half of this notebook is almost identical to the last exercise.
- Scroll down to around code cell 6, as shown here:

```
use_NAS = False
if use_NAS:
  IMG_SIZE = 224 # 299 for Inception, 224 for NASNet
  IMG_SHAPE = (IMG_SIZE, IMG_SIZE, 3)
else:
  IMG_SIZE = 299 # 299 for Inception, 224 for NASNet
  IMG_SHAPE = (IMG_SIZE, IMG_SIZE, 3)
```

- The addition of this code cell sets up the ability to swap the base model used for the nutritionist. By default, the model will use Inception. It is a simple matter to change the model to NasNetMobile or another base application of your choosing. Each base application, like Inception, has a preferred image size, and this block sets that size.

- Scroll down to the next cell and you will see the load_image function we already looked at. Inside this function, notice that we removed the hardcoded image shape and replaced it with the following:
```
img = tf.image.resize(img, (IMG_SIZE, IMG_SIZE))
```

- Continue scrolling down the notebook until you see the code that loads and processes the data using the load_images function. This is where we left off in the last exercise. Run all the cells up to this point by selecting Runtime → Run before from the menu.

- This takes us to our first new cell, as shown here:
```
tf.keras.backend.clear_session()

if use_NAS:
  # Create the base model from the pretrained model
  base_model = tf.keras.applications.NASNetMobile(input_shape=IMG_SHAPE,
    include_top=False,
    weights='imagenet')
else:
  # Create the base model from the pretrained model
  base_model = tf.keras.applications.InceptionResNetV2(input_shape=IMG_SHAPE,
    include_top=False,
    weights='imagenet')
```

- This section of code loads the base_model with a pre-trained model filled with weights trained on ImageNet. We again use the variable use_NAS to denote the type of model we want to build. The line of code at the top calling the clear_session function is used to free up GPU memory. If that doesn't work and you still experience Out of Memory errors, then you need to use the menu to factory-reset the Runtime. Be sure to also notice the include_top=False. Recall that in a transfer learning application, we do not include the top or output layer of the model. Thus we remove the top classification layer so that we can replace it with our own.

- Down to the next cell, and this time we can see the X and Y datasets we prepared are now getting converted into a dataset:

```
dataset = tf.data.Dataset.from_tensor_slices((X, Y))
dataset
batches = dataset.batch(64)
```

- The function `from_tensor_slices` is used to convert the X image data and Y nutrition labels into a dataset. After that we batch the data into batches of size 64. You can try different batch sizes, but be aware that this can cause memory issues. Larger batches require more GPU memory.

- After that we are going to extract a single test batch and feed it into our `base_model`. We need to do this in order to query the output feature shape, as shown in the following code:

```
for image_batch, label_batch in batches.take(1):
    pass

feature_batch = base_model(image_batch)
print(feature_batch.shape)

OUTPUTS
(64, 8, 8, 1536)
```

- We need to know the output shape of the `base_model` since we removed the top classification layer. This output shape will be the input into our new regression layer.

- Next, we want to make our `base_model` trainable but only partly so. The code that sets up the base model training is shown here:

```
base_model.trainable = True

if use_NAS:
    fine_tune_at = 100
else:
    fine_tune_at = 550

for layer in base_model.layers[:fine_tune_at]:
    layer.trainable =  False

base_model.summary()
```

- This code sets the model up for partial training. We still want to keep the base layers that do the heavy lifting intact. Changing the lower layers will allow us to better optimize the model for our purposes. This can be at the cost of additional training, so be careful about how much of a model you want to retrain.

- Scroll down some more, and the next few code blocks set up the new regression layer and add it to the model, as shown here:

```
global_average_layer = tf.keras.layers.GlobalAveragePooling2D()
feature_batch_average = global_average_layer(feature_batch)

prediction_layer = tf.keras.layers.Dense(3)
prediction_batch = prediction_layer(feature_batch_average)

model = tf.keras.Sequential([
  base_model,
  global_average_layer,
  prediction_layer
])
```

- Notice that we add a GlobalAveragePooling2D layer right on top. This is the first layer that will pool the features from the base_model. After that, we add the prediction layer, a Dense of size 3. We then put it all together using a sequential model.

- With the model built, we can move on to compiling it, as shown here:

```
base_learning_rate = 0.0001
model.compile(optimizer=tf.keras.optimizers.Nadam(lr=base_learning_rate),
    loss=tf.keras.losses.MeanAbsoluteError(),
    metrics=['mae', 'mse', 'accuracy'])

model.summary()
```

- The last sections of code compile the model with an Nadam optimizer and using a MeanAbsoluteError loss function. Finally, notice what metrics we are tracking: mae (mean absolute error), mse (mean squared error), and accuracy. MAE or MSE are not always very explanatory, so we add accuracy. It should be noted that accuracy is not a measure on which we should be basing loss off on since this is a regressor.

- Be sure to run all the code up to this point. If you experience out-of-memory errors, just factory-reset the runtime and run all the cells again.

- Since we want to preserve the training of this model, we are going to set up a checkpoint save folder. This will allow us to save the model as it is being trained. As well as allowing us to load the model later for use with our RL agent. Run the following code cell to mount your GDrive:

```
from google.colab import drive
drive.mount('/content/gdrive')

folder = '/content/gdrive/My Drive/Models'
if os.path.isdir(folder) == False:
  os.makedirs(folder)
```

- As soon as you run the above cell, you will prompted to enter a security code. Above the text box is a link. Click the link, and follow the directions to generate the security code for you. Paste the security code in and the next lines will run and create a new folder on your GDrive called *Models*.

- With the Models folder set up, you now run the next code cell that will create the model checkpoint function, shown here:

```
checkpoint_path = folder + "/cp-{epoch:04d}.ckpt"
checkpoint_dir = os.path.dirname(checkpoint_path)

cp_callback = tf.keras.callbacks.ModelCheckpoint(
    filepath=checkpoint_path,
    verbose=1,
    save_weights_only=True,
    period=5)
```

- This cell creates a `ModelCheckpoint` object that encompasses a function for saving the model every five epochs.

- In the next cell we can see where the `fit` function is called and the model is trained:

```
history = model.fit(batches,epochs=25, callbacks=[cp_callback])
```

- Here we can see fit being called on the model with the batches dataset. The model is to be trained for 25 epochs, and the `callback` function will intermediately save the model to the Models folder. You may notice we are not training the model with any validation or test data. This is intentional, and we will get to why shortly.

- Run the code up to this point, and let the model train. This may take 15 minutes, so be sure to get up and stretch your legs while waiting.

- When the model has completed training, you can visualize the output using the next cell. In this cell, it is the standard Matplotlib visualization code we have seen many times before. We won't need to review this here again.

At this point we have trained the nutritionist model to what should be an acceptable loss or accuracy. As we mentioned previously, we didn't train the model with any validation or test data. The data we trained our model is quite small to begin with. That means we could get wide variations in training results and test results. Indeed, running test and validation splits off of data works best with much larger datasets. That doesn't mean that splitting data for training and testing shouldn't be done. On the contrary. You should always plan to split your data with training, test, and possibly validation sets in mind.

In this case, we decide to use our training dataset for only training for a few reasons. First, the dataset is quite small, and this could skew our results. Second, food pictures in each category can vary widely. Third, and most important, is that we want to use real data for testing/validation, that is, we want to use our own food pictures or arbitrary ones pulled from the internet.

By using our own food pictures, we can better gauge if the output results make sense. It can also tell us if our model needs to be tweaked or if we need to modify the category nutrition values. This is also the benefit of breaking the agent up into an encoder model and an RL model. Understanding the encoder also allows us to gauge the importance of any formatting requirements. That means for this app we want to force our user to use clear, cropped, and focused images of individual food plates or items. Conceivably our app could take any picture of food, but this creates far too many options. More options mean more training and more training data.

In this next partial exercise we are going to complete the nutritionist model by testing the model. This exercise will require you to upload between 25 and 100 food images. If you don't have that many food images of your own, be sure to search the internet. Make sure to use foods in the designated food categories. You can find those categories in Example 9-1. After you have obtained those images, proceed to Example 9-3.

*Example 9-3. Building and testing the nutritionist encoder*

- Open *Chapter_9_Test_Nutritionist.ipynb*. The top cells of this notebook borrow code from the previous exercises.
- Run the first cell to connect to your GDrive, just as we have done before.
- Next, you can see we have a single function to create the nutritionist model called `create_model`. In this function resides all the code to set up and create the model resides.
- At this point we want to upload those test food images to the Colab folder. You can do that by expanding the folder section on the left side, then clicking the Upload button, as shown in Figure 9-4.

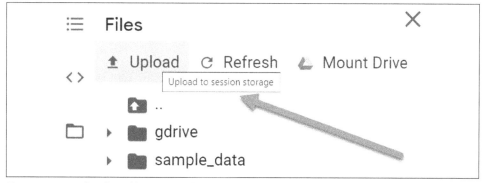

*Figure 9-4. Uploading files to Colab*

- Run all the code up to and including the following cell by selecting Runtime → Run Before and Runtime → Run Selection:

```
import os
from os import listdir
from shutil import copyfile

image_folder = my_drive + 'TestImages/'
if os.path.isdir(image_folder) == False:
  os.makedirs(image_folder)
  new_images = True
else:
  new_images = False

def save_test_image(image):
  copyfile(image, image)

def get_test_images(saved):
  if saved:
    directory = image_folder
  else:
    directory = '/content/'

  images = []
  for file in listdir(directory):
    if file.endswith(".jpg"):
      images.append(directory + file)
      if not saved:
        save_test_image(directory + file)
  return images

images = get_test_images(not new_images)
print(images)
```

- That entire code block loads up the test images you just uploaded and puts them in a list. It also saves those images to new folder called *TestImages*, also on your GDrive. This will allow us to reload those images in the future for further testing/ training.

- The next block of code tests to make sure the test images are loaded, and if they are, it loads the last previously saved version of the nutritionist:

```
if len(images) < 0:
  raise Exception('Test images need to be loaded!')
else:
  x, _ = load_image(images[0])
  img = x[np.newaxis, ...]  ❶

  model = create_model(img)
  model.summary()
```

- **❶** We need to batch dimension to our image so that it can be used as input into the model.

- The next section of code loads the model weights and may take some time to run. The reason is that this model has around 60 million weights to load:

```
latest = tf.train.latest_checkpoint(models)
latest
if latest != None:
  model.load_weights(latest)
```

- The last block of code sets up a helpful form for testing each of the images we uploaded, shown here:

```
#@title Image Prediction { run: "auto", vertical-output: true,
                           display-mode: "form" }

image_idx = 6 #@param {type:"slider", min:0, max:100, step:1}
cnt = len(images)
if  cnt > 0:
  image_idx = image_idx if image_idx < cnt else cnt - 1
  image = images[image_idx]
  x, _ = load_image(image)

  img = x[np.newaxis, ...]
  predict = model.predict(img)
  print(predict+5)
  print(image_idx,image)
  plt.imshow((x+1)/2)
```

- This code creates form with a slider. As you move the slider, it will load an image into the nutritionist model and output the results, as seen in Figure 9-5.

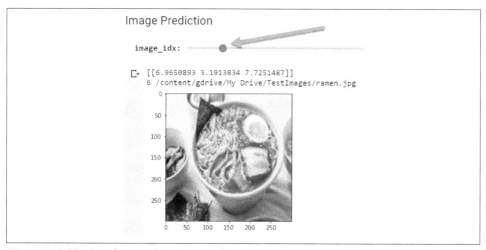

*Figure 9-5. Testing the nutritionist encoder*

- As you slide through the images, make sure you agree with the nutrition outputs. With the defaults, the first number represents a keto-friendly rating, or how high this dish is in protein. The second number represents the amount of carbohydrates. Finally, the third number denotes overall health, or what is considered healthy. If you find yourself not agreeing with the results, be sure to review the category assignments set in the *foods.txt* file. You can also update this file with your own ratings.

Training the nutritionist model to encode a food's arbitrary nutrition ratings has pros and cons. A pro is that we can reduce a complex feature space of an image into a 3D vector. Cons of this approach are potentially many. You may find some foods that fit well with the nutritional ratings, while others fit very well. This may require you to rethink your nutrition categories and ratings. However, an added benefit here is that you can be sure which foods are being identified well and which are not. This would likely not be the case if we were blindly testing and validating the results from data splits. We could, for instance, miss obvious shortcomings in some food categories.

 You should always train your models with training/testing and validation splits. However, you should never discount the value of testing raw real-world data on your models as the ultimate test.

Be sure that you are happy with the nutritionist encoding of your food images. If the results are less than satisfactory for foods that you eat, then go back and retrain with different hyperparameters. You may also think about altering the food nutrition values we set earlier in *foods.txt*. Another approach may be to export the results of the encoding into an embeddings output. Then you could use an embeddings projector to view in 3D how close foods are to each other. Recall that we used this method to determine how words could be embedded in NLP. In any case, if you are happy with the results, continue to the next section.

# Optimizing Deep Reinforcement Learning

Reinforcement learning is a powerful method for training smart agents. Results in recent years have been quite impressive, with agents able to beat humans in a number of tasks or games in which we never imagined a human could be bested by a smart AI. All of this has come with some extreme costs, though. Google has been quoted as saying that some of its RL agents would take 45 years to train on a typical modern-day desktop.

Obviously Colab could never provide that level of extensive training. We might have the option of going to a virtual hosted instance with a dedicated server VM. Yet this could also be quite expensive. Instead, we have decided to reduce the state space of our inputs using the nutritionist encoder. However, that will only take us so far, and we need to further optimize our RL agents.

As we saw in Chapter 8, choosing an RL algorithm can make a significant difference in solving the problem task. Different RL methods also work better for some tasks than others. There is also the issue of the algorithm implementation itself. Not all algorithms are implemented with performance in mind.

To demonstrate that fact, we are going to revisit a deep learning version of Q Learning called DQN. The DQN algorithm was the first to be successful in playing Atari games. It is also the simplest DRL method to implement, as we will see in Example 9-4.

*Example 9-4. Running a DQN agent*

- Open *Chapter_9_DQN_CartPole.ipynb*. This notebook is set up much like the *Chapter_8_A2C_LL.ipynb* example we reviewed at the end of the previous chapter. It shares much of the same code.

- Go ahead and run the notebook. From the menu, select Runtime → Run All. As the notebook is running, we will continue through the code cells.

- Scroll down to the top of the code cell that created the DQNAgent class, as shown here:

```
from collections import deque

class DQNAgent:
    def __init__(self, state_size, action_size):
        self.state_size = state_size
        self.action_size = action_size
        self.memory = deque(maxlen=2000)  ❶
        self.gamma = 0.95    # discount rate
        self.epsilon = 1.0  # exploration rate
        self.epsilon_min = 0.01
        self.epsilon_decay = 0.995
        self.learning_rate = 0.001
        self.model = self._build_model()
```

  ❶ Here we are giving the agent a memory using *deque*. Deque is a collection or object stack that will hold the agent's experiences.

- In this simple example, we can see that the inputs to the class are the state_size and action_size. After that, the rest of the parameters are hardcoded to similar values we used in previous Q Learning models. If you need to review what these hyperparameters do, return to Chapter 8.

- Just below that we can find a function called &#x5f;build&#x5f;model, which builds the agent's deep learning model:

```
def _build_model(self):
    # Neural Net for Deep-Q learning Model
    model = tf.keras.Sequential()
    model.add(tf.keras.layers.Dense(12,input_dim=self.state_size,
                                     activation='relu'))
    model.add(tf.keras.layers.Dense(6, activation='relu'))
    model.add(tf.keras.layers.Dense(self.action_size, activation='linear'))
    model.compile(loss='mse',
        optimizer=tf.keras.optimizers.Adam(lr=self.learning_rate))
    return model
```

- That code builds the agent's deep learning model. At this stage of the book, this should all look very familiar.

- Below that we have another function called memorize, shown here:

```
def memorize(self, state, action, reward, next_state, done):
    self.memory.append((state, action, reward, next_state, done))
```

- The memorize function is where the agent keeps a record of previous state, action, reward, next_state, and done output from a step.

- Below that we have the act function. act again selects the action the agent will take. Remember that we use the epsilon to denote how random an agent may take a random action. If not random, then the agent will take the maximum best action, as shown in the following code:

```
def act(self, state):
    if np.random.rand() <= self.epsilon:
        return random.randrange(self.action_size)
    act_values = self.model.predict(state)
    return np.argmax(act_values[0])
```

- Next, we can see the replay function. The replay function is where the agent model training is performed, essentially where we fit the deep learning model, shown here:

```
def replay(self, batch_size):
    minibatch = random.sample(self.memory, batch_size)
    for state, action, reward, next_state, done in minibatch:
        target = reward
        if not done:
            target = (reward + self.gamma *
                            np.amax(self.model.predict(next_state)[0]))
        target_f = self.model.predict(state)
        target_f[0][action] = target
        self.model.fit(state, target_f, epochs=1, verbose=0)
    if self.epsilon > self.epsilon_min:
        self.epsilon *= self.epsilon_decay
```

- Inside `replay`, we can first see that a minibatch of samples is taken from memory. Then we loop over each batch in the minibatch and train on the expected `target_f`. The equations used in this section of code are the same as we used for Q Learning. At the end of the code block, we decay epsilon if it still needs to be decayed.

- The rest of the code in this example is something we've already reviewed in previous examples from Chapter 8. We won't need to review the code here, but be sure to read it over to refresh your understanding.

- Let the agent run and train. Notice how long the agent takes to train, and compare these results to the LunarLander agent we developed at the end of Chapter 8.

One thing that should be obvious is how slowly the agent trains. This has to do with a simple and not-obvious problem with the training function replay we saw earlier. Go back and look at the replay function of the agent again. Notice that we're training on single elements in the minibatch instead of the whole batch. This slight oversight is what is causing the dramatically slow training times. It is also the reason we train deep learning models in batches, because it is computationally efficient. Remember that deep learning uses tensors for calculation. That means that larger batches are more efficient than single items.

So if this model is so inefficient, why was it made this way? Mostly because it is easier to handle the data or tensors this way. Tensor manipulation is not always so clean and can be quite messy. We can fix this DQN agent just by rewriting the replay function. In Example 9-5, we will look at an optimized DQN agent that handles the training tensors more efficiently.

*Example 9-5. Optimizing a DQN agent*

- Open *Chapter_9_DQN_Optimized.ipynb*. This is another DQN agent implementation that is very similar to the previous exercise. The main difference we will focus on in this example is the replay or `experience_replay` function.

- Run all the cells in the notebook by selecting Runtime → Run All from the menu.

- Scroll down to the DQN agent class called `DeepQNetwork` in this example. All of the code is very similar to the last exercise, so we will focus only on the `experience_replay` function, starting here:

```
def experience_replay(self, batch_size, episode):
    minibatch = random.sample( self.memory, batch_size )

    x = []
    y = []
    np_array = np.array(minibatch)
```

```
st = np.ones((0,self.nS))
nst = np.ones( (0,self.nS) )
```

- This function starts by setting up some NumPy arrays for collecting memory as a tensor. Notice that we are still pulling out a minibatch from memory at the start of the function.

- The next section of code loops over the np_array and appends the state and next state, as shown here:

```
for i in range(len(np_array)):
    st = np.append( st, np_array[i,0], axis=0)
    nst = np.append( nst, np_array[i,3], axis=0)
st_predict = self.model.predict(st)
nst_predict = self.model.predict(nst)
index = 0
```

- When the predict function is called on the state, we use the entire minibatch as opposed to looping through each entry.

- Below that we loop through the elements of the minibatch just as before, calculating the target_f or predicted target, as shown here:

```
for state, action, reward, nstate, done in minibatch:
    x.append(state)
    nst_action_predict_model = nst_predict[index]
    if done == True:
        target = reward
    else:
        target = reward + self.gamma * np.amax(nst_action_predict_model)
    target_f = st_predict[index]
    target_f[action] = target
    y.append(target_f)
    index += 1
```

- This is the same loop we saw in the last DQN agent, but this one collects all the target_f into the y array.

- The final important section of code is just below that and is shown here:

```
x_reshape = np.array(x).reshape(batch_size,self.nS)
y_reshape = np.array(y)
epoch_count = random.randint(1,5)
hist = self.model.fit(x_reshape, y_reshape, epochs=epoch_count, verbose=0)
```

- In this last section of code, we reshape the helper NumPy arrays x into x_reshape and y into y_reshape. This allows us to call model.fit on the whole minibatch of samples. This will greatly improve training efficiency. Last, note that this time we are setting the number of training epochs on fit to a random number from 1 to 5 using random.randint function. You could use other functions here to define epochs, but random will work for us for now.

- Let the agent run to completion. It should take only a few minutes. This agent should be able to solve the CartPole environment in 35–45 iterations. Notice that when the agent solves the environment, the training will exit early.

> On the OpenAI Gym site (*https://gym.openai.com*) there is a link on most environments that lists best-performing methods. The optimum RL agent to beat CartPole has been able to do so in around 13 training iterations. Quite impressive. This number of training iterations is the best method for comparing algorithms. Time can be reduced easily by adding computing resources.

As you can see from the last two exercises, there can be a significant difference in performance compared to the same agent algorithm. The optimized DQN agent we demonstrate here will be the algorithm we use to power our agent in Eat/No Eat. We will put that agent into practice in the next section.

# Building the Eat/No Eat Agent

Okay, we have all the pieces we need to build the agent, so now we need to put it all together. But wait—what we should do before building the full working app is to continue proving the concept—that is, train a DQN agent with nutritionist input and confirm the agent is making the correct suggestions. To do that, we need to build a starting set of training data. This form of training goes against trial-and-error learning, which we consider fundamental to RL.

The problem with trial-and-error learning at this stage is it would require us to be the environment, which would mean manually training the agent over hundreds or possibly thousands of iterations. Since we probably don't want to spend hours or possibly days training, we can apply a shortcut. It should be mentioned that this shortcut uses supervised learning, but that is our best option under the circumstances.

> There are a number of techniques that combine supervised learning with reinforcement learning for faster learning—everything from full planning to partial-supervised and unsupervised learning. To an RL purist, these methods may be considered cheating, although that mentality is quickly changing as well.

Before building the agent, then, we want to create a set of training data we can automatically feed into the DQN agent. We will use a form of supervised learning to create our dataset in Example 9-6.

*Example 9-6. Training the Eat/No Eat starter dataset*

- Open the *Chapter_9_EatNoEat_Training.ipynb* and run all the cells by selecting Runtime → Run All.

- This notebook uses the saved nutritionist model from the previous exercises. Be sure you have completed those exercises before running this notebook.

- Most of the code in this notebook will be familiar, except for the last few cells. Scroll down to the code cell shown here:

```
import ipywidgets as widgets
from IPython.display import display
from IPython.display import Javascript

test_states = []
```

- This block of code loads some imports of new libraries. We are going to use some interactive widgets in our next cell. Also note the initialization of the test_states array. This will hold our supervised training dataset.

- Move down to the next code block and notice the start of the code, as shown here:

```
#@title Eat/No Eat Training { run: "auto", vertical-output: true,
                              display-mode: "form" }
image_idx = 19 #@param {type:"slider", min:0, max:100, step:1}

val = f"Images Trained {len(test_states)}"
label = widgets.Label(
    value= val,
    disabled=False
)
display(label)
```

- This form cell is set to run automatically and allows us to change the image_idx with a slider. Below that is a block of code that uses a label widget to render how many images have been trained.

- Next is another familiar block of code for loading an image and using the nutritionist to encode the values:

```
cnt = len(images)
image_idx = image_idx if image_idx < cnt else cnt - 1
image = images[image_idx]
x, _ = load_image(image)
img = x[np.newaxis, ...]
predict = food_model.predict(img)
print(predict+5)
print(image_idx,image)
plt.imshow((x+1)/2)
```

- Below that we can see a toggle button and a regular button being created and then added to the form:

```
toggle = widgets.ToggleButtons(
    options=['Eat', 'No Eat'],
    disabled=False,
    button_style='', # 'success', 'info', 'warning', 'danger' or ''
    tooltip='Description',
#     icon='check'
)
display(toggle)

button = widgets.Button(description="Train!")
output = widgets.Output()

def button_clicked(b):
  # Display the message within the output widget.
  with output:
    test = (predict,toggle.index,image)
    test_states.append(test)

button.on_click(button_clicked)
display(button, output)
```

- This code cell will create the form shown in Figure 9-6. When the form is running, you the user can pretrain images for the Eat/No Eat DQN agent. Essentially, you will need to go through each image and select whether or not you should eat. Then click the Train! button to put the image features and action to memory in test_states.

- Go through all the images in your test dataset and set whether you should eat or not eat the food and press Train! It will be helpful to also review the nutritionist's encoding output in order to be sure you agree with that. Ideally, you want to train on one food picture for each category. So 101 images would be ideal. Another option is to just train on food images you would normally consume. About 20–30 images will work if you do that. That also means, though, that when testing later, you use the same categories of food.

- Finally, when you are done training, run the last cell in the notebook, shown here:

```
if len(test_states) > 0:
  if os.path.isdir(training_folder) == False:
    os.makedirs(training_folder)
  pickle.dump( test_states, open( training_folder + "food_test.p", "wb" ) )
```

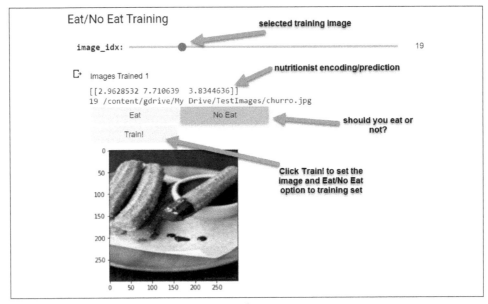

*Figure 9-6. Training the Eat/No Eat starter data*

- Running the last cell will save the `test_states` array into a file called *food_test.p* using `pickle.dump`. The pickle library allows us to serialize and deserialize Python objects.

At this stage of training development, we are just using positive rewards—that is, you tell the agent what you should or shouldn't be eating. We also found that introducing rewards at this state became too difficult for the human to train. It was too easy to get confused about how much reward to apply and for what. This simpler method also provides for better feedback when applying negative rewards later.

With the agent pre-training data saved, we can look next at setting up the DQN agent to consume output from the nutritionist. That means using the DQN agent not on a Gym environment but rather on an environment of our custom creation. This might seem like a lot of work, but it's quite simple, as we will see in Example 9-7.

*Example 9-7. Creating the Eat/No Eat agent*

- Open the *Chapter_9_DQN_EatNoEat.ipynb* and run all the cells by selecting Runtime → Run All.
- You have seen virtually all the code in this notebook, so we only need to focus on a couple of key cells. The first cell we will focus on is shown here:

```
#Create the agent
nS = 3
```

```
nA = 2
dqn = DeepQNetwork(nS, nA, learning_rate(), discount_rate(),
                   1, 0.001, 0.9985)

batch_size = batch_size()
```

- In this code block, we create the agent and set the state nS and action nA sizes. Notice that we are hardcoding the state and actions here. We have three input states output from the nutritionist encoder. The two actions are defined as Eat, action 0, and No Eat, action 1.

- The next key section of code we want to focus on is the agent training code, shown here:

```
foods = len(test_foods)
tests_per_food = 30  ❶
next_food = random.choice(test_foods)
tot_rewards = 0
for ft in nb.tqdm(range(tests_per_food * foods)):
  food = next_food
  state = food[0]
  action = dqn.action(state)
  reward = 1 if food[1] == action else -1  ❷
  tot_rewards += reward
  next_food = random.choice(test_foods)
  nstate = next_food[0]
  done = False
  dqn.store(state, action, reward, nstate, done) # Resize to store in memory
                                                 to pass to .predict
  with tf.name_scope('Training'):
    tf.summary.scalar('rewards', data=tot_rewards, step=ft)
    tf.summary.scalar('epsilon', data=dqn.epsilon, step=ft)
  if len(dqn.memory) > batch_size:
      dqn.experience_replay(batch_size, ft)
```

❶ The variable `tests_per_food` is defined. This is a setting that allows you to define how many training iterations you want to run per recorded food test state. Each test state is output that we trained in the last exercise.

❷ This is where the reward is set. A reward of 1 is returned if the action matches the predicted action; otherwise, a –1 reward is set.

- After the agent is trained, scroll down to the last cell, as shown here:

```
#@title Eat/No Eat Training {
  run: "auto", vertical-output: true, display-mode: "form" }
image_idx = 8 #@param {type:"slider", min:0, max:100, step:1}

cnt = len(test_foods)
image_idx = image_idx if image_idx < cnt else cnt - 1
food = test_foods[image_idx]
```

```
image = food[2]
x, _ = load_image(image)
print(image_idx,image)
action = dqn.action(food[0])
eat = "Eat" if action ==0 else "No Eat"
print(eat)
plt.imshow((x+1)/2)
```

- This cell creates another form that will allow you to test the agent. Figure 9-7 shows two example passes through a couple of foods. Notice that the agent is indeed identifying the correct state.

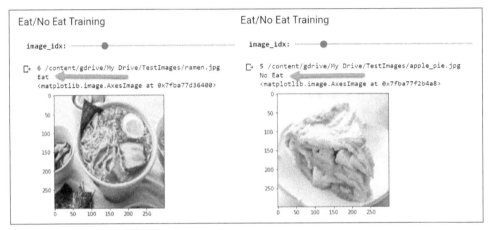

*Figure 9-7. Testing the Eat/No Eat agent*

We created, trained, and tested the agent in the last exercise. If your results are not what you expected but most choices are good, continue on to the next section. Your choices may need to be reinforced with greater rewards. If you are getting widely conflicting results, revisit your pretraining choices and rerun Example 9-6. For those of you with good results, by all means continue to the next section for further testing.

# Testing the AI Agent

Now that we have the nutritionist and agent constructed, trained, and tested, we can move on to validation. We also want to allow a user to train the agent in real time, essentially putting the app into a sort of production setting, allowing you as the user to upload new images, fully test them, and validate the results and teach the AI by augmenting results with rewards.

In order to test the full agent, we need to use all of the key pieces of code we have developed in this chapter. We are going to keep all of the code in a single notebook for simplicity. For a real production app, you likely want to create Python modules and/or libraries you can easily package and deploy. Having all the code viewable in a

---

single notebook can get heavy, but it also has the benefit of easier modification. Let's get started and jump into Example 9-8, where we build the Eat/No Eat app.

*Example 9-8. Building the Eat/No Eat app*

- Open the *Chapter_9_EatNoEat_App.ipynb*. Scroll down to the bottom of the notebook and the following text cell:

  ```
  Run all code to this point first. Then upload training test photos to the
  '/content' folder before running the next cell.
  ```

- As instructed, select this cell and run all of the code above this cell by selecting Runtime → Run Before from the menu. You will have to authenticate to allow mapping your GDrive.

- Next, we want to upload a new set of food images to the */content* folder. Ideally these should be images of foods you regularly eat. Choose images that include all your daily meals: breakfast, lunch, and dinner. At best, aim to upload 21 images, one for each meal over a week. If you eat fewer or more meals in a week, adjust accordingly.

- After uploading all the new images, select the previous text cell again. Select Runtime → Run After from the menu to finish running the entire sheet. It may take a few minutes to load the nutritionist model.

- With all the cells run, you can now scroll to the bottom cell, or the app, essentially. All of the work will take place in this single cell, the start of which is shown:

  ```
  #@title Eat/No Eat App {
      run: "auto", vertical-output: true, display-mode: "form" }
  image_idx = 6 #@param {type:"slider", min:0, max:100, step:1}
  reward = 10 #@param {type:"slider", min:-10, max:10, step:1}

  cnt = len(images)
  image_idx = image_idx if image_idx < cnt else cnt - 1

  state = observe_image(images[image_idx], nutritionist)
  action = dqn.action(state)
  eat = "Eat" if action ==0 else "No Eat"
  val = f"Suggested -> {eat}"
  label = widgets.Label(
      value= val,
      disabled=False
  )
  display(label)
  ```

- Previously we didn't care about the order in which we showed the images to the agent. However, RL is all about trajectory optimization. So for best results this time, we want to maintain an order to the images we test. Remember that Q Learning is off policy. That means our agent needs to explore first and then learn.

This means we need to set up a memory array to hold the record of previous testing/training iterations.

- The code to add a record set to memory and then train the agent is seen in the button click event handlers, shown here:

```
eat_button = widgets.Button(description="Eat")
noeat_button = widgets.Button(description="No Eat")
def eat_button_clicked(b):
    global test_it, nstate
    memory.append((state, 0, reward, nstate, done))
    if test_it > 0:
        mem = memory[test_it-1]
        dqn.store(mem[0],mem[1],mem[2],state, mem[4])
        dqn.experience_replay(batch_size, test_it)
    nstate = state
    test_it += 1

def noeat_button_clicked(b):
    global test_it, nstate
    memory.append((state, 1, reward, nstate, done))
    if test_it > 0:
        mem = memory[test_it-1]
        dqn.store(mem[0],mem[1],mem[2],state, mem[4])
        dqn.experience_replay(batch_size, test_it)
    nstate = state
    test_it += 1
```

- This means that when the user selects an option to eat or not eat, the agent won't be trained until the next action. We need to do this in order to record the state and next state of your food choices.

- The rest of the code for the form is shown here for completeness, but it should be self-explanatory:

```
eat_button.on_click(eat_button_clicked)
noeat_button.on_click(noeat_button_clicked)
display(eat_button, noeat_button)

file = open(images[image_idx], "rb")
image = file.read()
widgets.Image(
    value = image,
    format = "jpg",
    height = 200
)
```

- The code just adds the buttons to the form and outputs the training image.

- Run the cell and move the slider to select a food image. The agent will make a suggestion as to whether you should eat or not. As shown in Figure 9-8, you can choose to set a reward from –10 to 10 and select the actual action you will take.

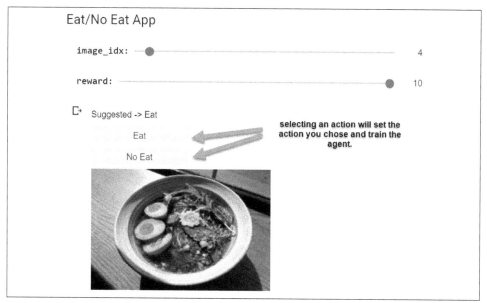

*Figure 9-8. Using the Eat/No Eat agent*

- By being able to set the reward, you can now rank the choices the agent gives you. If the agent tells you not to eat a food you sometimes consume, you may want to reduce the reward to –1. If you strongly agree or feel eating the food is good for you, then you would give a high reward and press the Eat button. This would teach the agent that this food is good for you. Conversely, if the agent suggests you eat a food, you can click the No Eat button and also give a positive reward. You would give the agent a negative reward if you followed the suggestion and the food was ultimately bad for you.

- As you test and work with the agent, be sure to keep the images in the order in which you may consume them during the day.

There are certain problem foods that may be hard to classify. Fried chicken is an excellent example of a food that could be keto diet–friendly but still register as No Eat. This has more to do with our nutritionist encoder than the DQN agent. Keep in mind that our encoder is one of the most sophisticated image classification networks available. We would be hard-pressed to do better, but there are other options, which we will discuss in the next section on commercializing the app.

# Commercializing the AI Agent

Before commercializing any product or software app, you want to be aware of possible shortcomings. It is naive to think any software app or AI you develop will be flawless. That doesn't mean you could never expect to develop the perfect AI, but then the question arises: what is perfect? Even if you are able to develop the perfect AI, you can often face other issues like user error or confusion. So what's the answer? One simple solution is to follow a key tenet of agile development and release early and often.

 The "Manifesto for Agile Software Development" (*https://agilemani festo.org*) was produced in 2001. The four key tenets of this manifesto are restated below:

1. Individuals and interactions over processes and tools.

2. Working software over comprehensive documentation.

3. Customer collaboration over contract negotiation.

4. Responding to change over following a plan. As the second point states, it is more important to have working software than a stack of documentation outlining how that software should work.

Software gets its name from being malleable. In most cases, we can easily fix the flaws or expand on features. It is the reason you need to get your software in users' hands early and often. Users are your best feedback, and they will be a far better guide than any feature list or other documentation. Does this same rule apply for the AI we develop? More than likely, yes. That means we need to have a plan to iterate our AI development and be prepared to scale up or down, as well as look to improve those shortcomings we may have identified earlier. We will look at how to identify potential app issues in the next section.

## Identifying App/AI Issues

In this chapter we developed out a proof of concept (POC) for the Eat/No Eat AI. We even went so far as to develop a simple user interface. Most importantly, though, we have an end-to-end working app. That means we didn't just build the AI portion or the user interface. This is an important step in achieving success with any software product, and that most certainly goes for AI apps. Don't expect that your cool AI project with raw output alone is going to attract user interest or attention. Remember, we want our software ready for consumption by users before proceeding to the next step.

With a working POC AI/app, we can move on to identifying issues we believe may arise. There will of course be many other issues identified by users. For now, though, we just want to identify potential issues through our own development and testings. Since we have the Eat/No Eat POC working, let's identify some potential issues:

*Lack of initial training data*

We use only a small 5,000-sample dataset. Future versions may require more initial training data for better results. As we mentioned earlier, there are much larger sets of food image data, but using those will require us to upgrade our training server.

*The nutritionist encoder*

The current encoder model should work for most foods but may fall short on others. Depending on the severity of issues with users, we may want to change the base encoder model. Fortunately, the way our app is currently built allows us to easily change the encoder later.

*Making the app multiuser*

We talked about this early in the chapter: what if we want the app to be shared among many users? That would require us to add further state input, perhaps in the form of age, weight, gender, and other factors. This causes two issues. First, we need to increase the training time due to increased state. Second, we could have data sensitivity issues. Users may not want to submit such personal information to a shared AI.

*Adding more user attributes*

Our current DQN agent is working more as a classifier than an RL agent. The reason for this is that we do little to track how and when a user eats. In order to use the full capability of our RL agent, we really should be tracking what times a user eats, at a minimum. Remember that RL is about finding the best trajectory or path through a problem. For the Eat/No Eat app, we can think of the path as the set of foods a user will eat. Activity and stress levels are other attributes we could/should track for users. Again, adding more attributes means larger state, and larger state means more training.

Figure 9-9 shows all these identified issues and how they connect with one another. It can actually be quite helpful to draw simple diagrams like this. They work as an excellent reminder and are very helpful in educating stakeholders or investors.

With the app problems identified, the next step is to get the app in front of users. Yes, even at this stage, it can be helpful to involve users. We will look at how to do that and proceed with development in the next section.

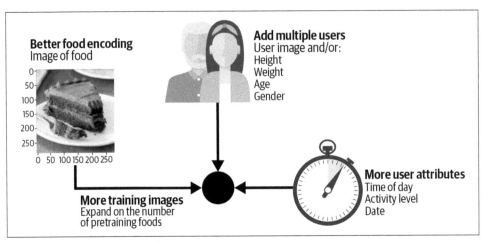

Figure 9-9. Identifying app shortcomings

## Involving Users and Progressing Development

Before you dive in and try to resolve the identified issues, you want to show users the POC first. Users should be those who will get value from using the app. That doesn't mean you want to do a public release. Think more of a smaller focus group of users who are outside your development circle or group. You want users to provide honest and constructive feedback. That also means you'll have to forget about using QA staff or interns. For best results, use real users.

Some organizations like to use blind focus groups or small groups of users to test POC or beta versions of apps. Use different users for different versions of the app. Never use the same user for two consecutive versions. For example, user A may test the POC, but not the first major release after the POC. That way user A will understand the app but still be blind to new changes.

After you first release the POC to users, expect most of the feature requests or issues to be UI- or workflow-related. At this stage, users may think the AI is cool, but their biggest issues will likely be around using the app, which is fine and what we want. It allows us to identify key concerns through the user using the app. Users can have unique insights into how to use apps that we as developers often overlook. By implementing their suggestions, we save time, avoiding pitfalls like developing features users don't need or want. Keep in mind, you likely will still need to guide the user at this stage, but also be sure to listen to them.

Figure 9-10 shows roughly how these development iterations may work for our Eat/No Eat app. Remember to be agile, and if situations dictate, be ready and open for change. For example, you should expect to get UI and workflow updates. If users come back and claim the AI is not working at all, then you need to address that first. Likewise, in later stages of development, you may still need major UI or workflow changes. It is important to be flexible and address what your users consider to be the biggest hurdles in using your app.

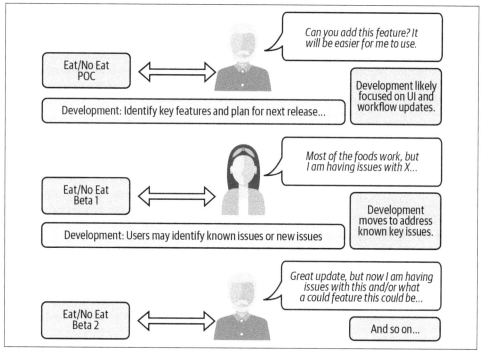

*Figure 9-10. App development iterations*

As your development progresses and the app gets more stable, introduce a wider audience of users. Again, you don't have to go fully public. At some point, though, you will be comfortable enough with your platform to do a general public release. Depending on your app, you may want to have many users testing beta versions. If we made the Eat/No Eat app, we would need a diverse set of users to thoroughly test it.

Another factor, less so with straight software apps, is advancing technology. The AI landscape is moving so fast, you may find some components or your agent becoming obsolete. For instance, you may find the base model you are using can be replaced by a far superior image encoder, one that can resolve encoding issues with foods like fried chicken. If that is the case, be prepared to upgrade or swap out components. Fortunately, for most AI projects, this may be a trivial concern since we develop in models with standard inputs/outputs. The ultimate thing to keep in mind is to prepare for change and be able to adapt.

The rest of your development process may vary substantially, including the source control system and the task tracking you use. At a minimum, you should use source control for your code and a tool to manage and track tasks or issues. There are plenty of free or paid options that can provide these services for you. Next, in the last section of this chapter, we leave you with some future considerations.

# Future Considerations

The architecture of the Eat/No Eat app will work for most small-scale requirements. However, if we start to add multiple users with many more foods, we could expect poor performance. We would likely get variations of users and foods our app has never seen before. Other issues could arise because our app can't encode certain food groups well or at all. In the following paragraphs, we discuss some possible next steps for upscaling the Eat/No Eat app:

*Remove the encoding layer*
> In fact, more deep reinforcement learning agents use raw input in the form of images. This means we could remove the encoding layer from the nutritionist and put it directly on top of the DQN agent, thus removing the encoding altogether and allowing the agent to train the loss not only back through the DQN model but through the nutritionist model as well. This would likely dramatically increase training times, but if you have thousands of users, that may be okay. The downside to this is the ability to add additional input features easily, which increases training times and makes the agent less stable.

*Expand the encoding categories*
> Another option is to expand the number of encoding dimensions we use. Instead of just 3, we could expand to 10 or possibly even 20 or more, thus allowing us more control over how we describe an encoded food. The downside to this is that we would need to break our foods down from general categories into more specific elements. This would require additional labeling of the foods themselves. The upside to this is having a better universal encoder. It also still allows us to add new input dimensions into the DQN.

*Develop a better nutritionist encoder*
> As you may have seen with fried chicken or other foods, the current encoder has limitations. We could get past those limitations by developing our own better image encoder. That is not a trivial task, mind you. However, with the ever-increasing wave of new methods, it may be an option. One such approach may be to use self-attention convolutional encoders or conditional GANs. Who knows—in a year or two there may be far better options as well.

Now that we have discussed the Eat/No Eat app at some length, we should perhaps finish out this chapter with the conclusion.

# Conclusion

The Eat/No Eat app concept is one practical example of combining multiple complex forms of AI into a working agent application—an agent that can take an image as input and provide the user with some form of guidance. This concept could be extended well beyond food to many other applications. It could be the basis for a whole range of AI applications that take user image input or perhaps even just monitor the users themselves.

In a few years, as technology advances, it is expected that smart phones will become more wearable. That likely means that these types of apps will be better integrated into our lives. Imagine having an Eat/No Eat agent watching every food you consume and then monitoring your health automatically, and feeding changes in your health back to the agent in terms of rewards. The possibilities are truly endless here.

With our Eat/No Eat done as a POC, we will take the next steps toward commercialization by building and deploying the app in the next chapter.

# CHAPTER 10

# Commercializing AI

Commercializing any product is really about putting it in front of users. For most software teams, this means building and deploying an app for customers, be it on the web, a mobile device, or a desktop. We discussed the need for putting software and AI in front of users early and often in the previous chapter. If you can achieve that in a workable product, you have commercialized.

Yet commercialization goes beyond just putting software in front of users. In this chapter, we go beyond talking about just deploying our app to discussing other factors. We will look at the ethical concerns that we as developers should consider when building a new AI. Then we will jump back to familiar territory and look at how to package up a Colab app for use. After that, we will look at various options for deploying your app and using it. Then we will finish up the last section by reviewing the future of AI apps and your next steps in building practical AI.

In this chapter, we look at a number of considerations when building new AI. Here is a preview of the main topics we will cover:

- The Ethics of Commercializing AI
- Packaging up the Eat/No Eat App
- Reviewing Options for Deployment
- Exploring the Future of Practical AI

To complete the exercises in this chapter, you will need to have completed the exercises in Chapter 9. Cutting-edge AI not only breaks technical boundaries, but it also addresses ethical and moral issues, which we will talk about in the next section.

# The Ethics of Commercializing AI

Commercialization is often seen as the biggest hurdle in any product development cycle. Many products consumed by people often face strict guidelines and testing. From prescription drugs to the food you consume at your local restaurant, it all gets tested internally and externally by government agencies looking to protect consumers. Yet these processes hardly exist for one of the main consumer products on earth, software. Software often is externalized as just a tool, one that we use at our own risk. This is all well and good for a spreadsheet or word processor, but what about an advanced AI app like Eat/No Eat?

With the advent of advanced AI and process automation, we now need to look at software differently. Software can not only help ease our lives, but also hurt or damage them. Consider the self-driving car, which we may consider an advanced form of AI. Developers of self-driving cars look to develop AI that can minimize risk, but under what rules? There are no government regulations (yet) that require developers to test that risk. There are no rules that dictate whether a self-driving car that is collision bound should do X given A, B, and C.

In the United States, roads and highways fall under the states' jurisdiction, so governance rules for self-driving cars will as well. While no state has formalized any rules yet, this will certainly come in time. That could mean that developers of such AI could face multiple rule sets or forms of AI for each state or country. Would that mean that as a vehicle crossed borders it would need to change AI? This could be a real possibility in the future, not just for self-driving cars but for all forms of AI.

For developers building new forms of AI like the Eat/No Eat app, this could be a significant problem. After all, government regulations are put in place to protect not only the consumer but also the manufacturer. Does that mean you as a developer should wait for better regulations on AI apps? Unfortunately, no. It really becomes a chicken-and-egg problem. We can't really develop regulations on something that only just came into existence today.

The Eat/No Eat app is an excellent example of an app that could both help and very much hurt individuals. Does that mean we should just wrap the product in legalese and license agreement protections, essentially telling the user to use it at their own risk? While that likely is the blanket solution, we should try to do better. We as developers of new AI need to set the precedent for how it is used, by whom, and when.

That may mean limiting the app's use or putting other rules in place. Some of these rules may be used to prevent user error, second-guessing the AI, and hacking or misuse. Using Eat/No Eat as an example, you could put a gate AI in place that makes sure user food images are food dishes and not pictures of other items. Other rules could monitor app use and the foods the user consumes. Perhaps a bit Big Brother, but this data could then be post-analyzed for anomalies to identify users who use the app incorrectly for any number of reasons.

 AI hacking is currently seen as the next big security concern of the 21st century. If you build any successful AI app, expect to be attacked by hackers.

Ethically, as developers we then need to consider how we can protect consumers, the AI, and ourselves. In some cases, those systems could be as expensive as constructing the AI itself. However, protecting consumers should never be an afterthought. It not only makes sense ethically, but also could certainly contribute to financial success in the long run as well.

In this chapter, we won't look at how to put any of those control systems in place other than to mention some suggested best practices. For most cases, developing such systems will be quite specific to the AI and the consumer base. However, as an example, let's look at the system we might put in place for Eat/No Eat:

*Food detection*
As mentioned earlier, we likely want an AI in front of the nutritionist encoder to detect whether an image is food. This would not only limit bad guesses but also allow us to better train the nutritionist itself. Such a system could also prevent attempted hacking or other surreptitious activity.

*Monitor user activity*
We likely want to monitor user activity for anomalies such as weight gain, weight loss, lethargy, or other factors. This could tell us if a user is losing or gaining weight too quickly, as well as help monitor how well the app is providing guidance. Of course, this whole monitoring process could define an app in and of itself, perhaps with other commercial applications.

*Override AI guidance*
A user or focused group of users could modify the AI to only suggest certain food categories. This could be detrimental to a multiuser version of the app, and that poses a real problem. The extent of such a problem would depend on the number of users. More users likely means better overall training. At times, though, we may still need to be careful about what guidance the AI gives for whom, and when.

*Baseline testing*
We could maintain continuous system testing of known users. One thing we should put in place is user baselines. This will help us make better and more informed decisions. Baselines can also establish guidance for other systems, like

AI overrides and user monitoring. Any AI application should consider ongoing baseline testing at a minimum.

These are only a few suggestions for systems that can help you be ethically and morally responsible to your users, which is something we need to consider more seriously when building AI and/or automated assistants. In the next section, we will show you how to package up and deploy the Eat/No Eat app in various configurations.

# Packaging Up the Eat/No Eat App

We have developed most of the apps in this book on the cloud using Colab. Now, that can be good and bad. With Colab, we know our apps are sure to work in most notebook environments, provided the correct dependencies are installed. However, the bad side of this is that our code is broken up into cells, which makes code management tricky and, quite frankly, ugly. A better option is to package up our code into Python files that we can reuse standalone or as modules. Modularizing code also has the benefit of being, well, modular. In Example 10-1, we will look at how to modularize the Eat/No Eat app.

*Example 10-1. Packaging up Eat/No Eat*

- Open *Chapter_10_EatNoEat.ipynb* and run the first code block to download the prepackaged code for the app. We have already packaged the code onto a GitHub repository for ease of deployment. Here is the code to download the source:
  ```
  !git clone https://github.com/cxbxmxcx/EatNoEat.git
  ```

- We will go over each module in this package to understand where the parts of Eat/No Eat reside. Packaging and pushing code as a Python app to GitHub makes a lot of sense. If you are not already familiar with Git as a source control platform, be sure to try out GitHub Desktop. Desktop is a UI tool that can help you easily manage cloning or building source repositories.

- The next code block imports a package called drive from EatNoEat:
  ```
  import drive as d

  drive, images, training = d.mount_drive()
  ```

- *drive.py* in the EatNoEat package contains a single function, mount_drive, which will connect to your GDrive and set the various folder paths, as we have seen previously. The cell just below this one will print out those paths.

- The next cell will import all of the code to build and train the DQN agent from a module/file called *dqn_agent.py*, shown here:
  ```
  import dqn_agent as agent

  dqn = agent.train_dqn(training)
  ```

- Running this cell will load the DQN agent and train it automatically on a set of saved test images just as we did before, but this time in a single line of code. Feel free to open the source folder and inspect the *dqn_agent.py* file in Colab. You can see that we have moved all of the model and training code to this file, thus allowing us to build and train the agent in a single line of code.

- Moving to the next cell, we can see a bit more code to load the nutritionist model and load the weights, shown here:

```
import tensorflow as tf
import numpy as np
import nutritionist as n

models = drive + 'Models'
print(models)
x, _ = n.load_image("apple_pie.jpg")
img = x[np.newaxis, ...]

nutritionist = n.create_model(img)
nutritionist.summary()
latest = tf.train.latest_checkpoint(models)

if latest != None:
  nutritionist.load_weights(latest)
```

- For reference, the file *apple_pie.jpg* has been included in the package source as a single test image. The other code creates the nutritionist model, summarizes it, and then loads the latest saved checkpoint model. This model is quite large and will take a while to load. The source for this model will be from the Models folder on your GDrive. We could, of course, save the model directly to GitHub using large file storage. However, at close to 500 MB, the file is quite large, so it is likely better pulled from your GDrive.

 GitHub is best used just with source code. It does have options to use large files, but it requires special configuration of an option called LFS, which stands for *large file storage*. LFS dictates which files can exceed the default limit.

- Next, we want to quickly test that the nutritionist has been loaded correctly using the simple line of code here:

```
print(n.observe_image("apple_pie.jpg", nutritionist)+5)
```

```
OUTPUT
[[2.936873 7.593238 5.764773]]
```

- This will output the nutrition ratings for the image. Remember that these values have been normalized to around 0. That means that to get a sense of the real values, we need to add 5 to each value. We can easily do this with a NumPy tensor by adding 5.

- The last code cell defines the working part of the app, shown here:

```
import webcam as wc
import ipywidgets as widgets
from IPython.display import display
from IPython.display import Image

try:
  filename = wc.take_photo()
  state = n.observe_image(filename, nutritionist)
  action = dqn.action(state)
  eat = "Eat" if action ==0 else "No Eat"
  val = f"Suggested -> {eat}"
  label = widgets.Label(
    value= val,
    disabled=False
  )
  display(label)
  display(Image(filename))
except Exception as err:
  print(str(err))
```

- In this cell, we import a new module called *webcam.py as wc*. This code sets up and enables the app to use the webcam as an input camera. The webcam module has a single function, `take_photo`, that does all the work. After that we can see similar code observing the image and then using that observation as state into the DQN agent action function. The results of that call to action provide the suggestion to eat or not.

- You can open up the *webcam.py* file as shown here:

```
from IPython.display import display, Javascript
from google.colab.output import eval_js
from base64 import b64decode

def take_photo(filename='photo.jpg', quality=0.8):
  js = Javascript('''
    async function takePhoto(quality) {
      const div = document.createElement('div');
      const capture = document.createElement('button');
      capture.textContent = 'Capture';
      div.appendChild(capture);

      const video = document.createElement('video');
      video.style.display = 'block';
      const stream =
```

```
    await navigator.mediaDevices.getUserMedia({video: true});

    document.body.appendChild(div);
    div.appendChild(video);
    video.srcObject = stream;
    await video.play();

    // Resize the output to fit the video element.
    google.colab.output.setIframeHeight(
      document.documentElement.scrollHeight, true);

    // Wait for Capture to be clicked.
    await new Promise((resolve) => capture.onclick = resolve);

    const canvas = document.createElement('canvas');
    canvas.width = video.videoWidth;
    canvas.height = video.videoHeight;
    canvas.getContext('2d').drawImage(video, 0, 0);
    stream.getVideoTracks()[0].stop();
    div.remove();
    return canvas.toDataURL('image/jpeg', quality);
  }
  ''')
display(js)
data = eval_js('takePhoto({})'.format(quality))
binary = b64decode(data.split(',')[1])
with open(filename, 'wb') as f:
  f.write(binary)
return filename
```

- The bulk of this code is JavaScript embedded into the Python code as a means to control the browser. We use a few interop techniques here to control communication between Python and JavaScript.

- Run the last code cell, and be sure you allow the browser to access the webcam. This example will work on a desktop or phone. As the app is running, just click the Capture button to take a picture of the current screen. The Eat/No Eat agent will use that image as input and make a recommendation.

The simple example we just looked at demonstrates how to break up the Eat/No Eat app into modules. Then we showed how to consume those modules with Colab. However, at this stage, we could deploy the app into multiple different settings, and we will review those options in the next section.

# Reviewing Options for Deployment

Deployment options for applications in all forms have come a long way. Not so long ago developers still struggled with installers and managing dependencies. When they were asked why an app wasn't working, the common retort was "It works on my machine."

Since those dark ages, we have come a long way toward making sure an app works where it should. Whole application suites like Docker and Kubernetes have sprung up to overcome deployment nightmares. Cloud platforms like GCP also provide numerous options to deploy an app. With all those options, it's often hard to decide what is best for your needs. In this section, we will look at a few options for deployment, as summarized in the following list:

*GitHub (open source)*
> Deploying your app to GitHub or another major repository as open source is often a great option. After all, developers are users too. Another common myth is that open source is free. While most OS apps start out free, they don't have to be. In fact, some of the biggest success stories in software started out as open source, one example being GitHub itself. The app itself also doesn't need to be developer focused.

*GCP instance*
> Since you already have a GCP account, you could use an instance or app server. This is a great option for apps that need to scale and gives you full control over the server itself. It can be the most expensive option.

*GCP Cloud Deploy*
> Instead of an instance, you can deploy an app directly to an app server that runs the Google Compute engine. This allows you to run TensorFlow models in the cloud at a cheaper price.

*Kubeflow*
> This option provides tools to deploy ML apps to Kubernetes. This often requires you to deploy the app on-premises on your own VM server instance.

*Other options*
> Other options could include everything from running an on-premises server to using other cloud services or deployments. Python and TensorFlow are both standard components and are supported by many other platforms.

For our purposes, we are going to look at deploying a simple TensorFlow/Keras app. To do that, we will look at a couple of basic options: GitHub and GCP Cloud Deploy. The other options on the list are outside of our scope (Kubeflow) or expensive. A GCP instance can quickly run up costs, and we will avoid putting that burden on you. Instead, we will focus on the cheaper and more widely accessible options, like GitHub.

## Deploying to GitHub

We have used git and GitHub throughout this book, and it is assumed you understand the value of source control. For coding, managing changes in your source is critical. If you don't use source control like GitHub on a day-to-day basis, you should. However, GitHub is more than source control. It is a platform by which we can engage users to review, test, and extend your app. An excellent example of this is the DeOldify project we looked at in Example 7-7.

If you jump to the DeOldify site (*https://github.com/jantic/DeOldify*), you can see a great example of a commercialized AI project delivered on GitHub. The home page contains excellent source documentation, as well as plenty of examples. It is as much a repository for code as it is for marketing and distributing the app. The site itself had over 10,000 stars, or what we call *likes* in GitHub, at time of writing. This demonstrates the power of this platform for app distribution.

Deploying to GitHub is not without issues, however. If you choose to open source, you are essentially placing a high bar for your app. In most cases, only developers will be inclined to look at or review your app, which can be a major problem if your app is designed for a broad user base. Eat/No Eat is an example that likely would not fare well if deployed to GitHub—at least, not in its current form—since the app is more targeted to general, nontechnical users.

Assuming you feel your app is a good fit for GitHub, the next step is documentation. Developers are smart people, but the more you can do to help them get started using your app, the better. DeOldify, for example, has a number of IPython notebooks that can be run from Colab or other platforms. Notebooks provide an easy point of entry to using your app, at least for developers or advanced users.

Okay, so you commercialize your app and deploy it to GitHub. Your next question is, how do you earn money? In most cases, deploying your app to GitHub won't manifest as direct consumer sales. There have been some cases where donate buttons have helped, but often not enough. Instead, the rewards are often deferred in the form of development assistance—that is, developers who are using your product for their own purposes needing your assistance to help them modify the base code or build a similar app concept.

In the vast number of open source projects, the apps never make any money. If you do open source, a good mindset to go in with is to expect not to make funds directly. Even if your app becomes hugely popular, there may still be a risk of knockoffs from all manner of competition, big or small. There have even been stories where open source projects have been replicated by big companies like Microsoft, Amazon, and others, with no compensation provided to the originating development team.

While some projects have done very well open sourcing, the majority do not. Does that mean open source projects are a bad idea? No, not at all. However, it is important to understand the audience for your app. It is also important to realize that just throwing your code online won't get users. You will still need to put in considerable effort to make your app usable. This means providing documentation and helpful quickstarts.

The other benefit to open sourcing an app or code base is in peer review and testing. If your app is popular and gets used, you will have some of the best free testing and code reviews available, not to mention free assistance in code contributions and possibly in tools. All of this can then be used to springboard your app to other commercial deployment options, like the one we'll review in the next section.

## Deploying with Google Cloud Deploy

The GCP provides a few options to deploy your app to use the Google Compute engine or server instances. Using Google Compute is likely the most economical option, but it is limited in the interface it exposes. This may mean breaking up your app into a web or application interface and the ML (TensorFlow) code, where the interface could run from a content delivery network (CDN) or other static site. The backend worker AI could then run on Google Compute.

CDN services are the best way to deliver your app's interface when using the cloud or the web. CDN is often distributed, and local servers can be set up to mirror your content worldwide. This leads to quicker loading times and better app performance. The downside to this is that your app needs to be dissected into an interface and server. Another drawback is that app communication can often be complex and fraught with issues. These are all things to keep in mind if you decide to take this plunge.

Another option to working with static, pure client-side sites is to use TensorFlow.js. TensorFlow.js can provide a TensorFlow platform in the browser using WebGL. You can still build your models with Python but then save the weights and reload them in TensorFlow.js.

Deciding how or what you need to deploy your app is fundamental. It is the reason we try and deploy an app to users ASAP. Doing so will unfold other considerations, such as any issues in the deployment itself. As we can see now, deployment can most certainly dictate the structure of your app, as well as either guide you or force you down certain paths. The simple option is often to just go with a server instance. However, this is far from the most economical or scalable option.

To demonstrate how you can deploy an app to Google Compute, we will use Colab. Another option is to install the Google Cloud console to your development machine. However, for simplicity we will stick with Colab for Example 10-2.

 This next exercise requires you to have billing enabled for your account and services. Running this exercise will incur costs to your account. The costs are minimal, a few dollars, but you should be aware that there will be charges. If you still have free credits from Google, this should be covered.

*Example 10-2. Deploying an app with Google Cloud Deploy*

- Open *Chapter_10_Deploy.ipynb* and run the first code block, shown here:
  ```
  !gcloud auth login
  ```
- Running this block will require you to authenticate your account and log in.
- Next, we need to set the working project we will use. In previous examples we have used practical-ai-gcp as the project. If you missed creating the project, go back and do that now. The code to set the project is shown here:
  ```
  !gcloud config set project practical-ai-gcp
  ```
- Then we come to creating a storage bucket for deploying the project, as shown in the code here:
  ```
  BUCKET_NAME = 'aigcp'
  REGION = 'us-central1'
  !gsutil mb -l $REGION gs://$BUCKET_NAME
  ```
- Be sure to change the REGION value to something closer to you, if need be. You can also change the bucket name, *aigcp*, to something else.
- Finally, we are going to pull down the code for the deployment examples from GitHub and deploy it with the following code:
  ```
  !git clone https://github.com/ryfeus/gcf-packs
  %cd gcf-packs/tensorflow2.0/example/
  !gcloud functions deploy handler --runtime python37 --trigger-http
                --memory 2048
  !gcloud functions call handler
  ```
- The last line in the preceding code block launches and calls the app handler.

This example shows how to deploy a simple app from GitHub to a Google Compute service. Compute also supports distributed environments as a means of scaling up, which can often be a good thing if needed. Keep in mind, though, that supporting this type of scalability requires more development best practices and workflows. It may not be well suited for teams just getting their feet wet. How you decide to deploy your app will depend on many factors.

The couple of options we looked at here are just good places to get started. There may be better options for you to pursue. A full cloud instance—though more expensive—can allow you to control all aspects of the environment. Google Compute, the cheapest option, will likely require a separation of interface and backend code. There are other factors to consider as well, such as advancing technology, your team's skill, and a host of others. We will address these in the next section.

## Exploring the Future of Practical AI

Virtually all of the material we have covered in this book is less than 10 years old. Aside from the perceptron, which dates back to the 1950s, all of our AI knowledge is fairly new. New technology and new development platforms can create a lot of fun. Yet they can also bring pain in the form of complex learning curves and changing technology. The current wave of AI is far from immune to this syndrome. In fact, the exceedingly fast pace at which AI has been advancing is causing problems with new development.

Many times when we look to develop a new product, platform, or technology, we need to consider where things will be in $X$ years. The current problem with AI is that no one has a good feel for what $X$ is. Think of $X$ as being the amount of time your product could function before needing an upgrade. Based on this value, you can then determine how much development time you have until things change, which in turn tells you how soon you need to release a working product. The problem now, though, is understanding how to determine $X$.

In a typical software development scenario, we may determine $X$ to be the number of years we estimate the current tech being viable for. For most programming languages and platforms, this is typically years or longer. However, AI projects now face constant upgrades in technology, process, languages, and toolkits. TensorFlow developers recently discovered this problem when TF upgraded to 2.0. However, this is a minor issue compared to the larger problem of AI best practices changing quickly.

 During the writing of this book, entire chapters were altered to accommodate changes in AI development best practices. While we hope that most of the practices in this book keep current for a couple of years, that could change.

As AI developers, we are now faced with an explosive landscape—a landscape populated with ever-changing tech, new innovations, and even fuzzier requirements. In order to make better decisions, we have identified a list of dos and don'ts below:

*Do...*

- ...keep your code modular and external. Avoid altering libraries or creating complex extensions to existing libraries. If you find you need to alter a library, consider looking for other options. This may be one reason to upgrade to PyTorch or another framework.

- ...consider writing a layer of abstraction. TensorFlow is a great platform, but it is rapidly changing. To avoid breaking changes, think about writing a layer of abstraction on top of your AI code. This layer can save you time later if things do change or you move to another platform. At the same time, writing abstractions creates a silo around your development, a silo new developers may struggle to learn or use.

- ...work with other platforms, technologies, or innovations. It is important to be open to change, especially when working in AI. When you are in a production development cycle, it can be difficult to get time to inspect other options. However, in AI it is critical, and you need to make time. That means occasionally scheduling time to look at new tech. That doesn't necessarily mean you need to abandon what you are doing, but it can alter timelines and expectations.

- ...isolate your AI models. Much like modularizing your code, you should construct your AI projects so models can easily be swapped out or upgraded. This is the same concept we followed in the development of Eat/No Eat.

*Don't...*

- ...wait for the next big thing. Don't put off development hoping for something new. It may not come, and if and when it does, it may not be what you expect. This is especially true for beta products, even from big companies like Google. New development doesn't always mean better. In many cases, developing on a new platform will require changes as the project matures, which in turn may cause several breaking changes in your project. It is better to develop on an established platform.

- ...be afraid to abandon development. This can be a hard decision, but it's one that is often required. At certain times, especially in AI, you may find that your development has quickly been eclipsed—that is, other, better products or services have emerged as you were developing. This is always a risk, and a higher one in AI projects. If and when this happens, don't be afraid to reroute or completely abandon a lost cause. However, be especially careful to be certain your cause is lost. This may require you to build a new project with the new technology. Of course, you should already be doing this as part of your "dos."

- ...keep your focus too narrow. Try to always look at the big picture of the tech you are working on. This may require taking the odd step back from the project to reassess what it is you are trying to deliver and build. Think about things you could do differently. What improvements or changes could be made with the AI or development? You want to try and do this on a monthly or perhaps biweekly basis.

- …back away from a challenge. AI is hard; it can be very hard. If it was easy, we would already have done it. That may mean struggling with models or development concepts for day or weeks. It may mean upgrading your knowledge in various areas, which is never a bad thing. Chances are that if you have built a working concept, your AI is well on its way to being a reality. If you are still struggling to build a working AI after a couple of days or weeks, you may want to revisit the problem and/or your skill set.

- …discount your abilities. Developers faced with complex challenges often encounter impostor syndrome. Impostor syndrome is where a person feels they lack the skills to do the job they are actually doing. This syndrome is common in highly technical areas, but for some reason more so in programming. Many blame this on the portrayal of programming in movies and media where we often see programmers blaze through and easily complete complex programming tasks in minutes, when in reality it can take weeks or months to do the task shown. Be confident in your abilities, and if you are uncertain, attend a software group or Meetup. Talk to others about the things you are working on and get their feedback.

 In the early days of Microsoft, during the mid '90s, a rumor was going around about programming quotas. The rumor suggested that Microsoft developers needed to write 1,000 lines of code a day. It wasn't until years later that Bill Gates came forward to squash that rumor, suggesting that in most cases it was the opposite—developers were encouraged to write fewer lines of well-written and tested code.

In the coming years, there will likely be a whole new collection of books dedicated to the process of building AI. While AI building will likely borrow from software best practices, it faces its own unique and ever-changing challenges that will surely become more complex as time goes by. Yet, as things become more complex, we also look to simplify tools. Deep learning is a testament to how well complexity has been simplified. Neural networks were complex and difficult to develop not more than five years ago. Now we can construct a simple deep learning model to analyze images in fewer than 30 lines of code. Quite an achievement, really.

We can almost assume that as AI becomes more complex, the tools we develop with will catch up and simplify the process. How that plays out remains to be seen, but it is already happening with TensorFlow and Keras. Assuming you follow that list of dos and don'ts, you should be prepared to adapt to those changes. In any case, we wish you all the best in your coming journey, and may you develop some great AI.

That about does it for this section and chapter, and we conclude with our final remarks in the next section.

# Conclusion

Commercialization of any application, be it a regular software product or AI, will always be a major milestone. It is a critical step not only in showcasing your development, but also in getting users to use it. Software and AI are nothing without users. Users can come in all forms, and while we often think of them as being human, that may not always be the case. In the future, we may build AI to be consumed by other AI, and so on. There may even be a day when specialized AI is developed for animals, be it our four-legged pets or animals in the wild. Imagine an AI agent that could care for and even perhaps walk your dog.

The possibilities are astounding and limitless. How we manifest these ideas into apps will require innovation in ideas and technology. At the same time, we can't forget the social, ethical, and moral implications of the AI that we develop. AI is quickly becoming a wild frontier filled with the good and the bad. It is unlike any frontier we have encountered as a species before. Every day, new AI emerges that could threaten the very fabric of our reality. How it is used will be up to us, the developers and creators. As the last words of this book, I leave you with a moving quote that reminds us of this:

> With great power there must also come great responsibility!
>
> —Spider-Man (Stan Lee)

# Index

future of practical AI, 358-361
packaging apps, 350-353
scope of, 347
conditional GAN (CGAN), 114, 241
connected network learning, 81
content classification, 144
content delivery networks (CDNs), 356
content generation (see generators)
continual learning, 279
continuous actions/states, 280
conversational AI (see chatbots and conversational AI)
convolutional neural networks (CNNs)
building comprehensive models, 89-91
concept of convolutions, 81-84
image channels and, 88
impact of, 81
improving models, 92-94
invention of, 79
training models, 91
using Keras application models, 99-107
using pretrained models, 95-99
corpus, 118
credit assignment, 265
cycle consistency, 249
CycleGAN, 242, 249-252

# D

data
bad data, 9
batching data, 31
data distribution, 230
data sparsity, 13
data variability, 13
duplicated data, 12
managing cloud data, 76
test, training, and validation data, 11
data discovery and preparation
hallmarks of good data, 12
recognizing bad data, 9
rules for preparing data, 12
rules for questioning your data, 13
training, test, and validation data, 11
data science
basics of, 2
classification and regression, 2-9
data discovery and preparation, 9-14
required skills, xi, xiv
DCGAN (dual convolutional GAN), 241

decrappification, 257
deep learning
basics of, 14-17
building deep learners, 36-41
effect on natural language processing, 118
how networks learn, 25-36
Perceptron Game, 17-24
required skills, xi, xiv
with images, 80-84
Deep Q Network (DQN), 297-301, 309
deep reinforcement learning (DRL)
benefits of, 296
Deep Q Network (DQN), 297-301
discrete versus continuous state, 296
optimizing with policy gradient methods,
301-306
POMDP (partially observable MDP), 297
DeepMind, 44
DeOldify, 257-260
dependent variables, 4, 8, 12
deployment
to GitHub, 355
with Google Cloud Deploy, 356
options for, 354
Desmos, 7
development guidelines, 358
development iterations, 342
Dialogflow chat agent, 161-168
Dietterich, Thomas G., 290
discrete actions/states, 280
document analysis, 150
downsampling, 244
DQN (Deep Q Network), 297-301, 309
dual convolutional GAN (DCGAN/DualGAN),
241
duplicated data, 12
Dynamic Programming (DP), 276, 278

# E

Eat/No Eat agent assistant
agent building, 331-336
build overview, 309
commercializing, 340-344
designing AI, 310-314
future considerations, 344
model training, 318-326
optimizing deep reinforcement learning,
326-331
purpose of, 309

network capacity, 41
neural translation
    AutoML translation engine, 140
    sequence-to-sequence learning, 137, 179
    Translation API, 138
    translation between languages, 136
next sentence prediction, 147
NoGAN, 257
normalization, 32, 86
not suitable for work (NSFW), 217
Nvidia, 242

# O

object detection, 107-110, 199-203
object tracking, 217
on- versus off-policy agents, 279, 301
one-hot encoding, 118
OpenAI Gym, 270-274, 282-296
OpenCV, 196, 206
optimization, 29, 39
options, 288
overfitting
    definition of, 40
    preventing with dropout and normalization,
        89, 186
    signs of, 59, 94, 134

# P

packaging apps, 350-353
paired translation, 243
parametric ReLU (PReLU) activation function,
    33
patience and fortitude, xi, xiv
PCA (principle component analysis), 128
Perceptron Game
    classification, 22-24
    game answers, 42
    goal of, 20
    materials and source code, 18
    options for learning weights, 20
    origins of, xvii, 17
    play area, 18
    softmax activation function and, 33
    solving with deep learners, 36
perceptrons
    activation functions and, 16
    code example, 17
    diagrammatic model of, 15
    mathematical firing of, 16

role in deep learning, 15
personal automation, x
Pix2Pix, 242, 244-248
placehoders, 216
planning method, 278
policy gradient improvement methods, 281,
    301-306
policy improvement methods, 281
POMDP (partially observable MDP), 297
pooling function, 93
positional encodings, 147
Postman, 76
prerequisite knowledge, xiv
principle component analysis (PCA), 128
probability density distribution, 230
ProGAN (progressive GANs), 242
protection, x
proximal policy optimization (PPO), 281

# Q

Q Learning
    Deep Q Network (DQN), 297-301
    development of, 268
Q Learning agent, 271
quality (Q), 268
questions and comments, xvi

# R

R squared (R2), 5, 68
rate of exploration, 274
recurrent neural networks (RNNs)
    classifying movie reviews, 133
    diagrammatic model of, 129
    feature extraction with, 129
    natural language processing with, 128
    retraining for improvement, 135
    RNN variations, 134
    training sentiment with, 130
    versus Transformer model, 168
regression (see classification and regression)
regularization, 32
reinforcement learning (RL) (see also Eat/No
    Eat agent assistant)
    algorithms selection, 327
    benefits of, 261
    deep reinforcement learning (DRL),
        296-306
    discrete versus continuous actions/states,
        280

## About the Author

**Micheal Lanham** is a proven software and tech innovator with 20 years of experience. During that time, he has developed a broad range of software applications, including games, and graphic, web, desktop, engineering, artificial intelligence, GIS, and machine learning applications for a variety of industries as an R&D developer. He currently resides in Calgary, Alberta, Canada with his family.

At the turn of the millennium, Micheal began working with neural networks and evolutionary algorithms in game development. He was later introduced to Unity and has been an avid developer, consultant, manager, and author of multiple Unity games, graphic projects, and books since.

Micheal has previously written *Augmented Reality Game Development*, *Game Audio Development with Unity 5.x*, *Learn ARCore—Fundamentals of Google ARCore*, *Unity ML-Agents—Fundamentals of Unity Machine Learning*, and *Hands-On Deep Learning for Games*, all published by Packt Publishing.

## Colophon

The animal on the cover of *Practical AI on the Google Cloud Platform* is a Bonelli's eagle (*Aquila fasciata*), a large bird of prey named for the Italian ornithologist Franco Andrea Bonelli. These eagles are found in southern Europe, northern Africa, and southern Asia, and a subspecies of the Bonelli's eagle, *A.f. renschi*, also inhabits parts of Indonesia. They typically live near mountainous, wooded areas where they nest in crags and hunt in the bushes and shrubs.

Adult Bonelli's eagles have long tails and relatively short rounded wings; their legs and feet are yellow and tipped with sharp black claws. The eagle's outer wings and upper body are dark brown, while the feathers on the throat, belly, and back are white streaked with black or brown. The female is typically larger, with more streaking on the underbelly. The eagle's diet consists of medium-sized birds and mammals such as pigeons, rabbits, ducks, and gulls, and even larger prey like herons, buzzards, and foxes. Most prey is caught on the ground, but they've been known to pursue and catch some of the flying birds while they are airborne.

Bonelli's eagles migrate during the winter, but they are very territorial over their nesting and breeding grounds. Like many eagles, both mates perform aerial displays by soaring over the breeding territory. These birds form long-term, monogamous pair-bonds that outlast the breeding season. Eggs are normally laid between early February and mid-March and take five to six weeks to hatch. The young stay in the nest for two or three months before eventually leaving in search of their own territory.

The Bonelli's eagle is usually silent, except when performing an aerial display or defending its nest. The species is currently classified as one of "Least Concern," but their numbers are declining due to hunting, destruction of habitat, and electrocution from electricity pylons—particularly in Europe. Many of the animals on O'Reilly covers are endangered; all of them are important to the world.

The cover illustration is by Karen Montgomery, based on a black and white engraving from Lydekker's *Royal Natural History*. The cover fonts are Gilroy Semibold and Guardian Sans. The text font is Adobe Minion Pro; the heading font is Adobe Myriad Condensed; and the code font is Dalton Maag's Ubuntu Mono.

# O'REILLY®

## There's much more where this came from.

Experience books, videos, live online training courses, and more from O'Reilly and our 200+ partners—all in one place.

Learn more at oreilly.com/online-learning

Milton Keynes UK
Ingram Content Group UK Ltd.
UKHW051859190124
436347UK00008B/485